THE INTERNET FAMILY

In *The Internet Family*, Drs. Katherine Hertlein and Markie Twist provide a current and comprehensive look at the effects of technology on couple and family relationships.

Beginning with an overview of the multifaceted ways in which technology impacts our relationships today, the authors discuss a wide range of topics pertinent to couple and family life. Chapters focus on issues such as online dating and infidelity, parenting and the Internet, video gaming, cyberbullying, and everyday usage of social and new media, before providing guidance on how the reader can successfully navigate the advantages and risks that emerge from the use of specific technologies. An online appendix offers a range of assessments and practical tools for identifying Internet-related problems and solutions.

A portion of the text is also devoted to the application of the Couple and Family Technology framework and how it can be effectively integrated into clinicians' current practice. Couple and family therapists will find this book highly informative, both to use in their own practice and for referring clients to as part of the treatment process.

Katherine M. Hertlein, PhD, LMFT, is a Professor in the Couple and Family Therapy Program in the School of Medicine's Department of Psychiatry and Behavioral Health at the the University of Nevada, Las Vegas, and has published eight books on couple and family therapy.

Markie L. C. Twist, PhD, LMFT, LHMC, CSE, is the Program Coordinator of the Graduate Certificate in Sex Therapy and Professor of Human Development and Family Studies at the University of Wisconsin-Stout, Wisonsin.

THE INTERNET FAMILY

FAMILY

Technology in Couple and Family Relationships

Katherine M. Hertlein and
Markie L. C. Twist

Routledge
Taylor & Francis Group

NEW YORK AND LONDON

First published 2019
by Routledge
52 Vanderbilt Avenue, New York, NY 10017

and by Routledge
2 Park Square, Milton Park, Abingdon, Oxon, OX14 4RN

Routledge is an imprint of the Taylor & Francis Group, an informa business

© 2019 Katherine M. Hertlein and Markie L. C. Twist

The right of Katherine M. Hertlein and Markie L. C. Twist to be identified as authors of this work has been asserted by him/her/them in accordance with sections 77 and 78 of the Copyright, Designs and Patents Act 1988.

British Library Cataloguing-in-Publication Data
A catalogue record for this book is available from the British Library

Library of Congress Cataloging-in-Publication Data
A catalog record for this title has been requested

ISBN: 978-1-138-47804-6 (hbk)
ISBN: 978-1-138-47805-3 (pbk)
ISBN: 978-1-351-10340-4 (ebk)

Typeset in Sabon
by Apex CoVantage, LLC

Visit the eResource: www.routledge.com/9781138478053

To Adam, Cora, Jack, and Luke—who will see technology integrated in their relationships in ways we cannot yet dream today. Use it well.

—Love, Mom/Auntie Kat

To Leif, my Ali—in the words of the late and still great Prince,[1] *"Technology is cool, but you've got to use it as opposed to letting it use you."*

—Love, Mom/Markie

---

1 Source: Nelson, P. N. (2004, March 15). *His purple highness* (M. Lauer, Interviewer). Retrieved from www.today.com/news/his-purple-highness-wbna4531634

Contents

APPENDICES – ONLINE ONLY
[can be accessed at www.routledge.com/9781138478053]

About the Authors

KATHERINE M. HERTLEIN, PHD, is a Professor in the Couple and Family Therapy Program in the Department of Psychiatry and Behavioral Health, School of Medicine, University of Nevada, Las Vegas (UNLV). She received her master's degree in marriage and family therapy from Purdue University Calumet and her doctorate in human development with a specialization in marriage and family therapy from Virginia Tech. Across her academic career, she has published over 75 articles, eight books and several book translations, and over 50 book chapters. She has co-edited a book on interventions in couples treatment, interventions for clients with health concerns, and a book on infidelity treatment. Recently, Dr. Hertlein published second editions of *Systemic Sex Therapy* and *A Clinician's Guide to Systemic Sex Therapy*. These two books are used in over 30 couple and family therapy training programs around the US. In 2017, *A Clinician's Guide to Systemic Sex Therapy* (2nd ed.) was awarded the 2017 Book Award and Integrative Sex Therapy Award from the American Association for Sexuality Educators, Counselors, and Therapists. Dr. Hertlein has also produced the first multitheoretical model detailing the role of technology in couple and family life published in her book *The Couple and Family Technology Framework*. Dr. Hertlein has won numerous awards including both research and teaching awards. Dr. Hertlein has also been awarded a Fulbright, which enabled her to teach and conduct research in technology and families at the University of Salzburg in Salzburg, Austria. Dr. Hertlein is the Editor-In-Chief of the *Journal of Couple and Relationship Therapy*. Dr. Hertlein's work has been featured in various media outlets including *Men's Health*, *The APA Monitor*, *The Atlantic*, and *The Huffington Post*. She lectures nationally and internationally on technology, couples, and sex. Dr. Hertlein maintains a private practice in Las Vegas, Nevada.

MARKIE LOUISE CHRISTIANSON (L. C.) TWIST, PHD, is the Program Coordinator of the Graduate Certificate in Sex Therapy Program, and

Professor in the Human Development and Family Studies Department and Marriage and Family Therapy Program at the University of Wisconsin-Stout. Markie received their master's degrees in education and marriage and family therapy with an emphasis in sex therapy from Northern Arizona University and University of Louisiana at Monroe respectively, and their doctorate in human development and family studies with a specialization in couple and family therapy from Iowa State University. Dr. Twist is a Licensed Marriage and Family Therapist (IA, NV) and Mental Health Counselor (IA), American Association for Marriage and Family Therapy Clinical Fellow and Approved Supervisor, and an American Association for Sexuality Educators, Counselors, and Therapists Certified Sexuality Educator and Certified Sexuality Educator Supervisor. Markie is co-author of the books *The Couple and Family Technology Framework: Intimate Relationships in a Digital Age*, and *Focused Genograms: Intergenerational Assessment of Individuals, Couples, and Families* (2nd ed.). Dr. Twist serves as the Editor-in-Chief of *Sexual and Relationship Therapy: International Perspectives on Theory, Research and Practice*. Markie is also co-editor of the book *Eco-Informed Practice: Family Therapy in an Age of Ecological Peril*. Markie has won numerous awards for mentorship and research. Markie regularly consults, presents, and researches in the following areas: eco-informed family therapy practices, Couple and Family Technology practices, and sexual, gender, erotic, and relational diversity. To learn more visit: drmarkie.com.

Preface

We have no business writing this book.

Those were my (KH) exact words to Markie as we sat eating chips and salsa, and drinking margaritas in a Mexican restaurant in the McCarran International Airport. This followed a conversation we were having with our respective children—two kids who seemingly knew more about YouTube than we did. In part, this comment was in jest. As parents, we know that our children are more "hip" than we are and up-to-date on the latest trends that we as parents may not follow or even be aware of. This fact was plainly clear, as each of our kids discussed their top five YouTube stars and sites. They continued their conversation into types of games that each liked and tried to organize a playdate for "Five Nights at Freddy's." As the conversation waned and our respective partners (one a software engineer and the other a social media manager) chimed in about their knowledge of what the kids were discussing, we continued to wonder if we, two family therapists and academics in psychotherapy by training, knew enough about specific software, hardware, and lingo to be writing a book telling people how to navigate these technologies in their relationships.

But, as the conversation unfolded, we realized: the technology (what we knew about it or what we did not know about it) did not ultimately matter. We could swap out the specific technology or device—cellphone, texting, social media, YouTube, etc.—and the net result was the same. It is about time on a screen. It is about interacting with something on screen seemingly in favor of another individual who may share the same space. It is about how to parent in a world where children are adapting more quickly than their care providers. It is about finding ways to use what children know to connect with them more fully. It is about identifying the circumstances in our romantic relationships that compromise the intimacy, trust, and communication, and finding innovative and applicable ways to repair these.

Markie and I (KH) have both long said that technology has not changed relationships and family systems in their daily tasks; families still accomplish the same tasks as they have in previous generations. We still must find ways to balance autonomy in raising our children and having them respond to rules. We still have to balance work life and home life, feeling crunched by the demands of both, and look for ways to spend more time together. No matter what exactly a specific type of technology is designed to do, there are predictable ways in which it affects our relationships and how our relationships influence the development of new technologies. And we, as couple and family therapy scholars, knew we were the perfect people for doing this job.

Purpose of the Book

The field of Couple and Family Technology (CFT) as identified by Katherine M. Hertlein (Hertlein, 2012; Hertlein & Blumer, 2013) addresses how technology affects couple and family life. The primary purpose of this book, *The Internet Family*, is to provide an updated look on how things have changed with technology for couples and families over time and provide a plan for readers to learn how to incorporate technology in their lives in thoughtful and helpful ways. In this book, we articulate the ways in which couples and families navigate their relationship with technology. This includes a discussion of the motivations of usage of specific technologies and social media, specific issues that emerge because of technology, and a presentation of risks relevant to ourselves and our relationships.

The audience for this book is practicing clinicians, instructors, and students. It is written to be a book that can be used by couple and family therapists as they work with relational systems; it is also written to be a book to which a clinician might refer an individual, couple, or family as part of a treatment process. A portion of this book is also devoted to the application of the CFT framework. Because it is multitheoretical, the introduction of the CFT framework does not imply that clinicians need to necessarily change their preferred clinical approach; instead, it serves as invitation to find ways to incorporate such a framework into current practice. We believe this is a more inclusive approach to working with couples and families, particularly around technology-related issues. Clinicians, students, and general readers will find information that will help them address the following kinds of common concerns:

- Internet or online infidelity
- Online pornography–related issues
- Online dating

- Parenting and the Internet
- Internet-related dissolutions
- Everyday usage of technology and new media
- Online video gaming
- The Internet in the developmental life cycle
- Cybersex and digisexuality
- Out-of-control technology-related behaviors
- Cyberbullying
- Cyberstalking
- Electronic intimate partner violence

Simply stated, our book is about the way that different technologies affect relationships in different ways and the way that relationships affect the use of different technologies. We present the state of the interdisciplinary research and scholarly thoughts on how new media is integrated into couple and family life. We also walk our readers through how to apply the CFT framework to their own lives, specifically assisting them in recognizing the scope of the Internet, the potential for risks and improvement in relationships via technology, and how to develop a plan to thoughtfully integrate technology into relationships.

Outline of Chapters

This book is divided into two sections. In Section One, we orient the reader to the issues and relevant topics of technology today. In Chapter 1, we review technology's penetration in our lives. We provide up-to-date information describing the devices people are using, what researchers tell us about how many messages and texts are being sent, how devices are being used, and how social media is used in couple and family life. In Chapter 2, we compare what the differences are between online and face-to-face communication. We also review personality characteristics and motivations of those engaging in electronically based communication, as well as review different types of online relationships.

The focus of Chapter 3 is on how couples and technology evolve together over the lifespan. Some specific areas of attention include how romantic relationships are initiated by electronic means, the use of technology in a couple's life as they raise children, and discussion of relationship termination in a digital age. In Chapter 4, we highlight key issues related to technology that may emerge in families/relational systems—namely, youth as digital natives, surveillance and tracking of children, age appropriate phone and technology usage, etc. This includes a discussion of education, parental monitoring, work life, and other critical issues.

Key issues related to technology that may emerge in couple treatment are highlighted in Chapter 5—namely, online infidelity, out-of-control technology-related behaviors, and online video gaming. We also address some of the larger areas, which may be secondary concerns related to these key areas such as accountability, shared time and interests, gender and power, and suspicion and jealousy. In Chapter 6, we review cyberbullying, cyberstalking, and technology-facilitated violence in couple relationships. We also discuss cyberbullying, adolescent usage of these technologies that lead to these things, and the role of the family in cyberbullying protection and awareness.

Rather than focusing on the problems, we then move to solutions in Section Two—how can myriad technologies be harnessed for our advantage? In Chapter 7, we detail how the qualities germane to the Internet affect a couple's satisfaction, structure, and processes. In Chapter 8, we review how the structure of relationships, as well as technology, affects relational functioning and the impact to relationship structure. We discuss roles by examining how aspects of technology described earlier affect couple and family roles, rules, and boundaries. The way technology influences processes, including relationship initiation, maintenance, and termination, is reviewed in Chapter 9. We provide detail on how parenting practices are affected by technologies, how children respond to these changes, and how adult children navigate relationships in a digital age.

In Chapter 10, we explore the presentation and management of advanced Internet issues such as the concept of out-of-control technology-related behaviors and video gaming. In Chapter 11, and highlighted specifically in the online Appendices, we present commonly used assessments and strategies to determine whether one is experiencing an Internet-related problem. In this chapter we also expand upon the technology-based focused genogram, as originally detailed in our last technology-related book (Hertlein & Blumer, 2013) and in one of our chapters (Blumer & Hertlein, 2015) in an edited work by one of our colleagues. We provide a series of questions to accompany this genogram contained within the Appendices provided on Taylor & Francis's website, www.routledge. com/9781138478053. Finally, in Chapter 12, we walk readers through how to create their own Technology Integration Plan (TIP) that outlines how to use technology well in one's relationships.

Key Terms

Throughout the course of this text, we will be using the terms "technology" and "new media." For our purposes, technology is defined as the application of innovations specifically within the fields of communication and electronics. New media is a term encompassing a broad range of technologies that enable electronic communication. These include objects such as smartphones and tablets, websites such as Facebook and other social media, and forms of art and entertainment such as video games and electronic art.

A Note on Timeliness

We also acknowledge that this book, as timely as it may be to the field now, may contain statistics and figures regarding technology usage that will be quickly outdated. Therefore, we want to assert that while the statistics may be flexible, the concepts related to the CFT framework and information about family and couple dynamics affected by technology will remain quite stable. We provide examples describing how common experiences (e.g., online dating, cyberbullying, parental monitoring, relationship maintenance, etc.) operate in couple relationships in the context of technology. Also explored in this book are the unique challenges that technology introduces into couple and family lives, as well as strategies for managing such issues. Our book is primarily aimed at assisting mental healthcare professionals working with relational systems, though we believe people interested in enhancing their relationships in an ever-growing digital age will find benefit in its pages as well.

We sincerely hope that couple and family therapists, academics, and students alike will find this book descriptive enough to be useful to apply in their own training, as well as to serve as a reference and a resource for couples and families they encounter in the therapy room. As technology and new media continue to evolve, we anticipate and embrace further exchange of ideas about this book and these topics for years to come.

Katherine M. Hertlein
Markie L. C. Twist

Acknowledgments

This book would not be possible without the invaluable assistance of many dedicated students, including Kaitlin Andrewjeski and Raven Cloud. Of course, I am also grateful for the support of my institution, the University of Nevada, Las Vegas, for its unwavering support of my career goals and areas of scholarly pursuit. Included in this group are Dr. Sara Jordan (Couple and Family Therapy Program Director), Dr. Alison Netski (Department Chair), and Dr. Sara Hunt (Assistant Dean) for their support of this program of research. It is a joy to go to work each day with these special women.

I am indebted to Mr. George Zimmar and the staff at Taylor & Francis for approaching Dr. Markie Twist and me with this opportunity to write this important text. Ms. Clare Ashworth, managing editor, served as a wonderful point person to ensure a quality project and has been supportive of the topics and writing style for this text, as well as assisting with navigating us through the publication process. A specific and very important thank you goes to Mrs. Kristi Sessions, who carefully edited the manuscript and offered substantive suggestions to expand and provide detailed content. She has offered both editorial support and emotional support in this process, and I am grateful for having a "partner in crime" in this endeavor. This book and the model have greatly benefited from her careful eye, her attention to detail, and her comprehensive and critical thinking of the material.

Personally, this book would not exist without the support of my friends and family. While I have many wonderful friends, specific to this text, thank you to Katie Matthews (who advised me on the proper use of Facebook to execute specific objectives), and Sheala Morrison and Brent Fladmo, for showing me how to maintain perspective and adopt new ones. I appreciate the time that my husband, Eric, affords me to stay up late and write in order to accomplish this project, and my son, Adam, for writing his own books alongside mine. I am grateful for this support of my career and look forward to an amazing new chapter as we manage technology together.

Personal and professional thanks go out to my (MLCT) colleague and friend Dr. Neil McArthur for his informing and innovative ideas regarding robot sex and digisexuality. Our dialogue around these technology-related practices has helped to shape my understanding of Couple and Family Technology (CFT) studies, which is reflected in my contributions regarding digisexuality in this text. Appreciation is also extended to my colleague and good friend Dr. Alex Iantaffi, whose support and encouragement of my work in the area of CFT studies lead to solid collaborations like co-editing a Special Issue on Sex and Technology for *Sexual and Relationship Therapy: International Perspectives on Theory, Research and Practice*. Gratitude is also extended to my friend Dr. Shayna S. Bassett, who, back in 2005, introduced and taught me how to use social media like Myspace and Facebook. As follow-up, a big thank you goes out to Rebecca Koonce, who several years later taught me how to actually use such social media well. Lastly, and most importantly, my deep gratitude goes out to my partner in life and love, Ryan B. Peterson, who works online, whom I met online, proposed to online, and live with online, and thankfully offline. Your experience with technology, and our experiences together as a couple and in our family/relational system, have opened my mind and heart up to the beauty and the benefits that technology has to offer, and have no doubt shaped my view of technology and how I write about it for the better—meaning in a more balanced and positive manner.

TUTORIAL ON TECHNOLOGY AND RELATIONSHIPS

ONE

Couples, Families, and Technology

Technology Invasion

It's "Facebook-official." The Internet and new technologies are in a relationship—with us. As heavy consumers of technology, we are tied to devices with an Internet connectivity nearly continuously. We check our emails in the morning, before bed, and an average of 15 times per day and ten times that if you are a millennial (Social Media Week, 2016). We set up alerts to notify us of any activities or incoming information so that we may be advised of any activities at a moment's notice. We can connect to others an ocean away or gain information about a topic that we could not possibly have accessed a decade ago. We rely on technology to help us more effectively move through the world, increase our social capital, gain information, socialize, and be entertained (Filipovic, 2013).

With these advances come some unintended (or unacknowledged) consequences. The ability we possess via these technologies to access others also provides a mechanism through which we, too, can be accessed. For example, we may be accessed at home and off-hours by those with whom we only have connections via work and career. Former partners, peers, and friends can make a connection to us or simply obtain updates on our daily life through quickly typing names into search engines. It is a way of staying connected without connecting. Further, the unintended consequences may have a substantial impact on others around us. The advances in technology are too fast and too numerous for anyone to keep up with all of them and their effects. By the time we identify how relationships are affected by these technologies, the technology we have figured out has been replaced by a new trend with its own set of implications and consequences.

Couples and families/relational systems who are living in today's world with technology as a prominent part in their organization of tasks and method of communication need to roll back the lens on what specific devices, software, and applications have contributed to the function (or dysfunction) in their relationships. Instead, we should evaluate how factors such as access, affordability, accommodation, and acceptability advance or interfere with a relationship's basic structure and functions. How, for example, does being accessible to anyone 24 hours a day and seven days a week affect how we communicate with those in our own home? How does the affordability and acceptability of having phones play into a parent's decision to gift a phone (and accessibility) to a child? How do we set rules to maintain the benefits of having these technologies in our lives, but limit what we may view as potential negatives?

With data from fields such as information technologies, education, sociology, psychology, biology, family studies, and psychotherapy, we are developing a rich library from which to develop appropriate adaptive responses to these questions. Family studies scholars are piecing together the circumstances in which the Internet can be used to augment relationships, as well as where the Internet may be contributing to problematic outcomes. In some cases, this distinction is easy to make. For example, cases of pathological Internet use, "addiction," or even Internet infidelity are commonly lumped into the negative outcomes category. It may be more difficult in other cases to quantify the net impact on our relationships without consideration of each couple's or family's unique characteristics and how they interact with technology and new media. For example, talking to an individual of a differing or similar gender via Facebook messaging may be perfectly permissible in one couple's relationship, but constitute a serious betrayal in another.

Prevalence of Technology in Our Lives

Technology is infused in the everyday experience for nearly half of the world's population. Of 7.4 billion people in the world, 50% (3.7 billion) indicated they are Internet users and 66% (or 4.92 billion) are identified as unique mobile phone users. This number represents a growth of 10% in Internet users and an increase of 21% in social media users over the last year alone (Hootsuites, 2017). Another 2.5 billion identify themselves as users of social media. Estimates of technological saturation in the population range anywhere from 30 to 99%, depending on where you are on the globe. For example, 88% of the population in North America are Internet users; this is in stark contrast to Africa or South Asia, where 29% and 33% of the population, respectively, are Internet users (Hootsuites, 2017). The United Arab Emirates has the highest penetration of Internet users at 99% and North Korea the lowest at 0.1% (Hootsuites, 2017). The difference in Internet usage between 11 developed countries (such as the United States, Canada, European countries, and developed Asian countries) and emerging countries is 33% (Greenwood, Perrin, & Duggan, 2016). Of those who use the Internet in developed countries, 75%

report accessing the Internet on a daily basis (Poushter, Bishop, & Chwe, 2018). Most frequently, global Internet users are using cellphones to text message, take photos and videos, access social media sites, get information, and make payments (Poushter et al., 2018).

Internet use is influenced by diverse intersectional elements like one's cohort or socioeconomic status (SES). For instance, vast majorities (98%) of Internet users are college-educated, make more than $75,000 annually, and are younger (between the ages of 18 and 29, or 18 and 34, depending on the study). Those who are accessing the Internet more than once a day are also more likely to fit these characteristics (Greenwood et al., 2016). For example, sub-Saharan Africa, which is classified as economically underdeveloped, has one of the lowest rates of adults who use the Internet (25%) (Poushter et al., 2018). In fact, Internet usage is highly correlated with a country's per capita income but has plateaued over the last few years in developed countries (Poushter et al., 2018).

Technology is immersed in our lives, with computers and tablets being a primary mechanism for usage. Somewhere on the order of 450 million hardware devices (e.g., computers, laptops, and tablets) are shipped annually. Specifically, people are opting for smaller and smaller devices, as the purchasing of desktops has decreased in favor of laptops and tablets (Anderson, 2015). One study found that the introduction of a smartphone reduced the use of laptops and, at least in some cases, increased media consumption in other parts of the day (Ley et al., 2013), in part because they may be viewed as more flexible devices and more convenient to accomplish a required task (Ley et al., 2013).

As prevalent as the Internet is in our lives, there still exists a small proportion of the population that is new to the Internet. Those who did not consider themselves Internet users, once given tablets, were still not all inclined to surf online: they also stated the reason they did not have access to technology in the first place was that they did not need the technology (Perrin & Bertoni, 2017). For the 61% who did some online exploration, top activities included looking up news and using applications (apps). In addition, new users reported struggles in using technology, including struggles with the password and login processes, using touch screens, and keeping the device charged (Perrin & Bertoni, 2017).

Mobile Connections by Device

Over time, our ability to be connected has grown even smaller. In the US, 95% of adults own a cellphone—which is a considerable jump from 2005, when 65% of American adults had a cellphone (Rainie, 2015), with no differences in ownership based on racial or ethnic identification. Of US adults who own devices, there has been a steady rise from about 65% to approximately 95% in the number of cellphone owners between 2004 and 2016 and a sharp rise of smartphone owners from nearly

35% to around 80% between 2011 and 2016, with a notable increase globally since 2013 (Greenwood et al., 2016), particularly in developed countries. Between 2013 and 2015, global ownership of smartphones increased from 45% to 54%. Countries such as Turkey, Brazil, Chile, and Malaysia experienced an increase in smartphone ownership of at least 25% (and, in the case of Turkey, up to 42%) (Greenwood et al., 2016). Specifically, there is greater smartphone usage in the US and Europe, and less usage in South Asia and Africa (Poushter et al., 2018). Mobile devices are in use globally, even if the phone is not technically a smartphone.

According to a study conducted by Hootsuites (2017) comparing global smartphone connections to total global mobile connections, the total of global connections across devices was 8.05 billion, the total of connections made on smartphones was 4.42 billion, and the total of connections used on feature-phone devices was 3.38 billion. They then compared the share of smartphone devices and share of feature-phone connections with the total connections. What they found was that the share of smartphone connections and the share of feature-phone connections were 55% and 45% respectively compared to total connections. Not surprisingly, Internet and smartphone penetration is related to a country's overall wealth (Poushter et al., 2018).

Another key advantage to new devices and applications is the flexibility in making connections to others (Barkhaus & Polichar, 2011). In a study examining why people use particular mediums, participants noted there was a great deal of choice and they chose a communication method based on the goal they were trying to meet. For example, if they were interested in making contact with someone due to an emergency, text messaging was preferred over other modalities. Other considerations included the sender's context and response time. For example, if one is going to be near their phone and that is the most convenient way to send a message, they may choose to use the phone. Flexibility was described as "paramount" in making such choices (Barkhaus & Polichar, 2011, p. 632).

The Rise of the Applications: Online Video Games

Today, 40% of adults report having a game console such as an Xbox or PlayStation. Only one-third of households, however, that earn $30,000 or less per year will own a game console compared to the 54% of adults in households that earn $75,000 or more per year. Young adults are particularly likely to play video games, as well as to identify as "gamers." About half of US adults (49%) "ever play video games on a computer, TV, game console or portable device like a cellphone," and 10% consider themselves to be "gamers" (Duggan, 2015). In fact, 77% of men aged 18 to 29 play video games, which is more than any other demographic group, in comparison with 57% of young women who play. Younger US males are the most likely to play video games (Brown, 2017). Of men and women, 24% of men said they play video games often, 23% reported sometimes with a net of 47% confirming video game use as opposed to women, where 19% said they played often, 21% sometimes with a net of 39%. Approximately 40% of people over 65 report playing video games online (Brown, 2017). People of Hispanic identities/backgrounds in the US tend to have the highest net of players at 48%, but persons of Black identities/experience have the highest percentage reporting that they play often at 24%. The highest percentage of gamers who claim to play were between the ages of 18 and 29 with a 60% net consisting of 29% of players saying they game often and 31% saying they game sometimes. Gamers aged 30 to 49 were the second most likely to participate in gaming (Brown, 2017). When looked at in terms of education level, those who had completed some college as opposed to earning a degree or a high school diploma netted the most reported gamers at 50% with 25% saying they play often and 25% saying they play sometimes. Those who had earned a high school diploma or less came in second with a net of 42%.

The Rise of the Applications: Social Networking

Social media is defined by Kaplan and Haenlein (2010, p. 61) as "a group of Internet-based applications that build on the ideological and technological foundations of Web 2.0 and that allow the creation and exchange of User Generated Content." Social media tools allow two-way information exchange, videos, free applications, and other services (Fusi & Feeney, 2016). In terms of messaging capabilities, over half of those using messaging apps between the ages of 18 and 29 use apps that auto-delete messages, significantly more than any other age group (Greenwood et al., 2016). Facebook boasts over one billion users, coming second in terms of Internet traffic only to Google. In fact, Facebook is increasing in its adoptions, whereas other social media sites are remaining steady in that regard (Greenwood et al., 2016). In contrast, 79% of the US population have at least one Facebook account; 32% use Instagram, followed by Pinterest at 31%, LinkedIn at 29%, and Twitter at 24% (Greenwood et al., 2016). The percentage of Facebook users now also represents a 7% increase from 2015 (Greenwood et al., 2016). Further, women are using social media more than men (83% versus 75% respectively), which is interesting given that men tend to use the Internet more than women (Greenwood et al., 2016; Rainie, 2015).

Accessing social media tends to be a regular occurrence in daily life. Some estimates indicate that access to social networking sites (SNSs) occurs approximately every 4 minutes. Data on social media use that looked at monthly active users reported by the most active social media platforms in each country found that there are 2.789 billion active social media users with 2.549 billion users accessing social media via mobile devices. This means that 37% of the total population is accessing social media, while 34% of the total population is accessing their social media through a mobile device (Hootsuites, 2017). Interestingly, countries with the lower proportion of Internet users have higher levels of social media usage, such as the Middle East, Africa, and Latin America. For example, while those in developing countries have less smartphone penetration than developed countries (Hootsuites, 2017), they are more likely to use social media when online (Greenwood et al., 2016). The 76% of those who use Facebook in the US report accessing the site daily (an increase from the 70% reporting such activity in 2015), with 55% reporting accessing sites multiple times per day (Greenwood et al., 2016).

Social media is also becoming the place where a majority of millennials get their news (Rainie, 2015)—via extelligence. Extelligence is described as knowledge gained externally; that is, it is the knowledge each of us contribute to as a collective entity, as well as the withdrawals we make from this collective (Stewart & Cohen, 1997). It describes the process of knowledge-creation in academia where one researcher takes the information provided by another and builds on it, both taking from the collective and contributing more, once they have concluded their studies (Friedman, Whitworth, & Brownstein, 2010). According to Brown, Campbell, and Ling (2011): "The Internet is an important means of acquiring and maintaining social capital" (p. 145), and is a primary reason why many millennials use the Internet. Wikipedia, for example, is one domain where multiple authors contribute to the knowledge presented to others. Sixty percent of those aged 51 to 68 obtain information and news about politics and the government via the television; 68% of millennials (aged 18 to 34), however, get their news about government and media through Facebook (Rainie, 2015). Younger individuals (aged 18 to 39) tend to use Instagram significantly more than older people. Specifically, 58% of those 18 to 29 used Instagram as compared to 33% of those 30 to 49 and 8% of those 65 and older (Greenwood et al., 2016). In fact, in a Greenwood et al. (2016) study, half of the respondents noted that they received information about the 2016 US presidential election from social media. As stated by one undergraduate student at my university: "I'm not big on research. I prefer social media because it's more current and explains better concepts." While access to Facebook may be universal, the way in which it is used is not. In a study on cultural differences in Facebook usage, Hong and Na (2018) found that Americans tend to perceive Facebook activities as individual, whereas Koreans see them as interdependent. These perceptions translate into activities on Facebook, as Koreans engaged in more interdependent activities on Facebook.

Effects of Technology on Our Individual Selves

The effects of technology can be either psychological or physical, or contain elements of both. We are human beings who live in context. That context has changed dramatically over the last 50 years. At present, 1% of US citizens own over one-third of the wealth (Schwartz, 2011). We are also living in an era with the highest proportion of families living in poverty, at 10.1% the same proportion that live without health insurance, a figure that is disproportionate to other geographic regions (U.S. Census Bureau, 2017a). In 2009, 43 million Americans were living in poverty—representing 14.3% of the population and the highest number since 1959 (Schwartz, 2011). We have grown from 1940 with 34,949 households to over 126,000 households in 2017. The number of married couples, however, has dropped. In 1940, 76% of the total households were married couples; in 2017, 47.6% were composed of married individuals (U. S. Census, 2017c). There have also been changes to the family structure. In the 1950s, the trend was for adult children to grow up and move away from the family home. As a consequence of unemployment, poverty, and other negative concerns this trend is reversing: as many as 8% of adults lived with extended family in 2009 and 3.9% of US citizens live in multigenerational households, with a higher proportion in California and the southern US than in other areas of the country (U.S. Census Bureau, 2017a). Since 1940, the number of single person households has steadily been increasing (U.S. Census Bureau, 2017b). On average, the number of persons per household has decreased from an average of 3.33 persons per household in 1960 to 2.54 in 2017.

Effects of Technology on Physical Well-Being

Like any activity, technology usage intersects with our physiology. For example, certain tasks on Facebook such as hitting the *like* button are associated with less cardiac involvement, suggesting it is a more automatic task than other directed Facebook activities (Alhabash, Almutairi, Lou, & Kim, 2018). Research has demonstrated that there are physical implications for young people who frequently use cellphones. The most common symptom is headaches, suffered by half of the respondents, followed extremely closely by irritability. Another symptom is impaired concentration (Acharya, Acharya, & Waghrey, 2013). For youth, consequences of using the Internet more than four hours per day include hypersomnia, skipping meals, and sleeping later (Kim et al., 2010).

Zheng, Wei, Li, Zhu, and Ning (2016) conducted probably the most comprehensive study on the effects of the Internet on our physical well-being. In a sample of 513 individuals, several negative physical impacts directly related to Internet use were observed. Over half of the sample suffered from dry eyes and declining eyesight (73.7% and 64.1% respectively). Nearly half of the sample reported cervical problems (48.1%). Worsening skin was also a problem associated with use, particularly for women (37.8% total, but reported by 26% of the men and 51% of the women). One-third of the sample reported headaches; another third reported lumbar pain and yet another third decreased sleep (34.1%, 31.8%, and 30.0% respectively). A related effect was decreased anti-fatigue for 27%, and nearly the same amount reported greasy hair (26.9%). Approximately 20% of the sample (19.9%) reported weight gain. This was followed by another 12.9% reporting finger numbness, 10.7% reporting wrist pain, 9.9% reporting hair loss, and 8.8% indicating they lose their appetite. Finally, the relationship was not tied to the relationship one developed with technology, but rather the frequency of use (i.e., number of hours online). In other words, the more you use the Internet, the more likely you will be to suffer these effects (Zheng et al., 2016).

There are also specific effects related to the use of mobile phone technologies. For example, 4 hours or more of exposure to the radiofrequency radiation in phones (at least 1800 MHz) was associated with cells with abnormal nuclei and cell death (Meena, Verma, Kohli, & Ingle, 2016). This is particularly true with heavy users and those under 20 years of age (Wojcik, 2016). Finally, in a review of 45 articles, Coenen, Howie, and Straker (2017) found evidence of significant musculoskeletal symptoms from using our touchscreen devices, including:

- Neck and shoulder issues in anywhere from one-quarter to two-thirds of university students using these devices
- Differences in postures when using smartphones as compared to when we do not use smartphones
- Neck and shoulder pain growing with more time on the devices
- Neck discomfort reported by half of high school students
- Pain reported in people who use a smartphone for at least 2 hours per day
- Increased frequency of using an awkward posture when using a tablet, thus contributing to discomfort
- A connection (albeit a weak one) between smartphone screen size and wrist pain
- More temporomandibular problems and wrist issues in those classified as being "addicted" to the smartphone as compared to non-addicted smartphone users
- Discomfort reported in those who play games on their tablet, particularly in the shoulder
- Differences in experience of pain based on the workstation and work type (i.e., keyboard, desktop, tablet, using a stylus, etc.)
- The presence of physiological responses such as muscle fatigue, pressure pain, nerve size, and hand function

On the other hand, such technologies have allowed people to have a more active and participatory role in their healthcare (Banos et al., 2014). For example, instead of waiting for a visit to a doctor to gain information about one's internal state, a host of devices can monitor our bodies and provide real-time information on blood sugar, heart rate, skin temperature, oxygen saturation, hand tremors, etc. (García-Magariño, Medrano, Plaza, & Oliván, 2016). The information provided online has also not interfered with the patient-physician relationship. In a study of approximately 3,200 participants, Murray et al. (2003) found one-third had looked for health information on the Internet in the past 12 months, 16% found health information relevant to themselves, and half of those took the information they found relevant and presented it to their physician. Of those who brought the information to their physician, they were more likely to ask the physician their opinion rather than demanding that the physician follow a particular intervention.

The same positive findings have occurred in promoting health behaviors in youth (Militello, Kelly, & Melnyk, 2012). The ability to text message others seems to increase frequency in blood glucose monitoring (Eng & Lee, 2013), liver transplant success (Miloh et al., 2009), and other healthy lifestyle reminders. Hill-Kayser, Vachani, Hampshire, Di Lullo, and Metz (2012) demonstrated the positive use of an Internet-based tool to create a plan after cancer, a tool that positively improved communication with the healthcare team and adherence to the developed plan. There also might be some data indicating that video games can improve health outcomes, though the quality of the studies is generally poor (Primack et al., 2012). For example, social media is being target as a way to increase awareness of melanoma in young people (Falzone et al., 2017).

Media Misinformation

Alternatively, the media may also produce misinformation regarding certain health conditions, which can compromise physical well-being. "Fake news" was probably one of the most infamous terms in 2017. Sadly, such "fake news" can have deleterious effects on our well-being, particularly for those who have the greatest level of exposure (Balmas, 2014). The more vast the Internet becomes, the greater the potential for misinformation. Part of the misinformation can be the presentation of symptoms linking to a certain condition that, upon reading, one might become concerned they have. As misinformation about conditions is present online, access to this information may create a condition called a *nocebo* effect—meaning that one may experience a detriment to their health because of what they have learned to expect based on the misinformation the Internet provides (Crichton & Petrie, 2015). The key to counteracting the nocebo effect is to provide positively framed messages where a different (and positive) expectation can be provided.

Sedentary Lifestyles

The debate around whether the Internet and new technologies contribute to a sedentary lifestyle is difficult to resolve. Sedentary lifestyles, defined as those that expend less than or equal to 1.5 metabolic equivalents (Prince, Reed, McFetridge, Tremblay, & Reid, 2017), are on an upward trend. Sedentary behaviors include activities such as watching television or using computers. Those who engage in more sedentary behaviors are at a higher risk for cardiac problems, cancers, and overall increased mortality (Wilmont et al., 2012). At this point, we are sitting for an average of 7.5 hours per day, with men sitting more than women and differences among cultural groups (Carson, Staiano, & Katzmarzyk, 2015). Researchers seem to agree that using a computer increases sitting time and, subsequently, increases risk for negative health outcomes (Fotheringham, Wonnacott, & Owen, 2000). This is also true in couples, as one partner's sedentary behavior affects the other partner's (Wood, Jago, Sebire, Zahra, & Thompson, 2015). The associations, however, between sitting time, socioeconomic status, type of setting in which one resides, and one's educational level may dictate how much time one sits. For example, looking at metabolic syndrome, there were no statistically significant differences between rural and urban individuals in how much time they sat during each day. When the dependent variable became measuring obesity, however, there was a difference in that rural individuals spent more than 4 hours a day on the computer.

On the flipside, when one excluded using a computer for work, individuals who lived in urban areas, had a higher level of education, and had higher incomes sat for longer periods of time (Prince et al., 2017). The other challenge is mitigating the negative health consequences attached to living a sedentary life. In one study, researchers discovered those who forego engagement in physical activity in favor of their cellphone have more negative outcomes, specifically those who self-identified as high-frequency cellphone users. In these cases, the more one used a cellphone the less likely one was engaged in cardiovascular activities. This finding was still true when controlled for gender, self-efficacy, and percentage of fat of participants. For example, the high-frequency cellphone users were also more likely to participate in sedentary behaviors more related to the phone. Finally, those who identified themselves as low-frequency users tended to use the cellphone to connect with others in social situations, including setting times to be physically active and engage in physical activities (Lepp, Barkley, Sanders, Rebold, & Gates, 2013). In another study, however, the effect of cellphone use was more tied to sedentary behavior, but not physical activity (Barkley, Lepp, & Salehi-Esfahani, 2016).

One peripherally related study examining transgenerational transmission of depression found depression-like symptoms in a sample of Siberian hamsters whose parents were exposed to nighttime illumination (i.e., much like the light we may be exposed to on computers) prior to mating (Cissé, Russart, & Nelson, 2017). The explanation for this finding is that early-life environments predispose certain individuals to particular conditions, and that stressful environments create toxins, which have an effect on how genes express themselves. Obviously, humans are not hamsters. But such findings beg the question as to whether there is similar transmission of stressful events and, consequently, how these events manifest in our genetic makeup. We already have evidence that some transmission of stressful events from parent to child occurs (Wolstenholme et al., 2012).

Sleep

Technology has also affected our sleep style—or rather whether we sleep at all. For children and adolescents, the results are clear: there is a detrimental effect to the amount of time spent online and their sleep schedule (Nose et al., 2017). Fifty-six percent of teens reported texting, tweeting, or messaging others while in bed, and 20% indicated they woke up to texts (Polos et al., 2015). The issues with sleep in young people are consistently present when one's Internet use is problematic, typically defined as excessive time spent online (Ferreira et al., 2017). Ferreira et al. (2017) asked seventh and eighth graders to complete a self-report inventory about their Internet use, their sleep habits, and their sleepiness during the day. Youth who fell into the Internet dependence category represented 19% of the sample, and were correlated with excessive daytime sleepiness, difficulty falling asleep, difficulty staying asleep, and using social media. In another study of 11 to 13 year olds, those who frequently used their mobile phones, played video games, engaged in social networking, and listened to music via devices had more difficulty falling asleep than their non-connected counterparts (Arora, Broglia, Thomas, & Taheri, 2014). In fact, those who listened to music had the most nightmares; those who watched TV were more likely to sleepwalk (Arora et al., 2014). Other problematic consequences include academic underperformance (Polos et al., 2015) and disruption to the next day's activities (Nose et al., 2017). More often than not, adolescents and young adults are using phones before bed, thus negatively impacting their sleep quantity and quality (Levenson, Shensa, Sidani, Colditz, & Primack, 2016).

For adults, the data is conflicting. An overwhelming majority of Americans (90%) report using some form of screen or technology prior to going to bed—with TV being the media used for 60%. At the same time, one study examined the amount of time one spends online prior to going to bed, with most (60%) noting TV was the media being used. Further, interactive technologies used within an hour of bedtime are associated with more problems in both falling asleep and obtaining restful sleep (Gradisar et al., 2013). While there is some evidence of the times at which adults' sleep schedules are shifting for those online more frequently (i.e., going to bed later and waking later), technologies such as TV or tablets in their bedroom do not seem to negatively impact sleep hygiene (Custers & Van den Bulck, 2012). In fact, in one study with a small sample (11 young adults), the amount they engaged in social exposure via media was affected by the sleep they got the night before (Butt, Ouarda, Quan, Pentland, & Khayal, 2015).

Finally, there are many ways in which technology is designed to augment sleep and deep relaxation. Countless apps for promoting deep sleep and relaxation are available, including websites and YouTube channels, and there are nearly 700 apps dedicated to mindfulness (Mani, Kavanagh, Hides, & Stoyanov, 2015), despite that their effectiveness is difficult to assess. The sheer number of apps advertised can be overwhelming and limit an individual's ability to sort through them all to find one that best fits or is evidence-based (Coulon, Monroe, & West, 2016). Handel (2011) outlined several apps that were characterized by good functionality, ease of use, workable interface, quality, ratings, and information provided, but apps change so constantly that this list may already be out of date. A branch of therapeutic intervention known as eco-wellness focuses on exposure and connection to nature settings as a way to promote relaxation. YouTube promotes methods by which one may tap into nature in sensory ways through watching a relaxing nature video and hearing natural sounds, such as ocean, waterfall, birds, streams, insects, rain, and thunder (Reese et al., 2016).

Effects of Technology on Psychological Well-Being

We are human beings who live in context. That context has changed dramatically over the last 50 years. Authors such as Stephen Ilardi (2009) point out that our lifestyle change from agricultural and rural beginnings to the life that many live now has been so drastic that we cannot help but have emotional, physical, and intellectual consequences. Younger age cohorts of the US are now five times more likely to exceed psychopathology cut off scores on the Minnesota Multiphasic Personality Inventory (MMPI), including in the areas of paranoia, hypomania (which 40% fit), psychopathic deviation, and depression (Twenge et al., 2010). Depression rates (and correlationally, suicide rates) have increased over the last 50 years, a fact in the US, and one that is not true in less-developed and more communal regions and cultures around the world. High school students report more subtle symptoms consistent with depression now than in cohorts before (Twenge, 2014), but fewer overt symptoms (i.e., less suicidal ideation and less likely to perceive themselves as being depressed). This increase in the US has prompted researchers to explore more how the environment may be a correlational factor in the increase. For example, teens who are exposed to chronic peer stress for three years are more likely to be diagnosed with depression later, a finding particularly true for girls (Hankin et al., 2015). One study of 816 teens explored the impact of social comparison and feedback seeking (a key part of social media usage, particularly for teens), and found adolescents were more likely to experience depressive symptoms if they engaged in higher levels of social comparison and feedback seeking. Further, adolescent boys with more depressive symptoms were more likely to continue to engage in social comparison and feedback seeking activities, thus potentially establishing a cycle of negative reinforcement (Nesi, Miller, & Prinstein, 2017).

The role of technology as a factor in contributing to depression continues to be explored. For instance, nationally representative annual survey research on 1.1 million 8th, 10th, and 12th graders between the years of 1991 and 2016 revealed a sudden and dramatic decrease in the psychological well-being of this adolescent population beginning in 2012 (Twenge, Martin, & Campbell, 2018). The researchers found that cyclical economic factors like unemployment and home loss due to foreclosure (as was occurring during the recession at the time of the study) were not significantly correlated with the well-being in this adolescent population, and were not the cause of the decreased well-being (Twenge et al., 2018). Instead, this decrease is believed to be related to the population's rapidly acquired smartphones and their related increased time spent communicating through and with technologies (e.g., social media, the Internet, texting, gaming) and less time spent engaging in non-technology-based activities (e.g., in-person social exchanges, sport/exercise, homework, attending cultural events) (Twenge et al., 2018). It is important to note that the adolescents in this population who were the happiest in terms of psychological well-being were those who spent time engaging in non-technology-based activities, but did also engage in technology-based activities—just for relatively shorter periods of time (Twenge et al., 2018)

We are not suggesting that cellphones and technology make people depressed and cause death. On the contrary, technologies have been and are used to intervene for someone having a difficult time or contemplating suicide, or for those who find benefit in keeping connections with peers and family, and enable them with a larger, more supportive, and immediate social network. In fact, Harwood, Dooley, Scott, and Joiner (2014) found no relationship between smartphone use and depression, and a negative relationship between depression and phone calls.

Integrating the research, the trend seems to be that while there are mixed reviews about the impact of technology on the psychology of adults, there appears to be more scholarly certainty of the negative impacts of technology on children and youth. For example, in a study of over 3500 children aged 10 and 11, those who used social networking sites and participated in online gaming fared worse psychologically than those who did not engage in such activities or did so to a lesser degree (Devine & Lloyd, 2012). So, what does the lack of sleep associated with the Internet do to our individual psychological selves? First, shorter sleep duration (related to excessive Internet use) increases the likelihood of some pretty significant negative outcomes, including depression, suicidal ideation, and obesity for young people (Demirci et al., 2015; Lemola, Perkinson-Gloor, Brand, Dewald-Kaufmann, & Grob, 2015) and behavior problems (Soni et al., 2017). These effects were both a direct result of Internet use, as well as indirectly the result of getting less sleep in favor of more time online.

The increased presence (or reliance) on social media is not unilaterally positive. Researcher Dr. Brian Primack suggests the net effect of the . . . er . . . "net" is *probably* leaning toward the negative, citing specifically the association of using social media and increased depression and feelings of isolation. People experience anxiety being away from their phones and seem to struggle with not living the ideal life that seems to be displayed on so many others' Facebook pages. He and his team also discovered that the more social media sites you use, the worse off you are in terms of mental health outcomes. In a meta-analysis of 23 studies including over 13,000 participants, a negative correlation was found between Facebook usage and well-being, as well as a positive correlation between Facebook usage and psychological distress, particularly for older individuals (Marino, Gini, Vieno, & Spada, 2018). On the other hand, from examining people's participation in dating apps (which are different than social media), Stanford sociologist Dr. Michael Rosenfeld suggests the Internet is indifferent—it is not positive or negative, but rather a tool people use to accomplish a task (Rosenfeld, 2018).

Video games also seem to have a detrimental impact on psychological well-being. For instance, for children, Gameboy usage was associated with lower levels of social acceptance (whereas high Internet usage was associated with lower academic competence) in a sample of 825 Norwegian school children aged 10 to 12 (Heim, Brandtzæg, Hertzberg Kaare, Endestad, & Torgersen, 2007). Impaired psychological well-being for youth has been found to be associated with greater video game usage, as well as using the Internet for communicative purposes, particularly for Black youth (Jackson et al., 2008). Similar findings were discovered for adults, where the amount of time participating in massively multiplayer online role-playing games (MMORPGs) is associated with poorer psychological outcomes (Kirby, Jones, & Copello, 2014).

The determination as to whether psychological effects are positive or negative may have something to do with the type of technology and platform used. For example, in the context of online gaming, those with higher levels of game-contingent self-worth are also more likely to develop Internet gaming disorders (Beard & Wickham, 2016). In the case for Facebook, for example, findings are mixed as to whether positives or negatives are dominant (Song et al., 2014). One study found that loneliness predicts Facebook use instead of the other way around (Song et al., 2014). In fact, those technologies where there is more richness in the media contribute to higher levels of satisfaction than media that are less rich (Goodman-Deane, Mieczakowski, Johnson, Goldhaber, & Clarkson, 2016). The function of why technology is used also may have an effect on the outcomes. In a study examining mental health and Internet usage, Panova and Lleras (2016) found a positive relationship between impaired mental health and problematic Internet usage, particularly when the Internet assists someone in avoiding negative feelings. The same was not true, however, when the Internet is used to manage boredom (Panova & Lleras, 2016). These same nuanced effects regarding playing MMORPGs—the impact of the game on one's psychological well-being—had to do with the motivation for playing (Shen & Williams, 2011). In fact, psychological resilience mitigates negative effects of social media use (Hou et al., 2017). In addition, children with cellphones were more likely to be nervous, have a bad temper, and be mentally distracted than children without phones. These behaviors were worse if the child had a phone at an early age (Divan, Kheifets, Obel, & Olsen, 2012).

Further, the impact on one's mental and emotional health has something to do with one's involvement and relationship with their device rather than use of the device itself. In a sample of 274 ranging in age from 16 to 59, researchers administered: (1) mood inventories (a depression/anxiety/stress inventory), (2) a series of questions assessing the purpose of Internet usage (i.e., information seeking, entertainment, etc.), (3) a series of questions regarding mobile phone involvement, and (4) an inventory on Internet "addiction" (Harwood et al., 2014). Contrary to previous research, they did not find associations with smartphone use and depression, stress, or anxiety; they did, however, distinguish smartphone involvement, such as obsessive phone checking, an activity that is not reported as phone usage, but that signifies a relationship with the phone without these mental health outcomes (Harwood et al., 2014). This is particularly important when we consider evidence that young people check their phone, on average, over 150 times per day (Social Media Week, 2016). Further support of media usage comes from the systematic review conducted by Seabrook, Kern, and Rickard (2016) in which they examined 70 studies on both passive and directed social networking site interactions. The interactions that were most frequently associated with poorer outcomes (i.e., depression and anxiety) were those that were negative interactions with others, and those that involved social comparison (Lin & Utz, 2015; further discussed in Chapter 3 in the present text). Intersecting with this type of usage is one's gender—girls, for example, who use Facebook passively are more likely to encounter harmful outcomes than girls who use it actively in either public or private settings; boys, on the other hand, have more negative outcomes when they use Facebook actively in a public setting only (Frison & Eggermont, 2015). These negative outcomes were exacerbated in cases where individuals had a tendency to ruminate about those negative interactions online. Finally, the more authentic a young person is online, the more social support they receive and, consequently, the more they are able to ward off depression (Xie et al., 2018).

Technology overload (defined by the number of hours using technology) is associated with a host of negative outcomes, including negative effects on self-esteem, the development of the inability to delay gratification, attention problems, problems with boundary settings, the emergence of personality disorders such as narcissism and antisocial behavior, and mood conditions such as depression and anxiety (Scott, Valley, & Simecka, 2016). In addition, young people (aged 30 or less) engage in the heaviest cellphone usage across groups. Taking measures including, but not limited to, the following: depending less on technologies, limiting time spent on technology, and finding ways technology is advantageous while mitigating the negative impacts might be worthwhile endeavors (Acharya et al., 2013). In fact, such technologies are developing to assist in monitoring mental health processes much in the same way that physical health may be monitored (Gaggioli et al., 2013). The effect of the benefits online may be tied to development. Less sleep in teens means a higher risk for suicidality (Lopes, Boronat, Wang, & Fu-I, 2016), particularly sleeping under 8 hours per night in Chinese youth and under 6 hours in Taiwanese youth (Yen, King, & Tang, 2010). In a rather disturbing study, Oshima et al. (2012) found a higher rate of mental health disturbance in both young and late adolescents associated with using a mobile phone after lights out bedtime. Specifically, those who used the phone after their bedtime were more likely to have suicidal thoughts and thoughts of self-harm, even after controlling for length of sleep.

The lack of sleep may have interpersonal and relational consequences (Gordon, Mendes, & Prather, 2017), in part because sleep is critical for the processing of emotions (Deliens, Gilson, & Peigneux, 2014). For example, in a study looking at husbands' and wives' sleep habits, heterosexual couples reported they were more satisfied if they had more hours of sleep (Maranges & McNulty, 2017). In fact, the more sleep husbands get, the more globally happy they are about the relationship (a finding not true for wives) (Maranges & McNulty, 2017). Lack of sleep in young people can have an impact in the development of depression, anxiety, and substance abuse (Lemola et al., 2015), which can in turn have indirect effects on relationship perception and satisfaction. For example, lack of sleep may have interpersonal consequences. In a study of 77 heterosexual couples, those who got less sleep and had lower quality sleep were more likely to report feeling hurt and rejected by their partner (Gilbert, Pond, Haak, DeWall, & Keller, 2015). Several studies found the reduction in sleep was associated with lower levels of empathy for one's partner and, consequently, an impaired ability to successfully resolve conflict (Gordon & Chen, 2014), but that inflammatory response is reduced when one is able to express their own feelings (Wilson et al., 2017).

In addition to the disruption to sleep quantity and quality, nighttime is also a time when sexual activity is more frequent. A couple's sex life, then, may be interrupted by a text message or email notification, as is now common (Wilmer & Chein, 2016). Finally, the information on life satisfaction and computer usage also may affect our relationships. Further, life satisfaction has an effect on relationship adjustment, and relationship adjustment can have an effect on overall life satisfaction (Stanley, Ragan, Rhoades, & Markman, 2012). And when that life satisfaction is mitigated by how we feel about ourselves, the conclusions we come to when we compare ourselves to others online, the constant checking and involvement in our cellphones, and the physical effects of screen times and small devices will ultimately have an impact on our relationships.

Life Satisfaction

Life satisfaction may be either positive or negative depending on the study. One study indicates life satisfaction for society is at an increase as compared to a decade ago—with the Internet as a key player in that change (Lissitsa & Chachashvili-Bolotin, 2016). As mentioned earlier, increased time on the computer may result in leading a more sedentary lifestyle. This not only has the physical implications listed earlier, but can also have psychological implications. For example, one study found that leisure time spent engaging in physical activity is related to higher levels of overall life satisfaction, as well as a lowered perception of stress (Schnohr, Kristensen, Prescott, & Scharling, 2005). In another study, however, life satisfaction was negatively correlated with amount of time spent online (Stepanikova, Nie, & He, 2010). Çelik and Odacı (2013) found that the more problematic Internet use was negatively associated with life satisfaction. In one study in Taiwan, positive impacts of the Internet were observed across many different domains. Liang, Peng, and Yu (2012) conducted phone interviews with 3,563 respondents aged 15 and over in Taiwan. They found that people who have a home computer and those who have the Internet at home have higher life satisfaction in many areas, including SES, physical health, social competence, and psychological pressure. Internet use is positively related to the development of empathy for Black American adolescents. Controlling for age, gender, and previous level of empathy, Black teens who use the Internet for race-related purposes scored higher on an empathy index one year later; however, that effect did not occur when the teen was exposed to discrimination online (Lozada & Tynes, 2017).

Other benefits of time online include increased opportunities for social connection and interaction (Chan, 2015). Connection through online experience is positively associated with the development of social relations to family members, friends, those with similar political and religious interests, and those in a similar profession (Oh, Ozkaya, & LaRose, 2014). The ability to participate in support groups or receive supportive messages is demonstrated to be significant in obtaining more positive health outcomes for both young people through older adulthood (Sims, Reed, & Carr, 2017), though frequency of involvement in social media does not seem to enhance the perception of social support (Shensa, Sidani, Lin, Bowman, & Primack, 2016). Text messaging among various support groups has had positive outcomes for the management of diabetes (Turner et al., 2013), and was associated with significantly fewer rejections after liver transplants (Miloh et al., 2009). But more friends does not equal increased subjective well-being across the board; the relationship is actually curvilinear (Kim & Lee, 2011). Specifically, fewer friends means less time becoming involved in others' lives, connected to a lower subjective well-being. As the number of Facebook friends increases, an investment in those friends likewise increases alongside one's subjective well-being. The subjective well-being, however, drops if even more friends are added to the point where the ability to be involved in their lives decreases due to the sheer number of friends (Kim & Lee, 2011).

Rainie (2013) argues that the Internet has made us more connected to others instead of being lonelier. Rather than turning to a physically close immediate family or network, we have shifted to larger, more loosely defined groups for connection. Both older and younger individuals cite Facebook and social media as a key factor in the maintenance of connections and increased quality of life (Quinn, Chen, Mulvenna, & Bond, 2016). This is specifically true when we use Facebook to maintain relationships we already have rather than establishing new ones—in that case, psychological outcomes tend to be worse (Erae & Lonborg, 2015). Our networks have, therefore, become more diversified.

Technology and Our Work Lives

Technology use has also had a significant effect on how we conduct ourselves in the workplace (Vitak, Crouse, & LaRose, 2011). Over half (53%) of Generation Y individuals (more commonly known as millennials) reported using social media at work; 53% of those older than Generation Y also reported using social media at work—but were more likely to use it for personal reasons than work-related (Holland, Cooper, & Hecker, 2016). In education, students indicate work is more collaborative when they have access to the Internet at school, but findings show they are more disengaged (Heflin, Shewmaker, & Nguyen, 2017). Some of these findings could be explained by the developmental level of the student. For example, freshmen in college who spend more time online have fewer friends, potentially negatively affecting their academic skills, whereas seniors actually benefit from their Facebook interactions, use it for social connection, and can limit it from interfering with their academics (Kalpidou, Costin, & Morris, 2011). One of the primary areas of investigation has been the extent to which having social media present in our workplaces has affected employee productivity. Part of this area of investigation has focused on the perception of managers of employees' social media use, and this research has shown that if managers perceive social media positively, they will regard others' usage as positive (Fusi & Feeney, 2016). Managers also play an unknowing but integral part in social media use at work. Social media is a tool used to accomplish many things—one of which is to gain social support. If supervisors provide social support for their staff in general, the staff is less likely to use social media (Charoensukmongkol, 2014). Additionally, one study found that top-level managers actually use social media for personal reasons at work more than their staff do (Andreassen, Torsheim, & Pallesen, 2014).

The terms "cyberloafing" and "cyberslacking" describe the phenomenon by which we engage in social media instead of working (Vitak et al., 2011). *Cyberloafing* is defined as using the Internet during work to engage in personal (non-workplace) business (Liberman, Seidman, McKenna, & Buffardi, 2011). Whether one engages in cyberloafing, however, depends on a complex interweave of factors. First, several studies have demonstrated that using the web during a task may be associated with several positive outcomes, including feeling less bored, more engaged, less stressed, and feeling a greater work-home balance (Andreassen et al., 2014; Malik, Saleem, & Ahmad, 2010). Second, those who tend to have a positive attitude toward using social media at work tend to be younger, more highly educated, and single (Andreassen et al., 2014). Cyberloafers more often have greater levels of autonomy in their position (also not surprising since that user would be able to get away with more activities that were not monitored (Andreassen et al., 2014). Other characteristics positively associated with cyberloafing include being younger, male, and in a minority group (Vitak et al., 2011). Finally, individuals who engage in cyberslacking may also rate more highly on the personality dimensions of extraversion and neuroticism scale of the Big 5 Personality test (Andreassen et al., 2014).

Using social media at work is also related to perceived job satisfaction (Koch, Gonzalez, & Leidner, 2012), potentially in part because policies that allow workers to use social media may increase morale (Bennett, Owers, Pitt, & Tucker, 2010), and consequently, productivity and performance (Nduhura & Prieler, 2017). Social media used for work, however, does not lend itself to more productivity (Leftheriotis & Giannakos, 2014). There is also age and generational differences, as one might expect with social media use. Holland et al. (2016) noted Generation Y-ers were more likely to voice concerns about work over social media if they were dissatisfied with their job. Looking at Facebook use specifically, those who more frequently use social media to connect are those who are part time workers or contract workers. In addition, the more some of these workers spent on Facebook, the more they perceived their job as a calling (Hanna, Kee, & Robertson, 2017. On the flipside, cyberloafing may also contribute to some negative outcomes as others may compare their status to what they see from others on Facebook (Andreassen et al., 2014). Finally, we are now becoming multi-taskers, which may impact learning. For example, in a study by Rosen and colleagues, students unlocked their phones over 50 times a day. Of course, adults are also people who are unlocking their phones (Rosen, Whaling, Rab, Carrier, & Cheever, 2012). This level of multi-tasking may interfere with work and emotional processing, and connect with some potentially negative outcomes.

Projecting What's Next for Technology in Our Lives

The latest technology trends in 2017 include both micro and macro changes. Micro changes include the presence of online harassment—a condition affecting 40% of overall Internet users, but 67% of younger users (Anderson, 2017). Social media is the venue by which most online harassment takes place (Rainie, 2017). The repeal of Net Neutrality is also a topic that will have impact on a micro level. In short, Net Neutrality protected consumers from Internet Service Providers' ability to speed up or slow down one's connection based on the information is sought. The country with the most protections to ensure a fair Internet service is India (Lyengar, 2018). With the repeal of Net Neutrality in the United States, Internet Service Providers will have more control over users' access, thus changing access, searches, communication, and information seeking ("Loss of Net Neutrality Could Harm Research", 2017). Another micro trend is the way in which we watch television—as we shift from cable and television networks to online streaming and a la carte viewing (Anderson, 2017). Macro impacts include the advent of driverless cars, the future of technology and automation in workplaces, and the integration of social media and technology in elections and political processes (Anderson, 2017).

In summarizing changes to society via new media, Rainie (2013) characterized the Internet and media as *"portable, participatory, and pervasive"* (Rainie, 2013). These precise characteristics demand more attention from couples and family therapy scholars. We are active participants in communication with others—our partners, our families—from anywhere. Vast majorities of us are making these connections to the Internet via a cellphone or tablet—both portable devices—and do so from virtually anywhere at any time. The opportunity to engage and interact with these technologies is everywhere you look and will continue to be everywhere (Rainie, 2015). Screens, for example, will be everywhere you look (Rainie, 2015). From a consumer perspective, there will be more encounters with media and more sharing of media. A second projection is that augmented reality will increasingly make its way into our offline lives. This will result in pointed information directed at us regarding our immediate location and advertising in local areas. A third trend will be the continued development and immersion in virtual reality, which may include more changes in one's brain due to the use of these technologies. We will also receive more alerts and notifications through media, which means that we will be checking media with more frequency than we already are. A fifth trend is the effect of automation on jobs and services, where such technologies will be even more integrated (and depended on) to complete certain jobs or assist us in accomplishing tasks (Rainie, 2015).

What Does All of This Mean for Relationships?

The Pathology of Pathology

A significant amount of literature early on in the field of Couple and Family Technology studies focused on the impact of the Internet on our personal lives and had a negative tinge. Part of this may be because the literature was written by therapists or others who viewed some of the problems with technology in daily life. For example, Hertlein and Webster (2008) concluded that scholars in the family therapy field default to resolve problems in our daily lives; therefore, the literature at the time largely reflected a pathological view of technology. Then again, this was around the time that the Internet was just becoming immersed in our lives, where much of the writing about it was negative.

Technology, however, is not inherently good or bad. Just like anything, technology can have negative implications based on how it is used. It can also be beneficial in our lives. We do not believe there is much value in pathologizing the Internet or social media, particularly because that pathology will get us nowhere. The Internet is here to stay, and we need to adopt a perspective on it that is helpful and adaptive rather than considering it unilaterally negative.

Our View—A Balanced Approach

There are many reasons that one could consider the computer and Internet unilaterally negative on people and relationships. As we have discussed earlier, there are associations to lack of sleep, depression, behavioral issues, and a host of other issues when these technologies are in use. In short, there is a general tendency in the media to present the idea that the computer and technology are a bad thing. The media is replete with the endorsement of a pathological perspective on technology as evidenced by news articles warning us of the dangers of technology "addiction" and cyberbullying of youth, and advising on how to become "unwired" to our devices, etc. This view, in our opinion, is neither accurate nor helpful. To simply assume that we can disconnect at this point is unrealistic: to only acknowledge the power of how the Internet can be used for maladaptive gains is also inaccurate and ignores the power and ways in which we can use the technology presented to augment our relationships and our development in healthy ways.

There are many implications of increased usage of technology in relationships. For instance, it could change how families interact with each other compared to other generations, but it could also look the same, simply with different language involved surrounding technology. How do these changes to information, automation, and connectivity change the way we accomplish the same tasks we did relationally? In addition to our interactions, the way we accomplish tasks has changed. For example, cellphones increased the likelihood adult women sustain contact with their mothers (Treas & Gubernskaya, 2018).

Conclusion

The purpose of this text is to answer these questions and to pose new ones about how technology shapes our roles, rules, boundaries, and relational processes. We will explore how these changes to our psychology, environment, and presentation in online venues impact how we initiate, structure, and terminate relationships. We will identify where technology is advantageous in our relationships and how we can tap into the resources technology has to offer to access its benefits, individually and relationally. Technology's role in our lives is not exclusively positive or negative. The ways in which it bridges us to others outside of our relationship may both enrich our relationships and create divisions and separations from each other. It may provide entertainment and greater opportunities to cultivate new ideas as much as it might promote isolation and foster a sense of disconnection. So what exactly is our relationship with technology? Let's just say "it's complicated."

References

Acharya, I., Acharya, J. P., & Waghrey, D. (2013). A study on some psychological health effects of cell-phone usage amongst college going students. *International Journal of Medical Research & Health Sciences, 2*(3), 388–394. doi:10.5958/j.2319-5886.2.3.068

Alhabash, S., Almutairi, N., Lou, C., & Kim, W. (2018). Pathways to virality: Psychophysiological responses preceding likes, shares, comments, and status updates on Facebook. *Media Psychology,* 1–21. doi:10.1080/15213269.2017.1416296

Anderson, M. (2015). *Technology device ownership: 2015.* Pew Research Center. Retrieved December 29, 2017, from www.pewInternet.org/2015/10/29/technology-device-ownership-2015

Anderson, M. (2017). *Key trends shaping technology in 2017.* PEW Research Center. Retrieved December 29, 2017, from www.pewresearch.org/fact-tank/2017/12/28/key-trends-shaping-technology-in-2017/

Andreassen, C. S., Torsheim, T., & Pallesen, S. (2014). Predictors of use of social network sites at work—A specific type of cyberloafing. *Journal of Computer-Mediated Communication, 19*(4), 906–921. doi:10.1111/jcc4.12085

Arora, T., Broglia, E., Thomas, G. N., & Taheri, S. (2014). Associations between specific technologies and adolescent sleep quantity, sleep quality, and parasomnias. *Sleep Medicine, 15*, 240–247. doi:10.1016/j.sleep.2013.08.799

Balmas, M. (2014). When fake news becomes real. *Communication Research, 41*(3), 430–454. doi:10.1177/0093650212453600

Banos, O., Villalonga, C., Damas, M., Gloesekoetter, P., Pomares, H., & Rojas, I. (2014). PhysioDroid: Combining wearable health sensors and mobile devices for a ubiquitous, continuous, and personal monitoring. *The Scientific World Journal, 2014*, 11–22.

Barkhaus, L., & Polichar, V. E. (2011). Empowerment through seamfulness: Smart phones in everyday life. *Personal and Ubiquitous Computing, 15*(6), 629–639. doi:10.1007/s00779-010-0342-4

Barkley, J. E., Lepp, A., & Salehi-Esfahani, S. (2016 [2015]). College students' mobile telephone use is positively associated with sedentary behavior. *American Journal of Lifestyle Medicine, 10*(6), 437–441. doi:10.1177/1559827615594338

Beard, C. L., & Wickham, R. E. (2016). Gaming-contingent self-worth, gaming motivation, and Internet gaming disorder. *Computers in Human Behavior, 61*, 507–515. doi:10.1016/j.chb.2016.03.046

Bennett, J., Owers, M., Pitt, M., & Tucker, M. (2010). Workplace impact of social networking. *Property Management, 28*(3), 138–148. doi:10.1108/02637471011051282

Brown, A. (2017). *Younger men play video games, but so do a diverse group of other Americans.* Retrieved December 8, 2017, from www.pewresearch.org/fact-tank/2017/09/11/younger-men-play-video-games-but-so-do-a-diverse-group-of-other-americans/

Brown, K., Campbell, S., & Ling, R. (2011). Mobile phones bridging the digital divide for teens in the US? *Future Internet, 3*(2), 144–158. doi: 10.3390/fi3020144

Butt, M., Ouarda, T. B., Quan, S. F., Pentland, A., & Khayal, I. (2015). Technologically sensed social exposure related to slow-wave sleep in healthy adults. *Sleep and Breathing, 19*(1), 255–261. doi:10.1007/s11325-014-1005-x

Carson, V., Staiano, A., & Katzmarzyk, P. (2015). Physical activity, screen time, and sitting among U.S. adolescents. *Pediatric Exercise Science, 27*(1), 151–159. doi:10.1123/pes.2014-0022

Çelik, C. B., & Odacı, H. (2013). The relationship between problematic Internet use and interpersonal cognitive distortions and life satisfaction in university students. *Children and Youth Services Review, 35*(3), 505–508. doi:10.1016/j.childyouth.2013.01.001

Chan, M. (2015). Mobile phones and the good life: Examining the relationships among mobile use, social capital and subjective well-being. *New Media & Society, 17*(1), 96–113. doi:10.1177/1461444813516836

Charoensukmongkol, P. (2014). Effects of support and job demands on social media use and work outcomes. *Computers in Human Behavior, 36*, 340–349. doi:10.1016/j.chb.2014.03.061

Cissé, Y. M., Russart, K. L. G., & Nelson, R. J. (2017). Depressive-like behavior is elevated among offspring of parents exposed to dim light at night prior to mating. *Psychoneuroendocrinology, 83*, 182–186. doi:10.1016/j.psyneuen.2017.06.004

Coenen, P., Howie, E., & Straker, L. (2017). The associations of mobile touch screen device use with musculoskeletal symptoms and exposures: A systematic review. *PLoS ONE, 12*(8), e0181220. doi:10.1371/journal.pone.0181220

Coulon, S. M., Monroe, C. M., & West, D. S. (2016). A systematic, multi-domain review of mobile smartphone apps for evidence-based stress management. *American Journal of Preventive Medicine*, *51*(1), 95–105. doi:10.1016/j.amepre. 2016.01.026

Crichton, F., & Petrie, K. J. (2015). Accentuate the positive: Counteracting psychogenic responses to media health messages in the age of the Internet. *Journal of Psychosomatic Research*, *79*(3), 185–189. doi:10.1016/j.jpsychores.2015.04.014

Custers, K., & Van den Bulck, J. (2012). Television viewing, Internet use, and self-reported bedtime and rise time in adults: Implications for sleep hygiene recommendations from an exploratory cross-sectional study. *Behavioral Sleep Medicine*, *10*(2), 96–105. doi:10.1080/15402002.2011.596599

Deliens, G., Gilson, M., & Peigneux, P. (2014). Sleep and the processing of emotions. *Experimental Brain Research*, *232*(5), 1403–1414. doi:10.1007/s00221-014-3832-1

Demïrcï, K., Akgönül, M., & Akpinar, A. (2015). Relationship of smartphone use severity with sleep quality, depression, and anxiety in university students. *Journal of Behavioral Addictions*, *4*(2), 85–92. doi:10.1556/2006.4.2015.010

Devine, P., & Lloyd, K. (2012). Internet use and psychological well-being among 10-year-old and 11-year-old children. *Child Care in Practice*, *18*(1), 5–22. doi: 10.1080/13575279.2011.621888

Divan, H. A., Kheifets, L., Obel, C., & Olsen, J. (2012). Cellphone use and behavioural problems in young children. *Journal of Epidemiology & Community Health*, *66*(6), 524–529. doi:10.1136/jech.2010.115402

Duggan, M. (2015, December). *Gaming and gamers*. Pew Research Center. Retrieved December 20, 2017, from www.pewInternet.org/2015/12/15/gaming-and-gamers/

Eng, D., & Lee, J. (2013). The promise and peril of mobile health applications for diabetes and endocrinology. *Pediatric Diabetes*, *14*(4), 231–238. doi: 10.1111/pedi.12034

Erae, J. R., & Lonborg, S. D. (2015). Do motivations for using Facebook moderate the association between Facebook use and psychological well-being? *Frontiers in Psychology*, *6*, 771. doi:10.3389/fpsyg.2015.00771

Falzone, A. E., Brindis, C. D., Chren, M. M., Junn, A., Pagoto, S., Wehner, M., & Linos, E. (2017). Teens, Tweets, and Tanning Beds: Rethinking the use of social media for skin cancer prevention. *American Journal of Preventive Medicine*, *53*(3), 86–S94. doi:10.1016/j.amepre.2017.04.027

Ferreira, C., Ferreira, H., Vieira, M. J., Costeira, M., Branco, L., Dias, Â., & Macedo, L. (2017). Epidemiology of Internet use by an adolescent population and its relation with sleep habits. *Acta Médica Portuguesa*, *30*(7), 524–533. doi:10.20344/amp.8205

Filipovic, J. (2013). The attractiveness of different online formats motives and frequencies of use. *Communications & Strategies*, *89*, 105–115.

Fotheringham, M. J., Wonnacott, R. L., & Owen, N. (2000). Computer use and physical inactivity in young adults: Public health perils and potentials of new information technologies. *Annals of Behavioral Medicine*, *22*(4), 269–275. doi:10.1007/BF02895662

Friedman, R., Whitworth, B., & Brownstein, M. (2010). Realizing the power of extelligence: A new business model for academic publishing. *The International Journal of Technology, Knowledge and Society*, *6*, 105–118. doi:10.18848/1832-3669/cgp/v06i02/56079

Frison, E., & Eggermont, S. (2015). Exploring the relationships between different types of Facebook use, perceived online social support, and adolescents' depressed mood. *Social Science Computer Review, 34,* 153–171. doi:10.1177/0894439314567449

Fusi, F., & Feeney, M. K. (2016). Social media in the workplace: Information exchange, productivity, or waste? *The American Review of Public Administration, 48*(5), 395–412. doi:10.1177/0275074016675722

Gaggioli, A., Pioggia, G., Tartarisco, G., Baldus, G., Corda, D., Cipresso, P., & Riva, G. (2013). A mobile data collection platform for mental health research. *Personal and Ubiquitous Computing, 17*(2), 241–251. doi:10.1007/s00779-011-0465-2

García-Magariño, I., Medrano, C., Plaza, I., & Oliván, B. (2016). A smartphone-based system for detecting hand tremors in unconstrained environments. *Personal and Ubiquitous Computing, 20*(6), 959–971. doi:10.1007/s00779-016-0956-2

Gilbert, L., Pond, R., Haak, E., DeWall, C., & Keller, P. (2015). Sleep problems exacerbate the emotional consequences of interpersonal rejection. *Journal of Social and Clinical Psychology, 34*(1), 50–63. doi:10.1521/jscp.2015.34.1.50

Goodman-Deane, J., Mieczakowski, A., Johnson, D., Goldhaber, T., & Clarkson, P. J. (2016). The impact of communication technologies on life and relationship satisfaction. *Computers in Human Behavior, 57,* 219–229. doi:10.1016/j.chb.2015.11.053

Gordon, A., & Chen, S. (2014). The role of sleep in interpersonal conflict. *Social Psychological and Personality Science, 5*(2), 168–175. doi:10.1177/1948550613488952

Gordon, A., Mendes, W., & Prather, A. (2017). The social side of sleep: Elucidating the links between sleep and social processes. *Current Directions in Psychological Science, 26*(5), 470–475. doi:10.1177/0963721417712269

Gradisar, M., Wolfson, A. R., Harvey, A. G., Hale, L., Rosenberg, R., & Czeisler, C. A. (2013). The sleep and technology use of Americans: Findings from the National Sleep Foundation's 2011 sleep in America poll. *Journal of Clinical Sleep Medicine, 9*(12), 1291–1299. doi:10.5664/jcsm.3272

Greenwood, S., Perrin, A., & Duggan, M. (2016, November). *Social media update 2016.* PEW Research Center; Information & Technology. Retrieved September 29, 2018, from www.pewInternet.org/2016/11/11/social-media-update-2016/

Handel, M. J. (2011). mHealth (mobile health)—Using apps for health and wellness. *Explore: The Journal of Science and Healing, 7*(4), 256–261. doi:10.1016/j.explore.2011.04.011

Hankin, B. L., Young, J. F., Abela, J. R. Z., Smolen, A., Jenness, J. L., Gulley, L. D., . . . Oppenheimer, C. W. (2015). Depression from childhood into late adolescence: Influence of gender, development, genetic susceptibility, and peer stress. *Journal of Abnormal Psychology, 124*(4), 803–816. doi:10.1037/abn0000089

Hanna, B., Kee, K. F., & Robertson, B. W. (2017). Positive impacts of social media at work: Job satisfaction, job calling, and Facebook use among co-workers. *SHS Web of Conferences, 33,* 12. doi:10.1051/shsconf/20173300012

Harwood, J., Dooley, J., Scott, A., & Joiner, R. (2014). Constantly connected—The effects of smart-devices on mental health. *Computers in Human Behavior, 34,* 267–272. doi:10.1016/j.chb.2014.02.006

Heflin, H., Shewmaker, J., & Nguyen, J. (2017). Impact of mobile technology on student attitudes, engagement, and learning. *Computers & Education, 107,* 91–99. doi:10.1016/j.compedu.2017.01.006

Heim, J., Brandtzæg, P. B., Hertzberg Kaare, B., Endestad, T., & Torgersen, L. (2007). Children's usage of media technologies and psychosocial factors. *New Media & Society*, *9*(3), 425–454. doi:10.1177/1461444807076971

Hertlein, K. M., & Webster, M. (2008). Technology, relationships, and problems: A research synthesis. *Journal of Marital and Family Therapy*, *34*, 445–460. doi:10.1111/j.1752-0606.2008.00087.x

Hill-Kayser, C., Vachani, C., Hampshire, M., Di Lullo, G. A., & Metz, J. M. (2012). Positive impact of Internet-based survivorship care plans on healthcare and lifestyle behaviors. *International Journal of Radiation Oncology, Biology, Physics*, *84*(3), 211–S212. doi:10.1016/j.ijrobp.2012.07.549

Holland, P., Cooper, B. K., & Hecker, R. (2016). Use of social media at work: A new form of employee voice? *The International Journal of Human Resource Management*, *27*(21), 2621–2634. doi:10.1080/09585192.2016.1227867

Hong, S., & Na, J. (2018). How Facebook is perceived and used by people across cultures: The implications of cultural differences in the use of Facebook. *Social Psychological and Personality Science*, *9*(4), 435–443. doi:10.1177/194855061 7711227

Hootsuites. (2017). Digital trends in 2017: 106 pages of Internet, mobile and social media data. *INSIGHTS*. Retrieved from https://thenextweb.com/insights/2017/01/24/digital-trends-2017-report-Internet/

Hou, X., Wang, H., Guo, C., Gaskin, J., Rost, D. H., & Wang, J. (2017). Psychological resilience can help combat the effect of stress on problematic social networking site usage. *Personality and Individual Differences*, *109*, 61–66. doi:10.1016/j.paid.2016.12.048

Ilardi, S. (2009). *The depression cure the 6-step program to beat depression without drugs* (1st Da Capo Press ed.). Cambridge, MA: Da Capo Lifelong.

Jackson, L. A., Fitzgerald, H. E., Zhao, Y., Kolenic, A., von Eye, A., & Harold, R. (2008). Information Technology (IT) use and children's psychological well-being. *CyberPsychology & Behavior*, *11*(6), 755–757. doi:10.1089/cpb.2008.0035

Kalpidou, M., Costin, D., & Morris, J. (2011). The relationship between Facebook and the well-being of undergraduate college students. *Cyberpsychology, Behavior, and Social Networking*, *14*(4), 183–189. doi:10.1089/cyber.2010.0061

Kaplan, A. M., & Haenlein, M. (2010). Users of the world, unite! The challenges and opportunities of Social Media. *Business Horizons*, *53*(1), 59–68. doi:10.1016/j.bushor.2009.09.003

Kim, J. H., Lau, C. H., Cheuk, K., Kan, P., Hui, H. L. C., & Griffiths, S. M. (2010). Brief report: Predictors of heavy Internet use and associations with health-promoting and health risk behaviors among Hong Kong university students. *Journal of Adolescence*, *33*(1), 215–220. doi:10.1016/j.adolescence.2009.03.012

Kim, J. H., & Lee, J. (2011). The Facebook paths to happiness: Effects of the number of Facebook friends and self-presentation on subjective well-being. *Cyberpsychology, Behavior, and Social Networking*, *14*(6), 359–364.

Kirby, A., Jones, C., & Copello, A. (2014). The impact of massively multiplayer online role playing games (MMORPGs) on psychological wellbeing and the role of play motivations and problematic use. *International Journal of Mental Health and Addiction*, *12*(1), 36–51. doi:10.1007/s11469-013-9467-9

Koch, H., Gonzalez, E., & Leidner, D. (2012). Bridging the work/social divide: The emotional response to organizational social networking sites. *European Journal of Information Systems*, *21*(6), 699–717. doi:10.1057/ejis.2012.18

Leftheriotis, I., & Giannakos, M. N. (2014). Using social media for work: Losing your time or improving your work? *Computers in Human Behavior, 31,* 134–142. doi.org/10.1016/j.chb.2013.10.016

Lemola, S., Perkinson-Gloor, N., Brand, S., Dewald-Kaufmann, J. F., & Grob, A. (2015). Adolescents' electronic media use at night, sleep disturbance, and depressive symptoms in the smartphone age. *Journal of Youth and Adolescence, 44*(2), 405–418. doi:10.1007/s10964-014-0176-x

Lepp, A., Barkley, J. E., Sanders, G. J., Rebold, M., & Gates, P. (2013). The relationship between cellphone use, physical and sedentary activity, and cardiorespiratory fitness in a sample of U.S. college students. *The International Journal of Behavioral Nutrition and Physical Activity, 10*(1), 79–79. doi:10.1186/1479-5868-10-79

Levenson, J. C., Shensa, A., Sidani, J. E., Colditz, J. B., & Primack, B. (2016). The association between social media use and sleep disturbance among young adults. *Preventive Medicine, 85,* 36–41. doi:10.1016/j.ypmed.2016.01.001

Ley, B., Ogonowski, C., Hess, J., Reichling, T., Wan, L., & Wulf, V. (2014). Impacts of new technologies on media usage and social behaviour in domestic environments. *Behaviour & Information Technology, 33*(8), 815–828. doi:10.1080/0144929X.2013.832383

Liang, T., Peng, J., & Yu, C. (2012). A simpler quality of e-life indicator: Does the Internet have a positive impact on the quality of life in Taiwan. *Quality & Quantity, 46*(4), 1025–1045. doi:10.1007/s11135-011-9446-9

Liberman, B., Seidman, G., McKenna, K. Y., & Buffardi, L. E. (2011). Employee job attitudes and organizational characteristics as predictors of cyberloafing. *Computers in Human Behavior, 27*(6), 2192–2199. doi:10.1016/j.chb.2011.06.015

Lin, R., & Utz, S. (2015). The emotional responses of browsing Facebook: Happiness, envy, and the role of tie strength. *Computers in Human Behavior, 52,* 29–38. doi:10.1016/j.chb.2015.04.064

Lissitsa, S., & Chachashvili-Bolotin, S. (2016). Life satisfaction in the Internet age—changes in the past decade. *Computers in Human Behavior, 54,* 197–206. doi:10.1016/j.chb.2015.08.001

Lopes, M., Boronat, A. C., Wang, Y., & Fu-I, L. (2016). Sleep complaints as risk factor for suicidal behavior in severely depressed children and adolescents. *CNS Neuroscience & Therapeutics, 22*(11), 915–920. doi:10.1111/cns.12597

Loss of net neutrality could harm research. (2017). *Nature, 552*(7684), 147.

Lozada, F. T., & Tynes, B. M. (2017). Longitudinal effects of online experiences on empathy among African American adolescents. *Journal of Applied Developmental Psychology, 52,* 181–190. doi:10.1016/j.appdev.2017.07.009

Lyengar, R. (2018). India now has the "world's strongest" net neutrality rules. *CNN Tech!* Retrieved from https://money.cnn.com/2018/07/12/technology/india-net-neutrality-rules-telecom/index.html

Malik, M. I., Saleem, F., & Ahmad, M. (2010). Work-life balance and job satisfaction among doctors in Pakistan. *South Asian Journal of Management, 17*(2), 112–123.

Mani, M., Kavanagh, D. J., Hides, L., & Stoyanov, S. R. (2015). Review and evaluation of mindfulness-based iPhone apps. *JMIR mHealth and uHealth, 3*(3), e82. doi:10.2196/mhealth.4328

Maranges, H. M., & McNulty, J. K. (2017). The rested relationship: Sleep benefits marital evaluations. *Journal of Family Psychology, 31*(1), 117–122. doi:10.1037/fam0000225

Marino, C., Gini, G., Vieno, A., & Spada, M. M. (2018). The associations between problematic Facebook use, psychological distress and well-being among adolescents and young adults: A systematic review and meta-analysis. *Journal of Affective Disorders, 226,* 274–281. doi:10.1016/j.jad.2017.10.007

Meena, J., Verma, A., Kohli, C., & Ingle, G. (2016). Mobile phone use and possible cancer risk: Current perspectives in India. *Indian Journal of Occupational and Environmental Medicine, 20*(1), 5–9. doi:10.4103/0019-5278.183827

Militello, L. K., Kelly, S. A., & Melnyk, B. M. (2012). Systematic review of Text-Messaging interventions to promote healthy behaviors in pediatric and adolescent populations: Implications for clinical practice and research. *Worldviews on Evidence-Based Nursing, 9*(2), 66–77. doi:10.1111/j.1741-6787.2011.00239.x

Miloh, T., Annunziato, R., Arnon, R., Warshaw, J., Parkar, S., Suchy, F. J., . . . Kerkar, N. (2009). Improved adherence and outcomes for pediatric liver transplant recipients by using text messaging. *Pediatrics, 124*(5), e844–e850. doi:10.1542/peds.2009-0415

Murray, E., Lo, B., Pollack, L., Donelan, K., Catania, J., White, M., . . . Turner, R. (2003). The impact of health information on the Internet on the Physician-Patient Relationship. *Archives of Internal Medicine, 163*(14), 1727. doi:10.1001/archinte.163.14.1727

Nduhura, D., & Prieler, M. (2017). When I chat online, I feel relaxed and work better: Exploring the use of social media in the public sector workplace in Rwanda. *Telecommunications Policy, 41*(7–8), 708–716. doi:10.1016/j.telpol.2017.05.008

Nesi, J., Miller, A. B., & Prinstein, M. J. (2017). Adolescents' depressive symptoms and subsequent technology-based interpersonal behaviors: A multi-wave study. *Journal of Applied Developmental Psychology, 51,* 12–19. doi:10.1016/j.appdev.2017.02.002

Nose, Y., Fujinaga, R., Suzuki, M., Hayashi, I., Moritani, T., Kotani, K., & Nagai, N. (2017). Association of evening smartphone use with cardiac autonomic nervous activity after awakening in adolescents living in high school dormitories. *Child's Nervous System, 33*(4), 653–658. doi:10.1007/s00381-017-3388-z

Oh, H. J., Ozkaya, E., & Larose, R. (2014). How does online social networking enhance life satisfaction? The relationships among online supportive interaction, affect, perceived social support, sense of community, and life satisfaction. *Computers in Human Behavior, 30*(C), 69–78.

Oshima, N., Nishida, A., Shimodera, S., Tochigi, M., Ando, S., Yamasaki, S., . . . Sasaki, T. (2012). The suicidal feelings, self-injury, and mobile phone use after lights out in adolescents. *Journal of Pediatric Psychology, 37*(9), 1023–1030. doi:10.1093/jpepsy/jss072

Panova, T., & Lleras, A. (2016). Avoidance or boredom: Negative mental health outcomes associated with use of information and communication technologies depend on users' motivations. *Computers in Human Behavior, 58,* 249–258. doi:10.1016/j.chb.2015.12.062

Perrin, A., & Bertoni, N. (2017, December 1). *First-time Internet users: Who they are and what they do when they get online.* Pew Research Center. Retrieved December 8, 2017, from www.pewresearch.org/fact-tank/2017/12/01/first-time-Internet-users-who-they-are-and-what-they-do-when-they-get-online/

Polos, P. G., Bhat, S., Gupta, D., O'Malley, R. J., DeBari, V. A., Upadhyay, H., . . . Chokroverty, S. (2015). The impact of sleep time-related information and communication technology (STRICT) on sleep patterns and daytime functioning in american adolescents. *Journal of Adolescence, 44,* 232–244. doi:10.1016/j.adolescence.2015.08.002

Poushter, J., Bishop, C., & Chwe, H. (2018, June). *Social media use continues to rise in developing countries, but plateaus across developed ones.* Retrieved September 29, 2018, from www.pewglobal.org/2018/06/19/social-media-use-continues-to-rise-in-developing-countries-but-plateaus-across-developed-ones/

Primack, B. A., Carroll, M. V., Mcnamara, M., Klem, M. L., King, B., Rich, M., . . . Nayak, S. (2012). Role of video games in improving health-related outcomes: A systematic review. *American Journal of Preventive Medicine, 42*(6), 630–638. doi:10.1016/j.amepre.2012.02.023

Prince, S. A., Reed, J. L., McFetridge, C., Tremblay, M. S., & Reid, R. D. (2017). Correlates of sedentary behaviour in adults: A systematic review. *Obesity Reviews, 18*(8), 915–935. doi:10.1111/obr.12529

Quinn, D., Chen, L., Mulvenna, M. D., & Bond, R. (2016). Exploring the relationship between online social network site usage and the impact on quality of life for older and younger users: An interaction analysis. *Journal of Medical Internet Research, 18*(9), 163–178. doi:10.2196/jmir.5377

Rainie, L. (2013). *Personal. portable. participatory. Pervasive the digital landscape in 2013 and its impact on communities.* Retrieved from www.pewInternet.org/2013/07/18/personal-portable-participatory-pervasive-the-digital-landscape-in-2013-and-its-impact-on-communities/

Rainie, L. (2015). *The changing digital landscape: Where things are headed.* Retrieved from www.pewInternet.org/2015/11/20/the-changing-digital-landscape-where-things-are-heading/

Rainie, L. (2017). *The reckoning for social media.* Retrieved December 29, 2017, from www.pewInternet.org/2017/08/01/the-reckoning-for-social-media/

Reese, R. F., Seitz, C. M., Stroud, D., Lehman, B., Caldwell, S., Ecklund, E., & Winn, A. (2016). YouTube nature preferences: A content analysis study. *The Journal of Humanistic Counseling, 55*(3), 183–199. doi:10.1002/johc.12033

Rosen, L. D., Whaling, K., Rab, S., Carrier, L.M., & Cheever, N. A. (2012). Is Facebook creating "iDisorders"? The link between clinical symptoms of psychiatric disorders and technology use, attitudes and anxiety. *Computers in Human Behavior, 29*(3), 1243–1254.

Rosenfeld, M. (2018). Are Tinder and dating apps changing the dating and mating in the USA? In J. van Hook, S. McHale, & V. King (Eds.), *Families and technology* (pp. 103–120). New York: Springer.

Schnohr, P., Kristensen, T. S., Prescott, E., & Scharling, H. (2005). Stress and life dissatisfaction are inversely associated with jogging and other types of physical activity in leisure time—The Copenhagen City Heart Study. *Scandinavian Journal of Medicine & Science in Sports, 15*, 107–112. doi:10.1111/j.1600-0838.2004.00394.x

Schwartz, S. A. (2011). Trends that will affect your future . . . . *EXPLORE: The Journal of Science and Healing, 2*(5), 394–398. doi:10.1016/j.explore.2006.06.007

Scott, D. A., Valley, B., & Simecka, B. A. (2016). Mental health concerns in the digital age. *International Journal of Mental Health and Addiction, 15*(3), 604–613. doi:10.1007/s11469-016-9684-0

Seabrook, E. M., Kern, M. L., & Rickard, N. S. (2016). Social networking sites, depression, and anxiety: A systematic review. *JMIR Mental Health, 3*(4), e50. doi:10.2196/mental.5842

Shen, C., & Williams, D. (2011). Unpacking time online: Connecting Internet and massively multiplayer online game use with psychosocial well-being. *Communication Research, 38*(1), 123–149. doi:10.1177/0093650210377196

Shensa, A., Sidani, J. E., Lin, L. Y., Bowman, N. D., & Primack, B. A. (2016). Social media use and perceived emotional support among US young adults. *Journal of Community Health*, *41*(3), 541–549. doi:10.1007/s10900-015-0128-8

Sims, T., Reed, A. E., & Carr, D. C. (2017). Information and communication technology use is related to higher well-being among the oldest-old. *The Journals of Gerontology Series B: Psychological Sciences and Social Sciences*, gbw130. doi:10.1093/geronb/gbw130

Social Media Week. (2016). *Millennials check their phones more than 157 times per day*. Retrieved November 15, 2017, from https://socialmediaweek.org/newyork/2016/05/31/millennials-check-phones-157-times-per-day/

Song, H., Zmyslinski-Seelig, A., Kim, J., Drent, A., Victor, A., Omori, K., & Allen, M. (2014). Does Facebook make you lonely?: A meta analysis. *Computers in Human Behavior*, *36*, 446–452. doi:10.1016/j.chb.2014.04.011

Soni, R., Upadhyay, R., & Mahendra, J. (2017). Prevalence of smartphone addiction, sleep quality and associated behavior problems in adolescents. *International Journal of Research in Medical Sciences*, *5*(2), 515–519. doi:10.18203/2320-6012.ijrms20170142

Stanley, S. M., Ragan, E. P., Rhoades, G. K., & Markman, H. J. (2012). Examining changes in relationship adjustment and life satisfaction in marriage. *Journal of Family Psychology*, *26*(1), 165–170. doi:10.1037/a0026759

Stepanikova, I., Nie, N. H., & He, X. (2010). Time on the Internet at home, loneliness, and life satisfaction: Evidence from panel time-diary data. *Computers in Human Behavior, 26*(3), 329–338. doi: 10.1016/j.chb.2009.11.002

Stewart, I., & Cohen, J. (1997). *Figments of reality: The evolution of the curious mind*. Cambridge: Cambridge University Press.

Treas, J., & Gubernskaya, Z. (2018). Did mobile phones increase adult children's material contact? In J. Van Hook, S. McHale, & V. King's (Eds.), *Families and technology* (pp. 139–151). New York, NY: Springer.

Turner, J. W., Robinson, J. D., Tian, Y., Neustadtl, A., Angelus, P., Russell, M., . . . Levine, B. (2013). Can messages make a difference? The association between E-Mail messages and health outcomes in diabetes patients. *Human Communication Research*, *39*(2), 252–268. doi:10.1111/j.1468-2958.2012.01437.x

Twenge, J. M. (2014). Time period and birth cohort differences in depressive symptoms in the U.S. 1982–2013. *Social Indicators Research*, *121*(2), 437–454. doi:10.1007/s11205-014-0647-1

Twenge, J. M., Gentile, B., DeWall, C. N., Ma, D., Lacefield, K., & Schurtz, D. R. (2010). Birth cohort increases in psychopathology among young Americans, 1938–2007: A cross-temporal meta-analysis of the MMPI. *Clinical Psychology Review*, *30*(4), 145–154. doi:10.1016/j.cpr.2009.10.005

Twenge, J. M., Martin, G. N., & Campbell, W. K. (2018). Decreases in psychological well-being among American adolescents after 2012 and links to screen time during the rise of smartphone technology. *Emotion*, *18*(6), 765–780. doi:10.1037/emo0000403

U.S. Census Bureau. (2017a). *Fast facts*. Retrieved December 29, 2017, from www.census.gov/quickfacts/fact/table/US/PST045217

U.S. Census Bureau. (2017b). *More children live with just their fathers than a decade ago*. Retrieved December 29, 2017, from www.census.gov/newsroom/press-releases/2017/living-arrangements.html

Vitak, J., Crouse, J., & LaRose, R. (2011). Personal Internet use at work: Understanding cyberslacking. *Computers in Human Behavior*, *27*(5), 1751–1759. doi:10.1016/j.chb.2011.03.002

Wilmer, H. H., & Chein, J. M. (2016). Mobile technology habits: Patterns of association among device usage, intertemporal preference, impulse control, and reward sensitivity. *Psychonomic Bulletin & Review, 23*(5), 1607–1614. doi:10.3758/s13423-016-1011-z

Wilmont, E. G., Edwardson, C. L., Achana, F. A., Davis, M. J., Gorely, T., Gray, L. J., . . . Biddle, S. J. H. (2012). Sedentary time in adults and the association with diabetes, cardiovascular disease and death: Systematic review and meta-analysis. *Diabetologia, 55*(11), 2895–2905. doi:10.1007/s00125-012-2677-z

Wilson, S. J., Jaremka, L. M., Fagundes, C. P., Andridge, R., Peng, J., Malarkey, W. B., . . . Kiecolt-Glaser, J. K. (2017). Shortened sleep fuels inflammatory responses to marital conflict: Emotion regulation matters. *Psychoneuroendocrinology, 79*, 74–83. doi:10.1016/j.psyneuen.2017.02.015

Wojcik, D. (2016). Primary brain tumors and mobile cellphone usage. *Cancer Epidemiology, 44*, 123–124. doi:10.1016/j.canep.2016.08.007

Wolstenholme, J. T., Edwards, M., Shetty, S. R., Gatewood, J. D., Taylor, J. A., Rissman, E. F., & Connelly, J. J. (2012). Gestational exposure to bisphenol a produces transgenerational changes in behaviors and gene expression. *Endocrinology, 153*(8), 3828–3838. doi:10.1210/en.2012-1195

Wood, L., Jago, R., Sebire, S. J., Zahra, J., & Thompson, J. L. (2015). Sedentary time among spouses: A cross-sectional study exploring associations in sedentary time and behaviour in parents of 5 and 6 year old children. *BMC Research Notes, 8*, 787–795. doi:10.1186/s13104-015-1758-8

Xie, X., Wang, X., Zhao, F., Lei, L., Niu, G., & Wang, P. (2018). Online real-self presentation and depression among Chinese teens: Mediating role of social support and moderating role of dispositional optimism. *Child Indicators Research, 11*(5), 1531–1544.

Yen, C. F., King, B. H., & Tang, T. C. (2010). The association between short and long nocturnal sleep durations and risky behaviours and the moderating factors in Taiwanese adolescents. *Psychiatry Research, 179*(1), 69–74.

Zheng, Y., Wei, D., Li, J., Zhu, T., & Ning, H. (2016). Internet use and its impact on individual physical health. *IEEE Access, 4*, 5135–5142. doi:10.1109/access.2016.2602301

TWO

From Digiteris to Tweeps
Understanding Online Communication Patterns

What Drives Patterns of Technology Use?

Theoretical Models of Motivations Applied to Social Media Use

Part of comprehending how people communicate online is understanding what drives them to use technology and in what ways they use the technologies available to them. There have been many studies exploring the motivation for participation in particular sites and Internet usage more globally. Many scholars have outlined their own categories of why people use social media. Some key reasons tend to be: social interaction, information seeking, to pass time, entertainment, relaxation, communicatory utility, convenience utility, expression of opinion, information sharing, and surveillance and/or to gain knowledge about others (Whiting & Williams, 2013). The primary goal of social networking sites (SNSs) is precisely that: networking (Filipovic, 2013). This technology allows users to connect to others, post pictures, share songs and other media, post thoughts and feelings, and have other users interact with them through likes, shares, etc. It can also be used as a personal diary (Syn & Sinn, 2015). As a result of the varied functions, social media is an important part of our lives.

Motivation theory has been applied to understand SNS usage to examine the perceived benefits of using such sites, including a site's utility and how much enjoyment the user experiences (Filipovic, 2013). Enjoyment is, as Lin and Lu (2011) found, the most critical factor in deciding to use SNSs. The more one enjoys the experience of social networking, the more they will participate. These positives are also subsequently reinforcing: if one individual has a good experience and enjoys the site, they will spend more time online, find new friends, develop a broader network, and likely have even more enriching experiences (Lin & Lu, 2011). In the case of Facebook, the primary motivator is to communicate with others, even more than individual personality factors in some cases (Ross et al., 2009).

The effects of the result of this networking may depend on the type of person using the media. Several studies have explored the personalities of those posting on social networking sites and explored whether, for some types of people, using Facebook is beneficial. For example, those who are extroverted tend to have more Facebook friends and be more active in social media (Wilson, Fornasier, & White, 2010). Consequently, those with a tendency toward introversion with Facebook profiles report feeling more disconnected than people with a similar level of introversion who do not have Facebook profiles (Stronge et al., 2015). This may be a result of the "grass is greener" through watching others' profiles and feeling as if one is not connected through comparing themselves to how others appear to be connected.

There are also some specific motivators in texting. In terms of personality, people who are anxious to take a face-to-face risk in communication are more motivated to use text than calling (Reid & Reid, 2007). In fact, the more someone has face-to-face interactions, the more they engage in texting (Jin & Park, 2010). Further motivations to use texting include searching for affection and feeling (Jin & Park, 2010). Park, Lee, and Chung (2016) suspected there was an association between the number of texts one sends on their cellphone (not time spent texting, but number) and feelings of loneliness—and they were right. The number of messages sent seemed to reduce subjective feelings of loneliness (Park et al., 2016).

The Importance of Being in Sync

Both the synchronous and asynchronous nature of interactive communicative technologies adds particular incentives to online communication and couple relationships. Synchronous communication is communication occurring at the same time—for example, chat rooms, text messaging, and other interactions conducted simultaneously. Asynchronous communications refer to communication occurring over time, such as email or instant messages not received immediately by the intended recipient. Synchronous communication has a built-in incentive of immediate response. Inquiries about one's whereabouts, activities, and directives are effectively transmitted instantly.

Research in the field of education suggests that a key incentive in the usage of asynchronous communication is the ability to be more thoughtful about one's message—having a chance to correspond at greater levels of depth (with the receiver focusing more on the message than the presenter) (Ocker & Yaverbaum, 1999). Further, those with a tendency to be shy may find more comfort in and be more motivated to participate in asynchronous than synchronous communicative methods (Krämer & Winter, 2008), so those uncomfortable in larger social surroundings may be drawn to forms of asynchronous communication and may communicate at a deeper level than those opting for synchronous communication. Those who are motivated to participate in asynchronous situations, however, also have to come to a decision about the rules of engagement: namely, frequency and timing of messages (Ocker & Yaverbaum, 1999). Confusion around this issue may prevent couples from moving forward.

Other research in the field of education can be used to understand interpersonal relationships. Much of the literature suggests the ability to process information presented through interactive communicative technology is dependent on the type of communication used. Synchronous communication may be more natural, but this style of communication may be more difficult to process because immediate responses are required in order to keep the conversation going. On the other hand, asynchronous communication may feel less natural and more purposive, but may be easier to process in some ways because there is little need to respond immediately (Hrastinski, 2008). Several studies have compared both modalities of communication in educational settings (see Hrastinski, 2008, for a complete analysis of studies) and, taken together, reveal a few important trends. First, many of the members who participated in online learning in synchronous chat formats had a greater sense of connection and social support with one another as compared to those who participated in asynchronous e-learning methods. Second, participation in asynchronous communication methods may be better when the focus of the communication is task-oriented. Third, asynchronous communication may be difficult to start when there are fewer people involved in the potential interaction; likewise, people interact more frequently when the communication method is synchronous (Hrastinski, 2008).

The differences described earlier have direct implications for couples, both positive and negative. In cases where the communication is problematic, it is often the case that synchronous and asynchronous types of communication are used inappropriately—that is, couples use asynchronous communication for synchronous communication or use synchronous communication in times when asynchronous communication would be more fitting. This application is supported by research examining couples' conflict resolution strategies in computer-mediated versus face-to-face communication. From a sample of 47 couples, there seemed to be little difference in the satisfaction level of resolving a conflict through a computer versus face-to-face. The participant's own responses indicated the use of computer-mediated communication was effective because there were fewer nonverbal distractions. In other words, there was little way to become angry at one's tone or facial expressions because there were none. Another benefit cited by participants was that asynchronous communication allowed for someone to not respond in the heat of the moment (Perry & Werner-Wilson, 2011).

Another facet of Internet communication related to synchrony is directed versus non-directed communication (Berger, 2013). In directed communication, we speak to one person or a group of people in particular. It is how most of our face-to-face communication operates. Personal information or feelings shared over Facebook statuses are seen by everyone, which is problematic for couples, where private matters are made public where a partner did not consent to the post. For individuals often they share deep personal problems and feelings in statuses and on blogs that are not appropriate and attract obligatory attention from other online members.

Relational Factors Influencing Social Media Use

The Desire for Social Capital

A common use of social media is to gain social capital (Aharony, 2016). The establishment of social capital is a mechanism for gaining more than networking (or bridging social capital). For example, if people are anxious, they are not typically going to reach out online to gain new friends, unless the anxiety around not having friends gets so overwhelming that it inspires reaching out online to make new friends—which, in turn, begets more reaching out and more friends (Weiqin, Campbell, Kimpton, Wozencroft, & Orel, 2016). In fact, extroverts end up winning out in online environments in terms of social capital, because of their ability to initiate the expansion of their social network (Weiqin et al., 2016).

The bonding type of social capital involves acquiring social support (Putnam, 2000). In the acquisition of social capital there is the ability to draw on that capital when needed. For example, one might be able to use a network to obtain a new job (Aharony, 2016). The potential resources to be gained from this network include emotional, personal, and financial support. Facebook, Twitter, Instagram, and LinkedIn are primary settings for the measurement of social capital. They retain information about how many friends, followers, and likes a post receives. Research conducted on social capital of social media (namely Facebook) discovered a strong relationship between both bridging and bonding types of social capital through the use of Facebook, though in some studies the relationship seemed to be strongest between Facebook and bridging capital (Burke, Wallen, Vail-Smith, & Knox, 2011) because Facebook helps with sustaining more associative relationships (Aharony, 2016). In a study looking specifically at youth, it was noted that those who felt more lonely were those who spent more time online communicating (i.e., disclosing intimate details about their lives) with others. Another study found the affiliation that one might receive from others as well as the feeling of being included were important motivators in phone and texting behaviors (Jin & Park, 2010). This leads scholars like Bonetti, Campbell, and Gilmore (2010) and Saxton and Waters (2014) to believe that the Internet provides a way for lonely youth to engage in developmentally appropriate socialization skills. This activity can combat the potential loneliness (Lee, Noh, & Koo, 2013). Finally, the way in which Facebook users post photos may be less about identity construction and more about relationship displays (Strano, 2008).

'Cuz You've Got . . . Personality (Disorders)?

Let us be clear on one point: it is not our intention to imply nor do we believe that the only people with personality disorders are the ones who post online or use social media. We do not believe this to be true, nor do we wish to communicate that in this section. We acknowledge that most people (1) do not have personality disorders, and (2) use the Internet regularly and in healthy ways. The purpose of this section is to merely present research that looks at the context and personality characteristics of some people who post and engage in interactions online.

In the early years of SNSs and Internet research, much time was spent examining who was participating in different facets of the Internet (Self-hout, Branje, Delsing, Ter Bogt, & Meeus, 2009; Zillien & Hargittai, 2009). Yet the significant proportion of individuals reporting they use at least one social media site (2.8 billion worldwide) has shifted researchers from examining the personalities of those online and instead evaluating processes in posting including assessing the circumstances under which posts are made. For example, shy people feel more comfortable when discussions are online versus when the discussions take place in person (Hammick & Lee, 2014). Shy people also tend to lead online conversations and forums as this does not challenge their anxiety in the same way that doing so in person would (Helm, Möller, Mauroner, & Conrad, 2013). Yet when the conversations are about intent to change some behavior, face-to-face interaction seems to be more effective (Hammick & Lee, 2014).

Regarding social media usage specifically, a notable amount of research examined those with more aggressive/problematic personality traits and their social media and Facebook usage. Buffardi and Campbell (2008) evaluated postings of those who have higher levels of narcissism and found they are more likely to post profile messages characterized by vanity than people who do not. Ong et al. (2011) found that those rating attractiveness of their own profile pictures had higher levels of narcissism and extroversion. Individuals with narcissistic personality traits reflect a high level of self-love, inflated self-view, sense of entitlement, and exaggerated sense of self-importance and uniqueness (Brailovskaia & Bierhoff, 2016). The utilization of technology and SNSs has allowed covert and open narcissists to indulge in their demand of attention, admiration, and popularity by establishing superficial relationships quickly with their viewers or followers. Consequently, narcissism is considered a predictor of social media use (Leung & Zhang, 2017). With the large audience they acquire, narcissists receive the attention they desire by creating an image of how they want others to perceive them via the amount and types of status updates and uploaded photos they post. Individuals with narcissistic personality traits tend to view their own SNS pages more frequently and spend more time on them (Brailovskaia & Bierhoff, 2016). Covert narcissists experience self-doubt, sensitivity, dissatisfaction, and social anxiety, which then results in a lack of social skills to gain public approval in face-to-face social interactions. They are, however, able to present their narcissism in an open manner via SNS platforms just as openly as open narcissists. Covert narcissists have time to plan and control their self-presentation that they otherwise would not be able to do in face-to-face interactions (Brailovskaia & Bierhoff, 2016). Likewise, Wolfradt and Doll (2001) found those with higher levels of narcissism or those with the potential for a personality disorder diagnosis tend to post more frequently, ostensibly to obtain validation from others. In another study, higher levels of narcissism and lower levels of self-esteem were associated with greater online social media usage as well as self-presentation (Mehdizadeh, 2010).

When exploring narcissism as a moderating behavior in social media, as Liu, Liu, Ding, Wang, Zhen, and Xu (2016) described it:

> When [adolescents] obtain a sense of competence, belong-ingness, and autonomy through disclosing private infor-mation on the Internet, they can become obsessed with network behavior. Due to a deficiency of self-control, young people might be caught in a vicious cycle.
>
> (p. 10)

This corresponds to other research that suggests the more positive feedback one gets from disclosure, the more disclosures they make; the more disclosure they make, the more positive feedback they receive (Liu & Brown, 2014).

Stead and Bibby (2017) explored the Big Five personality factors and their connection to Facebook usage. Using a cross-sectional design, neuroticism was unrelated to Facebook usage, whereas conscientiousness and extraversion were connected to use. Further, people who score higher on the "agree-able" scale are more likely to contact the person uploading the photo to make a change rather than unilaterally "untagging" (Lang & Barton, 2015). But personality is not the only factor that contributes to social media use, which might be because social networking is not social media's sole purpose. Social media users communicate with others, conduct business transactions, maintain long-term relationships, conduct research, and surveil others. This might explain the motivator known as "fear of missing out."

The Only Thing to Fear is Missing Out

Social media is not just about talking to someone else, but also sharing things that are going on in one's life (Utz, 2015) with both people known and unknown to the user. There are complex motivations in sharing information, posts, photos, and even our location with others. Another element affecting usage is one's end goal. For example, in the case of the research on narcissism and Facebook posting, the goal was to present oneself in such a way to obtain validation from others and to gain sympathy (Diefenbach & Christoforakos, 2017). In other cases, Facebook postings may be oriented to appear more socially desirable (Siibak, 2009; Yurchisin, Watchravesringkan, & McCabe, 2005).

Several studies have also tried to identify the fear of missing out's contribution in online communication and social media usage. For example, the fear of missing out is associated with higher levels of narcissism. In fact, the more pathology you have, the more you fear missing out (Wegmann, Oberst, Stodt, & Brand, 2017). For example, the lower one's self-esteem, the more one is subject to fear of missing out. On the other hand, lower levels of fear of missing out are associated with greater life satisfaction (Błachnio & Przepiórka, 2018). There is also some tie-in to how our brain operates and fear of missing out. Research tells us that people who score higher on a Fear of Missing Out Scale have a more activated right middle temporal gyrus in response to photos of social inclusions (Lai, Altavilla, Ronconi, & Aceto, 2016).

Fear of missing out has a significant impact in people's frequency of use of technology as well as how they use it. For example, fear of missing out is significantly related to one's use of social media: those who have a greater fear of missing out use social media more (Przybylski, Murayama, DeHaan, & Gladwell, 2013). Those who are more fearful of missing out are more willing to take risks that do not benefit them academically or personally. Specifically people who have more fear of missing out are more likely to use social media while they are driving, ordering, coursework, and lectures. This data is congruent with other data, and suggests the more people use Internet technologies, the more it interferes with their day-to-day life, and the more likely it is that they have an Internet communicative disorder. The assumption here is that fear of missing out might be the piece that mediates between Internet use and developing a disorder. For example, if someone has an Internet use disorder, it is likely that their Internet use is somehow compromising their day-to-day life and interfering with their well-being. Certainly, one could argue that using the Internet while you are driving and not paying attention or in lectures is an example of the Internet contributing to interfering with one's well-being. It is the presence of fear of missing out, which is idiosyncratic to each individual, bridging problematic Internet use and implications. While it is not described as a mediator or moderator, one group of researchers has looked at how fear of missing out contributes to what they described as online vulnerability. That may be a broader catch-all term for the development of Internet communication/use problems.

Fear of missing out is a substantial contributor to having problems online. It is connected to using social media during academic lectures and driving (Przybylski et al., 2013). While those who do not use phones when they drive or are in school think about dismissing this information, consider this: fear of missing out leads to other behaviors that constitute making oneself vulnerable online. First, the more one uses social media, the more one increases their vulnerability online. Second, the more one uses social media, the more they are afraid of missing out. The more one fears missing out, the more likely they are to say more online, share more, and try to make more friends, each of which increases one's vulnerabilities toward poor outcomes associated with online usage (Binder, Buglass, Betts, & Underwood, 2017). Using the term "new social anxiety," Wehrenberg (2018) discusses social media use in adolescents and the impact it has on young people. Wehrenberg agrees about fear of missing out. She also, however, ties it to a fear of failure, not just a fear of matching up. She connects this to a fear of anything that is not predictable. This, while not empirically supported, has some relevance when we talk about dating online.

Comparing Face-to-Face and Internet Communication Technologies

In general, Internet communication technologies allow us to be able to communicate with others in much the same way as we did prior to the innovations of technology, if not more frequently. For example, people can still talk to each other, express vulnerabilities, and share parts of their day with one another. They can build relationships steadily and progressively. The differences are in the way they accomplish these tasks, such as how they manage their impression online, and what the implications might be. Differences include self-presentation, nonverbal relationship signals, and the development of rituals and sense of "everydayness" (Hertlein & Blumer, 2013). The research is not clear on whether face-to-face or computer-mediated communication produces more disclosures (Ruppel et al., 2017). The current thinking is that there is no empirical support for hyperpersonal theory (Ruppel et al., 2017), which posits that people sending information can be strategic in their presentation; that a receiver cannot find out much information about the sender; and that the sender can intentionally misrepresent themselves. The positive response the sender gets reinforces similar presentations in the future (Walther, 1996). There is, however, seemingly some support for social information processing theory, which says that online relationships tend to have information exchanged more slowly, and while they may reach the same level of relationship development, it takes them a bit of time before they get there.

Markie and I originally described our viewpoints on the dimensions of commonalities and points of difference in *The Couple and Family Technology Framework* (Hertlein & Blumer, 2013). As originally constructed, the list contained a smaller set of domains on which comparisons could be made. Previously, these were described as also including a discussion of how time was spent, how nonverbal signals were communicated, and so forth. In this updated text, we have subsumed these domains into others and distinguished further domains. See Table 2.1.

Self-Presentation

Lasch (1979) made some stark predictions about US culture, with many if not all of them happening in our networked society. Lasch's (1979) premise was that, in response to the revolution and challenging political climate of the 1960s, US society would shift from looking outward and naturally begin to focus inward—with a specific focus on the attainment of our individual personal goals and happiness. In his text, he takes a somewhat critical view of psychotherapy as assisting with the development of the focus on self, but also presents a picture of, with that continued focus, what our community will look like. With the advent

Table 2.1 Comparing/Contrasting Face-to-Face (FtF) Versus Internet Communication Technologies (ICTs)

Domains	Similarity Between FtF and ICT	Differences Between FtF and ICT
Self-Presentation	Opportunities to manage your self-presentation exist.	Opportunities to manage your self-presentation are greater in ICT.
Sharing Data	Presentation involves the sharing of data.	Data in ICTs is composed of emoticons, lack of nonverbals, and potentially manipulated data.
Rituals	Rituals and traditions are developed.	The Internet is the primary medium for the ritual and may impact shared time/interests.
Everydayness	Conversation reflects a sense of comfortableness and everydayness.	In ICTs, everydayness may be less spontaneous and more structured.
Emotional Intimacy	Emotional intimacy is key to the development of relationships (couple and family).	Emotional intimacy is heavily dependent on text-based conversations in ICTs.
History-Gathering	History-gathering occurs through interaction and communication (primarily direct observation).	History-gathering may also include surveillance online (indirect observation).
Consent	Both parties are engaged in a consenting process to move a relationship forward.	Consent is implied in FtF and may have to be explicitly given in ICTs.

of technology, we are where he predicted us being. We use technology to focus on pursuing our individual happiness and goals, and are interested in how we present to others as a way to feel better about ourselves. Impression management in a voyeuristic world is critical (Kaylor, Jeglic, & Collins, 2016). Impression management in today's digital context is big business. One has the ability to critically evaluate and make decisions around what they wish to present about themselves and their lives to others (Krämer & Winter, 2008). For example, Saudi women aged 20–26 were shown to use the privacy offered by the Internet to hide their identity, give themselves aliases, and subsequently interact with others who were not culturally sanctioned (Guta & Karolak, 2015). Many companies boast the ability to create profiles or personas, to build friend lists, or to assist people in making more effective (or engaging) Facebook posts (Swani, Milne, Brown, Assaf, & Donthu, 2017). It was initially believed that people using social media had an ability to artfully manage their presentation online via its screen—and use it as a screen of anonymity (Hetsroni & Guldin, 2017).

In both face-to-face communication and Internet communication, users have a degree of control over what is presented to others. When relationships are initiated offline, the ability to manage one's self-presentation may be evident in one's physical presentation—their clothing, the way they care for their home, how they style their hair, and so on. Romantically, partners may opt to attend to their presentation in a way that would make them more attractive to the other. Some of the way in which presentations are managed change in the case of online communication. Goffman's (1959) theory of self-presentation has been used to explain Internet users' self-presentation (Hall & Caton, 2017). Hogan (2010) considered social media more an exhibition than presentation as exhibitions are subject to selective contributions and are posted for a duration of time that could be observed anytime by a third party at their leisure, and termed the social media user a curator rather than a presenter. Gabriel (2014) would agree with this perspective—teens and young adults need to be overly conscious about what they are presenting to the world and have to embark on visibility management. This is particularly true of young people who are sexual orientation minorities (lesbian, gay, and bisexual; LGB) who have a need for managing their visibility regarding the disclosure of their sexual orientation identity and relationships offline, as well as online, which scholars have termed "electronic visibility management" (Twist, Bergdall, Belous, & Maier, 2017). Goffman posited there were two ways in which people managed their presentation to others: explicitly and implicitly. Explicit presentation refers to our purposeful presentation to others. Implicit presentation is that which appears natural and is the one we try to manipulate when we are attempting to manage how others see us. Self-presentation on Facebook is associated with certain personality traits as well—predicting how one presents oneself was most closely linked to conscientiousness and neuroticism. In other words, motivation for using Facebook affects the relationship between personality and one's behavior. In particular, those who score high on agreeableness are more likely to use Facebook to achieve a sense of belongingness. Individuals scoring high on neuroticism, on the other hand, use Facebook for self-presentation and personal disclosure (Seidman, 2013).

Most people use social media in an attempt to "accurately" display elements of their lives and personas (Orehek & Human, 2017). In social media postings, early research examined five methods of self-presentation: ingratiation (wanting to be liked by others), competence (to appear skilled), intimidation (threats), exemplification (to be perceived as superior), and supplication (enticing others to come to your aid through appearing helpless). People may use the Internet to play out these strategies since one can easily identify targets for each of these skills (Dominick, 1999). Rather than focusing on theories of self-presentation, some authors have found profiles actually reflect personality instead of trying to gain a reaction from other users (Back et al., 2010). Alternatively, one theory with adequate support suggests users manage their posting to self-promote their ideal of how they appear in each situation rather than intentionally deceiving other users across the board (Diefenbach & Christoforakos, 2017). This misrepresentation is not typically malicious (Hall & Caton, 2017), though the information posted is selected by the user themselves (Oberst, Renau, Chamarro, & Carbonell, 2016). This self-selection bias may result in self-censorship (Hall & Caton, 2017), postings that are socially desirable (Siibak, 2009), and postings that are more likely to be reinforced and celebrated by the Internet audience (Marder, Houghton, Joinson, Shankar, & Bull, 2016), and potentially less accurate to one's lived experience and instead crafted (Michikyan, Subrahmanyam, & Dennis, 2015). What is shared depends on who is going to see the information posted. While on some other sites, a person who meets someone online eventually may get to the place of talking to them offline that is not true for Facebook (Ross et al., 2009). Those who expect to have some offline encounter with an individual will affect what they share and post (Ross et al., 2009).

There also are differences in self-esteem depending on what is posted (Yang & Bradford Brown, 2015). For example, positive postings are connected to boosting one's self-esteem (Yang, Holden, & Carter, 2017). The implications are that one may have a low self-esteem and want it boosted, thus providing a motivation for the post. The more deep information one posts, the more likely they are to have lower self-esteem, explained in part by the fact that with more information shared, there is more information of which an audience can be critical or judgmental (Yang et al., 2017). The anxiety tied to what is shared is precisely why people with social anxiety refrain from self-disclosures (Green, Wilhelmsen, Wilmots, Dodd, & Quinn, 2016). The finding about the potential critical nature of an audience, however, contradicts findings from other research that says that self-esteem is positively associated with positive self-disclosures presumably in an attempt to support one's positive view-of-self (Chen, 2017). For example, swapping instant messages with someone you do not know can provide a self-esteem boost for adolescents (but not young adults) (Gross, 2011). One final aspect for consideration is that someone else may put up a post tagging an individual who does not want that photo or event shared. In social media, self-presentation can also be other-presentation. In other words, what someone else chooses to present about you might contradict what you wish others to see about you. In fact, most people (84%) have had an experience of being tagged in a photo against their wishes (Lang & Barton, 2015). This has led some people to ask for consent or permission of a person in a picture before posting it online. For instance, teachers and pediatricians are the frontrunners of obtaining consent prior to taking and posting photos of students and patients, respectively (Bryson, 2013). Those photographing in these contexts not only take and post images with consent, they use the hashtag #withconsent every time they do so to demonstrate that this online act is being done with permission (Kunkel, Twist, McDaniel, & Theiler, 2016).

Me, My Selfie, and I

We cannot discuss self-presentation on social media without discussing the selfie. Selfies are defined as a picture you take involving only you or you and others that is presented to others via social media (Sorokowski et al., 2015), and was added to dictionaries as a term in 2013. It is one of the most prominent forms of media, with an estimated 93 million selfies posted daily (Brandt, 2014). This statistic, however, does not include users of iPhones, which are actually more popular than Android phones (Heisler, 2017). Selfies are clearly a means of self-expression. At the same time, social media users who want to appear a particular way can always edit, stage, or otherwise purposefully arrange the selfie they provide to ensure social desirability (Lin, Tov, & Qiu, 2014). People can be selective about what they present (Walther, 2011). Providing a selfie may also be a way to gain positive feedback from others, regardless of whether the selfie is realistic (Mehdizadeh, 2010).

Some argue that the selfie has transformed the emphasis of the activity and diluted the experience of what we are trying to capture. Frequently selfies look staged/organized as the individual is trying to get the perfect shot and instead loses the purpose of sharing the experience (Roman, 2014). In addition, selfies to some degree allow for comparisons between individuals. For adults this may not be a problem, but for young teens designed to obtain peer approval, the consequences of not meeting the bar set by others can have a host of negative consequences. For example, a host of research has uncovered that adolescent girls posting selfies are comparing themselves to their peers and encountering some pretty negative outcomes as they pertain to their self-esteem and body image (McLean, Paxton, Wertheim, & Masters, 2015).

Just as selfies may be staged or planned to reflect what one wants others to see (Lyu, 2016), selfies may also be edited post-production. Editing selfies is also becoming a common practice. The motivation behind editing selfies is less about dissatisfaction with the selfie itself, but more associated with the desire to appear more favorably to others (social comparison) (Chae, 2017). The decision to edit selfies seems to stem in part from a global trend toward posting selfies and the inherent social comparison that accompanies such activity. With more selfies in the world and more exposure to those selfies via social media, one can compare oneself to others and scrutinize one's appearance more. At the same time, some personality factors contribute to self-presentation. For example, there are some well-founded assertions that the platform of Facebook and posting of selfies are the result of or further cultivate a context to support narcissism (Błachnio & Przepiórka, 2018). This relationship between the two (selfie-taking and narcissism) is reciprocal—that is, the more narcissistic you are, the more selfies you take; the more selfies you post, the more narcissistic you become (Halpern, Valenzuela, & Katz, 2016). For example, people who wish to self-promote and self-disclose as a way to gain sympathy from others are more likely to feel positively about taking and posting selfies and do not see themselves as being narcissistic (Diefenbach & Christoforakos, 2017; Re, Wang, He, & Rule, 2016), perhaps a result of the way selfies are normalized on social media.

Because we know such posts are staged and can be edited (Marwick & boyd, 2011), the view of selfies from others is rather negative and critical. People in selfies tend to be viewed as less trustworthy, less attractive, and more narcissistic than the same person in photos taken by others (Krämer, Feurstein, Kluck, Meier, Rother, & Winter, 2017). This is particularly true for men who take selfies, specifically in the areas of narcissism and trustworthiness (Krämer et al., 2017). In fact, social media users actually prefer looking at standard photos on social media rather than selfies (Diefenbach & Christoforakos, 2017). In addition, selfies have been tied to loneliness and depression, with some devastating outcomes (Kaur & Vig, 2016). Others, however, believe that they are a regular part of everyday life and avoid linking them to pathology (Hunt, 2016).

Self-Presentation in Couples

Relationships that initiate online have to manage the issue of self-presentation differently. In short, there is a greater ability to edit one's presentation. Consequently, people's perceptions of the early days of online dating were that the type of people who chose to post profiles online could not be trusted, were shy, awkward, lonely, deceitful, and had difficulty with social interactions, thus resulting in them resorting to online engagements (Anderson, 2007). This becomes a critically important and early relationship task: determining the extent to which one has presented oneself accurately. In addition, once the information is tested, how much accuracy is sufficient to continue the relationship?

One way presentation may be edited is through management of mood state. This may include withholding information about one's mood and emotional condition or actively presenting inaccurate information (Lee, Cheung, & Thadani, 2012). Another area in which self-presentation manifests is regarding physical attributes. A host of research cites the challenges with online daters and their photo profiles. In face-to-face interactions, it may be relatively easy to observe aspects of one's physical appearance that may not be consistent with other photos or information received about oneself. We have the ability to make an assessment about our physical height, weight, hair color, physique, etc. in person. There also seem to be differences in gender. Men, for example, are more likely to exaggerate elements of their physique, where women are more likely to misrepresent hobbies and age (Ben-Ze'ev, 2004). Men are also more likely to present basic information about themselves on social media than are women (Special & Barber, 2012).

In essence, the Internet allows people to present whatever they want about themselves. In a study conducted on online dating, one individual reported that he would no longer trust anyone's online profile because he had one bad interaction with someone who was at least ten years older than that person's posted photo (Heino, Ellison, & Gibbs, 2010). Self-presentation, at least in front of an audience of friends, is strategic. In one study, there was no difference between the amount of positive messages between Facebook wall posts, status messages, and private messages. That is not true, however, for negative messages: there are significantly fewer negative messages on wall posts than there are in status messages and private messages (Bazarova, Taft, Choi, & Cosley, 2013). Finally, heterosexual couples who share profile pictures of them as a couple report feeling more satisfied with their relationship and closer to one another (Saslow, Muise, Impett, & Dubin, 2013). In LGB couples, those of a younger age/generation are not practicing a high degree of anonymity about their relationships on their social media—meaning they are "out" online to friends (Twist, Belous, Maier, & Bergdall, 2017), which is a change from previous generations and may be a sign of greater acceptance and social support for LGB relationships (Becker, 2012; Fingerhut, 2016).

Because of the ability to misrepresent, some individuals engage in a warranting procedure when first meeting. Warranting refers to a process by which an individual confirms the information provided by an individual's profile (Gibbs, Ellison, & Lai, 2011). This is a common practice in online dating, where anyone can post whatever is desired. For example, women under the age of 50 are more likely to be deceitful about their age in online dating profiles than older women (Hall, Park,

Song, & Cody, 2010). Warranting is partly accomplished through valu-ing information provided by a third party instead of the person with whom one is interacting because the information from the third party cannot be manipulated (Gibbs et al., 2011). Those who make a decision to continue the warranting process may experience a trade-off in trust: the recipient of the warranting process may experience anger about not being trusted. Further, those not using warranting procedures may have some difficulty in resolving inconsistencies once the relationship becomes more serious.

Despite both the anecdotal and empirical evidence that we may use creative license in our profiles and communications, what is not clear is how these inconsistencies are aired, acknowledged, or resolved. One easy way to resolve the observed inconsistency is terminating the relationship (Heino, Ellison, & Gibbs, 2010), particularly in the case of a mismatch in the description of physical characteristics (Whitty & Carr, 2006).

Self-Presentation in Families

As aforementioned, adolescents and young adults are the groups with the highest proportion of technology and media usage to facilitate social interactions. They make more calls and send more text messages per day than any other age group, and nearly half report being online "almost constantly" (Anderson & Jiang, 2018). Though a proportion of the research is dedicated to friendship and romantic relationships, youth use these technologies to also communicate with their families. Over half of college students note daily or nearly daily contact with their par-ents. Another quarter noted contact with parents a few times a week (Arnett & Schwab, 2012). In addition, digital technologies are evolving constantly, which may provide even more opportunities for connection (Stein, Osborn, & Greenberg, 2016) and opportunities for representation (or misrepresentation) between parents and their children. Teens tend to use email and phone calls to interact with older generations and text mes-saging and social media to communicate with peers (Brown, Campbell, & Ling, 2011).

In families with an adolescent who engages in online communication, a youth's online presentation may be to convince parents or care provid-ers who are monitoring one's activities that peers and others in a youth's social group adhere to household rules and standards (Siibak, 2009). On the contrary, many adolescents admit to having at least two social media profiles—one that their parents or care providers have "friended" where they can appear to be adhering to rules and expectations, and another profile through which they post information not permitted by their par-ents, care providers, or home rules.

One last piece of social networking affecting our relationships is the effect of networking on prosocial behavior. Those who post in a monologue style (one-to-many) exhibit fewer prosocial behaviors (Chiou, Chen, &

Liao, 2014).Certainly, there are plenty of reasons why someone would be posting in a monologue fashion in the first place—perhaps some narcissism as mentioned earlier, self-esteem issues, lack of social graces, etc. In any event, it is critical that we move forward to try to identify whether there is a contribution in any capacity regarding the actual use of media rather than the personality characteristics or social learning that occurs before the Internet gets involved.

Shared Data

Another similarity between face-to-face and computer-mediated communication is the sharing of nonverbal signals in one's communication pattern. Nonverbal interactions in humans related to courtship seem to follow predictable patterns (Moore, 2010). Most research, which focuses primarily on heterosexual couples, supports the idea that women typically initiate the earlier nonverbal interactions; however, the signs that women give tend to be subtle, and, when men respond, it appears as if the man is making the first move. Then men and women both respond in reciprocal ways, each interaction building on the next until one of two outcomes: successful relationship interaction, or one person stops reciprocating and opts out of the relationship.

These same patterns also seem to hold true in online interactions. Someone may initiate an interaction through an approach and then assess whether that invitation was received well. Women may play a more prominent role in the earlier stages of courtship, whereas men play a more prominent role in latter stages, such as just prior to sexual interaction. Nonverbal signals such as smiling and leaning forward to indicate interest seem to have emerged across multiple studies as playing an important role in the nonverbal courtship process (Moore, 2010).

In addition to verbal interactions, couples do indeed grow when they can assess and make meaning of one another's nonverbal interactions. A main difference between face-to-face and computer-mediated communication, however, is the way in which nonverbal signals are communicated. In online interactions, nonverbal signals are communicated by emoticons rather than by someone's facial expressions or body positioning. Emoticons can enhance communication through technology when one can accurately display a general nonverbal reaction to the communication that fits the circumstance and, moreover, can give the other person added information about the context in which one's message was received. For example, one middle-class, heterosexual EuroAmerican couple—Ryan and Anais—were discussing the most recent argument they had. Since the couple had the argument over a chat function, Anais brought in a print out of the argument. During the argument, one issue was the use of Anais's emoticons in communication. After a comment where she was trying to diffuse the powerful emotions that were building up, she inserted a smiling face emoticon. In Ryan's state of being upset, he misinterpreted the smile as her attempt to mock him, thus fueling his anger and escalating the conflict.

Problematic implications for online relationships are that users of communicative technologies may insert an emoticon to display a certain nonverbal signal that (a) may not be accurate to their true experience, and/ or (b) may be misinterpreted by the receiver. Holly and Damien, a lower-upper-class, heterosexual couple of mixed ethnic backgrounds, came into session arguing about an interaction they had over a text message earlier that day. In the message, Holly stated that she wanted Damien to be mindful of the time so that he would be on time for the session, especially given his tendency to run late. Since the message was not accompanied by any nonverbal signals, Damien took the message as a directive and as an attack about his time-management skills. Consequently, he reacted by socializing with his boss after work, partially to prove a point that he could be on time for the session without her managing his schedule for him, but ended up late to the session. The nonverbal signals not communicated were that Holly was interested in Damien and attempting to build the relationship. She was not intending to be critical toward him, which most likely would have been reflected in tone and attitude had she spoken to him in person rather than sending a text message.

Rituals and Everydayness

Another area in which face-to-face and computer-mediated communication are similar is the development of rituals and sense of everydayness that the couple shares. Rituals, defined as repetitive yet meaningful interactions, are a key piece of the relationship dynamic. Because of the positive impact of rituals on a sense of satisfaction and stability in the relationship (Bruess & Pearson, 2002), rituals can be a useful adjunct in treatment (Olson, 1993). Couples have found rituals useful as a way to process such events as forgiveness (Barnett & Youngberg, 2004) and infidelity (Winek & Craven, 2003). Examples include renewing their vows or engaging in some ritual creating a sense of having a unique boundary around their relationship. The rituals contribute to a couple's sense of shared identity (Berg-Cross, Daniels, & Carr, 1993) and can be used as a way to bind the couple together, provide a sense of predictability in their relationship, and identify elements of family life that they want to transmit to future generations (Crespo, Davide, Costa, & Fletcher, 2008). The establishment of rituals in relationships is also associated with increases in marital satisfaction for newer parents (Crespo et al., 2008). Various types of rituals exist for both married and unmarried couples. In married couples, rituals include those related to time, symbols, daily routines, communication, habits, intimacy, and spirituality (Bruess & Pearson, 1997). Unmarried couples have rituals distinct from those for married couples, such as gift giving, assistance giving, visiting with extended family, and planning for the future (Campbell, Silva, & Wright, 2011).

One way rituals differ in technology-mediated relationships is the use of the Internet as a mechanism for conducting the ritual. For example, Tramell and Yola, a, heterosexual, working-class, African American couple, had a ritual of holding hands and praying together before dinner each night. When the couple was separated by distance, however, they were unable to continue this ritual. Therefore, the ritual transitioned from praying together while touching to praying together without touching but over the webcam. This type of ritual can be evident in offline relationships as well, but the difference is that the Internet is not the form of mediation in the ritual. Further, the ritual can be compromised if there are technical difficulties in the participation in the ritual. Less than optimal rituals may also emerge in couples/relational systems (Olson, 1993). For example, each member of a system may play out a part in their dynamic that they admit is nonproductive and unhealthy, but in the moment, they cannot manage to do anything different. For example, Mark and David, a, gay couple of professional-class and mixed ethnic backgrounds, left a therapy session feeling hopeful about their relationship and worked to develop a plan for what they would do differently daily, weekly, and monthly for one another. At the end of the first week, however, neither one had participated in doing anything differently. In the second week, the couple decided on a ritual to designate every Tuesday night as "cooking class night" where they selected a new recipe they had never made before and spent time together working through the recipe.

Similarly, the concept of "everydayness" refers to the unstructured interactions and experiences people have with each other on a daily or regular basis. This includes seeing each other in less contrived ways, such as experiencing daily chores together, and negotiating aspects of the relations as they emerge. In both face-to-face and computer-mediated communication relationships, a sense of everydayness is shared. The difference, however, is that in relationships characterized by computer-mediated communication, the everydayness is structured. In other words, individuals in the relationship have to organize a time in which they share the everydayness with one another. Without this negotiation of time, a member of a couple/relational system is not privy to the day-to-day interactions, feelings, and experiences of another without an explicit invitation to do so.

Emotional Intimacy

Emotional intimacy is also very different from face-to-face versus online interactions. A key reason for this is the level of self-disclosure. Self-disclosure refers to the information about ourselves that we disclose to others (Cozby, 1973), including information about our present emotional state, our cognitive processes, and even our physical whereabouts and activities (Tidwell & Walther, 2000). This process involves disclosing with both breadth and depth (Greene, Derlega, & Mathews, 2006). In other words, it is characterized by the range of topics shared as well as how personally revealing or sensitive the shared information is. To some degree, the extent to which someone self-discloses online is tied to certain aspects of their personality (Chen, Widjaja, & Yen, 2015). Frequency and type of disclosure may also be tied to the size of one's network; those with more people in their network are more likely to disclose their emotions—primarily positive (Lin et al., 2014). Disclosures made via Facebook are also driven by emotional state. In a study on college students' social media usage, it was demonstrated that people tend to disclose more on social media when they are feeling stressed and these disclosures are intentional (Zhang, 2017). This finding supports previous findings of similar research investigating motivations for disclosures online; for example, those who tend to use online media to find fulfillment and receive affection from others find that they receive that affection and fulfillment when they make emotional disclosures—and, subsequently, are satisfied with their online relationships (Pornsakulvanich, Haridakis, & Rubin, 2008).

There are five dimensions of self-disclosure: intentionality, amount, valence, veracity, and depth (Wheeless & Grotz, 1976). A common misconception is that the type of self-disclosure that develops intimacy is heavily reliant on the depth type. In fact, intimacy can be developed through consistent/frequent self-disclosure about topics that seem rather benign. In this way, it feels as if the person disclosing one's partner has a high degree of social presence in the lives of others and is readily available for support. The dimensions change, however, when applied to self-disclosures made over social media like Facebook. Authors have found four distinct motivations for self-disclosure on Facebook: social, hedonic, utilitarian, and social investigation (Chang & Heo, 2014). Each of these motivations leads to a different path of self-disclosure. Those who tend to disclose basic, highly sensitive information tend to be those who are socially motivated.

Social presence was developed to explain communication via technology (Short, Williams, & Christie, 1976). Social presence describes the degree of salience one has in technological interactions. Those who have a higher degree of social presence (i.e., are more active on social media) are seen as more warm, caring, and likeable than those with a lower degree of social presence. Further, as someone discloses to you, you disclose to them in a reciprocal fashion. This reciprocity then affects how the relationship develops—known as social penetration theory (Altman & Taylor, 1973). This is critical in social networking. In fact, when negative messages are posted on a wall, the person with whom the user is most familiar has a quicker response time than those with whom the poster is less familiar, a fact that is not true when sending the same message via private messenger (Bazarova et al., 2013).

Part of why self-disclosure is so powerful in online relationships is due to the lack of nonverbal communications, resulting in a reliance on description of one's state and other descriptive cues to supplement context and facilitate greater understanding (Whitty, 2008). For example, a casual observer in near proximity to an individual may perceive that a person texting to another is visibly upset, as evidenced by a sorrowful expression, the appearance of tears, and other elements of their body language. The individual on the other end of the messages, however, without such information communicated, would experience far more difficulty being able to discern the texter's emotional state. From this lens, the observer in geographic proximity may be considered having a more intimate relationship with the texter than perhaps the person on the other end of the messages. On the other hand, if the individual texting chooses to completely describe their emotional experience, including a description of their facial expressions, thought processes, emotion, etc., the two communicating via text can develop a more intimate relationship with the person on the other end of the communications.

The decision to disclose online is subject to a series of considerations, not the least of which include privacy and trust (Contena, Loscalzo, & Taddei, 2015). In addition, self-disclosure may be tied to the social comparisons we conduct online. We share information about ourselves to receive validation or to compare what we have posted to the posts of others. At other times, self-disclosure is unplanned. We may disclose something without recognition that others who are not to see it will be able to do so, or may post a photo without realizing something in the photo discloses more about us than was intended. A statement we make may reveal more than what we are trying to communicate. The disclosures may also have some interpersonal consequences. Teachers, for example, are rated as being more credible when they disclose online (Mazer, Murphy, & Simonds, 2009).

Finally, there is a natural tension between what to post and what to keep private (Greene et al., 2006). In some ways, we rely on the others posting on social media to assist us with our own sense of self. Termed "collaborative disclosure," it means that we rely on others to help us maintain what is private versus what is shared (Farci, Rossi, Boccia Artieri, & Giglietto, 2017). A good deal of our management about what to post and what to keep private online relies on social comparison. We note what others write and post and leave feedback; we receive feedback from others; this mechanism, among many others, is a way to assist us with developing a sophisticated understanding of what is deemed appropriate sharing. It is this collaborative disclosure that also enhances intimacy development (Farci et al., 2017).

Disclosure also has implications for relationships. Farci et al. (2017) expanded on what exactly occurs in self-disclosure that promotes such closeness and intimacy. They identified five strategies people use on Facebook in particular to disclose: (1) showing rather than telling, (2) sharing implicit content, (3) tagging self and others, (4) expectation of mutual understanding, and (5) liking. In *showing rather than telling*, the old adage "a picture is worth a thousand words" seems to hold up. Viewers can imply certain meaning from the visual cue presented and can understand the "relational context existing behind the picture" (Farci et al., 2017, p. 790). Sharing implicit content, while it can also occur in the photos or images presented in the first type discussed, also means that one can imply certain things in their written text. This means that one can share a rather vague or ambiguous post where the intended audience (perhaps a very small group of intimate friends or connections) will understand its true meaning—a construct called social steganography (Oolo & Siibak, 2013). *Tagging* is a mechanism designed to expand the experience and post to others. It is viewed as collaborative, aimed at inviting social contact, and a method to improve group cohesion. *Mutual understanding* related to the reason and meaning behind one's post is implied in one's social network. Farci et al. (2017) assert that Facebook users have an ongoing assessment in their head evaluating the likelihood that their Facebook friends will be able to understand a given post and edit accordingly. Finally, *liking* is an easy way to stay connected to someone without more directly posting to them or interacting at length with them (Farci et al., 2017).

Because of their findings and these strategies leading to collaborative disclosures, Farci et al. (2017) introduced the concept of networked intimacy. Networked intimacy refers to an intimacy developed through collaborative disclosure, such as the disclosures we make on social media (and Facebook in particular). Users treat the disclosures both as disclosures and as information. As Farci et al. noted:

> Networked intimacy is, at one and the same time, a practice of *selective sociality* (Itō, Okabe, & Matsuda, 2005) that helps to maintain exclusive private intimacy, and a form of *social inclusion* that arises from the pleasure of belonging to what Nakajima, Himeno and Yoshii describe as a "full-time intimate community" (p. 137).
>
> (p. 795)

In other words, we are connected to each other in perpetuity—if we want to be. Users can make decisions about what to share, with whom, when, and how. They can interact with others to demonstrate reciprocity and enhance intimacy, and can choose to display their relationships with others.

History-Gathering

History-gathering takes a different turn in the age of the Internet and social media. History-gathering used to be a long assessment of time, various questions asked over many dinners or instances. In today's climate, however, history-gathering is primarily done online. It is quite easy to do a Google search for someone's name to try to identify whether the information about them is accurate. Using the Internet as a historian is another way to gain context about our peers and our colleagues. Not only can one establish the veracity of someone else's identity and background online, one can potentially identify key experiences through archived posts, photographs, and other memorabilia shared online. This includes information on one's medical history, relational history, employment history, and beyond (Aimeur & Lafond, 2013). In addition to gathering history on peers, there is also potential for professionals to gather history on an institution or each other. For example, literature in psychology and counseling discusses the ethical decision-making around searching for one's patients online. Some argue that is a violation of patient privacy; on the other hand, clinicians feel like it gives them a fuller picture of the patient when they are able to know some contextual information. Families also have the ability to become their own kind of family science scholars through creating genograms and connecting with others to explore their genealogy (Crowe, 2008).

Consent

Finally, many of these practices are activated without the consent of the other participant. So, for example, when you are gathering information about a peer or friend, they may not be aware that you are using the Internet to gain that information. Prior to advanced technologies, any gathering of information may have required the consent and/or volunteerism of the person with whom one was communicating. That is no longer always the case. Anybody can look up anybody without necessarily having to clear it with a person or obtain consent. This contributes to an unequal power dynamic developing in relationships from the beginning. As one person gains more information about their partner to the exclusion of their partner, they establish a dynamic where one person is not being very honest, and that can have implications that play out in the relationship later.

This domain refers to not just the gathering of information, but the sharing of it as well. This includes activities such as revenge pornography (revenge porn), the establishment of private social media accounts in youth, the recording of conversations without others' knowledge, etc. (Heistand & Weins, 2014; Johnson, Mishna, Okumu, & Daciuk, 2018). In many ways, these technologies allow for "plausible deniability" for the one who commits the action, creating even more distress for the victim (Johnson et al., 2018, p. 4). Aside from the dishonesty piece related to the variety of non-consensual activities noted earlier, other considerations may include the potential for abuse/coercion. In technology, one may have a certain level of power or control when they obtain information about another person that the person does not want shared. A partner may force their partner to provide information including surrendering their cellphone for checking, giving up email passwords, coercing a partner into being technologically available, monitoring, etc. For example, once someone declines a date, the other partner, if they have access to that person's cell number, can follow with an unlimited number of harassing text messages.

Conclusion

Clearly, the patterns that dictate one's decision to engage in a particular technology are a highly complex endeavor. The patterns reflect a synthesis of personality, social motivators, individual pathology, resiliencies, cognitive style, and stage of development. The decision, however, to present oneself in a particular way (or to have the power to present others in a particular way) can have significant implications for self-esteem and relationships.

References

Aharony, N. (2016). Relationships among attachment theory, social capital perspective, personality characteristics, and Facebook self-disclosure. *Aslib Journal of Information Management, 68*(3), 362–386. doi:10.1108/AJIM-01-2016-0001

Aimeur, E., & Lafond, M. (2013). The scourge of Internet personal data collection. Availability, Reliability and Security (ARES). *2013 Eighth International Conference,* 821–828. doi:10.1109/ARES.2013.110

Altman, I., & Taylor, D. (1973). *Social penetration: The development of interpersonal relationships.* New York, NY: Holt.

Anderson, M., & Jiang, J. (2018). *Teens, social media & technology 2018.* PEW Research Center; Internet and Technology. Retrieved September 29, 2018, from www.pewInternet.org/2018/05/31/teens-social-media-technology-2018/

Anderson, N. (2007). *Video gaming to be twice as big as music by 2011.* Retrieved March 20, 2011, from https://arstechnica.com/gaming/2007/08/gaming-to-surge-50-percent-in-four-years-possibly/

Arnett, J. J., & Schwab, J. (2012). *The Clark University poll of emerging adults: Thriving, struggling, and hopeful.* Worcester, MA: Clark University.

Back, M., Stopfer, J., Vazire, S., Gaddis, S., Schmukle, S., Egloff, B., & Gosling, S. (2010). Facebook profiles reflect actual personality, not self-idealization. *Psychological Science, 21*(3), 372–374. doi: 10.1177/0956797609360756

Barnett, J. K., & Youngberg, C. (2004). Forgiveness as a ritual in couples therapy. *The Family Journal, 12*(1), 14–20. doi:10.1177/1066480703258613

Bazarova, N., Taft, J., Choi, Y., & Cosley, D. (2013). Managing impressions and relationships on Facebook: Self-presentational and relational concerns revealed through the analysis of language style. *Journal of Language and Social Psychology, 32*(2), 121–141.

Becker, A. B. (2012). Determinants of public support for same-sex marriage: Generational cohorts, social contact, and shifting attitudes. *International Journal of Public Opinion Research, 24*(4), 524–533. doi:10.1093/ijpor/eds002

Ben-Ze'ev, A. (2004). *Love online: Emotions on the internet.* New York, NY: Cambridge University Press.

Berg-Cross, L., Daniels, C., & Carr, P. (1993). Marital rituals among divorced and married couples. *Journal of Divorce & Remarriage, 18*(1–2), 1–30. doi:10.1300/j087v18n01_01

Berger, J. (2013). Beyond viral: Interpersonal communication in the Internet age. *Psychological Inquiry, 24*(4), 293–296. doi:10.1080/1047840X.2013.842203

Binder, J. F., Buglass, S. L., Betts, L. R., & Underwood, J. D. (2017). Online social network data as sociometric markers. *American Psychologist, 72*(7), 668–678. doi:10.1037/amp0000052

Błachnio, A., & Przepiórka, A. (2018). Facebook intrusion, fear of missing out, narcissism, and life satisfaction: A cross-sectional study. *Psychiatry Research, 259*, 514–519. doi:10.1016/j.psychres.2017.11.012

Bonetti, L., Campbell, M. A., & Gilmore, L. (2010). The relationship of loneliness and social anxiety with children's and adolescents' online communication. *Cyberpsychology, Behavior, and Social Networking, 13*(3), 279–285. doi:10.1089/cyber.2009.0215

Brailovskaia, J., & Bierhoff, H. (2016). Cross-cultural narcissism on Facebook: Relationship between self-presentation, social interaction and the open and covert narcissism on a social networking site in Germany and Russia. *Computers in Human Behavior, 55*(PA), 251–257.

Brandt, R. (2014). *Google divulges numbers at I/O: 20 bullion texts, 93 million selfies and more.* Retrieved July 7, 2016, from www.bizjournals.com/sanjose/news/2014/06/25/google-divulges-numbers-at-i-o-20-billion-texts-93.html

Brown, K., Campbell, S. W., & Ling, R. (2011). Mobile phones bridging the digital divide for teens in the US? *Future Internet, 3*(4), 144–158. doi:10.3390/fi3020144

Bruess, C. J. S., & Pearson, J. C. (1997). Interpersonal rituals in marriage and adult friendship. *Communication Monographs, 64*(1), 25–46. doi:10.1080/03637759709376403

Bruess, C. J. S., & Pearson, J. C. (2002). The function of mundane ritualizing in adult friendship and marriage. *Communication Research Reports, 19*(4), 314–326. doi:10.1080/08824090209384860

Bryson, D. (2013). Current issues: Consent for clinical photography. *Journal of Visual Communication in Medicine, 36*(1/2), 62–63. doi:10.3109/17453054.2013.791256

Buffardi, L., & Campbell, W. (2008). Narcissism and social networking web sites. *Personality and Social Psychology Bulletin, 34*(10), 1303–1314.

Burke, S. C., Wallen, M., Vail-Smith, K., & Knox, D. (2011). Using technology to control intimate partners: An exploratory study of college undergraduates. *Computers in Human Behavior, 27*(3), 1162–1167. doi:10.1016/j.chb.2010.12.010

Campbell, K., Silva, L. C., & Wright, D. W. (2011). Rituals in unmarried couple relationships: An exploratory study. *Family and Consumer Sciences Research Journal, 40*(1), 45–57. doi:10.1111/j.1552-3934.2011.02087.x

Chae, J. (2017). Virtual makeover: Selfie-taking and social media use increase selfie-editing frequency through social comparison. *Computers in Human Behavior, 66*, 370–276. doi:10.1016/j.chb.2016.10.0070747-5632

Chang, C., & Heo, J. (2014). Visiting theories that predict college students' self-disclosure on Facebook. *Computers in Human Behavior, 30*, 79–86. doi:10.1016/j.chb.2013.07.059

Chen, H. (2017). Antecedents of positive self-disclosure online: An empirical study of US college students' Facebook usage. *Psychology Research and Behavior Management, 10*, 147–153. doi:10.2147/PRBM.S136049

Chen, J. V., Widjaja, A. E., & Yen, D. C. (2015). Need for affiliation, need for popularity, self-esteem, and the moderating effect of big five personality traits affecting individuals' self-disclosure on Facebook. *International Journal of Human-Computer Interaction, 31*(11), 815–831. doi:10.1080/10447318.2015.1067479

Chiou, W., Chen, S., & Liao, D. (2014). Does Facebook promote self-interest? Enactment of indiscriminate one-to-many communication on online social networking sites decreases prosocial behavior. *Cyberpsychology, Behavior, and Social Networking, 17*(2), 68–73. doi:10.1089/cyber.2013.0035

Contena, B., Loscalzo, Y., & Taddei, S. (2015). Surfing on social network sites: A comprehensive instrument to evaluate online self-disclosure and related attitudes. *Computers in Human Behavior, 49*, 30–37. doi:10.1016/j.chb.2015.02.04[KH1]

Cozby, P. C. (1973). Self-disclosure: A literature review. *Psychological Bulletin, 79*(2), 73–91. doi:10.1037/h0033950

Crespo, C., Davide, I. N., Costa, M. E., & Fletcher, G. J. O. (2008). Family rituals in married couples: Links with attachment, relationship quality, and closeness. *Personal Relationships, 15*(2), 191–203. doi:10.1111/j.1475-6811.2008.00193.x

Crowe, E. (2008). *Genealogy online* (8th ed., Fully rev. and updated. ed.). New York: McGraw-Hill.

Diefenbach, S., & Christoforakos, L. (2017).The selfie paradox: Nobody seems to like them Yet everyone has reasons to take them. An exploration of psychological functions of selfies in self-presentation. *Frontiers in Psychology, 8*(7). doi:10.3389/fpsyg.2017.00007

Dominick, J. R. (1999). Who do you think you are? Personal home pages and self-presentation on the world wide web. *Journalism & Mass Communication Quarterly, 76*(4), 646–658. doi:10.1177/107769909907600403

Farci, M., Rossi, L., Boccia Artieri, G., & Giglietto, F. (2017). Networked intimacy. Intimacy and friendship among Italian Facebook users. *Information, Communication & Society, 20*(5), 784–801. doi:10.1080/1369118X.2016.1203970

Filipovic, J. (2013). The attractiveness of different online formats motives and frequencies of use. *Communications & Strategies, 89*, 105–115.

Fingerhut, H. (2016). *Support steady for same-sex marriage and acceptance of homosexuality*. Retrieved from www.pewresearch.org/fact-tank/2016/05/12/support-steady-for-same-sex-marriage-and-acceptance-of-homosexuality/

Gabriel, F. (2014). Sexting, selfies and self-harm: Young people, social media and the performance of self-development. *Media International Australia, 151*(151), 104–112. doi:10.1177/1329878X1415100114

Gibbs, J. L., Ellison, N. B., & Lai, C. (2011). First comes love, then comes Google: An investigation of uncertainty reduction strategies and self-disclosure in online dating. *Communication Research, 38*(1), 70–100. doi:10.1177/0093650210377091

Goffman, E. (1959). *The presentation of self in everyday life*. New York: Anchor Books.

Green, T., Wilhelmsen, T., Wilmots, E., Dodd, B., & Quinn, S. (2016). Social anxiety, attributes of online communication and self-disclosure across private and public Facebook communication. *Computers in Human Behavior, 58*, 206–213. doi:10.1016/j.chb.2015.12.066

Greene, K. V., Derlega, J., & Mathews, A. (2006). Self-disclosure in personal relationships. In Vangelisti, A. L. & Perlman, D. (Eds.), *The Cambridge handbook of personal relationships* (pp. 412–413). New York, NY: Cambridge: Cambridge University Press.

Gross, E. F. (2011). Logging on, bouncing back: An experimental investigation of online communication following social exclusion. *Psychology of Popular Media Culture, 1*, 60–68. doi:10.1037/2160-4134.1.S.60

Guta, H., & Karolak, M. (2015). Veiling and blogging: Social media as sites of identity negotiation and expression among Saudi women. *Journal of International Women's Studies, 16*(2), 115–127.

Hall, J. A., Park, N., Song, H., & Cody, M. J. (2010). Strategic misrepresentation in online dating: The effects of gender, self-monitoring, and personality traits. *Journal of Social & Personal Relationships, 27*(1), 117–135. doi:10.1177/0265407509349633

Hall, M., & Caton, S. (2017). Am I who I say I am? Unobtrusive self-representation and personality recognition on Facebook. *PLoS ONE, 12*(9), e0184417. doi:10.1371/journal.pone.0184417

Halpern, D., Valenzuela, S., & Katz, J. E. (2016). 'Selfie-ists' or 'Narci-selfiers'?: A cross-lagged panel analysis of selfie taking and narcissism. *Personality and Individual Differences, 97*, 98–101. doi:10.1016/j.paid.2016.03.019

Hammick, J. K., & Lee, M. J. (2014). Do shy people feel less communication apprehension online? The effects of virtual reality on the relationship between personality characteristics and communication outcomes. *Computers in Human Behavior, 33*, 302–310. doi:10.1016/j.chb.2013.01.046

Heino, R., Ellison, N., & Gibbs, J. (2010). Relationshopping: Investigating the market metaphor in online dating. *Journal of Social and Personal Relationships, 27*(4), 427–447.

Heisler, Y. (2017, May). *Sorry, Android fans, but the iPhone is still the world's most popular smartphone.* Retrieved from http://bgr.com/2017/05/10/iphone-vs-android-sales-marketshare-2017/

Heistand, T. C., & Weins, W. J. (Eds.). (2014). *Sexting and youth.* Durham, NC: Carolina Academic Press.

Helm, R., Möller, M., Mauroner, O., & Conrad, D. (2013). The effects of a lack of social recognition on online communication behavior. *Computers in Human Behavior, 29*(3), 1065–1077. doi:10.1016/j.chb.2012.09.007

Hertlein, K. M., & Blumer, M. L. C. (2013). *The couple and family technology framework: Intimate relationships in a digital age.* New York: Routledge.

Hetsroni, A., & Guldin, D. A. (2017). Revealing images as Facebook profile pictures: Influences of demographics and relationship status. *Social Behavior and Personality, 45*(6), 987–998. doi:10.2224/sbp.6004

Hogan, B. (2010). The presentation of self in the age of social media: Distinguishing performances and exhibitions online. *Bulletin of Science, Technology & Society, 30*(6), 377–386. doi:10.1177/0270467610385893

Hrastinski, S. (2008). The potential of synchronous communication to enhance participation in online discussions: A case study of two e-learning courses. *Information & Management, 45*(7), 499–506. doi:10.1016/j.im.2008.07.005

Hunt, E. (2016). *Taking the self out of selfie? Most pictures not about vanity, says study.* Retrieved from www.theguardian.com/media/2016/oct/08/taking-the-self-out-of-selfie-most-pictures-not-about-vanity-says-study

Itō, M., Okabe, D., & Matsuda, M. (2005). *Personal, portable, pedestrian: Mobile phones in Japanese life*. Cambridge, MA: MIT Press. ISSN: 11578637.

Jin, B., & Park, N. (2010). In-person contact begets calling and texting: Interpersonal motives for cellphone use, face-to-face interaction, and loneliness. *Cyberpsychology, Behavior and Social Networking, 13*(6), 611–618. doi:10.1089/cyber.2009.0314

Johnson, M., Mishna, F., Okumu, M., & Daciuk, J. (2018). *Non-consensual sharing of sexts: behaviours and attitudes of Canadian youth*. Ottawa: MediaSmarts. Retrieved October 21, 2018, from http://mediasmarts.ca/sites/medi asmarts/files/publication-report/full/sharing-of-sexts.pdf

Kaur, S., & Vig, D. (2016). Selfie and mental health issues: An overview. *Indian Journal of Health and Wellbeing, 7*(12), 1149–1152.

Kaylor, L., Jeglic, E. L., & Collins, C. (2016). Examining the impact of technology on exhibitionistic behavior. *Deviant Behavior, 37*(10), 1152–1162. doi:10.108 0/01639625.2016.1169828

Krämer, N. C., Feurstein, M., Kluck, J. P., Meier, Y., Rother, M., & Winter, S. (2017). Beware of selfies: The impact of photo type on impression formation based on social networking profiles. *Frontiers in Psychology, 8*. doi:10.3389/fpsyg.2017.00188

Krämer, N. C., & Winter, S. (2008). Impression management 2.0: The relationship of self-esteem, extraversion, self-efficacy, and self-presentation within social networking sites. *Journal of Media Psychology, 20*(3), 106–116. doi:10.1027/1864-1105.20.3.106

Kunkel, H., Twist, M. L. C., McDaniel, R., & Theiler, A. F. (2016, November). *Consent and cosplay: Considerations for individuals and families*. Poster, Society for Scientific Study of Sexuality Annual Conference, Phoenix, AZ.

Lai, C., Altavilla, D., Ronconi, A., & Aceto, P. (2016). Fear of Missing Out (FOMO) is associated with activation of the right middle temporal gyrus during inclusion social cue. *Computers in Human Behavior, 61*(C), 516–521. doi:10.1016/j.chb.2016.03.072

Lang, C., & Barton, H. (2015). Just untag it: Exploring the management of undesirable Facebook photos. *Computers in Human Behavior, 43*, 147–155. doi:10.1016/j.chb.2014.10.051

Lasch, C. (1979). *The culture of narcissism: American life in an age of diminishing expectations*. New York: Norton.

Lee, K., Noh, M., & Koo, D. (2013). Lonely people are no longer lonely on social networking sites: The mediating role of self-disclosure and social support. *Cyberpsychology, Behavior, and Social Networking, 16*(6), 413–418. doi:10.1089/cyber.2012.0553

Lee, Z., Cheung, C. M., & Thadani, D. R. (2012). *An investigation into the problematic use of Facebook*. 45th Hawaii International Conference on System Sciences, Maui, HI, 2012, pp. 1768–1776. doi:10.1109/HICSS.2012.106

Leung, L., & Zhang, R. (2017). Narcissism and social media use by children and adolescents. In K. S. Young & C. N. de Abreu (Eds.), *Internet addiction in children and adolescents: Risk factors, assessment, and treatment*. New York: Springer.

Lin, H., Tov, W., & Qiu, L. (2014). Emotional disclosure on social networking sites: The role of network structure and psychological needs. *Computers in Human Behavior, 41*, 342–350. doi:10.1016/j.chb.2014.09.045

Lin, K., & Lu, H. (2011). Why people use social networking sites: An empirical study integrating network externalities and motivation theory. *Computers in Human Behavior*, *27*(3), 1152–1161. doi:10.1016/j.chb.2010.12.009

Liu, D., & Brown, B. B. (2014). Self-disclosure on social networking sites, positive feedback, and social capital among chinese college students. *Computers in Human Behavior*, *38*, 213–219. doi:10.1016/j.chb.2014.06.003

Liu, Y., Liu, R., Ding, Y., Wang, J., Zhen, R., & Xu, L. (2016). How online basic psychological need satisfaction influences self-disclosure online among Chinese adolescents: Moderated mediation effect of exhibitionism and narcissism. *Frontiers in Psychology*, *7*, 1279. doi:10.3389/fpsyg.2016.01279

Lyu, S. O. (2016). Travel selfies on social media as objectified self-presentation. *Tourism Management*, *54*, 185–195. doi:10.1016/j.tourman.2015.11.001

Marder, B., Houghton, D., Joinson, A., Shankar, A., & Bull, E. (2016). Understanding the psychological process of avoidance-based self-regulation on Facebook. *Cyberpsychology, Behavior & Social Networking*, *19*(5), 321–327. doi:10.1089/cyber.2015.0564

Marwick, A. E., & Boyd, d. (2011). I tweet honestly, I tweet passionately: Twitter users, context collapse, and the imagined audience. *New Media & Society*, *13*(1), 114–133.

Mazer, J. P., Murphy, R. E., & Simonds, C. J. (2009). The effects of teacher self-disclosure via Facebook on teacher credibility. *Learning, Media and Technology*, *34*(2), 175. doi:10.1080/17439880902923655

McLean, S. A., Paxton, S. J., Wertheim, E. H., & Masters, J. (2015). Photoshopping the selfie: Self photo editing and photo investment are associated with body dissatisfaction in adolescent girls. *International Journal of Eating Disorders*, *48*(8), 1132–1140. doi:10.1002/eat.22449

Mehdizadeh, S. (2010). Self-presentation 2.0: Narcissism and self-esteem on Facebook. *CyberPsychology, Behavior, and Social Networking*, *13*, 357–364. doi:10.1089/cpb.2009.0257

Michikyan, M., Subrahmanyam, K., & Dennis, J. (2015). A picture is worth a thousand words: A mixed methods study of online self-presentation in a multiethnic sample of emerging adults. *Identity*, *15*(4), 287–308. doi:10.1080/152 83488.2015.1089506

Moore, M. M. (2010). Human nonverbal courtship behavior- a brief historical review. *Journal of Sex Research*, *47*(2/3), 171–180. doi:10.1080/00224490903402520

Oberst, U., Renau, V., Chamarro, A., & Carbonell, X. (2016). Gender stereotypes in Facebook profiles: Are women more female online? *Computers in Human Behavior*, *60*, 559–564. doi:10.1016/j.chb.2016.02.085

Ocker, R. J., & Yaverbaum, G. J. (1999). Asynchronous computer-mediated communication versus face-to-face collaboration: Results on student learning, quality and satisfaction. *Group Decision and Negotiation*, *8*(5), 427–440. doi:10.1023/A:1008621827601

Olson, F. (1993). The development and impact of ritual in couple counseling. *Counseling and Values*, *38*(1), 12–20. doi:10.1002/j.2161-007X.1993.tb00816.x

Ong, E. Y., Ang, R. P., Ho, J., Lim, J. C., Goh, D. H., Lee, C. S., & Chua, Alton Y. K. (2011). Narcissism, extraversion and adolescents' self-presentation on Facebook. *Personality and Individual Differences*, *50*(2), 180–185. doi:10.1016/j.paid.2010.09.022

Oolo, E., & Siibak, A. (2013). Performing for one's imagined audience: Social steganography and other privacy strategies of Estonian teens on networked publics. *Cyberpsychology: Journal of Psychosocial Research on Cyberspace*, 7(1). doi:10.5817/CP2013-1-7

Orehek, E., & Human, L. (2017). Self-expression on social media. Do tweets present accurate and positive portraits of impulsivity, self-esteem, and attachment style? *Personality and Social Psychology Bulletin*, 43(1), 60–70. doi:10.1177/014 6167216675332

Park, N., Lee, S., & Chung, J. E. (2016). Uses of cellphone texting: An integration of motivations, usage patterns, and psychological outcomes. *Computers in Human Behavior*, 62, 712–719. doi:10.1016/j.chb.2016.04.041

Perry, M. S., & Werner Wilson, R. J. (2011). Couples and computer-mediated communication: A closer look at the affordances and use of the channel. *Family and Consumer Sciences Research Journal*, 40(2), 120–134. doi:10.1111/j.1552-3934.2011.02099.x

Pornsakulvanich, V., Haridakis, P., & Rubin, A. M. (2008). The influence of dispositions and Internet motivation on online communication satisfaction and relationship closeness. *Computers in Human Behavior*, 24(5), 2292–2310. doi:10.1016/j.chb.2007.11.003

Przybylski, A. K., Murayama, K., DeHaan, C. R., & Gladwell, V. (2013). Motivational, emotional, and behavioral correlates of fear of missing out. *Computers in Human Behavior*, 29(4), 1841–1848. doi:10.1016/j.chb.2013.02.014

Putnam, R. (2000). *Bowling alone: The collapse and revival of American community*. New York, NY: Simon & Schuster.

Re, D., Wang, S., He, J., & Rule, N. (2016). Selfie indulgence. *Social Psychological and Personality Science*, 7(6), 588–596. doi:10.1177/1948550616644299

Reid, D. J., & Reid, F. J. M. (2007). Text or talk? Social anxiety, loneliness, and divergent preferences for cellphone use. *CyberPsychology & Behavior*, 10(3), 424–435. doi:10.1089/cpb.2006.9936

Roman, M. W. (2014). Has "Be here now" become "Me here now"? *Issues in Mental Health Nursing*, 35(11), 814–814. doi:10.3109/01612840.2014.954069

Ross, C., Orr, R. R., Orr, E. S., Sisic, M., Arseneault, J. M., & Simmering, M. G. (2009). Personality and motivations associated with Facebook use. *Computers in Human Behavior*, 25(2), 578–586. doi:10.1016/j.chb.2008.12.024

Ruppel, E., Gross, C., Stoll, A., Peck, B., Allen, M., & Kim, S. (2017). Reflecting on connecting: Meta-analysis of differences between computer-mediated and face-to-face self-disclosure. *Journal of Computer-Mediated Communication*, 22(1). Retrieved from https://onlinelibrary.wiley.com/doi/full/10.1111/jcc4.12179

Saslow, L., Muise, A., Impett, E., & Dubin, M. (2013). Can you see how happy we are? Facebook images and relationship satisfaction. *Social Psychological and Personality Science*, 4(4), 411–418.

Saxton, G., & Waters, R. (2014). What do stakeholders like on Facebook? Examining public reactions to nonprofit organizations' informational, promotional, and community-building messages. *Journal of Public Relations Research*, 26(3), 280–299.

Seidman, G. (2013). Self-presentation and belonging on Facebook: How personality influences social media use and motivations. *Personality and Individual Differences*, 54(3), 402–407. doi:10.1016/j.paid.2012.10.009

Selfhout, M. H. W., Branje, S. J. T., Delsing, M., Ter Bogt, T. F., & Meeus, W. H. (2009). Different types of Internet use, depression, and social anxiety: The role of perceived friendship quality. *Journal of Adolescence*, 32(4), 819–833. doi:10.1016/j.adolescence.2008.10.011

Short, J., Williams, E., & Christie, B. (1976). *The social psychology of telecommunications*. Hoboken, NJ: John Wiley & Sons, Ltd.

Siibak, A. (2009). Constructing the self through the photo selection—Visual impression management on social networking websites. *Cyberpsychology: Journal of Psychosocial Research on Cyberspace*, 3(1).

Sorokowski, P., Sorokowska, A., Oleszkiewicz, A., Frackowiak, T., Huk, A., & Pisanski, K. (2015). Selfie posting behaviors are associated with narcissism among men. *Personality and Individual Differences*, 85, 123–127. 10.1016/j.paid.2015.05.004

Special, W. P., & Barber, K. T. (2012). Self-disclosure and student satisfaction with Facebook. *Computers in Human Behavior*, 28(2), 624–630. doi:10.1016/j.chb.2011.11.00

Stead, H., & Bibby, P. A. (2017). Personality, fear of missing out and problematic Internet use and their relationship to subjective well-being. *Computers in Human Behavior*, 76, 534–540. doi:10.1016/j.chb.2017.08.016

Stein, C. H., Osborn, L. A., & Greenberg, S. G. (2016). Understanding young adults' reports of contact with their parents in a digital world: Psychological and familial relationship factors. *Journal of Child and Family Studies*, 25, 1802–1814. doi:10.1007/s10826-016-0366-0

Strano, M. M. (2008). User descriptions and interpretations of self-presentation through Facebook profile images. *Cyberpsychology: Journal of Psychosocial Research on Cyberspace*, 2(2). Retrieved from https://cyberpsychology.eu/article/view/4212/3253

Stronge, S., Osborne, D., West-Newman, T., Milojev, P., Greaves, L. M., Sibley, C. G., & Wilson, M. S. (2015). The Facebook feedback hypothesis of personality and social belonging. *New Zealand Journal of Psychology*, 44(2), 4–13.

Swani, K., Milne, G., Brown, B., Assaf, G., & Donthu, N. (2017). What messages to post? Evaluating the popularity of social media communications in business versus consumer markets. *Industrial Marketing Management*, 62, 77–87. doi:10.1016/j.indmarman.2016.07.006

Syn, S., & Sinn, D. (2015). Repurposing Facebook for documenting personal history: How do people develop a secondary system use? *Information Research*, 20(4). Retrieved from http://InformationR.net/ir/20-4/paper698.html

Tidwell, L. C., & Walther, J. B. (2000). Getting to know one another a bit at a time: Computer-mediated communication effects on disclosure, impressions, and interpersonal evaluations. *Human Communication Research*, 28(3), 317–348. doi:10.1111/j.1468-2958.2002.tb00811.x

Twist, M. L. C., Belous, C. K., Maier, C. A., & Bergdall, M. K. (2017). Considering technology-based ecological elements in lesbian, gay, and bisexual partnered relationships. *Sexual and Relationship Therapy*, 32(3/4), 291–308.

Twist, M. L. C., Bergdall, M. K., Belous, C. K., & Maier, C. A. (2017). Electronic visibility management of lesbian, gay, and bisexual identities and relationships. *Journal of Couple and Relationship Therapy: Innovations in Clinical Educational Interventions*, 16(4), 271–285.

Utz, S. (2015). The function of self-disclosure on social network sites: Not only intimate, but also positive and entertaining self-disclosures increase the feeling of connection. *Computers in Human Behavior*, 45, 1–10. doi:10.1016/j.chb.2014.11.076

Walther, J. B. (1996). Computer-mediated communication impersonal, interpersonal, and hyperpersonal interaction. *Communication Research, 23*(1), 3–43. doi:10.1177/009365096023001001

Walther, J. B. (2011). *Theories of computer-mediated communication and interpersonal relations.* Retrieved October 21, 2018, from http://wiki.commres.org/pds/TheoriesInNewMedia/42241_14.pdf

Wegmann, E., Oberst, U., Stodt, B., & Brand, M. (2017). Online-specific fear of missing out and Internet-use expectancies contribute to symptoms of Internet-communication disorder. *Addictive Behaviors Reports, 5*, 33–42. doi:10.1016/j.abrep.2017.04.001

Wehrenberg, M. (2018). The New Face of Anxiety: Treating Anxiety Disorders in the Age of Texting, *Social Media* and 24/7 Internet Access. Seminar presented via PESI, December 2018.

Weiqin, E. L., Campbell, M., Kimpton, M., Wozencroft, K., & Orel, A. (2016). Social capital on Facebook: The impact of personality and online communication behaviors. *Journal of Educational Computing Research, 54*(6), 747–786. doi:10.1177/0735633116631886

Wheeless, L. R., & Grotz, J. (1976). Conceptualization and measurement of reported self-disclosure. *Human Communication Research, 2*(4), 338–346. doi:10.1111/j.1468-2958.1976.tb00494.x

Whiting, A., & Williams, D. (2013). Why people use social media: A uses and gratifications approach. *Qualitative Market Research: An International Journal, 16*(4), 362–369. doi:10.1108/qmr-06-2013-0041

Whitty, M. T. (2008). Liberating or debilitating? An examination of romantic relationships, sexual relationships and friendships on the Net. *Computers in Human Behavior, 24*(5), 1837–1850. doi:10.1016/j.chb.2008.02.009

Whitty, M. T., & Carr, A. N. (2006). Deviance and cyberspace. *Cyberspace Romance: The Psychology of Online Relationships,* 109–123. doi:10.1007/978-0-230-20856-8_6

Wilson, K., Fornasier, S., & White, K. M. (2010). Psychological predictors of young adults' use of social networking sites. *Cyberpsychology, Behavior, and Social Networking, 13*(2), 173–177. doi:10.1089/cyber.2009.0094

Winek, J. L., & Craven, P. A. (2003). Healing rituals for couples recovering from adultery. *Contemporary Family Therapy, 25*(3), 249–266. doi:10.1023/A:1024518719817

Wolfradt, U., & Doll, J. (2001). Motives of adolescents to use the Internet as a function of personality traits, personal and social factors. *Journal of Educational Computing Research, 24*(1), 13–27. doi:10.2190/anpm-ln97-aut2-d2ej

Yang, C., & Bradford Brown, B. (2015). Online self-presentation on Facebook and self development during the college transition. *Journal of Youth and Adolescence, 45*(2), 402–416. doi:10.1007/s10964-015-0385-y

Yang, C., Holden, S. M., & Carter, M. D. (2017). Emerging adults' social media self-presentation and identity development at college transition: Mindfulness as a moderator. *Journal of Applied Developmental Psychology, 52*, 212–221. doi:10.1016/j.appdev.2017.08.006

Yurchisin, J., Watchravesringkan, K., & McCabe, D. B. (2005). An exploration of identity re-creation in the context of Internet dating. *Social Behavior and Personality: An International Journal, 33*(8), 735–750. doi:10.2224/sbp.2005.33.8.735[KH5]

Zhang, R. (2017). The stress-buffering effect of self-disclosure on Facebook: An examination of stressful life events, social support, and mental health among college students. *Computers in Human Behavior*, *75*, 527. doi:10.1016/j.chb.2017.05.043

Zillien, N., & Hargittai, E. (2009). Digital distinction: Status-specific types of Internet usage. *Social Science Quarterly*, *90*(2), 274–291. doi:10.1111/j.1540-6237.2009.00617.x

THREE

Virtual Impacts on Real-Time Individual, Couple, and Family Developments

Technology Immersion Across Developmental Contexts

As we highlighted in Chapter 1, technology affords us both conveniences as well as challenges. Whether a certain aspect of technology and new media is positive or negative is influenced by where an individual is in their own lifespan, and at what point a couple, family, or relational system is at in its life cycle. One thing seems to be clear; technology is changing individuals and relationships (Lanigan, Bold, & Chenoweth (2009). How technology both changes and is influenced by relational systems across their developmental life cycle, however, remains considerably less explored in both research and practice. For example, the accessibility one has to online pornography may be either innocuous or deeply problematic depending on the time or circumstance it has introduced into one's lifespan. If introduced in a stage where the individual is a single adult, it may be innocuous. If, however, access to online pornography is introduced during early childhood, the results could be troublesome. If introduced while someone is partnered/in romantic relationships, the consequences could be benign, damaging, or anywhere on a continuum depending on the developmental stage and rules of the relationship.

The determination as to whether technology is an issue in a particular context is a confluence of where people are in their individual life cycle development and their relational life cycle. Successful development outcomes includes differentiating perception and response, controlling and directing one's own behavior, and coping effectively. The main tasks are: (a) differentiated perception and response; (b) directing and controlling one's own behavior; (c) coping successfully under stress; (d) acquiring knowledge and skill; (e) establishing and maintaining mutually rewarding relationships; and (f) modifying and constructing one's own physical, social, and symbolic environment (Bronfenbrenner & Ceci, 1994).

65

Individual Lifespan: Erikson Revisited

Children

Today I (KH) was taking a photo of myself and my 2 ½-year-old niece. The minute I turned the camera onto the two of us and she could see herself on my phone's screen, she exclaimed in her little baby voice: "We're taking a selfie!" The room erupted in laughter upon hearing such a little voice say such a non-child statement, but the truth was undeniable: even at such a young age, she already knew the vernacular related to technology and new media. In any culture, children seem to be the demographic that understands the cultural changes faster than the generations before them, to the point where their parents are often surprised by their adoptions and nuanced understanding of new technologies. In the US, most children quickly become familiar with a variety of technologies ranging from smartphones to digital streaming devices to computers to laptops to tablets to gaming devices to video calling with friends and family. Children as young as age 2 are interested in technologies like computers (Watt & White, 1999).

The relationship with technology remains constant throughout the development of relational systems; however, the types of technology and the way such media is managed at each point differ based on the point in development, the diversity of the members in the relationships, and the larger social web with whom the members are technologically connected. According to Nikken and Schols (2015):

> In accordance with Vygotsky's (1986) theory on child development, parental mediation is seen as a key strategy in developing children's skills to use and interpret the media, foster positive outcomes and prevent negative effects of the media on children. Physical, emotional and social experiences, such as media use, and social interactions related to these activities with parents and siblings, provide a scaffold for the child's development, especially when they occur within the child's zone of proximal development (Vygotsky, 1986). With regard to young children's media use, this means that when the child is engaged in specific media activities, the parent should apply a form of mediation that is developmentally appropriate (Clark, 2011).
>
> (p. 3424)

Clearly, as gatekeepers, parents and care providers shoulder a significant burden of the responsibility for assisting youth with navigating the responsible use of technology. In fact the exposure of young kids to smartphones has more to do with parents/care providers than the kids (Kim, Shin, & Jo, 2016).

Adolescence

Children are attracted to the Internet for specific reasons. In many ways, the Internet and new media provide ways for children to continue to meet their developmental psychosocial tasks and objectives laid out by Erikson (1982). Adolescence is the stage when youth try on different identities to form their own idea about whom they are (Steinberg, 2008). If this stage is successfully resolved, the adolescent will have a sense of identity. If the stage is not successfully resolved, the adolescent will experience identity foreclosure. Current technology now plays a key part in this developmental stage. Teens use technologies as a way to try on different identities, as a way to gain autonomy, and as a way to connect with their peers (Borca, Bina, Keller, Gilbert, & Begotti, 2015).

Adolescents also make use of technologies for a variety of reasons including gaming, social networking, and optimization of educational homework opportunities, to name a few (Hur, 2006). As a child moves into adolescence, once again boundaries, roles, and rules within the family system need be renegotiated (McGoldrick & Carter, 2001), including those around the role of technology. In addition, the myriad ecological influences around technology in the couple's, family's, and children's lives need to be reconsidered. Frequently the development tasks that couples need to consider in adolescence revolve around the negotiating of privacy, autonomy, and independence versus the degree to which one needs to retain parental and family control (Bacigalupe & Lambe, 2011). These same tasks are often central issues of teen-technology and parental/care provider–technology interactions (Bacigalupe & Lambe, 2011).

According to Choi and Lim (2016):

> First, examination of the effects of SNS use in young people is particularly important, as they are at a critical stage in the development of social skills. During adolescence, people need social skills, particularly those related to self-dependence, career orientation, and relationship maintenance, more than ever (Arnett, 2000). Because adolescence is the stage at which the initial step toward long-term well-being, identity formation, and the development and maintenance of friendships and family relationships is taken, SNS use is most important during this period (Connolly, Furman, & Konarski, 2000; Montgomery, 2005).
>
> (p. 246)

In other words, the ability for the Internet and new media to assist in this developmental stage makes it fertile ground for adolescents to try this task in a relatively non-threatening environment. For example, one can connect with a certain peer group, clique, or even ask someone out on a date via a text channel without necessarily letting anyone else know that they are connected with this group or were rejected from the date as these activities would take place without potential rejection occurring face-to-face. Another consideration is the nature of the individual. As Hou et al. (2017) noted, psychological resilience mitigates negative effects of social media use. In their study, college students who were more psychologically resilient were less likely to experience stress from the problems associated with social networking sites.

Another area of development to consider is that of cognition. To date, the research on the cognitive impact of technology on teens is not totally clear. On the negative side, researchers have discovered that those adolescents who are more connected to the Internet than other teens are less likely to find solutions when solutions are in front of them (Mills, 2016). When teens know that they can find information later, they tend to remember how to find the information rather than the information itself (Sparrow, Liu, & Wegner, 2011). The results, however, are conflicting when evaluating whether access to the Internet contributes to self-confidence (Ferguson, McLean, & Risko, 2015).

Young Adulthood

In young adulthood, the primary tasks include differentiation from one's family-of-origin, establishing an independent value set, and using the information one has about what they learned in the identity-formation stage to make decisions about career, relationships, and personal life. It is during this phase that young people search for their identity. Technology has a key place in this stage of development (Cyr, Berman, & Smith, 2015). Social media affords young people the opportunity to enact an identity and evolve it (Livingstone, 2008). In enacting an identity, adolescents may use stickers, colors, photos, and detailed descriptions in the Facebook profile questions; in fact, the lack of using these descriptives and details is also an enacted identity. The decision to display themselves as a certain type of identity is a function of first the norms of their peer group and second what interfaces are available on the social media platform (Livingstone, 2008).

A key task in young adulthood is the development of self-authorship (Baxter Magolda, 2001). Initially described by Kegan (1994) as a process by which someone's meaning-making shifts from external to internal, self-authorship is defined as "the capacity to author, or invent, one's own beliefs, values, sense of self, and relationships with others" (p. 3). It is the development of one's own perspective through balancing external pressures and beliefs with one's internally generated beliefs, with consideration of one's personal goals (Baxter Magolda, 2001).

The process of becoming self-authored follows a lengthy and intense period of reflection on how one knows one's beliefs because they are internally generated rather than influenced by others. It is the difference between following dreams and following footsteps. For example, one may decide to become a music major rather than taking over the family business. To accomplish this, one considers their beliefs, values, ideals, interpersonal loyalties, and related cognitions and begins to see them as separate from themselves as opposed to extensions of themselves. They carefully consider which elements truly represent them and which represent loyalties to others of the external world incongruent with whom they feel they are. Once the individual identifies which values, beliefs, ideals, and views they want to move forward, they emerge with a new and congruent identity—one that is congruent in both their personality and behavior. It is this new identity that is acted upon, is expressed, and coordinates action on behalf of the new self-authored individual.

Self-authorship does not mean, however, that the individual relies solely on their voice and ignores any other points of view. As with Bowen's (1978) concept of differentiation, self-authored individuals strike a healthy balance between the external world and their internal voices. In either condition (self-authorship or differentiation), to be on the end of the continuum one way or another actually reflects lower levels of differentiation. One is able to articulate their beliefs, goals, and choices after full consideration of others' (external) perspectives. Rather than managing relationships and external voices through separation, one is able to manage them through engagement, reflection, and decision-making without defensiveness or feeling threatened because they are grounded in knowing whom they are and authenticity (Kegan, 1994). It is also similar to Williamson's (1991) description of achieving personal authority in the family system.

Self-authorship has three components: trusting one's internal voice, building an internal foundation, and securing internal commitments. Trusting one's internal voice is characterized by understanding the difference between real-world events and one's reaction to those events, and acknowledgment that you could not change the event, but that you do have control over your response to the event, and that the meaning-making of that event is up to you (Baxter Magolda, 2001). Building internal commitments follows trusting one's internal voice and is exemplified by one developing a framework, model, or set of standards by which they will live their lives to be consistent with their internal voice. In this stage, one is both making decisions and actively living their new framework while making adjustments to follow their internal foundation with increasing consistency. The final stage, securing commitments, is evidenced by a greater sense of freedom as one becomes increasingly confident that they will be able to control the elements of a situation in a way that reflects their internal voice and internal foundation. It is a process where one strengthens their internal foundation and is able to feel more secure about how events will unfold (Baxter Magolda, 2001).

Self-authorship typically emerges in one's mid-20s. This is the stage when narratives describe conflict between one's internal voices and external voices (Baxter Magolda, 2001). As individuals move into their 30s, their narratives instead reflect a resolution to the dilemma present in their 20s and are characterized by trusting their internal voices and making sure that they organize their life in such a way that their internal voices can still be heard (Baxter Magolda, 2001). The process of achieving self-authorship is completed when an individual has the knowledge about their internal state, wishes, values, and desires, and can establish the necessary resources to be able to live their identity in an authentic way.

Self-Authorship in a Relationally Authored (and Heterogenic) Environment

At its core, self-authorship is a process toward meaning-making. As such, certain assumptions must be present as one seeks to achieve self-authorship. First, it is assumed that constructed knowledge is based on evidence. Second, the person on the self-authorship journey needs to make a decision on what to believe. Finally, it is assumed that each person has the capacity to make decisions. These assumptions are significantly compromised in the age of the Internet, thus making the process of self-authorship more challenging. As discussed in Chapter 1, the concept of extelligence means that we derive knowledge from a collection of other sources and, likewise, offer information back into that same pot to assist others in their understanding of a concept. Therefore, the first stage of developing self-authorship is about getting information and making decisions about what to believe; the Internet, or our setting through which we receive information (largely external and involving many opinions), is the environment in which we collect this evidence. Nichols (2014) calls this the death of expertise—the fact that people who have a voice are being given as much credence as resident experts in that field simply because the Internet now provides them with this microphone. The fact that the evidence collected may be rooted in extelligence can affect one's ability to develop their set of evidence through which to form their opinions, the second step in self-authorship. Finally, the capacity of decision-making my again be challenged in the age of the Internet because of the ease through which one may establish personal accounts or access information. Those deemed too young to make decisions (teens and young adults) or are incapable are heavy Internet users, with an estimated 39% of young adults (aged 18–29 years) online almost constantly (Perrin & Jiang, 2018). Approximately 45% of teens between the ages of 13 and 17 are online on a near-constant basis (Perrin & Jiang, 2018). Yet youth may mistakenly believe information provided online is evidence. This combined with the norm that youth are active online, and the displaying of the actions (or descriptions of actions) of their peers online, may convince youth they have the capacity for such decision-making.

To recall, the three key ingredients to self-authorship are trusting your internal voice, building your internal foundation, and securing commitments to be able to live in your world. Like the phases of self-authorship, these ingredients are also slightly altered in the age of technology. Trusting one's internal voice can be compromised when we live in a highly visible world. With 2.789 billion social media users and nearly 80% of the US population with social media accounts, one's internal voice, if posted, may be challenged by others who disagree (and who are vocal about it). In other words, one needs to be self-authored enough to post in the first place without allowing people's reactions to the post to affect them.

Rymarczuk and Derksen (2014) argue that social media sites such as Facebook can be considered heterotopic environments. Heterotopic environments, described by Foucault, are those that have a dual quality of both existing in space and not existing in a physical space simultaneously. This is accomplished by breaking down boundaries between spaces (Foucault, 1986, as cited in Rymarczuk & Derksen, 2014). Online spaces and social media in particular, due to their heterotopic nature, have some unique challenges that could also affect the development of self-authorship. Part of why cyberspace and Facebook in particular are considered heterotropic environments is because even when you leave (close, exit, etc.), you don't really leave. For example, you can log out of Facebook, but you are still "there." Someone can see your page, send a message, write a comment, etc. (Rymarczuk & Derksen, 2014). This ambivalent presence can be challenging in the development of self-authorship. One's ability to manage their identity is victim to previous comments, posts, and information that has been posted online, which may come back to haunt them. In many ways the Internet compromises our ability to see people as having evolved and changed over time because we have evidence of them at earlier stages in their emotional and intellectual development. As Rymarczuk and Derksen (2014) note, "A message once sent, a remark once made or a picture once posted could be fed back into the present at any time" (n.p.).

Ecological Life Cycle Models

Bronfenbrenner Revisited

While not the first scholar to describe the impact of environments on systems, Bronfenbrenner (1979) outlined how each system connects to and interacts with each other. Bronfenbrenner's model consisted of five different systems, each embedded within another. Development, therefore, is the result of the interaction of personal characteristics and one's context (Tudge et al., 2016). In the center is the individual. The individual is surrounded by the microsystem, which includes the networks in which the individual is embedded. In other words, the content and structure of the microsystem are the direct socializing/developmental influences on the individual. These include one's workplace, neighborhood, school system, peer group, and family. The microsystem is defined by one's roles in society, the patterns they exhibit, and the relationships in face-to-face settings (Bronfenbrenner, 1994). The content and structure of the microsystem dictates how we maintain development. The mesosystem is the interaction of microsystems that contains the developing person. For example, it is the system that is created when peers of the developing individual interact with the school system such as at a school event, when the family interacts with their religious faith by attending church, or when a family system interacts with the workplace such as at a holiday party. The mesosystem is embedded within the next level known as the exosystem.

The exosystem describes the connections and interactions between other systems, at least one of which does not directly involve the developing individual (Bronfenbrenner, 1979, 1994). For example, studies have consistently shown that the workplace of the parents of the developing individual, the social network of the family, and the context of the neighborhood have an impact on one's development (Bronfenbrenner, 1994). Beyond the exosystem exists the macrosystem. This system is the patterns in which micro-, meso-, and exosystems engage that reflect a set of beliefs, values, lifestyles, and customs. Finally, all of these systems are embedded in a certain era, age, or place in time. People's patterns, lifestyles, relationships with family, interactions with school, etc. are affected by the era in which one lives. This final layer is known as the chronosystem.

Probably the easiest place where technology's effects can be observed (and perhaps the most logical placement) is in the chronosystem. The advent of technology has shifted the way we think about this era as evidenced by phrases such as "age of technology," "digital age," "new media age," "computer age," "information age," and "Digital Revolution." We are certainly living in a digital culture that has established many new rules, customs, lifestyles, etc. related to computers/computation, information storage, and information transmission. A new vernacular has even emerged alongside the technological developments, including words like "noob," "bitcoin," "netocracy," "firewall," "bluetooth," and "avatar," to name just a very few. Words that were recently (2017) added to Webster's dictionary are words such as net neutrality, abandonware, botnet, ghost (verb), and binge-watch.

At the same time, the Internet's accessibility and one's daily (perhaps better described as intimate) contact with devices suggest the effect of the Internet might also be addressed among some of the intimate levels in Bronfenbrenner's ecological model because they involve more than just general trends and overarching cultural shifts. For example, one study found that mass media has an impact on parent involvement with junior high students as well as the attitudes of the teachers toward Taiwanese youth regarding English language achievement (Kung & Lee, 2016). In addition, Lee, Ho, and Lwin (2017) suggest that expanding theoretical directions for problematic social networking use in teens can be achieved through further exploration of Bronfenbrenner's model. At the microsystem level, parenting style (authoritative, authoritarian, permissive, and rejecting-neglecting) is linked to self-regulation, which may in turn influence a teen's motivation for using social networking sites (SNSs). In addition, the support that parents offer may also influence whether their child looks for that support online. In short, the more support a parent offers, it is hypothesized that their teens will be less likely to rely on SNSs in problematic ways to ascertain that support (Lee et al., 2017).

The placement of technology in our lives transcends each of these layers and, consequently, affects development for both individuals and families. Johnson (2010) presented an initial version of this construct in an ecological techno-subsystem. In this construct, Johnson (2010) describes Bronfenbrenner's systems in a different way. Johnson (2010) proposes a technological subsystem that is embedded within the microsystem. This techno subsystem includes portable devices, e-books, cellphones, computers, etc. This level branches out into the microsystem, which is described as the immediate environment. These effects spill out into the mesosystem, or the element that is the connection between systems. The mesosystem influences the exosystem, referred to by Johnson (2010) as the external system.

We agree with this conceptualization but wish to add one piece. The way in which Johnson and Puplampu (2008) depict it, the techno subsystem influences the microsystem layer, which in turn influences the mesosystem layer, then influencing the exosystem layer, and then onto the macro. In our experience, the Internet and media transcend each of the layers. In other words, it is possible that the individual usage directly affects systems above the microsystem. One's statement on Facebook, for example, may have direct implications on larger systems (i.e., employers and larger systems responding to one another) without having to go through the chain of systems outlined by Johnson (2010).

Social Comparison With Peers *à la* Festinger

Another key piece of the microsystem is peer relationships. It is also the case that young people, in their identity development, compare themselves to their peers (Appel, Gerlach, & Crusius, 2016). The social comparisons we make are also attributable to more than adolescents; they are human nature. Human beings are and have always been oriented to compare themselves to one another. There are several tenets to the theory of social comparison, and each of these tenets has implications for group formation and social interaction (Festinger, 1954). First, humans have a natural drive to appraise their opinions and abilities. This helps us to understand whether we are even in the ballpark with our opinions or whether there needs to be a change in our opinions and abilities. Social media is the perfect place for this. When people are able to share photographs, updates, and events, it is an automatic database for comparison. Second, people have a tendency to appraise such opinions and abilities by comparing them with other people. In other words, we are looking for whether we are the statistical norm. In the case of social media, this becomes a dual edged sword. While the population and database are there for the comparison, the question as to whether the events posted as a way to make that comparison are accurate is a different story.

A third hypothesis posed by Festinger (1954) is that we are less likely to compare ourselves with another person as we gather information corroborating our opinions and abilities. So, for example, the more information that I receive that confirms that I am on track, the less likely thatI will feel the need to seek out other people to corroborate it. This is particularly true when we obtain the abilities and opinions of others who are our peers. Because social media has an area for search terms, we can self-select the groups who agree with our skills, opinions, and abilities. Then, once we join those groups, we can begin to make those comparisons. It is an absolutely filtered way to select a peer group.

The fourth part of the theory of social comparison explains the divergence between opinions and abilities. For example, we expect in terms of ability that we always have to work toward doing something better, and that doing better would be more desirable and closer to the norm. In terms of opinions, however, there is not any intrinsic value for preferring one opinion over others: it is merely a subjective feeling one gets that one's opinion is based on fact and correct.

The fifth tenet of social comparison theory says that there may be things about the environment, our world, or the person themselves, that prevent us from improving our ability at a certain point; opinions, however, do not function with that same issue. There are very few things that prohibit someone from sharing their opinion.

The sixth hypothesis according to Festinger (1954) is that we stop comparing ourselves with others when the comparisons we are seeking result in negative consequences. This wildly abounds online, where people may receive that negative feedback swiftly and loudly. The seventh factor of social comparison theory states that any group that sets itself up to be a standard comparison group for an opinion or an ability will make sure that everybody who's part of that group is on the same page with regard to that opinion or ability. This exhibits itself most directly online in the form of groups, such as those groups formed on Facebook. To be a member of the group, the group administrator can identify certain criteria and screen for inclusion into the group. If comments are made that do not jibe with the group's philosophy, the user who made the offending comments is removed from the group. The eighth hypothesis is that when people think they are very similar to each other, they will try to establish differences between each other. Social media, then, exists as a perfect platform to attempt to refine, distinguish, and alter one's attitudes, beliefs, and values to promote some level of divergence in a group that appears homogeneous. The ninth hypothesis under social comparison theory states when there is a variety of opinions or abilities in a group, the strength of the pressure toward being the same is going to be more intense for people closer to the middle and surrounding the mean than for people who are on the outside of that bell curve (Festinger, 1954).

In application to online behavior, to substantiate one's experiences one may watch others online to gauge norms and make comparisons. At times these comparisons may be beneficial and allow one to experience positive affect, in that that comparison is favorably downward (i.e., one's performance is better than someone else's). When that comparison is unfavorably upward, however, there is a tendency to be associated with negative affect (Fuhr, Hautzinger, & Meyer, 2015). Technology provides a prime stage through which these comparisons can be made. Such consequences of unfavorable upward comparisons include envy, negative impact on self-esteem, increases in depression, etc. (Pera, 2018). To date, the literature suggests that negative information contributes to discomfort, particularly when there is a strong connection to the information. In other words, the less confident one is and the more negative the content they explore on Facebook, the more likely they will be negatively impacted by what they see on Facebook and the more negative they will feel about themselves after they make social comparisons (Pera, 2018) and the more jealous they will feel (Muise, Christofides, & Desmarais, 2009). Further, Facebook has some pretty negative consequences on the development of friendships for young people (Wang, Jackson, Gaskin, & Wang, 2014).

Taylor Revisited

Nearly 30 years after Bronfenbrenner's ecological model, Taylor (2008) posed another model describing how we interact with the world around us. Taylor's model builds on the work of Baxter Magolda (2001), Kegan (1994), and Bronfenbrenner (1994), offering a more in-depth look at psychological and sociological factors surrounding development in college-aged youth. Taylor expounded on the levels (with the exception of the chronosystem) identified by Bronfenbrenner (1994). Taylor classified the variables as occurring in one of two dimensions: individual variables and environmental variables. Individual variables include socially constructed identities, histories (defined as education, family histories, awareness, and experience of major events), attributes (tendency to internalize, self-confidence, persistence, and resilience), and one's style of knowing (either doubting or accepting new ideas).

These individual variables also need special consideration or a revision in our Internet-dominated society. For example, socially constructed identities are everywhere one looks. That is, in fact, the point of any posts on social media. Social media allows users to post information about themselves—as Chapter 2 mentions, in an edited, careful, and protective way. Histories are also critical in the digital age. Taylor (2008) includes the description of awareness and experience of major life events as part of one's history. As more information about traumatic events becomes available online, we adopt these histories (and traumatic events) as our own. Findings regarding the impact of viewing traumatic events via media has consistently been found to contribute to post-traumatic stress disorder (PTSD; Propper, Stickgold, Keeley, & Christman, 2007), though media viewing has not been shown to manifest in help-seeking for anxiety in a hospital setting (Claassen, Kashner, Kashner, Xuan, & Larkin, 2011). In addition, Propper et al.'s (2007) design was within group, meaning that the changes in one's dreams and visions could be directly tied to viewing the attacks. For children, print media more so than television broadcasting was more likely to be associated with enduring PTSD of events in which they were not involved (Pfefferbaum et al., 2003). The Internet, of course, is primarily print media. This means that the more kids read, the more likely PTSD is not too far behind.

Taylor also further describes the social context around the first four levels of Bronfenbrenner's model specific to the learning environment for young adults. Examples of microsystems in this context include friends and family. The microsystem is the dominating context for young adults, especially in a digital world. Today, the mere activity of going to get a coffee and noting it on Facebook alerts everyone in the microsystem to one's activities. In addition to the unfavorable upward comparisons, there are judgments and evaluations made via a comment section. This is one way in which social systems are embedded in social media. Further, the context in which things are posted (photos with other individuals, geographic regions, etc.) also expresses the larger system in which we are embedded.

Mesosystems refer to areas where a person's personal life and academic/ employment life interact with one another. This level has exploded in the age of the Internet because of what may be posted about the company (Smith & Kidder, 2010), because of the individual's personal postings independent of comments regarding their employers, and because the Internet can provide information about job applicants that might be used in determining whether one should be hired. Choosing to search an applicant on Facebook or Google can provide a great deal of information about a candidate—but there is a difference in what *could* be used versus what *should* be used in making decisions about hiring (Smith & Kidder, 2010). Employers need to consider the ethical responsibility they have to respect one's privacy (Lusk, 2014) as well as adhere to Facebook's policy that this information not be used for hiring or in making decisions about how much searching an employer does about a given candidate, despite the data indicating that 64% of employers do engage in this practice (Volz, 2013). In addition, in many cases, employers have retained the right to terminate employees based on their postings in social media (Supra, 2016).

Finally, Taylor's concept of exosystem examples are curriculum, university rules and administration, and policies. Macrosystem examples include cultural events that affect one's training, cultural beliefs important to success, etc. In a digital world, there is a substantial intersection between major policies and the individual. One key example is that of net neutrality. Net neutrality is the principle that Internet providers are to enable access to all sites and content without being able to control to what consumers have access. The repeal of Net Neutrality will dictate the content and sites that can be accessed. This limiting policy in the macrosystem will have a direct effect on the microsystem level. Likewise, the individual keystrokes and search terms are collected by Internet search engines as a way to develop themes and advertise to the user at a later time. The individual (microsystem) is affecting the macrosystem.

Technology Use Across Relational Developmental Stages

After one becomes a new parent/care provider there is a shift in what they use the Internet for to accommodate bringing a new person into the world, and it is not just through social media. Mothers use blogging as a way to connect with others, to develop a level of intellectual engagement and mental stimulation, to help others, to feel validated, and to enhance skills and abilities (both technologically and in terms of personal growth) (Pettigrew, Archer, & Harrigan, 2016). But, again, as with anything on the Internet, the effects are not unilaterally positive. Facebook is often described as a means for gaining social capital, or resources gained via relationships with others (Coleman, 1988). The processes to achieve social capital include bonding and bridging (Putnam, 2000). SNSs such as Facebook provide the opportunity for bridging through establishing a network of connections and suggestions of others you may know.

There are several publications related to family life cycle development. Families tend to go through life in predictable stages. A new couple forms and makes a decision about having children. For those who have children, parents typically move through predictable processes. These processes include challenges to their formerly held relational and household roles, as well as decisions about how to negotiate rules for the family and who will be the executor of those rules. Couples who decide not to (or cannot) have children have a slightly different trajectory than those who do not have children (Pelton & Hertlein, 2011). This may include addressing societal challenges related to this experience, visiting decisions multiple times across a lifespan and relationship, and managing the voices and pressures of family and peers. Technology now has an active role in managing the shifts from stage-to-stage for any of these family forms.

Technology, Anxiety, and Distress (Oh My!)

The prevalence of anxiety and depression changes based on the study you read. At least two studies combat the notion that the prevalence of anxiety and depression has substantially increased over the last few decades (Baxter et al., 2014). The increases of anxiety and depression globally have gone from 3.6% to 4.0% and 4.0% to 4.4% respectively (Baxter et al., 2014), but this is consistent with population changes. The prevalence of self-reported psychological distress, however, has significantly increased over time, most notably for women (Baxter et al., 2014). Further, between 1992 and 2001, hospitalizations for mental illness increased approximately 2% (Larkin, Claassen, Emond, Pelletier, & Camargo, 2005).

Anxiety plays a role in decisions about behavior, including decisions around cellphone usage. In one study exploring anxiety and phone usage, US teens were asked how often they used their phones for messaging, social interaction, and participation on SNSs (Pierce, 2009). Results suggested a positive relationship between social anxiety and interacting with others online. These findings for adolescents mirror those of adults (Prizant-Passal, Shechner, & Aderka, 2016). Women specifically were more likely than men to report that they feel more anxious talking to others in person and more comfortable talking to others online (Pierce, 2009). The explanation for the positive relationship between social anxiety and more comfort in online interactions is that there is a greater perception of control in online interactions, thus an ability to leave a situation more easily if one experiences unfavorable judgments (Lee & Stapinski, 2012). Finally, the avoidance becomes self-reinforcing and contributes to more avoidance of offline interactions as time goes on (Prizant-Passal, Shechner, & Aderka, 2016).

You're Never Fully Dressed Without a Phone

The literature on addiction might have you believe that we are just that— "addicted." Stories in the media highlight unique situations in which one might succumb to a problematic condition because of spending too much time online. Adolescents have demonstrated that they feel uncomfortable if they spend increasing time offline (López, Gutierrez, & Jiménez, 2015). This may be a result of our use of technology actually changing how our brain processes information (Rosen, 2012). In fact, early research has found when Internet use is problematic, it is associated with a decrease in the brain's grey matter (Altbäcker et al., 2016). The processes of the brain are also altered. Those who engage in "addictive" online gaming experience reactivity, impulsivity, and other patterns consistent with gambling disorders (Fauth-Bühler & Mann, 2017). In fact, because of the way in which contemporary technology is designed, the brain's pathways are being remapped and rerouted.

Attachment to Technology: The Missing Link?

While primarily anecdotal, there may be something to these claims. Recent evidence points to the fact that the Internet is in fact rewiring our brains. Internet use disorder, while not yet classified as a psychological disorder by the American Psychiatric Association in its own right, has been observed to have some similarities in brain structure as with those who suffer from substance use disorder. Internet use disorder has been tied to impairment in several cortexes in the brain—primarily the ones involved in reward processing, memory, motivation, and cognitive control (Parks, Han, & Roh, 2017). This is different both physiologically and psychologically from substance use disorders. As Park, Han, and Roh (2017) put it:

> Early neurobiological research results in this area indicated that Internet use disorder shares many similarities with substance use disorders, including, to a certain extent, a shared pathophysiology. However, recent studies suggest that differences in biological and psychological markers exist between Internet use disorder and substance use disorders.
>
> (p. 467)

Now we have two areas of evidence that anxiety, dependence, and changes to the brain are occurring connected to our technology usage. Let us say that again:

Anxiety.
Dependence.
Changes in the brain.

This sounds suspiciously similar to another highly popular construct in psychological and therapeutic literature: attachment.

Attachment is a highly popular construct in psychotherapy. It is our experience of being able to rely on others when we are in a time of need (Mikulincer, Florian, Cowan, & Cowan, 2002). It is described as a sense of security around others' reliability and responsiveness in times of need (Mikulincer et al., 2002). It is a critical variable in how one manages their emotions, develops schemas about relationships, and interacts with others in close relationships.

Technology: The Monkey on Your Back (And in Your Family?)

Harry Harlow, famed biologist, provided the evidence needed for Bowlby to make his claims about attachment having a biological basis (Suomi, van der Horst, & van der Veer, 2008). In conducting a study using rhesus monkeys, Harlow noticed monkeys had a strong emotional reaction when separated from soiled garments in their cage (Harlow, 1958). This finding led Harlow to engineer another study, where he further discovered monkeys displaying an attachment to cloth-and-wire versions of a mother (Harlow, 1961).

Two manifestations indicating one's attachment style are the presence of avoidance and anxiety (Mikulincer et al., 2002). Avoidance is when people disengage or are distant from others as a consequence of a belief that the world is full of people who are unsafe and do not operate out of good will; anxiety, on the other hand, stems from fear that one will not be able to access a confidant or safe person in times of stress. For example, research has found those high in relationship avoidance but low in relationship anxiety are those who are more likely to use technology to communicate in relationships (Cyr et al., 2015). In general, the more anxious and avoidant one is, the less they think of themselves and the less sensitive they are to a partner's needs (Mikulincer et al., 2002).

While most literature has talked about attachment as it pertains to attachment between people and not a cloth-and-wire object, we want to revisit the concept introduced by Harlow that mammals can develop attachments to objects, not only sentient beings. We certainly know that attachment styles may dictate how technology is used in interpersonal relationships. As evidence of this, Nitzburg and Farber (2013) found individuals with disorganized attachment styles were more likely to use social networking for communication over face-to-face. This was also true when controlling for age, ethnicity, gender, and socioeconomic status (SES). Further, the more attachment anxiety one has, the more they feel closer to others while using social networking (Nitzburg & Farber, 2013). It is our contention that smartphones and the Internet function as if they were individual members in our family system (Blumer & Hertlein, 2015; Hertlein & Blumer, 2013). In fact, we encourage families to consider that technology occupies a place in their system via a pictorial depiction or genogram.

Technology, Attachment, and Romantic Relationships

Harlow's groundbreaking research demonstrated that we as primates can develop attachments to inanimate objects, particularly when we perceive that inanimate object provides support (Keefer, Landau, & Sullivan, 2014). To date, literature has singularly focused on how new media, the Internet, and cellphones allow for the development of deep attachments to our romantic partners. For example, Chopik and Peterson (2014) clearly tie the decrease of anxious attachment over the last ten years to the emergence of cellphones. Morey, Gentzler, Creasy, Oberhauser, and Westerman (2013) would agree, as their research found those who communicate less online exhibit more attachment-avoidance, where more communication online is associated with higher levels of self-reported intimacy and support (Morey et al., 2013). We can also develop attachments to others online outside of our romantic partners or family members (Levine & Stekel, 2016; Lewis, Weber, & Bowman, 2008), in part again because of the accessibility (and responsiveness) that technology provides. In short, attachment is about connecting to people who support and respond to us. Like a human, today's technology responds to us and anticipates our needs. Alexa and Google listen to us. We can order things. It asks us if we want to repeat our last order. It knows us.

Attachment is not the same thing as "addiction" (see, for example, Kuss & Griffiths, 2011). Harlow's monkeys were not described as being addicted to their cloth-and-wire mother: the word used was "attachment." It is true that both addiction and attachment processes are represented in the brain (Park et al., 2017), but these processes do not necessarily lead to the same conclusions. Some evidence that we are beginning to develop attachment to our actual devices again comes from the constructs discussed earlier—anxiety and avoidance with regard to our phones. Anxiety when we are separated from our phones is a real event (Seunghee, Joon, & Hyun, 2017), and is characterized by two dimensions—*refuge* (defined as feeling safe with one's phone and uncomfortable with being distant from one's phone) and *burden* (where one experiences relief when away from one's phone) (Trub & Barbot, 2016).

Our conceptualization is there are four types of attachment we can hold to technology (Hertlein & Twist, 2018a, b) (see Table 3.1). For those who are securely attached to their phones, they will exhibit a pattern of low avoidance and low anxiety when separated. Those with preoccupied types of attachments with their phones will exhibit low levels of avoidance and high levels of anxiety when separated. One who is highly anxious about being separated from their phone and also highly avoidant in their phone usage and not anxious about checking their phone would have a dismissive style of attachment. Finally, those with a high level or complicated avoidance and high level of anxiety (those who have difficulty regulating their phone usage) are considered having a disorganized type of attachment with technology (see Table 3.1).

Conclusion

Technology use across the individual lifespan can be thought of from a variety of theoretical perspectives—including Erikson's (1982) developmental theory as it applies to children, adolescents, and young adults, Bronfenbrenner's ecological model (1979), Festinger's social model (1954), and Taylor's model for the development of young people (2008). Attachment is also a theoretical backdrop that cannot be ignored when it comes to understanding how our relationship with technology is influenced by and further affects our level of attachment. As our relationship with technology continues to evolve, these models can serve to illuminate what we might expect in terms of how the changing technologies will affect our individual psychosocial and relational development.

Table 3.1 Types of Attachment to Technology

Type of Attachment	Definition and Characteristics	Example
Secure	Appropriate use of technology; characterized by low avoidance and low anxiety regarding phone or Internet usage.	Does not avoid their phone, but also does not feel compelled to pick it up, check it, or otherwise interact with the phone when there is no distinct purpose.
Dismissive	High avoidance and low anxiety; not interested in checking the phone even when there could be some useful gains.	Refuses to interact with technology across multiple contexts (smartphones, tablets, etc).
Preoccupied	Low avoidance and high anxiety; constant checking of the phone even when there is no particular purpose nor apparent useful gains.	No ability to delay gratification in interacting with the phone; may be considered a nomophobe (King et al., 2014).
Unresolved-Disorganized	Complicated avoidance and high anxiety, but in an unpredictable and unpatterned way; technology represents a trauma; technology represents people who have traumatized them.	Experience with cyberbullying; trolling; electronic visibility management; intimate partner stalking, which contributes to a distancing from technology/phone usage.

References

Altbäcker, A., Plózer, E., Darnai, G., Perlaki, G., Horváth, R., Orsi, G., . . . Janszky, J. (2016). Problematic Internet use is associated with structural alterations in the brain reward system in females. *Brain Imaging and Behavior, 10*(4), 953–959. doi:10.1007/s11682-015-9454-9

Appel, H., Gerlach, A. L., & Crusius, J. (2016). The interplay between Facebook use, social comparison, envy, and depression. *Current Opinion in Psychology, 9*, 44–49. doi:10.1016/j.copsyc.2015.10.006

Arnett, J. J. (2000). Emerging adulthood: A theory of development from the late teens through the twenties. *The American Psychologist, 55*(5), 469–480. Retrieved from https://www.ncbi.nlm.nih.gov/pubmed/10842426

Bacigalupe, G., & Lambe, S. (2011). Virtualizing intimacy: Information communication technologies and transnational families in therapy. *Family Process, 50*(1), 12–26. doi: 10.1111/j.1545-5300.2010.01343.x.Baxter Magolda, M. (2001). *Making their own way: Narratives for transforming higher education to promote self-development.* New York: Stylus Publishing.

Baxter, A. J., Scott, K. M., Ferrari, A. J., Norman, R. E., Vos, T., & Whiteford, H. A. (2014). Challenging the myth of an "epidemic" of common mental disorders:

Trends in the global prevalence of anxiety and depression between 1990 and 2010. *Depression and Anxiety*, *31*(6), 506–516. doi:10.1002/da.22230

Blumer, M., & Hertlein, K. M. (2015). The technological genogram: Tool for exploring intergenerational communication patterns around technology use. In C. Breuss (Ed.), *Family communication in the digital age* (pp. 471–490). New York: Peter Lang International Publishers.

Borca, G., Bina, M., Keller, P., Gilbert, L., & Begotti, T. (2015). Internet use and developmental tasks: Adolescents' point of view. *Computers in Human Behavior*, *52*, 49–58. doi:10.1016/j.chb.2015.05.029

Bowen, M. (1978). *Family therapy in clinical practice*. Lanham, MD: Rowman & Littlefield.

Bronfenbrenner, U. (1979). *The ecology of human development: Experiments by nature and design*. Cambridge, MA: Harvard University Press.

Bronfenbrenner, U. (1994). Ecological models of human development. *The International Encyclopedia of Education*, *3*(2), 1643–1647. Retrieved from www.stolaf.edu/people/huff/classes/Psych130F2010/Readings/Bronfenbrenner1994.pdf

Bronfenbrenner, U., & Ceci, S. (1994). Nature-nurture reconceptualized in developmental perspective: A bioecological model. *Psychological Review*, *101*(4), 568–586. doi:10.1037//0033-295x.101.4.568

Choi, S. B., & Lim, M. S. (2016). Effects of social and technology overload on psychological well-being in young South Korean adults: The mediatory role of social network service addiction. *Computers in Human Behavior*, *61*, 245–254. doi:10.1016/j.chb.2016.03.032

Chopik, W., & Peterson, C. (2014). Changes in technology use and adult attachment orientation from 2002 to 2012. *Computers in Human Behavior*, *38*, 208–212. doi:10.1016/j.chb.2014.05.031

Claassen, C., Kashner, T. M., Kashner, T. K., Xuan, L., & Larkin, G. L. (2011). Psychiatric emergency "surge capacity" following acts of terrorism and mass violence with high media impact: What is required? *General Hospital Psychiatry*, *33*(3), 287–293. doi:10.1016/j.genhosppsych.2011.01.015

Clark, L. (2011). Parental mediation theory for the digital age. *Communication Theory*, *21*(4), 323–343.

Coleman, J. S. (1988). Social capital in the creation of human capital. *American Journal of Sociology*, *94*, S95–S120. Retrieved from www.jstor.org/stable/2780243

Connolly, J., Furman, W., & Konarski, R. (2000). The role of peers in the emergence of heterosexual romantic relationships in adolescence. *Child Development*, *71*(5), 1395–1408.

Cyr, B., Berman, S. L., & Smith, M. L. (2015). The role of communication technology in adolescent relationships and identity development. *Child & Youth Care Forum*, *44*(1), 79–92. doi:10.1007/s10566-014-9271-0

Erikson, E. H. (1982). *The life cycle completed*. New York, NY: Norton.

Fauth-Bühler, M., & Mann, K. (2017). Neurobiological correlates of Internet gaming disorder: Similarities to pathological gambling. *Addictive Behaviors*, *64*, 349–356. doi:10.1016/j.addbeh.2015.11.004

Ferguson, A. M., McLean, D., & Risko, E. F. (2015). Answers at your fingertips: Access to the Internet influences willingness to answer questions. *Consciousness and Cognition*, *37*, 91–102. doi:10.1016/j.concog.2015.08.008

Festinger, L. (1954). A theory of social comparison processes. *Human Relations*, *7*(2), 117–140. doi:10.1177/001872675400700202

Foucault, M. (1986) [1967]. Of other spaces, heterotopias, trans. J. Miskowiec, *Diacritics, 16*, 22–27.

Fuhr, K., Hautzinger, M., & Meyer, T. D. (2015). Are social comparisons detrimental for the mood and self-esteem of individuals with an affective disorder? *Cognitive Therapy and Research, 39*(3), 279–291. doi:10.1007/s10608-014-9656-2

Harlow, H. F. (1958). The nature of love. *American Psychologist, 13*(12), 673–685. doi:10.1037/h0047884

Harlow, H. F. (1961). The development of affectional patterns in infant monkeys. In B. M. Foss (Ed.), *Determinants of infant behaviour I* (pp. 75–97). London/New York, NY: Methuen/Wiley.

Hertlein, K. M., & Blumer, M. L. C. (2013). *The couple and family technology framework: Intimate relationships in a digital age.* New York, NY: Routledge.

Hertlein, K. M., & Twist, M. L. C. (2018a). Attachment to technology: The missing link. *Journal of Couple and Relationship Therapy: Innovations in Clinical Educational Interventions, 17*(1), 2–6.

Hertlein, K. M., & Twist, M. L. C. (2018b). Me, myself, and I(phone): Attachment revisited. *Family Therapy Magazine*, 33–35.

Hou, X., Wang, H., Guo, C., Gaskin, J., Rost, D. H., & Wang, J. (2017). Psychological resilience can help combat the effect of stress on problematic social networking site usage. *Personality and Individual Differences, 109*, 61–66. doi:10.1016/j.paid.2016.12.048

Hur, M. H. (2006). Demographic, habitual, socioeconomic determinants of Internet addiction disorder: An empirical study of Korean teenagers. *CyberPsychology & Behavior, 9*(5), 514–525. doi:10.1089/cpb.2006.9.514

Johnson, G. M. (2010). Internet use and child development: Validation of the ecological techno-subsystem. *Journal of Educational Technology & Society, 13*(1), 176–185. doi:10.21432/t2cp4t

Johnson, G. M., & Puplampu, P. (2008). A conceptual framework for understanding the effect of the Internet on child development: The ecological techno-subsystem. *Canadian Journal of Learning and Technology, 34*, 19–28. doi:10.21432/t2cp4t

Keefer, L. A., Landau, M. J., & Sullivan, D. (2014). Non-human support: Broadening the scope of attachment theory: Non-human support. *Social and Personality Psychology Compass, 8*(9), 524–535. doi:10.1111/spc3.12129

Kegan, R. (1994). *In over our heads: The mental demands of modern life.* Cambridge, MA: Harvard University Press.

Kim, S. J., Shin, Y., & Jo, W. D. (2016). Analysis factors that influence smartphone exposure and use from ages 3 to 5 years. *Journal of the American Academy of Child & Adolescent Psychiatry, 55*(10), S204. doi:10.1016/j.jaac.2016.09.511

King, A., Valença, A., Silva, A., Sancassiani, F., Machado, S., & Nardi, A. (2014). "Nomophobia": Impact of cell phone use interfering with symptoms and emotions of individuals with panic disorder compared with a control group. *Clinical Practice and Epidemiology in Mental Health: CP & EMH, 10*(1), 28–35. doi: 10.2174/1745017901410010028

Kung, H., & Lee, C. (2016). Factors influencing junior high school students' English language achievement in Taiwan: A Bronfenbrenner's ecological system approach. *Journal of Educational Practice and Research, 29*(1), 35–66.

Kuss, D. J., & Griffiths, M. D. (2011). Online social networking and addiction—A review of the psychological literature. *International Journal of Environmental Research and Public Health*, 8(9), 3528–3552. doi:10.3390/ijerph8093528

Larkin, G. L., Claassen, C. A., Emond, J. A., Pelletier, A. J., & Camargo, C. A. (2005). Trends in US emergency department visits for mental health conditions, 1992 to 2001. *Psychiatric Services*, 56(6), 671–677. doi:10.1176/appi. ps.56.6.671

Lee, E., Ho, S., & Lwin, M. (2017). Explicating problematic social network sites use: A review of concepts, theoretical frameworks, and future directions for communication theorizing. *New Media & Society*, 19(2), 308–326. doi:10.1177/ 1461444816671891

Lee, B., & Stapinski, L. (2012). Seeking safety on the internet: Relationship between social anxiety and problematic internet use. *Journal of Anxiety Disorders*, 26(1), 197–205. *doi:* 10.1016/j.janxdis.2011.11.001

Levine, D. T., & Stekel, D. J. (2016). So why have you added me? Adolescent girls' technology-mediated attachments and relationships. *Computers in Human Behavior*, 63, 25–34. doi:10.1016/j.chb.2016.05.011

Lewis, M., Weber, R., & Bowman, N. (2008). "They may be pixels, but they're MY pixels": Developing a metric of character attachment in role-playing video games. *Cyberpsychology & Behavior*, 11(4), 515–518. doi:10.1089/cpb.2007. 0137

Livingstone, S. (2008). Taking risky opportunities in youthful content creation: Teenagers' use of social networking sites for intimacy, privacy and self-expression. *New Media & Society*, 10(3), 393–411. doi:10.1177/1461444808089415

López de Ayala López, M., Sendín Gutierrez, J., & García Jiménez, A. (2015). Problematic Internet use among Spanish adolescents: The predictive role of Internet preference and family relationships. *European Journal of Communication*, 30(4), 470–485. doi:10.1177/0267323115586725

Lusk, R. (2014). Facebook's newest friend—Employers: Use of social networking in hiring challenges U.S. privacy constructs. *Capital University Law Review*, 42(3), 709–762.

McGoldrick, M., & Carter, B. (2001). Advances in coaching: Family therapy with one person. *Journal of Marital and Family Therapy*, 27(3), 281–300. doi:10.1111/ j.1752-0606.2001.tb00325.x

Mikulincer, M., Florian, V., Cowan, P. A., & Cowan, C. P. (2002). Attachment security in couple relationships: A systemic model and its implications for family dynamics. *Family Process*, 41(3), 405–434. doi:10.1111/j.1545-5300.2002.41309.x

Mills, K. (2016). Possible effects of Internet use on cognitive development in adolescence. *Media and Communication*, 4(3), 4–12. doi:10.17645/mac.v4i3.516

Montgomery, M. J. (2005). Psychosocial intimacy and identity: An early adolescence to emerging adulthood. *Journal of Adolescent Research*, 20(3), 346–374. doi: 10.1177/0743558404273118

Morey, J. N., Gentzler, A. L., Creasy, B., Oberhauser, A. M., & Westerman, D. (2013). Young adults' use of communication technology within their romantic relationships and associations with attachment style. *Computers in Human Behavior*, 29(4), 1771–1778. doi:10.1016/j.chb.2013.02.019

Muise, A., Christofides, E., & Desmarais, S. (2009). More information than you ever wanted: Does Facebook bring out the green-eyed monster of jealousy? *Cyberpsychology & Behavior*, 12, 441–444. doi:10.1089/cpb.2008.0263

Nichols, T. (2014). The death of expertise. *The Federalist.* Retrieved January 2, 2018, from http://thefederalist.com/2014/01/17/the-death-of-expertise/

Nikken, P., & Schols, M. (2015). How and why parents guide the media use of young children. *Journal of Child and Family Studies, 24*(11), 3423–3435. doi: 10.1007/s10826-015-0144-4.

Nitzburg, G. C., & Farber, B. A. (2013). Putting up emotional (Facebook) walls? Attachment status and emerging adults' experiences of social networking sites. *Journal of Clinical Psychology, 69*(11), 1183–1190. doi:10.1002/jclp.22045

Park, B., Han, D. H., & Roh, S. (2017). Neurobiological findings related to Internet use disorders. *Psychiatry and Clinical Neurosciences, 71*(7), 467–478. doi:10.1111/pcn.12422

Pelton, S., & Hertlein, K. (2011). A proposed life cycle for voluntary childfree couples. *Journal of Feminist Family Therapy, 23*(1), 39–53. doi: 10.1080/08952833. 2011.548703

Pera, A. (2018). Psychopathological processes involved in social comparison, depression, and envy on Facebook. *Frontiers in Psychology, 9*, 22. doi:10.3389/ fpsyg.2018.00022

Perrin, P., & Jiang, J. (2018). About a quarter of U.S. adults say they are "almost constantly" online. Retrieved December 8, 2018, from: http://www.pewresearch. org/fact-tank/2018/03/14/about-a-quarter-of-americans-report-going-online-almost-constantly/

Pettigrew, S., Archer, C., & Harrigan, P. (2016). A thematic analysis of mothers' motivations for blogging. *Maternal and Child Health Journal, 20*(5), 1025–1031. doi:10.1007/s10995-015-1887-7

Pfefferbaum, B., Seale, T., Brandt, E., Pfefferbaum, R., Doughty, D., & Rainwater, S. (2003). Media exposure in children one hundred miles from a terrorist bombing. *Annals of Clinical Psychiatry, 15*(1), 1–8. doi:10.3109/10401230309085664

Pierce, T. (2009). Social anxiety and technology: Face-to-face communication versus technological communication among teens. *Computers in Human Behavior, 25*(6), 1367–1372. doi:10.1016/j.chb.2009.06.003

Prizant-Passal, S., Shechner, T., & Aderka, I. M. (2016). Social anxiety and internet use – A meta-analysis: What do we know? What are we missing? *Computers in Human Behavior, 62*, 221–229. doi: 10.1016/j.chb.2016.04.003

Propper, R., Stickgold, R., Keeley, R., & Christman, S. (2007). Is television traumatic? Dreams, stress, and media exposure in the aftermath of September 11, 2001. *Psychological Science, 18*(4), 334–340. doi:10.1111/j.1467-9280.2007.01900.x

Putnam, R. D. (2000). *Bowling alone: The collapse and revival of American community.* New York, NY: Simon & Schuster.

Rosen, L. (2012). *iDisorder: Understanding our dependency on technology and overcoming our addiction.* New York, NY: Palgrave Macmillan.

Rymarczuk, R., & Derksen, M. (2014). Different spaces: Exploring Facebook as heterotopia. *First Monday, 19*(6). Retrieved December 6, 2018, from https:// firstmonday.org/ojs/index.php/fm/article/view/5006

Seunghee, H., Joon, K. K., & Hyun, K. J. (2017). Understanding Nomophobia: Structural equation modeling and semantic network analysis of smartphone separation anxiety. *Cyberpsychology, Behavior, and Social Networking, 20*(7), 419–427. doi:10.1089/cyber.2017.0113

Smith, W. P., & Kidder, D. L. (2010). You've been tagged! (Then again, maybe not): Employers and Facebook. *Business Horizons, 53*(5), 491–499. doi:10.1016/j. bushor.2010.04.004

Sparrow, B., Liu, J., & Wegner, D. (2011). Google effects on memory: Cognitive consequences of having information at our fingertips. *Science* (New York, N.Y.), *333*(6043), 776–778. doi:10.1126/science.1207745

Steinberg, L. (2008). *Adolescence*. Boston, MA: McGraw Hill

Suomi, S. J., van der Horst, F. C., & van der Veer, R. (2008). Rigorous experiments on monkey love: An account of Harry F. Harlow's role in the history of attachment theory. *Integrative Psychological & Behavioral Science, 42*(4), 354–370. doi:10.1007/s12124-008-9072-9

Supra, J. D. (2016). *Employer not responsible for employee defaming customer on Facebook*. Retrieved June 2, 2018, from http://scholar.aci.info/view/1464ec 3df006b730146/15357aaafa900140003

Taylor, K. (2008). Mapping the intricacies of young adults' developmental journey from socially prescribed to internally defined identities, relationships, and beliefs. *Journal of College Student Development, 49*(3), 215–234. doi:10.1353/ csd.0.0005

Trub, L., & Barbot, B. (2016). The paradox of phone attachment: Development and validation of the young adult attachment to phone scale (YAPS). *Computers in Human Behavior, 64*, 663–672. doi:10.1016/j.chb.2016.07.050

Tudge, J. R. H., Payir, A., Merçon-Vargas, E., Cao, H., Liang, Y., Li, J., & O'Brien, L. (2016). Still misused after all these years? A reevaluation of the uses of bronfenbrenner's bioecological theory of human development. *Journal of Family Theory & Review, 8*(4), 427–445. doi:10.1111/jftr.12165

Volz, D. (2013, November 26). Facebook helps employers discriminate. Can we avoid it? *National Journal Daily AM (USA)*. Retrieved from http://infoweb. newsbank.com/resources/doc/nb/news/14A5A7682F76B9F0?p=AWNB

Vygotsky, L. S. (1986). *Thought and language*. Cambridge, MA: MIT Press.

Wang, J. L., Jackson, L. A., Gaskin, J., & Wang, H.-Z. (2014). The effects of Social Networking Site (SNS) use on college students' friendship and well-being. *Computers in Human Behavior, 37*, 229–236. doi:10.1016/j.chb.2014.04.051

Watt, D., & White, J. M. (1999). Computers and the family life: A family development perspective. *Journal of Comparative Family Studies, 30*(1), 1–15. Retrieved from https://psycnet.apa.org/record/1999-10027-001

Williamson, D. (1991). *The intimacy paradox: Personal authority in the family system*. Guilford Family Therapy Series. New York, NY: Guilford Press.

FOUR

Family "Net" working

Digital Family Communication

Researchers have examined the role of electronic communication on social and familial relationships. Lanigan, Bold, and Chenoweth (2009) conducted a survey study involving 103 participants, including parents of children under 12, parents of children 12 and up, post-parenting families, and couples without children. Their study explored family adaptability and cohesion, alternative use of technology time, and perceived impact of technology on family relationships. Unsurprisingly, the majority of the participants (n = 79, 89%) reported that technology had affected their family relationships (Lanigan et al., 2009). Perhaps, what might come as a surprise is the direction of said impact. The majority (n = 36, 45%) shared that computers had a mostly positive impact, whereas less than one-quarter (n = 16, 20%) reported a negative impact. The remaining participants shared that the impact of technology on family relationships was mixed (positive and negative; n = 19, 25%).

Further discussion of the Lanigan et al. (2009) findings revealed that time spent with technology, like computers, generally replaced time that would have been spent alone or involved with other forms of technology like television rather than time that would have been spent with family members (Lanigan et al., 2009). Interestingly, those few participants who did perceive that the computer interfered with family time were more likely to classify the rules and roles within the family as being less flexible (Lanigan et al., 2009). Other authors have also found that the more time youth spend on their phones, the more poorly those same adolescents rated their connection with their parents (Padilla-Walker, Coyne, & Fraser, 2012). For some, the increased permeability of boundaries between the family and the outside world via technology negatively affected family relationships and reduced family time (Lanigan et al., 2009). But, for most, the use of computers improved family communication, served as a shared activity, helped members meet a variety of needs like entertainment, information gathering, and household management, and increased efficiency resulting in more free family time (Lanigan et al., 2009).

Generally speaking, there are a couple of different dimensions of communication patterns in families. The first dimension refers to context a family creates in having conversations (Ledbetter, 2010). Families may fall anywhere on a continuum in this dimension, with low-communication families being rather closed and having limited space for few topics, whereas families high in this dimension encourage open communication about a variety of topics, including emotional expression (Koerner & Fitzpatrick, 2002). The second dimension in family communication patterns is the degree to which a family is homogeneous (and conforms) in their attitudes, beliefs, and values. Families high on the continuum are those where parental authority is highly valued; low conforming families do not have the same hierarchical structure, may be chaotic, or have few rules (Koerner & Fitzpatrick, 2002). In reference to technology, there is some evidence that family communication about appropriate technology usage connects to better competence in using technology. The attitude a family holds about online communication influences the competence of the youth user. According to Ledbetter (2010, p. 112):

> conversation orientation emerges as a potential theoretical mechanism via which conformity orientation influences subsequent schemata for the role of technology in interpersonal relationships. In other words, conformity orientation may not influence children's online communication attitude unless the family emphasizes frequent interpersonal communication (i.e., conversation orientation) among family members; yet when families do exhibit high conversation orientation, attitude toward online self-disclosure varies greatly depending on the family's level of conformity orientation.

In other words, the high conversation families beget youth who know how to use technology more effectively. Further, competence is enhanced in high conversation families when those families also have a moderate level of conformity—not too flexible to be chaotic, but also not overly rigid (Ledbetter, 2010).

Schofield-Clark (2013) noted that families with technology have opportunities for expressive empowerment and respectful connectedness. Expressive empowerment as it pertains to technology means that mobile phones provide us more ways to empower ourselves through expression. Children with phones may feel empowered to answer the phones on their own, or even to make decisions about whether to take an incoming call. Adolescents may feel empowered to have a social media account without friending their parents and may express themselves through posting on such accounts with little recognition of the risks they are taking with certain posts. In many ways, they may abdicate any cautions around safety for the excitement of their independence in those decisions. Empowered expression, however, does not have to be negative; in many families, the expressive empowerment can be beneficial and is developmentally appropriate. It can be a way of testing the waters toward self-expression and being able to experiment with independence when done so in relatively safe channels.

Respectful connectedness (Schofield-Clark, 2013) refers to the idea that media can be used as a way to connect and communicate with those in our families. It can reinforce values and provide opportunities for family togetherness. It may even provide opportunities for youth to engage in relatively safe activities, as opposed to the alternatives. Using media also provides an opportunity for trust to be exhibited from parents toward their children.

Few scholars have examined how technological communication varies by individual life course developmental stage (Adams & Stevenson, 2004), and/or the role of technology across the couple and family life cycle (Hughes & Hans, 2001). In a study by Morrison and Krugman (2001) involving 105 participants, the influence of in-home media technologies on the social environment of the home concerning social facilitation, rulemaking, attitudes toward technologies, and shifts and expansions around media usage was explored. Participants broke down into two different types—families using low/moderate technologies (i.e., continuous technologies like television) and those using high-level technologies (i.e., discontinuous technologies like computers). The largest theme of the study was that of the "valuing" of media technologies (Morrison & Krugman, 2001). Those with higher-level technologies tended to place more value on media technologies than those with low/moderate technologies (Morrison & Krugman, 2001). The researchers discuss that variances in the valuing of technologies might be related to the evolution of the family over their life cycle (Morrison & Krugman, 2001) and advocate for examination of the way that technology grows and changes as the family grows and changes (Morrison & Krugman, 2001), which is the focus of this chapter.

It is important to note that despite the difficulties that technology can pose in family relationships, the literature regarding the role of technology on parent-child and family relationships remains mixed. Some researchers have found that computers reduce familial contact, yet others have demonstrated either no change or an increase in family contact resulting from home computer use (Lanigan et al., 2009). These results seem to demonstrate that it is not necessarily the inclusion of technology in children's and their parents' lives that creates problems, but rather how they attend to technology that makes the difference. For instance, when parents and children collaborate on technological activities together it can actually improve their communication (Mesch, 2006). In addition, parents who are in need of support, assistance finding extracurricular activities, and childcare providers can find these services much more readily using online access (Mesch, 2006). With the rise of new media and home computers more parents have been able to work from home, meaning that there is often more time for them to spend at home with children (Watt & White, 1999). Finally, for parents who work outside of the home, the use of new media like smartphones has provided a more consistent bridge through which to stay in contact with and monitor children who arrive home before their parents (Watt & White, 1999).

Children under the age of 5 experience difficulty understanding and communicating remotely via the phone (Ballagas, Kaye, Ames, Go, & Raffle, 2009). The social and cognitive challenges of using telephones faced by young children decreases their motivation for use (Ballagas et al., 2009). Kids up to age 9 are relatively unmotivated to communicate via telephony (Ballagas et al., 2009). Interestingly, according to a 2009 Pew Research Center Internet and American Life Project Survey of parents of children with cellphones, roughly 3% of children under the age of 10, 6% of 10 year olds, and 11% of 11 year olds had cellphones of their own (Lenhart, 2010). This means that some children may be receiving cellphones before they have the capabilities to successfully negotiate their use or are motivated to use them apart from their parents. When parents are a part of the calling process, however, many of the barriers that exist for telephony by young children are diminished (Ballagas et al., 2009). Another way that the issues faced with telephony can be circumvented for young children is using video calling (Ballagas et al., 2009).

Another key part is to whom these children are talking. In the case of divorce, children who have access to a cellphone may serve as the mediators between separated or divorced parents, which also changes the dynamics of family communication. In the case of divorce, young adults were more likely to feel caught in the middle when their parents were antagonistic with one another (Schrodt & Shimkowski, 2013). In cases where parents are antagonistic toward one another, they may be more likely to rely on having their children be the intermediary in terms of communication between parents because technology in the child's hands would inherently mean distance between the parents.

One ill effect of children serving in the role of the intermediary may be parental alienation. As one parent has direct access to their children, the likelihood of parental alienation is increased because there is not a buffer regarding what is said (Johnston, 2005). In the case of cellphones where that communication is private and can be deleted and not traced, the potential for alienation may be even greater. Further, it allows the child a choice in whether they will accept the visitation, which may or may not be developmentally appropriate, given the developmental stage.

What involvement with technology by parents of infants and young children means for themselves in the future is that they will most likely not ever have an identity apart from technology. Their pictures, videos, and stories are told online before they are able to give permission and consent offline to others in doing this or before they are able to be mindful about what they share themselves. The implications of this is that the responsible adults and parents in their lives need to be mindful of their web print before they can be mindful of it themselves. Care providers are the gatekeepers of children's web prints and, in some cases, have been prosecuted for not taking this responsibility seriously. Lawsuits have been filed against parents non-consensually sharing private information about their children online (DW, 2016).

Youth and Online Communication

One of the difficulties in negotiating this has historically been that adolescents typically hold a higher degree of technological literacy than those at other points in the e-developmental lifespan (DiMaggio, Hargittai, Neuman, & Robinson, 2001). Many adolescents are and have always been digital natives—meaning they are native speakers of the language of technology because they have been raised in a world where it has always been present (Prensky, 2001). "Digital natives" is a controversial term (Selwyn, 2009). It describes people born after 1993 who use the Internet and new media, but due to the changes in technology, there are two different types: first generation digital natives and second generation. It is not surprising that second generation digital natives are more likely to use email more frequently and to also rate their experience of using technology and email as more positive than first generation natives, though first generationers also report positive experiences (Joiner et al., 2013). The adolescents of today, particularly those born from 1996 and later, are really the first generation who has grown up digital (Heim, Brandtzæg, Hertzberg, Endestad, & Torgersen, 2007). Why 1996? Because this was the year that Internet use began to rise and become more common in homes in the United States (Coffman & Odlyzko, 1998). Since this time more and more people have been raised side-by-side with technology, and while at one time there was a so-called "digital divide" that separated those that had technology from those that did not, this has almost entirely disappeared in the US (Horrigan, 2009; Rushing & Stephen, 2011). The generation of digital natives differs from most of their parents, who more than likely are either digital immigrants, meaning that they were not born into a digital age and thus have not easily adopted the digital language, or digital settlers (Prensky, 2001). Digital settlers grew up in an analog world, but are now e-bilingual in that they speak both the digital and analog languages to varying degrees (Prensky, 2001). The evidence seems to suggest that "digital natives" really differ only in terms of quantity of their technology usage rather than in substantive qualitative ways (Margaryan, Littlejohn, & Vojt, 2011).

Differences in terms of digital languaging and other areas of digital competency, between parents and adolescents can make the negotiating of this e-developmental period difficult for relational systems with adolescents. After all, management of technology usage requires technological understanding that many adolescents acquire before their parents.

Survey research by Mesch (2006) of 754 children aged 12 to 17 and their parents revealed that adolescent-parent conflicts with regard to Internet usage are strongly related to the parental perception of their child as a computer expert. This means that often one of the most difficult things for parents to negotiate in relation to re-establishing roles, rules, and boundaries with adolescents is the balancing of power and re-establishing of hierarchy within the family, as adolescents often become the people with the most technological knowledge and highest degree of digital literacy (Aarsand, 2007).

Perhaps what is most interesting about teen use of technology is that their patterns are distinctly different than those of any other age group (Jordan, Trentacoste, Henderson, Manganello, & Fishbein, 2007). Little is known, however, about their motives, perceptions, and awareness around use (Hundley & Shyles, 2010). Ninety-five percent of teens have access to a smartphone and describe themselves as "online constantly," with YouTube and Snapchat being the most common platforms used by teens (Anderson & Jiang, 2018).

While adolescent girls might be doing more texting, teen boys are engaging in more gaming (Rushing & Stephens, 2011). Many care providers worry about the effects of gaming on their kids, ranging from worrying over isolationism to exposure to explicit sexual and violent aggression (Villani, Olson, & Jellinek, 2005). Surprisingly, however, there is also correlational research linking reduced aggression offline to digitally violent gaming. No doubt myriad individual, cultural, developmental, familial, and parental differences account for outcomes in these various research studies (Villani et al., 2005). Since research remains inconclusive, it is essential that parents be available to monitor technological (including gaming) content, interactions, and timing (Villani et al., 2005).

Often it is the case that teens in the US are using more than one platform at a time, and they themselves are not clear on the impact of social media on their lives—whether it be positive or negative (Anderson & Jiang, 2018). Estimates are as high as 45% of US teens between ages 13 and 17 years being online via mobile devices at a near-constant basis (Anderson & Jiang, 2018). While online, most teens are visiting Snapchat (35%), YouTube (32%), Instagram (15%), or Facebook (10%) (Anderson & Jiang, 2018). There are differences around gender, ethnicity/race, and economic status in terms of which online platform is used most and least frequently by teens. Teens of lower-income backgrounds use Facebook more often than those of higher-income backgrounds (22% versus 4%) (Anderson & Jiang, 2018). Girls are more likely than boys to use Snapchat most frequently (42% versus 29%), whereas boys are more likely than girls to use YouTube (39% versus 25%; Anderson & Jiang, 2018). White and Hispanic teens are most likely to use Snapchat (41% and 29%, respectively), and Black teens are most likely to use Facebook (26%; Anderson & Jiang, 2018). Finally, while teens may be aware of the digital devices that they own, they experience a high degree of temporal displacement while using them—meaning that they are frequently not aware of the amount of time spent with their technology (Hundley & Shyles, 2010).

Parenting in a Digital World

Parents and Online Communication

Parenting is hard in the best of circumstances. Many things about technology make it easier to parent. Most of the research regarding technology and communication in relationships that has to do with family is focused on mothers. Blogs, for example, are a common method by which mothers seek to ascertain support and connection with other mothers (Gabbert, Metze, Bührer, & Garten, 2013), perhaps in an attempt to mitigate the stress of parenting (Leahy-Warren, McCarthy, & Corcoran, 2011). The average time new mothers spend on the computer is approximately 3 hours, and these 3 hours are mostly spent using the Internet. The major reason new mothers cite for logging on is to keep a connection to family and friends—presumably to provide updates about the infant and family/relational system life (McDaniel, Coyne, & Holmes, 2012). On the other hand, others have found that frequent use of Facebook is associated with greater parenting stress (Bartholomew, Schoppe-Sullivan, Glassman, Dush, & Sullivan, 2012). Mothers also use technology to get advice about issues related to parenting (Duggan, Lenhart, Lampe, & Ellison, 2015).

The ways in which fathers use technology are not wholly different from others. In one qualitative study exploring how fathers of preterm babies used the social media discovered similar themes to Duggan et al.'s (2015) findings about mothers—including looking for support and education (Kim, Wyatt, Li, & Gaylord, 2016). Stay-at-home fathers also use the Internet to blog, and single fathers use the Internet to identify role models (Ammari & Schoenebeck, 2015).

Technology Interference in Parenting

Recently at a family-oriented restaurant, we began taking note of every other parenting group or family around us. The sight was astonishing: we noticed the abdicating of parenting to the devices in front of us with regularity and, alarmingly, comfort. Parents would arrive with their children and slap a set of headphones on the child attached to a small tablet in a child-friendly case (rubber and looking like a robot). What we began to wonder was how children are learning to be able to regulate emotions? Anxiety? To be patient? To order food themselves? To talk to their parents? There are some good reasons that parents may have for abdicating their responsibilities as parents to technology. Parenting is an emotionally and physically demanding endeavor. It is tough to be able to have a conversation with a partner when one or more of the children are dysregulated. They may wish to want to talk to one another without the hindrance of warning little Sally to move her arm before she spills her milk, or having to entertain the kids to prevent them from disrupting other patrons. It may have been the first time in a long time that parents could talk to each other. We get it; we understand it; but the question is whether that is the best decision for children.

Given that 94% of parents are on social media and 70% are posting frequently (Duggan et al., 2015), it is highly likely that some aspects of one's parenting will be impacted by technology usage. A qualitative study conducted by Johnson (2017) was designed to determine the extent to which parents are aware of their own phone usage behavior. Parents admitted to being "distracted" by phones in their parenting, a finding that corroborated the work of McDaniel and Coyne (2016). When observing others' behavior in using the phone instead of attending to their children, participants reported a sense of shaming and judgment. When discussing themselves, however, mothers justified their decision as needing that time. Part of what may contribute to this distraction is in fact a sense of urgency that is brought on by the expectations of the outside world to respond to every little ring, vibration, and alert (McDaniel & Coyne, 2016). Related to Hertlein's (2012; Hertlein & Blumer, 2013) concept of accessibility, we are all accessible via phone, which increases our anxiety around not responding, as the unstated expectation is if we are accessible, we are *implored* to respond, lest we feel the anxiety of *not* responding. Some people in the study reported that they attempted to establish boundaries between the phone and their family life, but that in some cases, the boundaries were not upheld due to the nature of the contact made from the outside world (i.e., a supervisor or another individual in a position of hierarchy making contact might warrant a response).

Technology and Adoption

Technology and social media in particular have drastically changed the way in which members of adoptive families/relational systems communicate with one another. The rationale for adoptions to be "closed" (in other words, the child and the family not having information about the biological other family) was to limit the stigma and confusion that the child might experience, and to limit the opportunity for interference from the biological parents on the bonding between adoptive parents and the child (Black, Moyer, & Goldberg, 2016).

As adoptions have more frequently become "open" (knowledge of placement and/or communication between adoptive and birth parents), the Internet and social media have played a huge role in providing a space for making connections. One of the primary issues is about maintaining boundaries, and families need to negotiate what would be the appropriate boundaries in communicating with family members. Approximately 20% of adoptive families have had some passive contact with birth families via Facebook or other social media and have downloaded information that may be used later, and 50% have made contact via technology (Black et al., 2016). Specifically, researchers have discovered that our Couple and Family Technology framework (Hertlein, 2012; Hertlein & Blumer, 2013) offers a useful guide in that it provides a space to both build and exhibit mutual trust (Black et al., 2016). In addition, diffuse boundaries are more common in a digital world and, in adoption, may shift people away from making contact with either the adoptive families or the birth families, as people may be unsure whether the people they are contacting will be able to maintain appropriate boundaries. Two other pieces of the Couple and Family Technology framework—accessibility and affordability—also contribute to how these families navigate social interactions. They allow birth parents to surveil their birth child while being relatively unobstructive.

Privacy, Technology, and Family Relationships

Privacy is a huge issue with online interactions. The latest news regarding Facebook and its data breach (where the sharing of private information occurred) has hundreds of thousands of people deactivating or totally deleting their accounts (Kelly, 2018). Yet our concerns about privacy do not necessarily result in behavior change with Internet usage (Hallam & Zanella, 2017). Privacy, while problematic for adults online, is equally an issue with teens and kids. There really is not a value in privacy as youth rush online to share the smallest of feelings (Taylor & Rooney, 2017). The Internet and new technologies provide ways for youth to have more levels of privacy than in the past. Youth can (and more often than we want to believe) create fake email accounts or obtain social media profiles without alerting their parents. In addition, both youth and adults can join any number of media sites or register for websites via a name generator, and use these email addresses as a way to bypass a system in order to obtain a benefit without having to give away their personal email address. It is a way to stay private while expecting the rest of the world does not.

Another issue that intersects with stages of development is how technology alters the developmental tasks specifically with regard to autonomy, privacy, and boundary management—key skills for emerging adults (van den Broeck, Poels, & Walrave, 2015). Emerging adults (aged 18 to 25) tend to be the group that uses social media at a higher rate than other groups, and a huge part of this is self-disclosure (van de Broek et al., 2015). The development of Facebook and decisions about how to interact with parents (or whether one should) is considered to be a significant dilemma (Child & Westermann, 2013). First, social media is a primary way in which adolescents communicate with their peers. Second, they also communicate with their parents less frequently as they shift through this developmental stage as a way to develop autonomy (Keijsers & Poulin, 2013). The "friending" of parents on Facebook is inversely related to the relationship offline: in other words, the worse a relationship between parent and child is offline, the more likely they are to "not friend" on social media (De Wolf, Willaert, & Pierson, 2014).

At the same time, young adults and teens do not feel that they can necessarily decline when a parent sends a Facebook friend request (Mullen & Hamilton, 2016), likely because of the hierarchy involved in the request and ramifications for declining that request (Child & Westermann, 2013). There are three actions that can be taken once a parent has requested to "friend" their teen: the teen can choose to ignore, accept, or decline the request (Child & Westermann, 2013). Of those who do grant their parents access to their online profiles, only 20% interact with their parents daily on those sites (Coyne, Padilla-Walker, Day, Harper, & Stockdale, 2014). Some youth, particularly Black urban youth, prefer to text message with their parents, as they feel that they are in more control of the information they share with their parent(s) versus connecting on social media (Racz, Johnson, Bradshaw, & Cheng, 2017). Finally, there are many parents who simply do not monitor their children's social media, citing reasons such as that their child is an emerging adult, that they do not want to violate their child's trust, and that the parents themselves have other things to do with their time (Vaterlaus, Beckert, & Bird, 2015).

From Helicopter-Parents to Drone-Parents: Surveillance, Spying, and Other Monitoring Strategies

The term "helicopter parent," coined by Cline and Fay (1990), refers to a cluster of behaviors that characterize a parent as overprotective across many domains including financial, physical, and emotional (Reed, Duncan, Lucier-Greer, Fixelle, & Ferraro, 2016). Those parents on the negative spectrum of these behaviors communicate with their children with a high frequency, insert themselves or flat-out intervene in a child's decision-making in a way that is inconsistent with their child's developmental stage, remove barriers to ensure their children's success, and are highly (and personally) invested in their children's goals (Odenweller, Booth-Butterfield, & Weber, 2014). While maladaptive helicopter parenting typically emerges from well-educated, well-resourced, and well-intentioned parents (Kantrowitz & Tyre, 2006), it is tied to worse outcomes for young people. Children of helicopter parents have higher rates of prescription drug use, painkiller use, and experience lower self-esteem (Reed et al., 2016). They are less adjusted in their development, are less mature, and are less independent (Reed et al., 2016). Further, they have more difficulty in problem-solving (Odenweller et al., 2014), which may have a marginal impact to their physical health due to the indirect effect of the psychological issues (Reed et al., 2016), and seem to be more entitled (LeMoyne & Buchanan, 2011). Academically, they suffer from lower levels of engagement in school and lower grades (Shoup, Gonyea, & Kuh, 2009). Helicopter parenting does not work out well for communication either. Just because helicopter parents are doing more talking does not mean that more communication is happening: that is, the conversations are not about private and personal matters (Odenweller et al., 2014).

Digital technologies are removing the need for people to be helicopter parents and instead are allowing us to revert to being drone parents— those who watch from afar, inconspicuously, and then have video evidence of the observations we are making. Not only do we retain the ability to intervene in our children's lives in an instant, we can now have digital evidence that our child needs us or is not following our prescription, thus rationalizing more surveillance. According to Taylor and Rooney (2017):

> Common idioms, such as "keeping an eye on the kids", expose the inherent complexities and contradictions harbored by surveillance practices; on the one hand, surveillance can be perceived as a protective measure to stave off exposure to potential dangers; on the other hand, it can refer to assurance that young people do not cause trouble or mischief (Taylor, 2016). There is certainly ambiguity regarding the applications of surveillance. Lyon (2003) suggests that the underlying reasons for surveillance can be situated along a "continuum from care to control", arguing that "some element of care and some element of control are nearly always present". Similarly, Nelson and Garey (2009) view the motivations of care and control "in a dialectical relationship with each other, and not a simple dichotomous one."
>
> (pp. 1–2)

One case demonstrates this concept brilliantly. An upper-class family of mixed ethnic backgrounds living on the West Coast of the US came to therapy seeking assistance with their 15-year-old son. He was experimenting with marijuana and cocaine and ended up in the emergency room as a consequence of one of those experiments. His parents, both practicing physicians, were very concerned for his physical well-being and, when the crisis of the physical issues resolved, turned toward addressing his compliance and lack of obedience. The parents had constructed a monitoring system based on the youth's phone location and using a global positioning system (GPS) application (app). They would ask where he was going and wait for an answer; they would allow him to leave and use the GPS device to locate where he was, then drive out to where he was to ensure that he was not with people of whom they did not approve. These actions may sound as if they are rather benign or an appropriate reaction to protect and advocate for the welfare of their son. As time progressed, however, as the 15 year old became more trustworthy, his parents stepped up their surveillance to include every manner of electronic surveillance to catch him in the slightest transgression, and enabling them to apply severe punishments.

The 15 year old was, naturally, highly aversive to the surveillance methods used by his parents. In fact, he was only partially aware of all of the methods used, and the ones he did know about contributed to his feeling untrustworthy, damaged, etc. As a consequence, he began to act out by engaging in more lying as a way to develop autonomy His parents responded swiftly with more punishments: the cycle of who was in control of this youth escalated into a dangerous game. The parents went so far as to continue to track him not only on his phone, but also using GPS on his car when he went to college across the country, and throughout his college career, despite him performing well academically. In this case, the surveillance clearly demonstrates Taylor and Rooney's (2017) concept of the continuum of care to control; their attempts to track originated as a way to demonstrate caring and protection of their son. It ended up as a way to control and (attempt to) ensure that he would follow their directives, rules, and mandates.

Developmentally, computers and camera technology have introduced us to a new world of surveillance—beginning with surveillance of the self. Digital recording of events allows us to relive and re-experience the world. Terming it the "society of the spectacle" (p. 47), Lasch (1979) noted:

> We live in a swirl of images and echoes that arrest experience and play it back in slow motion. Cameras and recording machines not only transcribe our experience but alter its quality, giving to much of modern life the character of an enormous echo chamber, a hall of mirrors. Life presents itself as a succession of images or electronic signals, or impressions recorded and reproduced by means of photography, motion pictures, television, and sophisticated recording devices. Modern life is so thoroughly mediated by electronic images that we cannot help responding to others as if their actions—and our own—were being recorded and simultaneously transmitted to an unseen audience or stored up for some close scrutiny at some later time.
>
> (p. 47)

The constant proliferation of images, however, can also lead us to a pervasively distorted view of the world. Some authors such as Sontag (1977) argued that we use photos and images to verify that we are living, breathing beings. The problem with this use is that we learn to depend on this media to develop our sense of whom we are, which could potentially lead us to challenge our view of reality. Lasch and Sontag made these points in the 1970s, but the proliferation of audio visual media has continued, thereby making these points striking commentaries on today's society.

Surveillance is commonly used by parents to identify whether their children are safe. Another way that parents often ameliorate some of their e-concerns is by interacting with their teens in online environments, such as playing on the same team when online gaming, or friending their children on SNSs. This serves as yet another example of the balancing act that parents participate in during this stage of development. This act involves balancing trusting their teens to act autonomously while also maintaining some semblance of control over their actions. This is a task that parents have been doing for a very long time with their teenagers; however, now it is just being done in the context of technology. It may bring some comfort to know that the fourth theme in the Hundley and Shyles (2010) study revealed that teens have a palpable sense of risk associated with using online mediums like SNSs. They reported having a keen sense of the need to avoid those who may be dangerous to them online. The ways in which they accomplished this include altering or omitting sensitive information, friending only people they know in their actual offline social world, routinely blocking those people who are unknown to them offline, taking necessary precautions to help ensure safety from hackers, and building a new profile page/new gaming world if they get bothered or hacked.

Though it appears that some adolescents have a fair level of knowledge and management skills around negotiating some of the risks associated with online interactions, it is still wise for parents to practice monitoring teen Internet use. It is important, however, to do so in ways that do not create a distancing or defensiveness effect, as is the case with managing other issues in this developmental stage via parenting practices (Rushing & Stephens, 2011). According to Mesch (2006) intergenerational conflicts between adolescents aged 12–17 and their parents are higher in families where the parents express concern over the negative consequences of technological usage. Yet, common sense would suggest: "if you can't talk about technology you probably shouldn't be using it," and this logic would also seem to apply to adolescents and their parents as well. So how is a parent to express their concerns with regard to teen techno-practices in a way that is more likely to lead to a productive conversation and promotion of healthy practices in this developmental stage and ones yet to come? Perhaps a dialogue can be weighted more toward the positive consequences of technology in their teens' lives, and with some conversation regarding how they are to successfully negotiate the potential negative consequences, including the ways in which parents may act as allies rather than enemies in managing these concerns (Lanigan et al., 2009; Rushing & Stephens, 2011).

Surveillance Habituation

As described earlier, surveillance is becoming more challenging for parents as youth are often using devices that are single-user such as online games and social media sites via cellphones (Ferreira et al., 2017). In many ways, however, we are becoming habituated to being watched and monitored (Taylor & Rooney, 2017). We begin a process of technology-mitigated surveillance in the earliest stages of pregnancy via ultrasounds and 3D imaging. We then progress to baby monitors and Smart Nurseries, which ensure that we can connect all of our monitoring devices together and operate them from a single application on our phones. In Taylor and Rooney's (2017, p. 5) words: "the video camera becomes the surrogate parent, observing the child's activity and development, absent yet continually 'present.'"

We can all agree that parents need to supervise and monitor their children in some capacity. The question becomes how much? And what does that look like in a digital world? While it may be tempting to "drone" parent, surveilling our youth may have some impact on their internalizing and externalizing behaviors (Taylor, Lopez, Budescu, & McGill, 2012). Specifically, parents who are supportive emotionally to their children and are engaged in activities with them have children who are less likely to abuse substances (see, for example, Gaylord-Harden, Campbell, & Kesselring, 2010; Ghazarian & Roche, 2010). Children whose parents monitor them more diligently are at reduced risk of violence, have a lower likelihood of engaging in behaviors that compromise their health and safety, and tend to be better adjusted. At the same time, the effectiveness of control exerted by a parent varies in effectiveness based on the social context. For example, family relationships with demanding kin as well as psychological control from moms was associated with internalizing. Further, the factors tend to balance each other out—if your kin are more demanding, you need less control from parents, while if there is a lot from parents, you need less demanding kin (Taylor et al., 2012). In a digital world, it is incredibly difficult to monitor and understand the child's exact context and assess the level of risk when the context is also digital (and, in some cases, invisible to parents and caregivers). This can potentially create more difficulty in determining how much control one needs to effectively monitor their kids. In addition, kids may respond differently to surveillance and control depending on their age and the context in which the surveillance is levied. When kids are younger and the purpose is surveillance, the relationship between parents and kids suffers (Padilla-Walker et al., 2012).

In older adolescents who feel that they are retaining their autonomy, the goal is communication, not surveillance. Therefore, they tend to report more positive outcomes (Coyne et al., 2014).

We also expect to be surveilled, and our children are being raised under the burden of this expectation. Just today, my son and I (KH) were in a small roadside shop, and he started looking around to see if he could find the cameras. Further, people's behavior changes when they are being surveilled (Simons, Beltramo, Blalock, & Levine, 2017). This is part of what we do with SNSs like Twitter—we edit, articulate differently, delete, and post strategically, constantly aware of the audience around us (Papacharissi, 2012). Known as the Hawthorne effect, the principle describes the way in which others being observed begin to act in more socially appropriate ways upon the knowledge they are being observed. The way in which we surveil across technology is no different. The change in kids' behavior under surveillance is particularly true for children in the age of digital surveillance. Kids have even figured out how to behave when they know that they are on camera. When cameras are in the classroom, children adjust their behavior to exhibit less creativity and have less spontaneous interactions with others.

Family Negotiation of the "Net"

As cellphone technologies increase in our homes, families have to respond in certain ways (Hodge et al., 2012). As with most things with children, they emulate and model how to interact with the world around them from their primary caregivers. They learn how to develop relationships, how to talk, how to show affection, etc. The same is true with phone usage. Children watch their parent's phone behavior and emulate it. They are able at very young ages to replicate their parent's phone behavior. You have probably seen young kids grab their parent's phone. They are able to swipe, delete, open windows, and perform simple tasks, etc. Parents can teach children how to manage their phones in ways that are responsible, not only by overseeing their phone usage, but also by also modeling appropriate and balanced usage ourselves. Parents have to send better messages by establishing better mobile phone usage themselves—and modeling that behavior for their children (Hefner, Knop, Schmitt, & Vorderer, 2018).

Part of how to solve this might be through rule setting and through negotiation of the rules. Certainly not every family will be able to have devices for each individual in the system or agree on how a particular device should be used. Ley et al., 2013 noted some family conflict may emerge around who gets to use what device and under what circumstances. Parents who are more highly educated are more likely to monitor their children's devices (Wang, Bianchi, & Raley, 2005). Schofield-Clark (2013) emphasizes setting rules around family time, such as making family time a priority. In her text, she even provides a media agreement for family members, which clearly outlines the limits of media usage in a family system. Such an agreement is less about setting rules for media, and more about balancing family time with media time, generating a sense of connection both with and without media, and changing the conversation around technology in the family.

Conclusion

Digital family communication affects our families and relationships. Just as there are differences in how literate certain people are with technologies, there are also differences in how parents choose to use some of these technologies to monitor their children. Surveillance is clearly a huge issue in families related to technology. We are evolving into families that are constantly under surveillance—from one another. Negotiation of these rules and boundaries will be critical as the technologies increase their capacity to eavesdrop.

References

Aarsand, P. A. (2007). Computer and video games in family life: The digital divide as a resource in intergenerational interactions. *Childhood*, *14*(2), 235–256. doi:10.1177/0907568207078330

Adams, R., & Stevenson, M. (2004). A lifetime of relationships mediated by technology. In F. Lang & K. Fingerman (Eds.), *Growing together: Personal relationships across the lifespan* (pp. 368–393). New York, NY: Cambridge University Press.

Ammari, T., & Schoenebeck, S. (2015). *Understanding and supporting fathers and fatherhood on social media sites*. Proceedings of the 33rd Annual ACM Conference on Human Factors in Computing Systems, pp. 1905–1914.

Anderson, M., & Jiang, J. (2018). *Teens, social media & technology 2018*. PEW Research Center.

Ballagas, R., Kaye, J., Ames, M., Go, J., & Raffle, H. (2009). *Family communication*. Proceedings of the 8th International Conference on Interaction Design and Children—IDC '09. doi:10.1145/1551788.1551874

Bartholomew, M. K., Schoppe-Sullivan, S. J., Glassman, M., Kamp Dush, C. M., & Sullivan, J. M. (2012). New parents' Facebook use at the transition to parenthood. *Family Relations*, *61*(3), 455–469. doi:10.1111/j.1741-3729.2012.00708.x

Black, K. A., Moyer, A. M., & Goldberg, A. E. (2016). From face-to-face to Facebook: The role of technology and social media in adoptive family relationships with birth family members. *Adoption Quarterly*, *19*(4), 307–332. doi:10.1080/10926755.2016.1217575

Child, J. T., & Westermann, D. A. (2013). Let's be Facebook friends: Exploring parental Facebook friend requests from a Communication Privacy Management (CPM) perspective. *Journal of Family Communication*, *13*(1), 46–59. doi:10.1080/15267431.2012.742089

Cline, F. W., & Fay, J. (1990). *Parenting with love and logic: Teaching children responsibility*. Colorado Springs, CO: Pinon.

Coffman, K., & Odlyzko, A. (1998). The work of the encyclopedia in the age of electronic reproduction. *First Monday, 3*(10). doi:10.5210/fm.v3i10.620

Coyne, S., Padilla-Walker, L., Day, R., Harper, J., & Stockdale, L. (2014). A friend request from dear old dad: Associations between parent–child social networking and adolescent outcomes. *Cyberpsychology, Behavior, and Social Networking, 17*(1), 8–13.

De Wolf, R., Willaert, K., & Pierson, J. (2014). Managing privacy boundaries together: Exploring individual and group privacy management strategies in Facebook. *Computers in Human Behavior, 35*, 444–454. doi:10.1016/j.chb.2014.03.010

DiMaggio, P., Hargittai, E., Neuman, W. R., & Robinson, J. P. (2001). Social implications of the Internet. *Annual Review of Sociology, 27*(1), 307–336. doi:10.1146/annurev.soc.27.1.307

Duggan, M., Lenhart, A., Lampe, C., & Ellison, N. B. (2015). *Parents and social media*. Pew Research Center. Retrieved from www.pewInternet.org/2015/07/16/parents-andsocial-media/

DW (2016, September). *Teen sues parents for sharing embarrassing childhood photos online*. Retrieved April 4, 2018, from www.thenewsminute.com/article/teen-sues-parents-sharing-embarrassing-childhood-photos-online-49973

Ferreira, C., Ferreira, H., Vieira, M. J., Costeira, M., Branco, L., Dias, A., & Macedo, L. (2017). Epidemiology of Internet use by an adolescent population and its relation with sleep habits. *Acta Medica Portuguesa, 30*(7–8), 524–533. doi:10.20344/amp.8205

Gabbert, T., Metze, B., Bührer, C., & Garten, L. (2013). Use of social networking sites by parents of very low birth weight infants: Experiences and the potential of a dedicated site. *European Journal of Pediatrics, 172*(12), 1671–1677. doi:10.1007/s00431-013-2067-7

Gaylord-Harden, N. K., Campbell, C. L., & Kesselring, C. M. (2010). Maternal parenting behaviors and coping in African American children: The influence of gender and stress. *Journal of Family Psychology, 19*, 579–587. doi:10.1007/s10826-009-9333-3

Ghazarian, S. R., & Roche, K. M. (2010). Social support and low-income, urban Mothers: Longitudinal associations with adolescent delinquency. *Journal of Youth and Adolescence, 39*, 1097–1108. doi:10.1007/s10964-010-9544-3

Hallam, C., & Zanella, G. (2017). Online self-disclosure: The privacy paradox explained as a temporally discounted balance between concerns and rewards. *Computers in Human Behavior, 68*, 217–227. doi:10.1016/j.chb.2016.11.033

Hefner, D., Knop, K., Schmitt, S., & Vorderer, P. (2018). Rules? role model? relationship? The impact of parents on their children's problematic mobile phone involvement. *Media Psychology*, 1–27.

Heim, J., Brandtzæg, P., Hertzberg, B., Endestad, K., & Torgersen, L. (2007). Children's usage of media technologies and psychosocial factors. *New Media and Society, 9*(3), 425–454. doi:10.1177/1461444807076971

Hertlein, K. M. (2012). Digital dwelling: Technology in couple and family relationships. *Family Relations, 61*(3), 374–387.

Hertlein, K. M., & Blumer, M. L. C. (2013). *The couple and family technology framework: Intimate relationships in a digital age*. New York, NY: Routledge.

Hodge, C., Zabriskie, R., Fellingham, G., Coyne, S., Lundberg, N., Padilla-Walker, L., & Day, R. (2012). The relationship between media in the home and family functioning in context of leisure. *Journal of Leisure Research*, 44(3), 285–307. doi:10.1080/00222216.2012.11950266

Horrigan, J. B. (2009). *Mobile Internet use increases sharply in 2009 as more than half of all Americans have gotten online by some wireless means.* Retrieved from www.pewInternet.org/2009/07/22/mobile-Internet-use-increases-sharply-in-2009-as-more-than-half-of-all-americans-have-gotten-online-by-some-wireless-means/

Hughes, R., & Hans, J. D. (2001). Computers, the Internet, and families. A review of the role new technology plays in family life. *Journal of Family Issues*, 22(6), 776–790. doi:10.1177/019251301022006006

Hundley, H. L., & Shyles, L. (2010). US teenagers' perceptions and awareness of digital technology: A focus group approach. *New Media & Society*, 12(3), 417–433. doi:10.1177/1461444809342558

Johnson, D. (2017). *Parents' perceptions of smartphone use and parenting practices.* ProQuest Dissertations and Theses.

Johnston, J. R. (2005). Children of divorce who reject a parent and refuse visitation: Recent research and social policy implications for the alienated child. *Family Law Quarterly*, 38(4), 757–775.

Joiner, R., Gavin, J., Brosnan, M., Cromby, J., Gregory, H., Guiller, J., . . . Moon, A. (2013). Comparing first and second generation digital natives' Internet use, Internet anxiety, and Internet identification. *Cyberpsychology, Behavior, and Social Networking*, 16(7), 549–552. doi:10.1089/cyber.2012.0526

Jordan, A., Trentacoste, N., Henderson, V., Manganello, J., & Fishbein, M. (2007). Measuring the time teens spend with media: Challenges and opportunities. *Media Psychology*, 9(1), 19–41. doi:10.1080/15213260709336801

Kantrowitz, B., & Tyre, P. (2006). The fine art of letting go; As parents, boomers face their final frontier: How to stand aside as their children become independent adults. Where's the line between caring and coddling? *Newsweek*, 147(22), 48–60.

Keijsers, L., & Poulin, F. (2013). Developmental changes in parent-child communication throughout adolescence. *Developmental Psychology*, 49(12), 2301–2308. doi:10.1037/a0032217

Kelly, H. (2018). *Facebook says Cambridge Analytica may have had data on 87 million people.* Retrieved April 5, 2018, from http://money.cnn.com/2018/04/04/technology/facebook-cambridge-analytica-data-87-million/index.html

Kim, H. N., Wyatt, T. H., Li, X., & Gaylord, M. (2016). Use of social media by fathers of premature infants. *The Journal of Perinatal & Neonatal Nursing*, 30(4), 359–366. doi:10.1097/JPN.0000000000000214

Koerner, A. F., & Fitzpatrick, M. A. (2002). Toward a theory of family communication. *Communication Theory*, 12, 70–91.

Lanigan, J., Bold, M., & Chenoweth, L. (2009). Computers in the family context: Perceived impact on family time and relationships. *Family Science Review*, 14(1), 16–32.

Lasch, C. (1979). *The culture of narcissism.* New York, NY: W. W. Norton & Company.

Leahy-Warren, P., McCarthy, G., & Corcoran, P. (2011). First-time mothers: Social support, maternal parental self-efficacy and postnatal depression. *Journal of Clinical Nursing*, 21(3–4), 388–397. doi:10.1111/j.1365-2702.2011.03701.x

Ledbetter, A. M. (2010). Family communication patterns and communication competence as predictors of online communication attitude: Evaluating a dual pathway model. *Journal of Family Communication*, *10*(2), 99–115. doi:10.1080/15267431003595462

LeMoyne, T., & Buchanan, T. (2011). Does "hovering" matter?: Helicopter parenting and its effect on well-being. *Sociological Spectrum*, *31*(4), 399–418. doi: 10.1080=02732173.2011.574038

Lenhart, A. (2010, December 1). *Is the age at which kids get cellphones getting younger?* Retrieved from http://pewInternet.org/Commentary/2010/December/Is-the-age-at-which-kids-get-cell-phones-getting-younger.aspx

Ley, B., Ogonowski, C., Hess, J., Reichling, T., Wan, L., & Wulf, V. (2013). Impacts of new technologies on media usage and social behaviour in domestic environments. *Behaviour & Information Technology*, *33*(8), 815–828. doi:10.1080/0144929X.2013.832383Lyon, D. (2003). *Surveillance as social sorting: Privacy, risk, and digital discrimination.* London; New York: Routledge.

Margaryan, A., Littlejohn, A., & Vojt, G. (2011). Are digital natives a myth or reality? University students' use of digital technologies. *Computers & Education*, *56*, 429–440. doi:10.1016/j.compedu.2010.09.004

McDaniel, B. T., & Coyne, S. M. (2016). Technology interference in the parenting of young children: Implications for mothers' perceptions of coparenting. *The Social Science Journal*, *53*(4), 435–443. doi:10.1016/j.soscij.2016.04.010

McDaniel, B. T., Coyne, S. M., & Holmes, E. (2012). New mothers and media use: Associations between blogging, social networking, and maternal well-being. *Maternal and Child Health Journal*, *16*(7), 1509–1517. doi:10.1007/s10995-011-0918-2

Mesch, G. S. (2006). Family relations and the Internet: Exploring a family boundaries approach. *The Journal of Family Communication*, *6*(2), 119–138. doi:10.1207/s15327698jfc0602_2

Morrison, M., & Krugman, D. M. (2001). A look at mass and computer mediated technologies: Understanding the roles of television and computers in the home. *Journal of Broadcasting & Electronic Media*, *45*(1), 135–161. doi:10.1207/s15506878jobem4501_

Mullen, C., & Fox Hamilton, N. (2016). Adolescents' response to parental *Facebook* friend requests: The comparative influence of *privacy* management, parent-child relational quality, attitude and peer influence. *Computers in Human Behavior*, *60*, 165–172.

Nelson, M., & Garey, A. (2009). *Who's watching?: Daily practices of surveillance among contemporary families.* Nashville, TN: Vanderbilt University Press.

Odenweller, K. G., Booth-Butterfield, M., & Weber, K. (2014). Investigating helicopter parenting, family environments, and relational outcomes for millennials. *Communication Studies*, *65*(4), 407–425. doi:10.1080/10510974.2013.811434

Padilla-Walker, L. M., Coyne, S. M., & Fraser, A. M. (2012). Getting a high-speed family connection: Associations between family media use and family connection. *Family Relations*, *61*(3), 426–440.

Papacharissi, Z. (2012). Without you, I'm nothing: Performances of the self on Twitter. *International Journal of Communication*, *6*, 1989–2006. doi:1932-8036/2012000

Prensky, M. (2001). Digital natives, digital immigrants pa 1. *On the Horizon*, *9*(5), 1–6. doi:10.1108/10748120110424816

Racz, S., Johnson, S., Bradshaw, C., & Cheng, T. (2017). Parenting in the digital age: Urban black youth's perceptions about technology-based communication with parents. *Journal of Family Studies*, 23(2), 198–214. doi:10.1080/132294 00.2015.1108858

Reed, K., Duncan, J., Lucier-Greer, M., Fixelle, M., & Ferraro, C. (2016). Helicopter parenting and emerging adult self-efficacy: Implications for mental and physical health. *Journal of Child and Family Studies*, 25(10), 3136–3149. doi:10.1007/s10826-016-0466-x

Rushing, S. C., & Stephens, D. (2011). Use of media technologies by Native American Teens and young adults in the Pacific Northwest: Exploring their utility for designing culturally appropriate technology-based health interventions. *Journal of Primary Prevention*, 32, 135–145. doi:10.1007/s10935-011-0242-z

Schofield-Clark, L. (2013). *The parent app*. New York, NY: Oxford University Press.

Schrodt, P., & Shimkowski, J. (2013). Feeling caught as a mediator of co-parental communication and young adult children's mental health and relational satisfaction with parents. *Journal of Social and Personal Relationships*, 30(8), 977–999. doi:10.1177/0265407513479213

Selwyn, N. (2009). The digital native—Myth and reality. *Aslib Proceedings*, 61(4), 364–379. doi:10.1108/00012530910973776

Shoup, R., Gonyea, R. M., & Kuh, G. D. (2009). *Helicopter parents: Examining the impact of highly involved parents on student engagement and educational outcomes*. Retrieved November 28, 2018, from http://cpr.indiana.edu/uploads/2009%20AIR%20Forum%20-%20Helicopter%20Slides.pdf

Simons, A. M., Beltramo, T., Blalock, G., & Levine, D. I. (2017). Using unobtrusive sensors to measure and minimize Hawthorne effects: Evidence from cookstoves. *Journal of Environmental Economics and Management*, 86, 68–80. doi:10.1016/j.jeem.2017.05.007

Sontag, S. (1977). *On photography*. New York: Farrar, Straus an Giroux.

Taylor, E. (2016). Teaching us to be "smart"? The use of RFID in schools and the habituation of young people to everyday surveillance. In *Surveillance futures: Social and ethical implications of new technologies for children and young people*. Emerging Technologies, Ethics and International Affairs (pp. 67–78). New York, NY: Routledge.

Taylor, E., & Rooney, T. (2017). Digital playgrounds: Growing up in the surveillance age. In E. Taylor & T. Rooney's (Eds.), *Surveillance, childhood and youth: Social and ethical implications of new technologies for children and young people*. Emerging Technologies, Ethics and International Affairs (pp. 1–16). New York, NY: Routledge.

Taylor, R. D., Lopez, E. I., Budescu, M., & McGill, R. K. (2012). Parenting practices and adolescent internalizing and externalizing problems: Moderating effects of socially demanding kin relations. *Journal of Child and Family Studies*, 21(3), 474–485. doi:10.1007/s10826-011-9501-0

Van den Broeck, E., Poels, K., & Walrave, M. (2015). Older and wiser? Facebook use, privacy concern, and privacy protection in the life stages of emerging, young, and middle adulthood. *Social Media Society*, 1(2), 1–11. doi:10.1177/2056305115616149

Vaterlaus, J. M., Beckert, T. E., & Bird, C. V. (2015). At a certain age it's not appropriate to monitor one's child': Perceptions of parental mediation of emerging adult interactive technology use. *Emerging Adulthood, 3*(5), 353–358. doi:10. 1177/2167696815581277

Villani, V. S., Olson, C. K., & Jellinek, M. S. (2005). Media literacy for clinicians and parents. *Child and Adolescent Psychiatric Clinics of North America, 14*(3), 523–553. doi:10.1016/j.chc.2005.03.001

Wang, R., Bianchi, S. M., & Raley, S. B. (2005). Teenagers' Internet use and family rules: A research note. *Journal of Marriage and Family, 67*(5), 1249–1258.

Watt, D., & White, J. M. (1999). Computers and the family: A family development perspective. *Journal of Comparative Family Studies, 30*(1), 1–15.

FIVE

The iCouple

Common Couple Issues in a Digital Age

If you believe everything in the news, technology, phones, and Facebook are generally regarded as significant threats to partnered relationships. The popular media is replete with stories about online infidelity, text messaging to partners who are not your own, and the development of secrecy. Current technology and new media reintroduce couples to age-old issues in relationship formation and maintenance as well as introduce new issues into couple relationships. Issues emerging in relationships related to technology and new media include but are not limited to: how the couple has organized to spend time with one another, how power is experienced in the relationship, and how couples handle the idiosyncrasies around each partner's usage of technology and new media. Each of these issues (shared time, sexual technology or digisexuality, cybersex, online infidelity/non-consensual non-monogamy, and online gaming) introduces challenges into relationships.

Technology, relationships, and our personal emotions have gotten a fair bit of attention historically and recently in the media. In an article entitled "Thought-Reading Machines and the Death of Love," Jason Pontin (2018) explores the all-too-near future we have coming. As we write this, Facebook engineers are working to develop the ability to have one's THOUGHT transcribed into text format. We realize this sounds far-fetched; but we recall a time not long ago when our kids' age (11 years old) and video calling were also impossible. And Facebook is not the only company, according to Pontin (2018), that is working to decode and see the brain's process. The theory behind this type of work is that if the brain has a process, it can be measured. And if the brain's process can be measured, we can identify the patterns and make meaning of those patterns by pairing those patterns with other contexts (cognitions, actions, self-report). Pontin's (2018) question is a simple yet significant one: what happens when our thoughts are no longer private?

Attention to the differences between computer-based conversation and face-to-face communication has led to a discussion of the valuation of this mode of communication on relationships. Specifically, the involvement of technology in relationships has created controversy about whether technology is good or bad for relationships (Hertlein & Webster, 2008). Both anecdotal and empirical evidence from couples in treatment highlights the issue in relationships associated with technology usage, including a redefining of what it means to be unfaithful (Hertlein & Piercy, 2012). The truth is technology may be both good and bad for relationships: the ways in which technology can strengthen a relationship may also be ways in which it interferes with a relationship (Hertlein & Blumer, 2013).

The determination as to whether technology interferes with relationships or supports them is largely dependent on the couple and how each individual and the couple use technology. Abbasi and Alghamdi (2017) cite the chicken and the egg conundrum in social media and infidelity: did issues in the couple relationship precede infidelity, or did infidelity create problems in the relationship? From a cognitive perspective, we certainly have a problem with technology in our lives. Study after study confirms the same thing: the multi-tasking involved in phone usage and the presence of a phone take our attention away from other things (Wilmer, Sherman, & Chein, 2017). In fact, just having a phone present is enough to impair cognitive performance (Thornton, Faires, Robbins, & Rollins, 2014). Given that we are all at home with our phones right next to us suggests that there is a level of impairment constantly in our homes—that means in our relationships.

The presence of a phone can have some effect on relationships, either positive or negative. Duran, Kelly, and Rotaru (2011) examined the dialectic between autonomy and connectedness provided by cellphones. Phones can be used to feel connected to one another; at the same time, we can choose to be autonomous by ignoring incoming text or calls, or turning off the phone altogether and shutting off the ability for others in the outside world to reach out. Couple relationships are a balance between autonomy and independence—too much independence can result in disengagement, and too little can look like enmeshment or fusion. The notion of "perpetual contact" with our romantic partners, as can be the case with cellphones (Katz & Aakhus, 2002, p. 2), can encroach on the feeling of independence and create a set of unreachable expectations in terms of couple support (Duran et al., 2011).

Cellphones are both a source of conflict in couple relationships, as well as an area where couples report they need to establish rules. People who were more controlling over their partner's phone usage were the ones who were less satisfied in their relationships, less satisfied with how phones were used in their relationships, and less satisfied with the time spent together (Duran et al., 2011).

Survey Says

There is some direct evidence pointing to the benefit of technology in relationships. For example, technology allows us to be available to our romantic partners when a personal emergency arises, when we need emotional soothing and support, and when we need human contact (Parker, Blackburn, Perry, & Hawks, 2012). In a study specifically looking at how couples used technology, Pettigrew (2009) found that specific use of text messaging was reported by couples to be a key tool that allowed them to communicate and stay connected all day long. Part of the reason that couples identified this as something that increased their intimacy and connection to one another was because the text messages go directly to a person instead of a place where multiple people could overhear the information. These results were corroborated in another study looking at married heterosexual couples and their use of technology, where married couples acknowledged using technology more frequently during the day than those who are dating (Coyne, Stockdale, Busby, Iverson, & Grant, 2011). Texting is also used to express affection of married couples in highly satisfying relationships. Those who were less satisfied in their relationship, however, tended to use texting for confrontation with their partner and problem solving (Coyne et al., 2011).

Hertlein and Ancheta (2014) conducted a survey of over 400 young people and inquired about the positives and challenges technology introduced into their relationships. As far as the positives go, there were quite a few. Technology permits couples to meet in new ways. This was particularly true when people wanted to develop relationships with others who had similar beliefs and habits, or even hobbies. Another piece that the participants discussed was the ability to pace getting to know someone. The participants in this study reported having some level of control over the relationships as they progressed, and that was something that was more comfortable for a lot of people. In this way, the use of the Internet in developing relationships might be mediating some of what might be natural anxiety around the developmental processes. Another thing that the participants talked about was the level of emotional support that could be gained in text-based relationships. Instead of being able to contact one person and have a conversation while other people are around, the Internet and texting pretty much give us direct and private access to whomever we want all the time.

Participants also discussed the educational nature of technology. That is, it was easier to identify resources for relationships online as opposed to going to a library or looking up support in physical form. Finally, they acknowledged that the Internet could be used to find ways to address conflict in the relationship. While in previous responses the participants talked about being in constant communication and having that be in some ways a relationship accelerator, in other ways it gives people the ability to slow down and really consider their responses before committing them to a text or email, or memorializing them in some written fashion (Hertlein & Ancheta, 2014).

Another advantage noted in the same study was the ability to participate in long-distance relationships in ways that were previously not possible. In some ways, this might mean a demonstration of commitment to one another. To be able to participate in that relationship at a distance means that there is some level of commitment to organize time together to be able to do video calls or to talk. By the same token, the commitment one feels in a relationship can be shared publicly through the sharing of photos, changing relationship statuses, and other demonstrations of relationship status (Hertlein & Ancheta, 2014). There is also a significant degree of flexibility in the way that technology can be used in a relationship. Participants in the same study talked about flexibility from a perspective of being able to expand on one's fantasy life and being able to fulfill partners sexually through the presentation of seductive pictures or engagement in other sexually explicit strategies to be able to augment and supplement one's relationship. On the other hand, some people noted that technology communication methods such as texting or email are rather impersonal. In other words, it allows for people to be able to respond at a distance without having to take ownership in terms of managing or moderating or even experiencing the other person's emotions. One participant even characterized sexting as dehumanizing, and it takes away a lot of the physical factors that become really important in communication. How many times have you been with someone and in the middle of what you think is a dinner or a conversation, they simply pick up and check their phones? In Hertlein and Ancheta's (2014) study, this type of behavior was also identified as problematic. A partner might want to spend time with a partner, and this partner is staring at their phone. That contributes to feeling ignored and not important in the relationship, and may raise questions about what exactly is so important on the phone, thus creating jealousy. One of the things that also came up in the survey study was that there may be opportunities for impaired trust (Hertlein & Ancheta, 2014). One of the things that we will discuss later in this book is the surveillance that can occur in relationships more frequently now than ever. Historically, any conversations that came from a house were conducted on a phone, which was generally centrally located. Now, people can connect with anybody directly, discreetly, and privately, which introduces a level of distrust in relationships that has not been previously present.

Another finding from the Hertlein and Ancheta (2014) study was the challenges around ambiguity in text-based messages. Quite often, because messages were not accompanied by any other nonverbals, it was really challenging for some couples to try to interpret what their partner was saying and how they were saying it. Because one cannot see their partner face-to-face things might be out of context and they might not have an awareness that their partner is upset because they cannot see all the nonverbals, and consequently, the partner might hide that they are upset because they have the ability to do so. In a study of individuals in lesbian, gay, and bisexual (LGB) partnered relationships by Twist, Belous, Maier, and Bergdall (2017) they found the same kind of expressed ambiguity in text-based communications between the partners in that there were reportedly more arguments, miscommunications, and misunderstandings via texting than other offline and online ways of communicating. Each of these creates challenges for a relationship.

Hertlein and Ancheta's (2014) work was supported by earlier work conducted by Pettigrew (2009). In lengthy interviews with 19 couples, they agreed that texting gave them permission to stay connected all day long. They also agreed that when they were texting with one another, that constant connection and the ability to disclose information were things that helped them feel close and connected to one another. This is especially helpful in long-distance or geographically distant relation-ships, as those couples use social media with more intensity and more frequency than couples who are geographically close (Billedo, Kerkhof, & Finkenauer, 2015).

Just the Two of Us

Individuals move together across the course of their couplehood. In many cases, relationships develop through common interests, experiences, and activities. There are two current views on shared couple time. First, couples are now, more than ever, experiencing disruptions in their daily lives that interfere with time they can spend together. At the same time, there is an increased importance placed upon shared time in relationships (Hickman-Evans, Higgins, Aller, Chavez, & Piercy, 2018; Voorpostel, Lippe, & Gershuny, 2009). Newlyweds, for example, place a great importance on time spent together (Hickman-Evans et al., 2018).

Shared time together for couples has also changed over the years. Between 1965 and 2003, individuals reported spending more minutes on leisure activities, from 171 to 179 minutes for women and men, respec-tively, to 206 and 230 minutes (an increase of 20% for men and 28% for women). Men generally reported the proportion of time they spent with a partner seemed to be about 68%, a percentage that stayed fairly constant over the 38 years of data; women, on the other hand, increased the proportion of time spent with the presence of a partner, from 53% in 1965 to 65% in 2003 (Voorpostel et al., 2009). That being said, one of the important aspects of time spent together is the quality of the experi-ence over the time spent in the leisure experience (Ward, Barney, Lund-berg, & Zabriskie, 2014). Partners who spend time together participating in shared activities report higher levels of relational satisfaction and more stability as compared to time where couples engage in individual pursuits

(Hill, 1988; Holman & Jacquart, 1988; Johnson and Anderson, 2013; Johnson, Zabriskie, & Hill, 2006; Rogers & Amato, 1997). They report more opportunities for communication (Sharaievska, Kim, & Stodolska, 2013) as well as learning more about their partner (Hickman-Evans et al., 2018).

On the other hand, relationships where partners actively spend more time together are also associated with feelings of the time as not being enough. This can result in one feeling upset the time spent did not meet their expectations and they were somehow disillusioned (Daly, 2001). Further, when couples participate in individual activities, wives in heterosexual relationships are more likely than husbands to report relationship dissatisfaction specifically in those cases where the extracurricular activity is disliked by the wife (Crawford, Houts, Huston, & George, 2002).

In some cases, the selection of the shared activity may depend on each partner's value system (Kalmijn & Bernasco, 2001). For example, some couples may discover participating in a shared religious ideology or particular traditions might enhance the meaning of these activities and enjoyment each receives within the relationship. In other cases, however, there is an inherent risk to moving to a place of greater leisure time in the couple relationship. In a study on fathers and leisure time negotiation, it was found that fathers are most often the people in the relationship initiating the adoption of leisure time. Most often, this is intended as a way to relieve the partner of her responsibilities. Yet, even with the invitation, the female partner has difficulty giving up the role because of the power associated with being the person who runs the household schedule (Dyck & Daly, 2006). It is also possible a resistance to engage in leisure time may emerge from a fear (real or imagined) that bad things will happen should the person who is in charge leave that position to participate in leisure time without assisting with household duties.

Researchers have sought to understand the circumstances under which couples fare better with regard to separate versus shared activities. One longitudinal study (Crawford et al., 2002) demonstrated that the dissatisfaction in relationships where each member of a couple participates in different activities is more problematic for the wife and relationship when husbands participate in activities disliked by wives. In addition, the dissatisfaction experienced by the wives contributed positively to the participation of their spouse in continuing to participate in that particular activity. In another study (Johnson, Zabriskie, & Hill, 2006), couples were asked to complete a survey composed of a number of questionnaires, including the Marital Activity Profile, the Satisfaction of Married Life Scale, and demographic information. "Overall, couples in this study indicated it was not the level or amount of couple leisure involvement or the satisfaction with the amount of time spent together, but the satisfaction with couple." (Johnson et al., 2006). There also seem to be differences in how individuals in different couple types (dual-earner versus one-earner, versus both unemployed) spend time together and the impact on their relationship. Men in dual-earner couples indicated they spend less time with their partners, whereas for women the opposite was true. When both members of a couple, however, were unemployed, women were less likely than men to spend their leisure time in the presence of their partner (Voorpostel et al., 2009). Lower levels of relational satisfaction are particularly true in the case of video gaming, where only one of the two partners plays massively multiplayer online role-playing games (Ahlstrom, Lundberg, Zabriskie, Eggett, & Lindsay, 2012).

The extent to which one in an intimate relationship participates in individually based electronic activities has much validity in an electronic age. In most cases, participation in online activities occurs at one computer or device, most likely because these machines are too small to afford space for multiple users. Individual/separate leisure activities may sometimes be a source of contention in cases where one partner participates in online activities and the other partner is not interested or included. Further, the leisure time that we do spend may be in front of a computer—where we are at increased risk for obesity and other outcomes of a sedentary lifestyle (Vandelanotte, Sugiyama, Gardiner, & Owen, 2009), which may in turn have relational consequences. The fact the couples now multitask may also be an impediment to couple relationships, with 62% of respondents in a recent study indicating that there was at least one interruption per day (McDaniel & Coyne, 2016). In fact, the more interference via technology in a couple's life, the less satisfaction, more depression, and lower global life satisfaction (McDaniel & Coyne, 2016).

Of course, the computer and new media present other ways to share time. A common way is through video gaming (Bergstrom, 2009). In positive ways, couples who game together were able to use this as a continued point of connection and as shared leisure time. Also reported by these same couples, which negatively impacted their marital satisfaction, were one person neglecting the household tasks or child-rearing, disagreements, and disparate bed times (Ahlstrom et al., 2012). In the virtual world, couples also had lower levels of satisfaction if they were both in a guild (while online gaming) and one person did not perform their roles well enough to make progress on a task. At the same time, if the person who games more often can have the opportunity to teach their partner how to navigate the game, this leads to more positive interactions/leisure time, and therefore increases satisfaction (Ahlstrom et al., 2012).

An Affair to Delete

Shirley Glass, in her book *Not Just Friends* (2002), described the slippery slope that occurs as people are becoming acquainted and developing intimate relationships with one another. As discussed in Chapter 2, emotional intimacy is driven significantly by the type of disclosures that are made between individuals online. Dr. Glass notes that as people are making the self-disclosures and increasing their level of emotional intimacy with one another, they remain relatively unaware of where they are headed. She describes people's level of reciprocal and progressive disclosures as this slippery slope. She posits that by the time people realize where they are in the couple relationship, they are already too far into emotional connection to be able to disengage.

This process of moving quickly into a romantic relationship when that was not the intention is also described by Abbasi and Alghamdi (2017) and Cravens and Whiting (2013). It has also fueled the development of emotional affairs and confuses couples as to what exactly *is* infidelity. Sexual infidelity is pretty easy to understand: it refers to physical, sexual contact with another person outside of the primary relationship. (Guitar et al., 2017). One of the primary issues in addressing online infidelity is trying to understand the definition. Historically the definition of infidelity was rather straightforward: it was about genital contact with another person. That is not the case anymore. As a society, we have moved to understand and provide value to emotional affairs. Emotional infidelity refers to the type that is developed where the self-disclosures are made to one another to the exclusion of the primary relationships (Valenzuela, Halpern, & Katz, 2014). These types of affairs are common online, as much of the communication occurs with one self-disclosing in great detail to another without the benefit of context and nonverbal accompaniments, and out of ear shot of one's primary partner.

Cyber affairs can have components of both emotional and physical affairs. They may have originated as traditional friendships, where there are disclosures that are made that are reciprocal. In these friendships, the disclosures really communicate a level of commitment and depth of knowing somebody perhaps more deeply than you know others, or perhaps being more intimately familiar with someone than their friends or peer group is. On the other hand, there may be cyber affairs that are sexually based only. Under the cloak of anonymity, you can say anything to anybody and see if there is some response. If the response is not favorable, you can move on without ever having exposed yourself or taking a significant risk. If the risk pays off, you might be able to become sexually gratified with someone whom you perhaps do not even know.

In some ways, the ability to make disclosures to others would be really beneficial for relationships trying to get off the ground. Today, people are quite busy with work and other engagements, and it can be really difficult to carve out time to spend and get to know someone else. The Internet and new technologies, as accessible as they are, enable people to connect in ways without having a particular time carved out. But the slippery slope is also very seductive. Yes, disclosures are very powerful and do progress a relationship into high levels of commitment and high levels of intimacy over a short period of time because of the level of disclosure. In fact, one-third of divorces cite Facebook (and one spouse's inappropriate communications with other users) as a primary cause (Moscaritolo,

2012). This finding was corroborated in a research study of people across the lifespan (aged 18–82) conducted by Clayton, Nagurney, and Smith (2013), where those who used Facebook more frequently were the same people who were saddled with more negative relationship outcomes—including cheating (both emotional and physical affairs) or terminating the relationship. This finding was true for those who had been in relationships a relatively short duration of time—less than three years.

On the other hand, we must remember that a lot of the research tells us that not all of our disclosures are honest. We may tell people certain things in order to look a certain way or appear a certain way to receive a positive valuation or to be regarded positively, and this lack of authenticity may compromise relationships. It's not about the fact that social media exists at all and that couples use it: it's about the fact that the way in which we use it may create or compromise existent couple relationships, which can subsequently lead to separation, disillusionment, and divorce (Valenzuela et al., 2014). In fact, Valenzuela et al. (2014) just found a correlation between having a Facebook profile and people who have problems in their relationship and get divorced.

It is not just Facebook or the use of it; it is what is done with it. This includes sending messages to your exes, sending private messages to other people, and perhaps making notes, likes, or commenting on other people's pictures, and in some cases the relationship rules of the primary relationship do not allow for that. Research on jealousy and cheating suggests that the more ambiguous behaviors are the ones that create suspicion in partnerships (Buss, 2002). Flirting may be a prime example of this. Abbasi and Alghamdi (2017) noted it is often difficult to tell the difference between when somebody is chatting with somebody else and when they are flirting. The way in which this is defined now is when there is a romantic signal that is sent from one person to somebody else outside the relationship. The problem with this is in a technological world, that happens daily. We are texting people and communicating on some level in private messaging, direct chats, and public posts with people outside of the relationship. Further, because of the ambiguity that surrounds these messages, it is easy to over interpret those communications as romantic symbols, or perhaps even under interpret. In many ways, just the simple act of talking to someone else might be in one person's relationship acceptable, and considered inappropriately romantic to somebody else. The effect on a relationship also has something to do with one's gender, sexual orientation, relational orientation, and whether the behavior was emotional or sexual in nature. Specifically, scenarios where someone was described as having sex or falling in love with someone other than their partner online evoke feelings of betrayal, anger, and jealousy; scenarios where someone develops an emotional connection with another online evokes a threat type of jealousy (Dijkstra, Barelds, & Groothof, 2013). Women were also more likely to report more jealousy than men when faced with a potential cheating scenario online. Finally, those in similar-gender relationships reported feeling less jealousy than those in heterosexual relationships with regard to scenarios describing one partner's engagement in extradyadic sex (Dijkstra et al., 2013). And partners in consensually non-monogamous relationships often report feeling the opposite of jealousy, what has been termed "compersion" (Furchgott, 1985), when their partner(s) start developing a new affectional relationship offline or online in the context of there being consent already agreed upon within the relationship to do so.

Gerson (2011) identified three unique elements of betrayal in an online world. Gerson (2011) argued that online betrayal is sudden when it is discovered. In other words, when one aspect of an online affair is discovered, it is akin to the pull of a thread unraveling an entire sweater. One email expressing some level of betrayal may lead to a literally virtual treasure trove of betrayal as it connects to a chain of other emails, photos, or other recorded proof of an affair. The second unique characteristic, privacy, refers to the betrayal associated with the fact that the behaviors were often conducted in privacy while actively engaged in the relationship—that is, while the participating partner was still in the home, perhaps right next to the primary partner. The last component—permanence—refers to the quality where the record of the behavior is archived, saved, and cannot be extinguished or removed from servers or the web.

There is also data suggesting that newer relationships may be more prone to Facebook affecting their relationship than relationships of a longer duration. One of the other things that happens with infidelity is that the perception of online infidelity versus offline infidelity is about the same. In two different studies, online behaviors are considered infidelity, and online behaviors have emotional or sexual components, and still constitute the same level of betrayal in relationships (Parker & Wampler, 2003). The consequences of online infidelity are about the same as offline. Partners get hurt. They do not believe they can trust one another. And in some cases, the relationship ends. The other challenge in Internet infidelity is that it is perceived as having more of an emotional component than sexual, because of the ability to be able to seek out someone and exchange specific and private messages.

In a key study by Cravens and Whiting (2014), over 600 students were given a story completion test where they were asked to write what happens next. Participants were given one of two versions of a story. In Version A, a female realizes after reading her male partner's private messages that he's developed a relationship with someone else. In Version B, the male makes the discovery that his female partner has sent private messages to somebody else. Approximately half of the participants interpreted this as some act of infidelity. In fact, only 3% stated it was not infidelity, and the remainder, 46%, did not indicate whether it was infidelity or not. Further, approximately 25% of the people in the study felt that the privacy of the individual who wrote the message in the first place was violated, particularly women. When asked about the end of the relationship or what came after, two-thirds of the participants said the relationship would have ended, with half of them saying the reason it ended was because the person read the message and broke up with the person who wrote the message. A very small percentage, under 10% of those who thought the relationship ended, said it would have ended because the other person felt that their privacy was violated. These findings supported the work of Schneider, Weiss, and Samenow (2012), who found infidelity committed online had some of the same negative impacts as offline infidelity, including lack of trust and feeling traumatized.

As sexual technologies (sextech) develop past "swiping right," toward second wave digisexualities such as virtual reality sex, and robot sex (McArthur & Twist, 2017; Twist, 2018) what will constitute cheating or non-consensual non-monogamy then? In the present age of first-wave digisexualities people already do not always agree on a definition of online cheating because of ecological elements experienced in one's relationship with each other and one's technology like ambiguity around said definition, differences in acceptability in engagement in certain technology-related behaviors, and the degree to which the sextech approximates actual offline sex (McArthur & Twist, 2017). For example, in a study by Thompson and O'Sullivan (2016) of 810 predominantly heterosexual partnered adults, 50% of the participants reported that they saw the viewing of online pornography as cheating, and the other half did not—this seems to be a clear example of ambiguity.

Ambiguity around what constitutes non-consensual non-monogamy will remain and perhaps intensify in this emerging second-wave of digisexualities, because there will be an ongoing debate over what kind of sextech is acceptable to use in (and out) of partnered relationships, and because these technologies will approximate offline sex in ways not ever possible before (McArthur & Twist, 2017). For instance, despite the fact that at the time of the writing of this book, realistic sex robots (sexbots) do not yet exist (note: sex dolls do exist), people are already expressing ambiguity over whether or not having sex with a sexbot while in a monogamous relationship constitutes cheating (McArthur & Twist, 2017; Twist, 2018). Responses from a recent YouGov (2013) poll show that 42% of respondents said "yes" when asked, "If it were possible for humans to have sex with robots, do you think that a person in an exclusive relationship who had sex with a robot would be cheating?" Twenty-six percent reported being "not sure," and the remaining third (31%) said "no."

With the advancement of second-wave digisexualities the likelihood of more people forgoing human partnered relationships altogether increases. People who do and will forgo human connection in favor of technology-based connection may be said to have a sextech orientation of being a digisexual (McArthur & Twist, 2017; Twist, 2018). If one is a digisexual will they even have a human partner to debate whether sex with a robot is cheating or will they be asking their robot partner(s) if sex with a human is cheating? We just do not yet know.

Social Media and Romantic Relationships

Romantic relationships and social media are big business. Social media is heavily involved in the phases of couple relationship development, maintenance, and dissolution (Brody, LeFebvre, & Blackburn, 2016). Use of social media, however, has also been tied to lower marital quality and satisfaction in the US (Valenzuela et al., 2014). For example, as couples share more about one another and their lives online, there is less tolerance for independent activities, and that can create issues for autonomy while in a relationship and increase conflict in one's relationship (Fox, Osborn, & Warber, 2014).

Social media has a predominant role in couples' relationships. Relationships where members post more description and give more cues have higher levels of relationship satisfaction than couples whose postings are more ambiguous (Goodman-Deane, Mieczakowski, Johnson, Goldhaber, & Clarkson, 2016). Toma and Choi (2015) discovered that the couples who make it a point to post on each other's walls and to connect with each other on Facebook are actually the couples whose relationship deteriorates and ends more often than not. While this does not necessarily make sense from the data earlier on how social media assists with establishing connection and reducing some isolation, it may fit better when one considers the information presented in Chapter 3 about narcissism, authenticity, and people's self-presentation. It could be argued that one is trying to present themselves in a particular way that is not accurate to the relationship, but that makes them feel better about where things are at in the relationship. Instagram does not seem to be any better. When people post selfies on Instagram, their body image satisfaction goes up, which increases conflict in their relationship related to Instagram, which then, in turn, is associated with a negative relational outcome (Ridgway & Clayton, 2016).

Social media displays may become very important in the couple's life and have significant consequences for the relationship (Papp, Danielewicz, & Cayemberg, 2012). In some cases, the social media displays are our way to present and throw off those using social media and some of the problems in our relationships; other times, the displays may promote some level of conflict. The connection to one another that sites like Facebook give us also introduces stress into our relationship (Fox & Moreland, 2015). One of the facets of social media that becomes important in relationships is the similarity in Facebook presentations. What might explain some of the issues related to Instagram is that one person is taking selfies and posting and the other is not. Dissimilarities in presentation might in fact underlie the relational conflict rather than the post itself.

When people's method of posting and process around posting are more similar, they tend to do better in their relationship. There do seem to be gender differences. For example, when both men and women post their status and include of their partner in the profile picture, that's linked to greater relationship satisfaction. At the same time, there may be differences in how men and women value other things posted on Facebook and the meaning that they make from those posts (Papp et al., 2012).

Blair (2017) adopted the position that couples who overshare on social media are insecure. To this point, we agree. Think again about the literature on sharing on social media, the exhibition and narcissism qualities that are involved in the "society of the spectacle" (Lasch, 1979). People do not act unless they are getting a benefit or some payback from that activity. So what would be the payback? In a society of the spectacle, the payback is reward from those who comment, like, share, and otherwise endorse the post. Blair's argument is that when someone feels secure, they do not need the applause from others as they are already content in their relationships. It is this insecurity online that may prompt members of a relationship to use social media to engage in mate-retention actions. Brem, Spiller, and Vandehey (2015) explored how people use mate-retention strategies via Facebook in a sample of about 200 college students. Their results revealed four types of mate-guarding and retention fostered in Facebook: expressions of care and affection, surveillance, punishment, and threats of infidelity. Specifically, one partner may feel jealous, which fuels their drive to spy and surveil, which they are doing when they are often feeling angry and aggressive toward their partner offline.

Texting and Romantic Relationships

Texting is a highly popular activity for both individuals and people communicating in couple relationships. It is defined as a quick message sent between one mobile phone and another. Texting is now the backbone of communication in our interpersonal relationships. These text messages allow people to feel a greater sense of being connected to one another and a greater sense of emotional closeness (Hwang & Lombard, 2006).

To date, there are some mixed to positive findings about the use of technology and texting in particular and interpersonal relationships. For example, one study found that texting specifically in romantic relationships was associated with negative outcomes (Luo, 2014). On the other hand, another study found no relationship between texting and relationship outcomes at all (Jin & Peña, 2010). These findings seem to support the bilateral findings related to positives and negatives of technology in relationships (Hertlein & Ancheta, 2014) discussed in the previous section. Sexting and being able to text allow for enhanced communication and support of long-distance relationships, which would speak to positive outcomes: they also provide fertile ground for the development of trust issues, and ambiguity in terms of communication, thus potentially complicating the relationship. Case in point: in a study examining the sending of positive messages to relational partners, there were no statistically significant positive associations between sending these positive messages and overall happiness and relational satisfaction (Luo & Tuney, 2015). The explanation the authors provided was that because the positive messages were scripted, they did not mimic what was typical in the couple's relationship and therefore may have created some level of confusion.

Other research has looked specifically at the association between texting and attachment style. In this case, attachment might be the moderator or the missing piece between the actual texting behavior and relationship satisfaction. Said differently, is there a particular attachment style that predicts texting, and therefore, is somehow tied to satisfaction in the relationship? Jin and Peña (2010) looked at attachment and mobile phone use and did not see avoidance or anxiety increasing the use of texting. Another study found that avoidance and anxiety actually negatively predicted sharing emotions over text (Luo, 2014). Luo (2014) also demonstrated that technology supports long-distance relationships in that people share more texts and disclose more, which helps support their relationship development. There is also a different way to think about technology and couple relationships. Halpern and Katz (2017), for example, discuss how using texting while in an offline couple interaction can be damaging. It communicates a sense of not caring and disengagement with the partner, and that leads to some negative relational outcomes.

I Spy With My Little "I": Surveillance in Couples

In an earlier chapter, we discussed surveillance between parents/care providers and children. We also discussed privacy issues for individuals generally or rather will discuss it more completely in Chapter 6 when we talk about risk. But, surveillance is a different story, and in the case of surveillance between parents and children, there is a natural hierarchy. There is some expectation that surveillance is present in parent-child relationships because of the inherent dynamic: parents have a responsibility and a role to monitor and protect children. As annoying as this is for adolescents, adolescents somehow are aware of this and are becoming increasingly accepting of surveillance as generations evolve with technology as a part of their day-to-day lives (Fulton & Kibby, 2017).

The case of couples can make the meaning of surveillance very different. Surveillance in couples often stems from hurt, betrayal, or suspicions, and is also predicted by uncertainty in the relationships (Fox & Warber, 2013), though one study disputes this (Muise, Christofides, & Desmarais, 2009). The more time that one spends on Facebook, the more surveillance, which reciprocally contributes to higher levels of jealousy, which likewise results in more surveillance (Muise et al., 2009). Surveillance methods used by couples are a point of confusion in the law as to what is considered a violation of privacy (Calman, 2005). The anonymity and the privacy that are a function of and built into the technology can be a hotbed for deceitful behaviors (Hertlein, Dulley, Cloud, Leon, & Chang, 2017). The way technology is designed is that it inadvertently facilitates secrecy. These messages to one another can be private and can be deleted, and there are any number of apps that permit private texting where that text itself ends up being destroyed. Further, technology also makes it easier to surveil. Just as there are apps that ensure private texting, there are also apps that assist one with surveillance and monitoring their partner's behaviors, keystrokes, and phone calls. This behavior is similar to the concept of "mate guarding." In Abbasi and Alghamdi's (2017) description of it, mate-guarding is associated with surveillance and monitoring of a partner, but mate-guarding may also be another mechanism to claim someone as your own in a very public forum.

Engaging in surveillance strategies online is fairly commonplace (Park, Shin, & Ju, 2015). It is present in jealous individuals as well as loving individuals (Marshall, Bejanyan, Castro, & Lee, 2013). Helsper and Whitty (2010) note that approximately one-third of couples have had at least one partner who is engaged in surveillance. Finally, surveillance is connected in some ways to a couple's power dynamic. There is a lot of research that talks about how egalitarian relationships, at least in Western culture, have higher levels of relationship and sexual satisfaction. The presence of surveillance alters that power dynamic and sets a relationship on its proverbial head. There are also different ways we can monitor others online, anywhere on a continuum from passive strategies such as watching from a distance to soliciting information about the target from mutual friends or acquaintances (Fox & Warber, 2013).

There are four characteristics of social networking sites (SNSs) that contribute to what Tokunaga (2011) terms "interpersonal electronic surveillance." Accessibility, as mentioned earlier in Chapter 1 and described in greater detail in Chapter 7, is the first key factor. As Hertlein and Blumer (2013) stated, the Internet and new media introduce people you know into your relationship as well as people you do not. We are accessible to others, and others are accessible to us—making everyone their very own private eye. And it is not just that we are accessible—it is that so much of our lives is accessible via the data that is posted and shared, including photos, conversations with others, location tags, etc. This can be particularly problematic as photos might be rather ambiguous and can lead the viewer to make inaccurate interpretations or interpret the photos broadly. Another characteristic about social media is that the information is archived—which makes it searchable. There is a history of activities, interactions, and statements that is (1) permanent and (2) searchable. As a prime example, news journalist Joy Reid lost the *Straight for Equality in Media* award after a search of her social media accounts revealed her previous posts reflecting a prejudicial stance on LGB individuals (CBS News, 2018). Finally, the person who is being searched is unaware that they are being searched and/or surveilled. In one case, a client we had in treatment was shaken up after being alerted by someone she once knew that they had created a fake Facebook account to be able to watch her on hers because she had blocked their account. This type of surveillance might answer questions in relationships, but also might create new ones (Fox & Warber, 2013).

Another factor driving social media behaviors and how information online is interpreted is one's attachment style. Individuals with an anxious or preoccupied attachment style (and with lower levels of relationship satisfaction) are more likely to become jealous over their partner's Facebook activity and, consequently, engage in surveillance on social media (Tokunaga, 2015). For those who are anxiously attached, the reason that they surveil more is because they trust their partners less (Marshall et al., 2013), but also feel more intimate while using social media (Nitzburg & Farber, 2013). Those who are insecurely attached also have a tendency to post pictures of them and their partner as a profile picture rather than themselves (Shu, Hu, Zhang, Ma, & Chen, 2017) and use surveillance to mitigate their anxiety (Wang, Zhou, & Zhang, 2017). Unfortunately, anxiety attachment was also associated with increased likelihood of infidelity behavior (McDaniel, Drouin, & Cravens, 2017). In a large study exploring attachment style, perception of emotion, and Facebook posts, Fleuriet, Cole, and Guerrero (2014) assessed attachment style of over 800 undergraduate students and randomly assigned them to one of many Facebook post conditions emphasizing differences in use of photos, emoticons, capitalization, and punctuation. They found that the use of a face-wink emoticon was associated with a negative emotional response; that those who tended to post more attractive photos online were those who were looking for connections with those who were gender-attractive to them; that women were more likely to be upset by posts of perceived rivals; and that those with a dismissive attachment style actually had low levels of negative emotion with a troublesome Facebook post, likely because they dismissed information generally. This may be similar to the findings of those who suffer from attachment-avoidance and avoid their partner's Facebook pages (Marshall et al., 2013), and consistent with other findings that suggest that those who are avoidant do not engage in methods of communication that would produce immediate contact (Wardecker, Chopik, Boyer, & Edelstein, 2016).

Developing Trust Online

One final challenge in the development of relationships and online activities is the development of trust (Hertlein & Ancheta, 2014). There are several key criteria that make up the development of trust in relationships.

Building trust is a reciprocal process (Bartle, 1996). The expectation is that neither will harm the other. Part of this might have to do with temperament; some people are more trusting than others (Zentner & Shiner, 2012). One of the keys to building trust, however, is the first impression. If it is positive, there is a potential for the relationship to grow and develop. If, on the other hand, the initial meeting is not good, trust does not follow (Bekmeier-Feuerhahn & Eichenlaub, 2010). Other important ingredients include similarity and familiarity (Bekmeier-Feuerhahn & Eichenlaub, 2010). This can be particularly tricky in an online world where someone might easily be able to tell another how similar they are, but in reality be dissimilar and instead be portraying that they are similar because there are no reality checks (more on this in Chapter 7). The process of being able to conduct those reality checks is considered a warranting procedure, and was mentioned earlier in this text. In other words, when people present information online about themselves, observers will often look for information on their own to corroborate or dispute what is presented (Walther, Van Der Heide, Hamel, & Shulman, 2009). Any information that is discovered by the observer inconsistent with the self-presentation could negatively impact the development of trust, or destroy it completely.

Conclusion

Online infidelity, digisexual activities, digital miscommunications and misunderstandings, partner surveillance and privacy, and the challenges of developing trust via online environments are important risk factors introduced by present day technologies. Just as technology provides opportunities for introducing these risks, however, it also can provide several avenues for relationship enrichment and enhancement if used properly.

References

Abbasi, I. S., & Alghamdi, N. G. (2017). When flirting turns into infidelity: The Facebook dilemma. *American Journal of Family Therapy*, 45(1), 1–14. doi:10.1080/01926187.2016.1277804

Ahlstrom, M., Lundberg, N. R., Zabriskie, R., Eggett, D., & Lindsay, G. B. (2012). Me, my spouse, and my avatar: The relationship between marital satisfaction and playing Massively Multiplayer Online Role-Playing Games (MMORPGs). *Journal of Leisure Research*, 44(1), 1–22. doi:10.1080/00222216.2012.11950252

Bartle, S. (1996). Family of origin and interpersonal contributions to the interdependence of dating partners' trust. *Personal Relationships*, 3(2), 197–209. doi:10.1111/j.1475-6811.1996.tb00112.x

Bekmcier-Feuerhahn, S., & Eichenlaub, A. (2010). What makes for trusting relationships in online communication? *Journal of Communication Management*, 14(4), 337–355. doi:10.1108/13632541011090446

Bergstrom, K. (2009). *Adventuring together exploring how romantic couples use MMOs as part of their shared leisure time.* ProQuest Dissertations and Theses.

Billedo, C. J., Kerkhof, P., & Finkenauer, C. (2015). The use of social networking sites for relationship maintenance in long-distance and geographically close romantic relationships. *Cyberpsychology, Behavior, and Social Networking, 18*(3), 152–157. doi:10.1089/cyber.2014.0469

Blair, O. (2017). *There's a very good reason not to envy those gushing couples on Facebook.* Retrieved from www.independent.co.uk/life-style/love-sex/couples-social-media-oversharing-facebook-instagram-twitter-relationship-insecurities-experts-nikki-a7530911.html

Brem, M. J., Spiller, L. C., & Vandehey, M. A. (2015). Online mate-retention tactics on Facebook are associated with relationship aggression. *Journal of Interpersonal Violence, 30*(16), 2831–2850. doi:10.1177/0886260514554286

Brody, N., LeFebvre, L. E., & Blackburn, K. G. (2016). Social networking site behaviors across the relational lifespan: Measurement and association with relationship escalation and de-escalation. *Social Media + Society, 2*(4) doi:10.1177/2056305116680004

Buss, D. M. (2002). Human mate guarding. *Neuroendocrinology Letters, 23*(4), 23–29.

Calman, C. (2005). Spy vs. spouse: Regulating surveillance software on shared marital computers. *Columbia Law Review, 105*(7), 2097–2134.

CBS News. (2018). *LGBT advocacy group rescinds award to Joy Reid.* Retrieved May 4, 2018, from www.cbsnews.com/news/lgbt-advocacy-group-rescinds-award-to-joy-reid/

Clayton, R. B., Nagurney, A., & Smith, J. R. (2013). Cheating, breakup, and divorce: Is Facebook use to blame? *Cyberpsychology, Behavior & Social Networking, 16*(10), 717–720. doi:10.1089/cyber.2012.0424

Coyne, S. M., Stockdale, L., Busby, D., Iverson, B., & Grant, D. M. (2011). "I luv u:)!": A descriptive study of the media use of individuals in romantic relationships. *Family Relations, 60*(2), 150–162. doi:10.1111/j.1741-3729.2010.00639.x

Cravens, J. D., & Whiting, J. B. (2014). Clinical implications of Internet infidelity: Where Facebook fits in. *The American Journal of Family Therapy, 42*(4), 325–339. doi:10.1080/01926187.2013.874211

Crawford, D. W., Houts, R. M., Huston, T. L., & George, L. J. (2002). Compatibility, leisure, and satisfaction in marital relationships. *Journal of Marriage and Family, 64*(2), 433–449. doi:10.1111/j.1741-3737.2002.00433.x

Daly, K. J. (2001). Deconstructing family time: From ideology to lived experience. *Journal of Marriage and Family, 63*(2), 283–294. doi:10.1111/j.1741-3737.2001.00283.x

Dijkstra, P., Barelds, D. P. H., & Groothof, H. A. K. (2013). Jealousy in response to online and offline infidelity: The role of sex and sexual orientation. *Scandinavian Journal of Psychology, 54*(4), 328–336. doi:10.1111/sjop.12055

Duran, R., Kelly, L., & Rotaru, T. (2011). Mobile phones in romantic relationships and the dialectic of autonomy versus connection. *Communication Quarterly, 59*(1), 19–36. doi:10.1080/01463373.2011.541336

Dyck, V., & Daly, K. (2006). Rising to the challenge: Fathers' role in the negotiation of couple time. *Leisure Studies, 25*(2), 201–217. doi:10.1080/02614360500418589

Fleuriet, C., Cole, M., & Guerrero, L. K. (2014). Exploring Facebook: Attachment style and nonverbal message characteristics as predictors of anticipated emotional reactions to Facebook postings. *Journal of Nonverbal Behavior, 38*(4), 429–450. doi:10.1007/s10919-014-0189-x

Fox, J., & Moreland, J. J. (2015). The dark side of social networking sites: An exploration of the relational and psychological stressors associated with Facebook use and affordances. *Computers in Human Behavior, 45*, 168–176. doi:10.1016/j.chb.2014.11.083

Fox, J., Osborn, J. L., & Warber, K. M. (2014). Relational dialectics and social networking sites: The role of Facebook in romantic relationship escalation, maintenance, conflict, and dissolution. *Computers in Human Behavior, 35*, 527–534. doi:10.1016/j.chb.2014.02.031

Fox, J., & Warber, K. M. (2013). Social networking sites in romantic relationships: Attachment, uncertainty, and partner surveillance on Facebook. *Cyberpsychology, Behavior & Social Networking, 17*(1), 3–7. doi:10.1089/cyber.2012.0667

Fulton, J. M., & Kibby, M. D. (2017). Millennials and the normalization of surveillance on Facebook. *Continuum: Journal of Media & Cultural Studies, 31*(2), 189–199. doi:10.1080/10304312.2016.1265094

Furchgott, E. (1985). Glossary of Keristan English (abridged). *Scientific Utopianism and the Humanities, 1*(4). Retrieved from http://kerista.com/kerdocs/glossary.html

Gerson, M. (2011). Cyberspace betrayal: Attachment in an era of virtual connection. *Journal of Family Psychotherapy, 22*(2), 148–156. doi:10.1080/08975353.2011.578039

Glass, S. P. (2002). *Not "just friends"*. New York, NY: Simon & Schuster.

Goodman-Deane, J., Mieczakowski, A., Johnson, D., Goldhaber, T., & Clarkson, P. J. (2016). The impact of communication technologies on life and relationship satisfaction. *Computers in Human Behavior, 57*, 219–229. doi:10.1016/j.chb.2015.11.053

Guitar, A. E., Geher, G., Kruger, D. J., Garcia, J. R., Fisher, M. L., & Fitzgerald, C. J. (2016). Defining and distinguishing sexual and emotional infidelity. *Current Psychology, 36*(3), 434–446. doi:10.1007/s12144-016-9432-4

Halpern, D., & Katz, J. E. (2017). Texting's consequences for romantic relationships: A cross-lagged analysis highlights its risks. *Computers in Human Behavior, 71*, 386–394. doi:10.1016/j.chb.2017.01.051

Helsper, E. J., & Whitty, M. T. (2010). Netiquette within married couples: Agreement about acceptable online behavior and surveillance between partners. *Computers in Human Behavior, 26*(5), 916–926. doi:10.1016/j.chb.2010.02.006

Hertlein, K. M., & Ancheta, K. (2014). Advantages and disadvantages of technology in relationships: Findings from an open-ended survey. *The Qualitative Report, 19* (article 22), 1–11. Retrieved December 6, 2018, from https://nsuworks.nova.edu/tqr/vol19/iss11/2

Hertlein, K. M., & Blumer, M. L. (2013). *The couple and family technology framework: Intimate relationships in a digital age*. New York, NY: Routledge

Hertlein, K. M., Dulley, C., Cloud, R., Leon, D., & Chang, J. (2017). Does absence of evidence mean evidence of absence? Managing the issue of partner surveillance in infidelity treatment. *Sexual and Relationship Therapy, 32*(3–4), 323–333. doi:10.1080/14681994.2017.1397952

Hertlein, K. M., & Piercy, F. P. (2012). Essential elements of Internet infidelity treatment. *Journal of Marital and Family Therapy, 38*, 1–14. doi:10.1111/j.1752-0606.2011.00275.x

Hertlein, K. M., & Webster, M. (2008). Technology, relationships, and problems: A research synthesis. *Journal of Marital and Family Therapy*, 34(4), 445–460. doi:10.1111/j.1752-0606.2008.00087.x

Hickman-Evans, C., Higgins, J. P., Aller, T. B., Chavez, J., & Piercy, K. W. (2018). Newlywed couple leisure: Couple identity formation through leisure time. *Marriage & Family Review*, 54(2), 105–127. doi:10.1080/01494929.2017.1297756

Hill, M. S. (1988). Marital stability and spouses' shared leisure time: A multidisciplinary hypothesis. *Journal of Family Issues*, 9, 427–451. doi:10.1177/019251388009004001

Holman, T. B., & Jacquart, M. (1988). Leisure-activity patterns and marital satisfaction: A further test. *Journal of Marriage and the Family*, 50, 69–77. doi:10.2307/352428

Hwang, H. S., & Lombard, M. (2006). Understanding instant messaging: Gratifications and social presence. *Bulletin of Science Technology & Society*, 30(5), 350–361. doi:10.1177/0270467610380009

Jin, B., & Peña, J. (2010). Mobile communication in romantic relationships: Mobile phone use, relational uncertainty, love, commitment, and attachment styles. *Communication Reports*, 23(1), 39–51. doi:10.1080/08934211003598742

Johnson, H. A., Zabriskie, R. B., & Hill, B. (2006). The contribution of couple leisure involvement, leisure time, and leisure satisfaction to marital satisfaction. *Marriage & Family Review*, 40(1), 69–91. doi:10.1300/J002v40n01_05

Johnson, M. D., & Anderson, J. R. (2013). The longitudinal association of marital confidence, time spent together, and marital satisfaction. *Family Process*, 52, 244–256. doi:10.1111/j.1545-5300.2012.01417.x

Kalmijn, M., & Bernasco, W. (2001). Joint and separated lifestyles in couple relationships. *Journal of Marriage and Family*, 63, 639–654. doi:10.1111/j.1741-3737.2001.00639.x

Katz, J. E., & Aakhus, M. A. (2002). Introduction: Framing the issues. In J. Katz & M. Aakhus (Eds.), *Perpetual contact: Mobile communication, private talk, public performance* (pp. 1–14). Cambridge, UK: Cambridge University Press.

Lasch, C. (1979). *The culture of narcissism: American life in an age of diminished expectations*. New York, NY: Norton.

Luo, S. (2014). Effects of texting on satisfaction in romantic relationships: The role of attachment. *Computers in Human Behavior*, 33, 145–152.

Luo, S., & Tuney, S. (2015). Can texting be used to improve romantic relationships? The effects of sending positive text messages on relationship satisfaction. *Computers in Human Behavior*, 49, 670–678. doi:10.1016/j.chb.2014.11.035

Marshall, T. C., Bejanyan, K., Di Castro, G., & Lee, R. A. (2013). Attachment styles as predictors of Facebook-related jealousy and surveillance in romantic relationships. *Personal Relationships*, 20(1), 1–22. doi:10.1111/j.1475-6811.2011.01393.x

McArthur, N., & Twist, M. L. C. (2017). The rise of digisexuality: Therapeutic challenges and possibilities. *Sexual and Relationship Therapy*, 32(3/4), 334–344.

McDaniel, B. T., & Coyne, S. M. (2016). "Technoference": The interference of technology in couple relationships and implications for women's personal and relational well-being. *Psychology of Popular Media Culture*, 5(1), 85–98. doi:10.1037/ppm0000065

McDaniel, B. T., Drouin, M., & Cravens, J. D. (2017). Do you have anything to hide? Infidelity-related behaviors on social media sites and marital satisfaction. *Computers in Human Behavior*, 66, 88–95. doi:10.1016/j.chb.2016.09.031

Moscaritolo, A. (2012). Facebook cited in third of U.K. divorces. *PC Magazine*, 1.

Muise, A., Christofides, E., & Desmarais, S. (2009). More information than you ever wanted: Does Facebook bring out the green-eyed monster of jealousy? *CyberPsychology & Behavior*, 12(4), 441–444. doi:10.1089/cpb.2008.0263

Nitzburg, G. C., & Farber, B. A. (2013). Putting up emotional (Facebook) walls? Attachment status and emerging adults' experiences of social networking sites. *Journal of Clinical Psychology*, 69(11), 1183–1190. doi:10.1002/jclp.22045

Papp, L. M., Danielewicz, J., & Cayemberg, C. (2012). "Are we Facebook official?" Implications of dating partners' Facebook use and profiles for intimate relationship satisfaction. *Cyberpsychology, Behavior, and Social Networking*, 15(2), 85–90. doi:10.1089/cyber.2011.0291

Park, M., Shin, J., & Ju, Y. (2015). A taxonomy of social networking site users: Social surveillance and self-surveillance perspective. *Psychology & Marketing*, 32(6), 601–610. doi:10.1002/mar.20803

Parker, T. S., Blackburn, K. M., Perry, M. S., & Hawks, J. M. (2012). Sexting as an intervention: Relationship satisfaction and motivation considerations. *The American Journal of Family Therapy*, 41(1), 1–12. doi:10.1080/01926187.2011.635134

Parker, T. S., & Wampler, K. S. (2003). How bad is it? Perceptions of the relationship impact of Internet sexual activities. *Contemporary Family Therapy*, 25, 415–429. doi:10.1023/A:1027360703099

Pettigrew, J. (2009). Text Messaging and connectedness within close interpersonal relationships. *Marriage & Family Review*, 45(6–8), 697–716. doi:10.1080/01494920903224269

Pontin, J. (2018, April 16). *TED 2018: Thought-reading machines and the death of love*. Retrieved from www.wired.com/story/ideas-jason-pontin-openwater/

Ridgway, J. L., & Clayton, R. B. (2016). Instagram unfiltered: Exploring associations of body image satisfaction, instagram# selfie posting, and negative romantic relationship outcomes. *Cyberpsychology, Behavior, and Social Networking*, 19, 2–7. 10.1089/cyber.2015.0433

Rogers, S., & Amato, P. (1997). Is marital quality declining? The evidence from two generations. *Social Forces*, 75(3), 1089–1100. doi:10.2307/2580532

Schneider, J. P., Weiss, R., & Samenow, C. (2012). Is it really cheating? Understanding the emotional reactions and clinical treatment of spouses and partners affected by cybersex infidelity. *Sexual Addiction & Compulsivity*, 19(1–2), 123–139. doi:10.1080/10720162.2012.658344

Sharaievska, I., Kim, J., & Stodolska, M. (2013). Leisure and marital satisfaction in intercultural marriages. *Journal of Leisure Research*, 45(4), 445. doi:10.18666/jlr-2013-v45-i4-3894

Shu, C., Hu, N., Zhang, X., Ma, Y. X., & Chen, X. (2017). Adult attachment and profile images on Chinese social networking sites: A comparative analysis of sina weibo and WeChat. *Computers in Human Behavior*, 77, 266–273. doi:10.1016/j.chb.2017.09.014

Thompson, A. E., & O'Sullivan, L. F. (2016). I can but you can't: Inconsistencies in judgments and experiences with infidelity. *Journal of Relationships Research*, 7, e3. doi:10.1017/jrr.2016.1

Thornton, B., Faires, A., Robbins, M., & Rollins, E. (2014). The mere presence of a cellphone may be distracting implications for attention and task performance. *Social Psychology*, 45, 479–488. doi:10.1027/1864-9335/a000216

Tokunaga, R. S. (2011). Social networking site or social surveillance site? Understanding the use of interpersonal electronic surveillance in romantic relationships.

Computers in Human Behavior, 27(2), 705–713. doi:10.1016/j.chb.2010.08.014

Tokunaga, R. S. (2015). Interpersonal surveillance over social network sites: Applying a theory of negative relational maintenance and the investment model. *Journal of Social and Personal Relationships, 33*(2), 171–190. doi:10.1177/0265407514568749

Toma, C. L., & Choi, M. (2015). The couple who facebooks together, stays together: Facebook self-presentation and relationship longevity among college-aged dating couples. *Cyberpsychology, Behavior, and Social Networking, 18*(7), 367–372.

Twist, M. L. C. (2018, June). *Digisexuality: What the tech is it?* Invited Lecture, College of Sexual and Relationship Therapists, London, England, United Kingdom.

Twist, M. L. C., Belous, C. K., Maier, C. A., & Bergdall, M. K. (2017). Considering technology-based ecological elements in lesbian, gay, and bisexual partnered relationships. *Sexual and Relationship Therapy, 32*(3/4), 291–308.

Valenzuela, S., Halpern, D., & Katz, J. E. (2014). Social network sites, marriage well-being and divorce: Survey and state-level evidence from the United States. *Computers in Human Behavior, 36*, 94–101. doi:10.1016/j.chb.2014.03.034

Vandelanotte, C., Sugiyama, T., Gardiner, P., & Owen, N. (2009). Associations of leisure-time Internet and computer use with overweight and obesity, physical activity and sedentary behaviors: Cross-sectional study. *Journal of Medical Internet Research, 11*(3), E28. doi:10.2196/jmir.1084

Voorpostel, M., Van der Lippe, T., & Gershuny, J. (2009). Trends in free time with a partner: A transformation of intimacy? *Social Indicators Research, 93*(1), 165–169. doi:10.1007/s11205-008-9383-8

Walther, J. B., Van Der Heide, B., Hamel, L. M., & Shulman, H. C. (2009). Self-generated versus other-generated statements and impressions in computer-mediated communication: A test of warranting theory using Facebook. *Communication Research, 36*(2), 229–253. doi:10.1177/0093650208330251

Wang, K. X., Zhou, M. J., & Zhang, Z. (2017). Can insecurely attached dating couples get compensated on social network sites? The effect of surveillance. *Computers in Human Behavior, 73*, 303–310. doi:10.1016/j.chb.2017.03.046

Ward, P. J., Barney, K. W., Lundberg, N. R., & Zabriskie, R. B. (2014). A critical examination of couple leisure and the application of the core and balance model. *Journal of Leisure Research, 46*(5), 593–611. doi:10.1080/00222216.2014.11950344

Wardecker, B. M., Chopik, W. J., Boyer, M. P., & Edelstein, R. S. (2016). Individual differences in attachment are associated with usage and perceived intimacy of different communication media. *Computers in Human Behavior, 59*, 18–27. doi:10.1016/j.chb.2016.01.029

Wilmer, H. H., Sherman, L. E., & Chein, J. M. (2017). Smartphones and cognition: A review of research exploring the links between mobile technology habits and cognitive functioning. *Frontiers in Psychology, 8*. doi:10.3389/fpsyg.2017.00605

YouGov. (2013, February 23). *Omnibus poll*. Retrieved from http://big.assets.huffingtonpost.com/toplinesbrobots.pdf

Zentner, M., & Shiner, R. (2012). *Handbook of temperament*. New York, NY: Guilford Press.

SIX

Relational Malware

Risks of Technology in Relationships

The Trouble With Tech

The Internet gets the blame for all sorts of things—somehow it gets blamed for why children do poorly in school, their clandestine arrangements with peers, why partners cheat, the development of various out-of-control technology-related behaviors, including video gaming, shopping, and the use of pornography, and why our world has become more violent. The Internet becomes the scapegoat for all things negative. Earlier in Chapter 1, we presented information on why the Internet and technology could be challenging for individuals and families. For example, there is more eye strain, more signs of depression, bad posture, and sleep problems. We further explored some of these issues in the book to this point, where we described in greater detail the consequences of getting wrapped up in a digital world while living in a physical one. People who get absorbed in the Internet are not connecting or being fully present with the world around them. For example, recently I (KH) was volunteering in my son's classroom. There were four additional parent volunteers. Two of us did not have our phones with us at all; the other three parents had their phones visibly displayed, with one of them constantly typing on their phone the entire time while there. I began to wonder why this parent had volunteered in the first place. At some point in the 3 hours we were there, his daughter actually approached him while he was on his phone and began tugging his arm as a way to engage him in what was happening in the front of the room. He did not take his eyes (or fingers) off his phone. So at what point is this father's behavior problematic usage? Or is it an addiction? Where does he fall on the Internet use continuum? Would it be different for us or would we feel differently about it if we saw him reading a newspaper or book the entire time instead? How do we know he wasn't?

There are some specific major themes on the future of the "Internet of things"[1] and connected life. One is that people are highly motivated by being linked to one another, and the Internet is the perfect key to fit into that craving lock, in part because there is very little effort involved in making these connections. In fact, it is almost impossible to not have the Internet at your disposal—it is on our watches, our phones, our cameras, our workstations, our televisions, etc. There is also a subset of people, however, who will not get involved and stay rigidly away from integration if they can. Further, as privacy breaches occur, an increasing number of users will disband their accounts and limit their social media presence, if not disconnecting altogether, as a way to maintain control over their privacy. Another important piece that directly corresponds to risk management is that while most people know the dangers and dark side of the Internet, they do not believe the negatives are going to happen to them. In fact, the advances in technology will be in part an attempt to make using the Internet safer for us, but it will be difficult to have privacy protection strategies catch up to the technologies that are being developed.

Risky Business

While technology like computers can play a positive role in children's lives there is also concern over the effect that such technologies can have on children and on families. The most abundant concern that parents have with regard to their children and technology is their online experiences (Adams & Stevenson, 2004). These experience may occur while a child is out of the eyes of a watchful parent. Unmonitored online experiences of children raise all kinds of concerns ranging from cyberbullying, to interactions with cyber predators to privacy issues (Adams & Stevenson, 2004), to concern over what kids might see and hear that may not be age appropriate (Mesch, 2006), to fear of identity theft of one's child (Smardon, 2012), to concern for children not getting enough exercise, leading to a sedentary lifestyle and not getting enough sleep (Van den Bulck, 2004).

Despite the frequency in the use of social networking sites (SNSs), many parents with children worry about the risks associated with online interactions, particularly with regard to potential victimization by online sexual predators and/or cyberbullies (Crooks & Baur, 2011). Cyberbullying is attended to more specifically later in the book which focuses on some of the most frequent "e-risks" (Hertlein & Blumer, 2013). Though parents/care providers may express a high degree of worry around e-risks, specifically involving online predators, this is the category about which the family therapy professionals in one of our studies inquired the least of the clinical participants with whom they worked (Hertlein, Blumer, & Smith, 2014). Forty-one percent (n = 93) reported they do not ask about engagement in online predatory behaviors at all, and 28.2% (n = 64) reported not inquiring about safety with regard to online sexual predators (Hertlein et al., 2014).

Online sexual predators visit chat rooms and SNSs seeking out unsuspecting, attention needing children to confuse with notions of sexuality and then lure them into meeting so they can sexually assault them (Crooks & Baur, 2011). Although companies such as CompuServe and America Online (AOL) have created "guards" and monitoring devices to protect youth online (Crooks & Baur, 2011), Mesch (2006) notes that increased surveillance of an adolescent's online activities can also create arguments over their growing need for autonomy. Additionally, in many instances, parents may not have the time nor ability to monitor their youth's online activity in this manner. Even if they could successfully exert this much control over the limiting of online exposure that comes with new media, how is this helping to optimize the development of their teen and future young adult (Rushing & Stephens, 2011)?

Many adults are concerned about how to interact and communicate with adolescents in their lives in online environments. Engagement in online family and social networking seems fraught with confusion and uncertainty in terms of practice management. It may also, however, offer some benefit when used in helpful and adjunctive ways. Parental concerns around teen use go beyond those already mentioned, and often include that young people might not be as mindful as they do not primarily focus on risks from those outside of them (e.g., strangers, acquaintances, predators, bullies, etc.), but rather are more concerned with their own techno-involvement. Researchers have found that teenagers also struggle with Internet and online gaming "addiction" (Hur, 2006), which are two more technological areas that family therapy professionals in our study infrequently inquired about in their clinical work (Hertlein et al., 2014). Associations between pathological Internet use and problem drinking (Ko et al., 2008), depression, relationship problems, aggressive behaviors, ill health (Lam & Peng, 2010), and obesity (American Academy of Pediatrics, 2013) have also been noted as cyber-related problems in adolescence. Cellphone use has even been correlated, albeit weakly, with increased body mass index (BMI) levels in adolescents aged 11 to 17 (Lajunen et al., 2007).

Despite the potential drawbacks associated with adolescent engagement with technologies and new media there are some positives to use in this stage of family e-development. For adolescents, the Internet serves as a resource for coping, escapism, regulation of emotions (Lam, Peng, Mai, & Jing, 2009), the gaining of a sense of control, an outlet for negative energy, and reducing stress (Grüsser, Thalemann, & Griffiths, 2007). Even after controlling for family income, the accessing of computers has been associated with higher test scores in school, and may play a major part in future success in higher education (Koivusilta, Nupponen, & Rimpela, 2011). Finally, some researchers suggest that technology-based interventions like the accessing of health websites (e.g., WebMD.com), the use of smartphones and applications (apps) aimed at promoting well-being, and the playing of video games that encourage health practices can help inform and change health related behaviors in adolescents (Rushing & Stephens, 2011). In a quantified study involving 405 American

Indian/Native American youth aged 13–21, technology-based interventions, particularly those involving the accessing of health websites, demonstrated effectiveness in terms of informing and changing participant health behaviors. A full 75% (n = 303.75) of participants searched online for health information in this study (Rushing & Stephens, 2011).

Anxiety management is a huge piece of what drives online behavior. As mentioned in an earlier chapter, Wehrenberg (2018) discusses the role of social anxiety and how that dominates some of our online interactions. According to Wehrenberg (2018), technology produces a new type of stress response. When we hear technology-related sounds like notifications, it puts our body in a state of stress. And when those dings and notifications go off all the time, and they do, our body is in a state of chronic stress. That state of chronic stress has implications for the way in which we interpret messages and the way in which we respond. Some of the literature actually already talks about this. In terms of our posture, Hansraj (2014) found when we are receiving a text and responding, our shoulders and neck are positioned in such a way that looks like anxiety, and consequently, messages that come in are interpreted with our bodies being in a physical place of holding more stress and more tension than when we are not holding the phone. This damages our health and makes us more tired.

The other piece about social media, stress, and anxiety is that there is tremendous success that is posted for more peer groups on social media. There are many ways in which we can compare ourselves to our peers, as we mentioned with Festinger (1954), and one of the biggest features of social anxiety is that we are constantly scrutinizing how we are appearing to others online, based on what others are presenting.

Privacy

Your Penetralia is Showing

Control is an important psychological construct. When people have a sense of control, they believe that they have some level of power over their environment, and that what happens to them is a consequence of their choices and actions (Rotter, 1966). The ability to be able to feel that one is in control is a critical developmental task according to many scholars, not the least of which include Erikson (1982), Piaget (1977), and Mirowsky (1997). The Internet gives some illusion of control through giving us search engines through which we can search for exactly what we are looking for and nothing else; we are able to control (or so we think) the information that we receive because we specifically look for that information and only that information. We are able to feel more in control of our intimacy development, and obtain financial rewards and other relational benefits (De Wolf, Williart, & Pierson, 2014).

Sense of agency, a construct closely related to control, can be established in a digital environment by managing three primary elements:

sense of self-location, sense of body ownership, and sense of agency (Jeunet, Albert, Argelaguet, & Lecuyer, 2018). Sense of self-location describes one's orientation in the digital world. For example, when in an environment where one is regarded as a third person, they would rate their sense of location as lower than those who are operating from a first-person perspective. Sense of body refers to the quality where one person is able to note similarities between their offline and online self. When there is more congruence between these two entities, there is a greater sense of feeling agency. Finally, environments are created where one has some degree of control in what happens next (as is very often the case with blogging, social media exhibitions, etc.).

When these three elements come together, the greater one's sense of digital agency, potentially, the greater their experience of being able to be in control (or at least the importance of establishing that feeling). The development of agency is critical to establishing a sense of privacy. In a virtual world, sense of agency means a great deal, because we believe that it allows us to control our private information and the way in which people access us. Privacy is defined as "the feeling that one has the right to own private information, either personally or collectively" (Petronio, 2002, p. 6). Internet use is associated with privacy in one way or another. The feeling of privacy is augmented by the belief that we are in control. If we believe we are in control, we believe that we can control our level of privacy.

As much control as we may think we have and believe sharing online gives us (Petronio, 2002), privacy is not guaranteed in an online world. Consider the recent example of Facebook, which has gotten into some hot water in its handling of private data. In two breaches that affected 90 million users, Facebook shared personally identifiable information of its users to outside forces, and then these forces used this information in an effort to sway users' opinions and affect how they vote. While Facebook initially expressed apologies about these breaches and even initiated a public relations campaign to make a commitment to better protect privacy, it quietly moved its headquarters to a new location out of reach of European privacy laws (which happen to be much stricter than in the United States; www.mercurynews.com/2018/04/19/facebook-moving-most-users-from-protection-of-eu-privacy-law/). This event, however, was not the first time. A similar incident occurring in 2008 also led Facebook to widely issue a "mea culpa" to those complaining about breaches in privacy.

In 2008, however, the complaints to Facebook about privacy were not centered on selling of information but rather the way in which people were able to access information on the News Feed. It was not that more information was being shared; it was that this information was now accessible via the development of a "search bar," thus overstepping current social mores. As Boyd (2008) stated:

> Search disrupted the social dynamics. The reason for this is that privacy is not simply about the state of an inanimate object or set of bytes; it is about the sense

of vulnerability that an individual experiences when negotiating data. Both Usenet and Facebook users felt exposed and/or invaded by the architectural shifts without having a good way of articulating why the feature made them feel "icky."

(p. 14)

In cyberspace, both exposure and invasion contribute to our feeling vulnerable and that our privacy is violated (Boyd, 2008). In exposure, we post things, and they become announced to others. At times, we are aware that others are made aware of certain actions, postings, and events; at other times, we are unaware of what is being told to others about us, and how to check the veracity of such statements. For example, LinkedIn may alert you that someone is looking for you . . . but are they really? Or is it LinkedIn's attempt to have you log in and use its services? Once exposed, invasion occurs. People can access you and the exposed information about you without you being aware that they are becoming a student of, well, you. One final example of the privacy issue is the development of what are known as "ambient apps" (Tene & Polonetsky, 2014, p. 61). These apps are those that identify and disclose one's geographic locations to other social media and Internet users. For example, an app called Highlight 6 allows others in the area to know that you are also in the area and displays your profile. You may also interact with those who are nearby through highlighting them via the Highlight 6 app or social media apps such as Facebook, Twitter, and Tinder (Tene & Polonetsky, 2014). Further, we acknowledge there exists the possibility of unintended privacy breaches (Krasnova, Veltri, & Günther, 2012); but this potential consequence may lose out when weighed against the benefits and convenience of access and ability to forge connections.

Privacy Considerations: The People

Demographics of Internet users affect what we need to consider in terms of privacy. Managing privacy may involve directly limiting the audience (Kramer-Duffield, 2010) or adjusting settings built into social media sites to delete posts (Litt, 2013). Teens respond to the concern that there may be privacy violations by leaking specific information where the primary message will be hidden from those not in the know, but apparent to those who do know, a concept known as social steganography (Boyd & Marwick, 2011). They also are more vocal (and scrutinize people) when information is shared about them they do not wish to be shared (Trottier, 2012). Alternatively, those from collectivist backgrounds tend to be less likely to share personal information on social media, whereas those from individualistic cultures are more likely to self-disclose (Krasnova et al., 2012). Finally, the way that teens use technology (and their exposure to risk) also changes across their lives. For young teens, there is more of an emphasis on engaging with others and using what social media has to offer. This increased exposure accentuates their risk.

Privacy Considerations: The Space

One of the other issues that confuses the privacy issue is the actual space. As mentioned earlier in this text, social media presents an environment that blurs the boundaries between offline and virtual environments (Gabriel, 2014). As Boyd (2008) described it:

> Offline, people are accustomed to having architecturally defined boundaries. Physical features like walls and limited audio range help people have a sense of just how public their actions are. The digital world has different properties and these can be easily altered through the development of new technologies, radically altering the assumptions that people have when they interact online. As a result of new technological developments, social convergence is becoming the norm online, but people are still uncomfortable with the changes.
>
> (Boyd, 2008, p. 14)

In other words, we have to make adjustments in how we interact with others as the boundary between us in our homes and them in their homes is different than walls—it does not exist—but we often do not make those adjustments.

Crossing Boundaries in Unbounded Space (Spy-Berspace?)

Cyberbullying

Cyberbullying includes a wide range of bullying behaviors using an equally wide range of electronic communication as the medium of delivery. While there is no commonly agreed upon definition, there are a few definitions that are more commonly cited in the literature (Li, Smith, & Cross, 2012). Belsey (2004) defines cyberbullying as:

> the use of information and communication technologies such as email, cellphone and pager text messages, instant messaging, defamatory personal websites, and defamatory online personal polling websites, to support deliberate, repeated, and hostile behavior by an individual or group that is intended to harm others.
>
> (n.p.)

Two years later, Willard (2006) provided a more basic definition by framing cyberbullying as "sending or posting harmful or cruel text or images using the Internet or other digital communication devices" (p. 1). Smith, on the other hand, adds intentionality and victim positioning to the definition. Another widely adapted definition is proposed by Smith and colleagues, who define cyberbullying as "an aggressive, intentional act carried out by a group or individual, using electronic forms of contact, repeatedly and over time against a victim who cannot easily defend him or herself" (Smith et al., 2008, p. 376).

Some activities commonly characterizing cyberbullying include sending threatening emails, sending repetitive emails, repeatedly sending upsetting messages, blackballing certain individuals from chat or message groups, and slandering others online (Goebert, Else, Matsu, Chung-Do, & Chang, 2011). Bullying activities can occur across a variety of mediums, including: email, text messages, instant messengers including via SNSs, websites, chat rooms, online games, and digital images (Kowalski, Giumetti, Schroeder, & Lattanner, 2014). While some studies pin the prevalence at 4.6% (Waasdorp & Bradshaw, 2015), others report the prevalence has increased from 2006 to 2012 by 6 percentage points among youth (increasing particularly for girls), from 15% to 21% (Schneider, O'Donnell, & Smith, 2015), though some estimate the range to be as high at 72% for school-aged children (Juvonen & Gross, 2008). Another estimate of those who cyberbully others may be as high as 29.7% in a sample of school-aged youth (Wade & Beran, 2011). The rates of cyberbullying are even more significant when diverse sexual orientations and genders are factored in, as lesbian, gay, bisexual, transgender, questioning (LGBTQ) youth experience such bullying at higher rates in comparison to their heterosexual counterparts (Kann et al., 2018). Results from the nationwide 2017 Youth Risk Behavior Survey of US high school students found that 27.1% of those students identifying as LGBTQ experienced cyberbullying in the past year, whereas only 13.3% of their heterosexual peers experienced cyberbullying in the same year (Kann et al., 2018). Part of the prevalence of cyberbullying may be due to the fact that we are living in a world of constant connection and constant risk (Rao, Bansal, & Chandran, 2018).

There are different types of cyberbullying as identified by Willard (2007). Flaming refers to an online fight where at least one individual is bullied. Harassment occurs when repetitive, negative messages are sent to the target. Outing and trickery refer to circumstances where an individual takes another's personal information and disseminates it without the target's knowledge or consent. Impersonation (sometimes termed masquerading) refers to pretending to be someone else and using that identity to communicate with others. Cyberstalking, to be discussed in a later section, is using technology to send threatening messages. Exclusion is where it is made clear to an individual that they have been excluded from a group or an event (Kowalski et al., 2014).

While girls may be more likely to be cyberbullied (if we include data on cyberstalking, a form of cyberbullying) (Ortega et al., 2012), they are just as likely as boys to be the bully (Beckman, Hagquist, & Hellström, 2013). Young men are victimized online more often if they have a lower level of education (Festl & Quandt, 2016). Those who cyberbully tend to get less and poorer quality sleep, are of a male gender, score higher on extroversion and neuroticism scales, and are less conscientious (Kırcaburun & Tosuntaş, 2018). What may positively affect or even reduce the presence of cyberbullying is the development of empathy and a positive school climate around the reduction of bullying. What seems to be negatively related is whether the individual has out-of-control technology-related behaviors, uses the Internet more often, engages in more risky online behavior (more common in people who use the Internet more), and lacks control (there is that word again) of the personal information one posts online (Festl & Quandt, 2016).

From a relational perspective, power dynamics in relationships seem to affect engagement in cyberbullying. Specifically it seems to occur more often in relationships where there is a power imbalance like in the forms of heterosexism, cisgenderism, racism, sexism, etc. (Kowalski et al., 2014; Twist, Bergdall, Belous, & Maier, 2017). Bullies themselves do not seem to have a sense of their actions, and the victims experience further marginalization among their peers (Cowie & Myers, 2014). In fact, those who are cyberbullied are more likely to be bullied in their relationship, and more often the person who cyberbullied them was a friend (Waasdorp & Bradshaw, 2015).

The consequences of cyberbullying seem to be equal opportunity destroyers, though at least one study has young school-aged males as bearing consequences more intensely (Kowalski & Limber, 2013). The effects of being a victim of cyberbullying can lead to depression, paranoia, and anxiety problems. In addition, victims of cyberbullying have more suicidal ideation, as well as more suicide attempts (Kowalski et al., 2014). Experiences related to being cyberbullied like depression, suicidal ideation, misuse of drugs and alcohol, and risky sexual behavior are even greater in LGBTQ youth (Kann et al., 2018). Furthermore, suicidal ideation is associated with both roles—the bully and the target (Kowalski & Limber, 2013). Those who are cyberbullied also have a lower level of self-esteem (Patchin & Hinduja, 2010b). Depression seems to be a mediating factor for girls between traditional bullying and suicide, but it does not mediate cyberbullying and suicide (Bauman, Toomey, & Walker, 2013), nor does being the offender in cyberbullying predict depression or anxiety (Goebert et al., 2011). In addition, those who have less social support have a higher risk of experiencing cyberbullying (Kwak & Oh, 2017). Finally, compared to the effects of traditional bullying, cyberbullying is associated with stronger indirect effects on well-being (Muhonen, Jönsson, & Bäckström, 2017).

This is not to say there is no risk. Negative consequences of cyberbullying do indeed exist. For both victim and offender, engagement or experience with cyberbullying was associated with higher levels of suicidal ideation and suicide attempts, with victims experiencing more suicidal thoughts (Patchin & Hinduja, 2010a). Girls, as mentioned earlier, are both more likely to be cyberbullied and also more likely to internalize as a response (Brown, Demaray, Tennant, & Jenkins, 2017). Cyberbullying victims are more likely to use substances, binge drink, or use marijuana (by a rate of 2.5 times), are twice as likely to be depressed, and are over three times more likely to attempt suicide (Goebert et al., 2011). There are also significant academic consequences. For example, children who are cyberbullied are more likely to be absent from school and report school-related illnesses (Kowalski & Limber, 2013). For instance, 10% of LGB students and 6.1% of hetersexual students report not going to school because of safety concerns related to cyberbullying (Kann et al., 2018). Furthermore, among students who identify as "questioning" their sexual orientation, they report being cyberbullied at a rate of 22% a year, and 10.7% reported not going to school because of related safety concerns (Kann et al., 2018).

Partly because of the risks of being bullied and/or cyberbullied, some LGBTQ youth are not "out" offline or online about their sexual orientation and/or gender identity—what is called "visibility management" or "e-visibility management," respectively (Twist et al., 2017). While this might serve as a mechanism to diminish bullying experiences, there are significant drawbacks to not being out, as well. For instance, research has shown that being out is associated with greater positive social adjustment (Kann et al., 2018), increased opportunities to meet potential dating partners and supportive friends, and access to supportive psychological, relational, and wellness-based resources and communities (Twist et al., 2017).

Technology-Based Dating Violence

The Internet and social media also have a role in dating violence. As positive as it can be for relationships, technology also can facilitate coercion, threats, abuse, stalking, harassment, intimidation, and controlling behaviors (Stonard, Bowen, Walker, & Price, 2017). Common experiences for the victim include embarrassing posts about them (photos or otherwise), the Internet being used as a platform to spread rumors, and threats being made. Men tend to be the culprits behind sexual technology-assisted violence, whereas women seem to initiate non-sexual types (Stonard, Bowen, Walker, & Price, 2017). Part of what happens with technology regarding younger people is that there is an ability to ask for a password and check a partner's phone—an option exercised more frequently by adolescent girls, which is actually controlling behavior. Further, because events are memorialized online or in text, there is a record that one may revisit and can play in one's mind.

Sexting

As if cyberbullying was not enough, add sex into the mix and we all get confused. Sexting refers to the exchanging of sexually explicit material via a mobile phone's text messaging function. Those who sext are more likely to be connected to their peer group and less connected to their parents (Campbell & Park, 2014). The good news is that, as much attention as it gets, sexting is a relatively infrequent activity among youth. Approximately only 7% of youth report receiving such messages and 2% of those aged 10 to 17 (Mitchell, Finkelhor, Jones, & Wolak, 2012), but another study reports that number could be anywhere from 15% to 40% (Ringrose, Gill, Livingstone, & Harvey, 2012, as cited in Stonard et al., 2017). Fifteen percent report sending such messages, and those teens also seem to be more sexually active (Gamez-Guadix, De Santisteban, & Resett, 2017). Sexting can include:

> Sending (1) sexually suggestive photos or videos, (2) photos or videos wearing lingerie, (3) nude photos or videos, (4) sexually suggestive text messages, (5) text messages propositioning sex, and (6) forwarding on or showing others sexts which were meant to be kept private.
> (Scholes-Balog, Francke, & Hemphill, 2016, p. 2)

There may be many motivations for engaging in sexting. For youth, one motivation may be linked to their stage of development. Experimenting with different behavior is a normative process of youth, and they may perceive sending a text, even if it is sexually explicit, to someone as a relatively benign way of expressing the developmental impulsivity and identity-formation process. A second motivation (for both youth and adults) may be the relationship currency that is established through sexting (Judge, 2012). For example, while in a romantic relationship, adults with anxious types of attachment tend to send sexts to get a response or some level of engagement back, not necessarily expecting a sexual encounter as a result (Weisskirch & Delevi, 2011). Other motivations include thrill-seeking, hopes of beginning a relationship with someone, and/or to keep their partners happy (Scholes-Balog et al., 2016). With regard to sensation-seeking, it may be that the moderator between sensation-seeking and sexting is relationship expectations (Scholes-Balog et al., 2016).

Once sexual material is included in an electronic transmission, the person who included the graphic material no longer has control of where that information and subject matter are distributed. If the information is distributed widely, significant psychological distress may follow (Van Ouytsel, Walrave, Ponnet, & Heirman, 2015). Further, young people often are unaware of the consequences of sexting, which makes them more vulnerable to its effects (Ahern & Mechling, 2013). Consequences of sexting include being seen by unintended individuals and the potential for an encounter to go too far (Renfrow & Rollo, 2014). Examining the behaviors of over 700 youth, Benotsch, Snipes, Martin, and Bull (2013) found significant associations between sexting and higher levels of substance abuse, as well as engaging in sex with multiple partners. Individuals who are more likely to send sexts are in a relationship, and those who do not send them tend to have higher levels of self-esteem (Scholes-Balog et al., 2016). On the other hand, at least one study disputes these findings. Gordon-Messer, Bauermeister, Grodzinski, and Zimmerman (2012) found while sexting is used in place of physical sex when there is not an available partner, there was no increase in the number of sexual partners, and no increase in unprotected sex. Further, they found no association with low self-esteem, depression, or anxiety among those who engaged in sexting.

"Sometimes It's Hard to Be a Woman"

Sexting within a committed relationship may have different implications for the relationship based on its culture and gender. The truth is women have it rough and are exposed to many risks from sexting (Albury & Byron, 2014). Teen girls who do not participate in sexting or respond to sexts are generally shunned by peers, fueling isolation (Lippman & Campbell, 2014). In heterosexual relationships in particular, if the woman receives a sext and she does not respond, there are negative ramifications. In the case of similar-gender romantic relationships, however, there do not seem to be negative ramifications for not reciprocating a message (Currin, Jayne, Hammer, Brim, & Hubach, 2016). It is essential to note that in general there is very little scholarly information focused on understanding the experiences, benefits, and risks of sexting for people of sexually and gender diverse backgrounds, identities, and relationships (Albury & Byron, 2014). What little scholarly information is available shows that adolescents and young people of sexually and gender diverse backgrounds display a range of creative techniques for navigating digisexual cultures (McArthur & Twist, 2017; Twist, 2018), and need to have strategies for negotiating safety and risk within offline and online sexual cultures (Albury & Byron, 2014; Twist et al., 2017).

In an attempt to understand what is happening to women, one study looked at the stories of over 450 adolescent girls and the dilemma they face when a nude photo appears or the request for such a photo is received (Thomas, 2018). There were three critical questions facing these teens: the decision as to whether to send photographs, the decision as to how to manage the consequences of sending the photos, and self-concept in relation to sending photos. Considerations for sending photos include love, desire for status, expectations of what a girlfriend normally does, fear of anger, complying to requests, experiencing repeated requests, responding to a threat, or other consequences to the relationship (Thomas, 2018). Adolescent girls reported a series of options in how to respond to these requests. Of course, adolescent girls can choose to acquiesce to such requests or decline. Other strategies teen girls reported using include delay tactics (such as sending photos of generic women online), seeking guidance asking others how to respond, and seeking help (but not from adults; Thomas, 2018).

Sweet Revenge?

Revenge pornography (porn) is a relatively new risk associated with our digital age. Revenge porn is the sharing of pornographic images of an individual without their knowledge or consent. Most commonly it is executed via online forums. The non-consensual distribution of these images is becoming a common revenge strategy for ex-partners, particularly male partners non-consensually sharing pornographic images of their female ex-partners (Hall & Hearn, 2017). In revenge porn, women are the victims 90% of the time (Hall & Hearn, 2017). Over 35 states in the US have revenge porn laws (www.cybercivilrights.org/revenge-porn-laws/), though at times those laws are challenged with laws around free speech (Larkin, 2014).

Cyberstalking

At a basic level, cyberstalking is defined as repeated use of the Internet and/or electronic communications to cause distress in another person (Nobles, Reyns, Fox, & Fisher, 2014). There are some definitions that involve the desire to create fear, but the establishment of this as a motivator can be difficult to determine (Nobles et al., 2014). In the US, the prevalence of cyberstalking varies widely, from 1% to 40%, with most estimates hovering near 20% (Nobles et al., 2014). Approximately one-quarter of women using dating sites indicate that they have been victims of cyberstalking through that mechanism (Jerin & Dolinsky, 2001, as cited in Nobles et al., 2014). In the European Union, an estimated nine million women per year are the victim of cyberstalking every 12 months, with most of these women between the ages of 18 and 29 (Horsman & Conniss, 2015). Constructs associated with cyberstalking victimization include the extent to which one exposes themselves to risks online generally, the attractiveness of the target, the extent to which the Internet users were monitored, and how deviant one was (Reyns, Henson, & Fisher, 2011).

There are four different types of cyberstalking. Vindictive cyberstalking is the type that is inspired by ill-wishes, malice, and intent to harm (Jansen van Rensburg, 2017). This type is characterized by extensive spamming via email and/or identity theft (Pittaro, 2007) and may transition into physical offline stalking (McFarlane & Bocij, 2003). Another type, composed cyberstalking, is where the stalker does not have the same intense ill-intention as the vindictive type, but instead is attempting to be a nuisance to the target (Jansen van Rensburg, 2017). Intimate cyberstalking is the type where the one doing the stalking is interested in capturing the attention of the target. Intimate cyberstalking, because it is designed to entice the target, is characterized by gathering specific and personal details about the target and reflecting this information to the target as a way to demonstrate the level of intimate connection through many phone calls, emails, and/or texts (Jansen van Rensburg, 2017). Finally, any of these types can be engaged in by two or more people, which is called collaborative cyberstalking. In this case, one target is identified, and it may include impersonation (Jansen van Rensburg, 2017).

In one study, both those engaging in the stalking and their targets engaged in different strategies to monitor their counterpart. These strategies include five different categories: primary contact attempts, secondary contact attempts (i.e., contacting others connected to the target), monitoring or surveillance, expressions, and invitations. From the offender perspective, this makes sense—they are keeping tabs on their target. From the target's perspective, however, they can also keeps tabs on who is keeping tabs on them. Bear in mind that these are not just keeping tabs; it means that the person who is keeping tabs is doing so in such a way that it looks like relational intrusion or has an obsessional quality (Chaulk & Jones, 2011). The development of cyberstalking is fueled by the characteristics of the Internet itself, such as anonymity—or at least perceived anonymity (Horsman & Connis, 2015).

As you might expect (and probably based on the different monitoring strategies used), consequences of cyberstalking can be highly damaging. These include psychological distress, a sense that one's privacy was invaded, and fear. Manifestations of psychological distress include stress, anger, irritation, paranoia, lack of concentration, betrayal, helplessness, annoyance, and depression. Targets of cyberstalking fear their reputation would be harmed, fear for their personal security, and fear that the online harassment and stalking would escalate to offline activities

(Jansen van Rensburg, 2017; Marcum, Higgins, & Ricketts, 2014). Finally, the ways in which the target may attempt to protect oneself typically involve more money than those in offline stalking experiences (Nobles et al., 2014).

Conclusion

Families may experience several risks related to technology and their relationships, including the introduction of online sexual predators, cyberbullying, video and online gaming, privacy considerations, cyberstalking, technology-based dating violence, sexting, and revenge pornography. As these issues continue to emerge, we have to stay one step ahead of these emerging technologies as a way to curb any negative impact and perhaps even reduce the instances of when technology is used inappropriately.

Note

1. The term "Internet of things" was coined by Kevin Ashton in 1999 and is used to refer to the capability of computers/technologies to sense things for themselves rather than only sensing what humans tell them (Ashton, 2009).

References

Adams, R., & Stevenson, M. (2004). A lifetime of relationships mediated by technology. In F. Lang & K. Fingerman (Eds.), *Growing together: Personal relationships across the lifespan* (pp. 368–393). New York, NY: Cambridge University Press.

Ahern, N. R., & Mechling, B. (2013). Sexting: Serious problems for youth. *Journal of Psychosocial Nursing and Mental Health Services, 51*(7), 22. doi:10.3928/02793695-20130503-02

Albury, K., & Byron, P. (2014, November). *Queering sexting and sexualisation.* Media International Australia Incorporating Culture and Policy, 153.

American Academy of Pediatrics. (2013). Policy statement: Children, adolescents, and the media. *Pediatrics, 132,* 958–961. doi:10.1542/peds.2013-2656

Ashton, K. (2009). That "Internet of things" thing: In the real world, things matter more than ideas. *RFID Journal.* Retrieved from https://www.rfidjournal.com/articles/view?4986

Bauman, S., Toomey, R. B., & Walker, J. L. (2013). Associations among bullying, cyberbullying, and suicide in high school students. *Journal of Adolescence, 36*(2), 341–350. doi:10.1016/j.adolescence.2012.12.001

Beckman, L., Hagquist, C., & Hellström, L. (2013). Discrepant gender patterns for cyberbullying and traditional bullying: An analysis of Swedish adolescent data. *Computers in Human Behavior, 29*(5), 1896–1903. doi:10.1016/j.chb.2013.03.010

Belsey, B. (2004). *Cyberbullying.* Retrieved July 15, 2018, from www.cyberbullying.ca

Benotsch, E. G., Snipes, D. J., Martin, A. M., & Bull, S. S. (2013). Sexting, substance use, and sexual risk behavior in young adults. *The Journal of Adolescent Health: Official Publication of the Society for Adolescent Medicine, 52*(3), 307–313. doi:10.1016/j.jadohealth.2012.06.011

Boyd, D. (2008). Facebook's privacy trainwreck: Exposure, invasion, and social convergence. *Convergence: The International Journal of Research into New Media Technologies, 14*(1), 13–20. doi:10.1177/1354856507084416

Boyd, D., & Marwick, A. (2011). Social privacy in networked publics: Teen's attitudes, practices, and strategies. *Microsoft Research*, 1–29. Retrieved from www.danah.org/papers/2011/SocialPrivacyPLSC-Draft.pdf

Brown, C. F., Demaray, M. K., Tennant, J. E., & Jenkins, L. N. (2017). Cyber victimization in high school: Measurement, overlap with face-to-face victimization, and associations with social-emotional outcomes. *School Psychology Review, 46*(3), 288–303.

Campbell, S. W., & Park, Y. J. (2014). Predictors of mobile sexting among teens: Toward a new explanatory framework. *Mobile Media & Communication, 2*(1), 20–39. doi:10.1177/2050157913502645

Chaulk, K., & Jones, T. (2011). Online obsessive relational intrusion: Further concerns about Facebook. *Journal of Family Violence, 26*(4), 245–254. doi:10.1007/s10896-011-9360-x

Cowie, H., & Myers, C. (2014). Bullying amongst university students in the UK. *International Journal of Emotional Education, 6*(1), 66–75. Retrieved from https://files.eric.ed.gov/fulltext/EJ1085613.pdf

Crooks, R., & Baur, K. (2011). *Our sexuality* (11th ed.). Belmont, CA: Thomson Wadsworth.

Currin, J. M., Jayne, C. N., Hammer, T. R., Brim, T., & Hubach, R. D. (2016). Explicitly pressing send: Impact of sexting on relationship satisfaction. *American Journal of Family Therapy, 44*(3), 143–154. doi:10.1080/01926187.2016.1145086

De Wolf, R. D., Williart, K., & Pierson, J. (2014). Managing privacy boundaries together: Exploring individual and group privacy management strategies in Facebook. *Computers in Human Behavior, 35*, 444–454. doi:10.1016/j.chb.2014.03.010

Erikson, E. H. (1982). *The life cycle completed.* New York, NY: Norton.

Festinger, L. (1954). A theory of social comparison processes. *Human Relations, 7*(2), 117–140. doi:10.1177/001872675400700202

Festl, R., & Quandt, T. (2016). The role of online communication in long-term cyberbullying involvement among girls and boys. *Journal of Youth and Adolescence, 45*(9), 1931–1945. doi:10.1007/s10964-016-0552-9

Gabriel, F. (2014). Sexting, selfies and self-harm: Young people, social media and the performance of self-development. *Media International Australia, 151*(1), 104–112.

Gamez-Guadix, M., De Santisteban, P., & Resett, S. (2017). Sexting among Spanish adolescents: Prevalence and personality profiles/Sexting entre adolescentes espanoles: Prevalencia y asociacion con variables de personalidad. *Psicothema, 29*(1), 29–34. doi:10.7334/psicothema2016.222

Goebert, D., Else, I., Matsu, C., Chung-Do, J., & Chang, J. (2011). The impact of cyberbullying on substance use and mental health in a multiethnic sample. *Maternal and Child Health Journal, 15*(8), 1282–1286. doi:10.1007/s10995-010-0672-x

Gordon-Messer, D., Bauermeister, J. A., Grodzinski, A., & Zimmerman, M. (2012). Sexting among young adults. *Journal of Adolescent Health*, *52*(3), 301–306. doi:10.1016/j.jadohealth.2012.05.013

Grüsser, S. M., Thalemann, R., & Griffiths, M. D. (2007). Excessive computer game playing: Evidence for addiction and aggression? *Cyberpsychology & Behavior: The Impact of the Internet, Multimedia and Virtual Reality on Behavior and Society*, *10*(2), 290–292. doi:10.1089/cpb.2006.9956

Hall, M., & Hearn, J. (2017). Revenge pornography: Gender, sexuality, and motivations. *NOTA News*, 16–18. doi:10.4324/9781315648187

Hansraj, K. K. (2014). Assesment of stresses in the cervical spine causes by posture and position of the head. *Surgical Technology International*, *25*, 277–279. Retrieved from https://motamem.org/wp-content/uploads/2016/06/spine-study.pdf

Hertlein, K. M., & Blumer, M. L. C. (2013). *The couple and family technology framework*. New York, NY: Routledge.

Hertlein, K. M., Blumer, M. L. C., & Smith, J. (2014). Marriage and family therapists' use and comfort with online communication with clients. *Contemporary Family Therapy*, *36*, 58–69. doi:10.1007/s10591-013-9284-0

Horsman, G., & Conniss, L. R. (2015). An investigation of anonymous and spoof SMS resources used for the purposes of cyberstalking. *Digital Investigation*, *13*, 80–93. doi:10.1016/j.diin.2015.04.001

Hur, M. H. (2006). Demographic, habitual, and socioeconomic determinants of Internet addiction disorder: An empirical study of korean teenagers. *Cyberpsychology & Behavior: The Impact of the Internet, Multimedia and Virtual Reality on Behavior and Society*, *9*(5), 514–525. doi:10.1089/cpb.2006.9.514

Jansen van Rensburg, S. K. (2017). Unwanted attention: The psychological impact of cyberstalking on its survivors. *Journal of Psychology in Africa*, *27*(3), 273–276. doi:10.1080/14330237.2017.1321858

Jerin, R., & Dolinsky, B. (2001). You've got mail! You don't want it. *Journal of Criminal Justice and Popular Culture*, *8*(1). Retrieved from https://www.albany.edu/scj/jcjpc/vol9is1/jerin.pdf

Jeunet, C., Albert, L., Argelaguet, F., & Lecuyer, A. (2018). "Do you feel in control?": Towards novel approaches to characterise, manipulate and measure the sense of agency in virtual environments. *Visualization and Computer Graphics, IEEE Transactions on*, *24*(4), 1486–1495. doi:10.1109/TVCG.2018.2794598

Judge, A. M. (2012). "Sexting" among U.S. adolescents: Psychological and legal perspectives. *Harvard Review of Psychiatry*, *20*(2), 86–96. doi:10.3109/10673229.2012.677360

Juvonen, J., & Gross, E. F. (2008). Extending the school grounds? Bullying experiences in cyberspace. *Journal of School Health*, *78*(9), 496–505. doi:10.1111/j.1746-1561.2008.00335.

Kann, L., McManus, T., Harris, W. A., Shanklin, S. L., Flint, K. H., Queen, B., . . . Ethier, K. A. (2018). Youth risk behavior surveillance—United States, 2017. *Morbidity and Mortality Weekly Report Surveillance Summary*, *67*(8), 1–114. doi:10.15585/mmwr.ss6708a1Kırcaburun, K., & Tosuntaş, S. B. (2018). Cyberbullying perpetration among undergraduates: Evidence of the roles of chronotype and sleep quality. *Biological Rhythm Research*, *49*(2), 247–265. doi:10.1080/02723646.2017.1352918

Ko, C. H., Yen, J. Y., Yen, C. F., Chen, C. S., Weng, C. C., & Chen, C. C. (2008). The association between Internet addiction and problematic alcohol use in adolescents: The problem behavior model. *Cyberpsychology & Behavior, 11*(5), 571–576. doi: 10.1089/cpb.2008.0199

Koivusilta, L., Nupponen, H., & Rimpela, A. (2011). Adolescent physical activity predicts high education and socioeconomic position in adulthood. *The European Journal of Public Health, 22*(2), 203–209. doi:10.1093/eurpub/ckr037

Kowalski, R. M., Giumetti, G. W., Schroeder, A. N., & Lattanner, M. R. (2014). Bullying in the digital age: A critical review and meta-analysis of cyberbullying research among youth. *Psychological Bulletin, 140*(4), 1073–1137. doi:10.1037/a0035618

Kowalski, R. M., & Limber, S. P. (2013). Psychological, physical, and academic correlates of cyberbullying and traditional bullying. *Journal of Adolescent Health, 53*(1), S13–S20. doi:10.1016/j.jadohealth.2012.09.018

Kramer-Duffield, J. (2010). *Beliefs and uses of tagging among undergraduates.* ProQuest Dissertations and Theses.

Krasnova, H., Veltri, N. F., & Günther, O. (2012). Self-disclosure and privacy calculus on social networking sites: The role of culture. *Business & Information Systems Engineering, 4*(3), 127–135. doi:10.1007/s12599-012-0216-6

Kwak, M., & Oh, I. (2017). Comparison of psychological and social characteristics among traditional, cyber, combined bullies, and non-involved. *School Psychology International, 38*(6), 608–627. doi:10.1177/0143034317729424

Lajunen, H., Keski-Rahkonen, A., Pulkkinen, L., Rose, R. J., Rissanen, A., & Kaprio, J. (2007). Are computer and cellphone use associated with body mass index and overweight? A population study among twin adolescents. *BMC Public Health, 7*(1), 24–24. doi:10.1186/1471-2458-7-24

Lam, L. T., & Peng, Z. W. (2010). Effect of pathological use of the Internet on adolescent mental health: A prospective study. *Archive of Pediatric Adolescent Medicine, 164*(10), 901–906. doi:10.1001/archpediatrics.2010.159.

Lam, L. T., Peng, Z. W., Mai, J. C., & Jing, J. (2009). Factors associated with Internet addiction among adolescents. *Cyberpyschology & Behavior, 12*(5), 551–555. doi: 10.1089/cpb.2009.0036

Larkin, P. (2014). Revenge porn, state law, and free speech. *Loyola of Los Angeles Law Review, 48*(1), 57–117. doi:10.2139/ssrn.2385620

Li, Q., Smith, P. K., & Cross, D. (2012). Research into cyberbullying. In Q. Li., D. Cross, & P. K. Smith (Eds.), *Cyberbullying in the global playground: Research from international perspectives.* Hoboken, NJ: Wiley-Blackwell.

Lippman, J. R., & Campbell, S. W. (2014). Damned if you do, damned if you don't . . . If you're a girl: Relational and normative contexts of adolescent sexting in the United States. *Journal of Children and Media, 8*(4), 371–386. doi:1 0.1080/17482798.2014.923009

Litt, E. (2013). Measuring user's Internet skills: A review of past assessments and a look toward the future. *New Media & Society, 15*(4), 612–630. doi:10.1177/1461444813475424

Marcum, C. D., Higgins, G. E., & Ricketts, M. L. (2014). Juveniles and cyber stalking in the United States: An analysis of theoretical predictors of patterns of online perpetration. *International Journal of Cyber Criminology, 8*(1), 47–56. Retrieved from https://libres.uncg.edu/ir/asu/f/Marcum_catherine_2014_Juvenilles_and_Cyber_orig.pdf

McArthur, N., & Twist, M. L. C. (2017). The rise of digisexuality: Therapeutic challenges and possibilities. *Sexual and Relationship Therapy, 32*(3/4), 334–344.

McFarlane, P., & Bocij, L. (2003). Cyberstalking: The technology of hate. *The Police Journal: Theory, Practice and Principles, 76*(3), 204–221. doi:10.1350/pojo.76.3.204.19442

Mesch, G. S. (2006). Family relations and the Internet: Exploring a family boundaries approach. *The Journal of Family Communication, 6*(2), 119–138. doi:10.1207/s15327698jfc0602_2

Mirowsky, J. (1997). Age, subjective life expectancy, and the sense of control: The horizon hypothesis. *The Journals of Gerontology, 52*(3), S125–134. doi:10.1093/geronb/52B.3.S125

Mitchell, K. J., Finkelhor, D., Jones, L. M., & Wolak, J. (2012). Prevalence and characteristics of youth sexting: A national study. *Pediatrics, 129*(1), 13–20. doi:10.1542/peds.2011-1730

Muhonen, T., Jönsson, S., & Bäckström, M. (2017). Consequences of cyberbullying behaviour in working life: The mediating roles of social support and social organisational climate. *International Journal of Workplace Health Management, 10*(5), 376–390. doi:10.1108/ijwhm-10-2016-0075

Nobles, M., Reyns, B., Fox, K., & Fisher, B. (2014). Protection against pursuit: A conceptual and empirical comparison of cyberstalking and stalking victimization among a national sample. *Justice Quarterly, 31*(6), 986–1014. doi:10.1080/07418825.2012.723030

Ortega, R., Elipe, P., Mora-Merchán, J. A., Genta, M. L., Brighi, A., Guarini, A., . . . Tippett, N. (2012). The emotional impact of bullying and cyberbullying on victims: A European cross-national study. *Aggressive Behavior, 38*(5), 342–356. doi:10.1002/ab.21440

Patchin, J. W., & Hinduja, S. (2010a). Bullying, cyberbullying, and suicide. *Archives of Suicide Research, 14*(3), 206–221. doi:10.1080/13811118.2010.494133

Patchin, J. W., & Hinduja, S. (2010b). Cyberbullying and self-esteem. *Journal of School Health, 80*(12), 614–621. doi:10.1111/j.1746-1561.2010.00548.x

Petronio, S. (2002). *Boundaries of privacy: Dialectics of discolsure 6.* Albany, NY: State University of New York Press.

Piaget, J. (1977). *The essential Piaget.* New York, NY: Basic Books.

Pittaro, M. L. (2007). Cyberstalking: An analysis of online harassment and intimidation. *International Journal of Cyber Criminology, 1*, 180–197. doi:10.5281/zenodo.18794

Rao Sathyanarayana, T., Bansal, D., & Chandran, S. (2018). Cyberbullying: A virtual offense with real consequences. *Indian Journal of Psychiatry, 60*(1), 3–5. doi:10.4103/psychiatry.IndianJPsychiatry_147_18

Renfrow, D. G., & Rollo, E. A. (2014). Sexting on campus: Minimizing perceived risks and neutralizing behaviors. *Deviant Behavior, 35*(11), 903–920. doi:10.1080/01639625.2014.897122

Reyns, B. W., Henson, B., & Fisher, B. S. (2011). Being pursued online: Applying cyberlifestyle—Routine activities theory to cyberstalking victimization. *Criminal Justice and Behavior, 38*(11), 1149–1169. doi:10.1177/0093854811421484

Ringrose, J., Gill, R., Livingstone, S., & Harvey, L. (2012). *A qualitative study of children, young people, and "sexing": A report prepared for the NSPCC.* London, England, UK: National Society for the Prevention of Cruelty to Children. Retrieved from http://eprints.lse.ac.uk/44216/

Rotter, J. B. (1966). Generalized expectancies for internal vs. external control of reinforcements. *Psychological Monographs, 80*, 1–28. doi:10.1037/h0092976

Rushing, S. C., & Stephens, D. (2011). Use of media technologies by Native American Teens and young adults in the Pacific Northwest: Exploring their utility for designing culturally appropriate technology-based health interventions. *Journal of Primary Prevention, 32*, 135–145. doi:10.1007/s10935-011-0242-z

Schneider, S. K., O'Donnell, L., & Smith, E. (2015). Trends in cyberbullying and school bullying victimization in a regional census of high school students, 2006–2012. *The Journal of School Health, 85*(9), 611–620. doi:10.1111/josh.122908

Scholes-Balog, K., Francke, N., & Hemphill, S. (2016). Relationships between sexting, self-esteem, and sensation seeking among Australian young adults. *Sexualization, Media, & Society, 2*(2). doi:10.1177/2374623815627790

Smardon, A. (2012). *Identity theft: "Kids don't know they're victims"*. Retrieved December 6, 2018, from http://m.npr.org/story/153030774

Smith, P. K., Mahdavi, J., Carvalho, M., Fisher, S., Russell, S., & Tippett, N. (2008). Cyberbullying: Its nature and impact in secondary school pupils. *Journal of Child Psychology and Psychiatry, 49*(4), 376–385. doi:10.1111/j.1469-7610.2007.01846.x.

Stonard, K., Bowen, E., Walker, K., & Price, S. (2017). "They'll always find a way to get to you": Technology use in adolescent romantic relationships and its role in dating violence and abuse. *Journal of Interpersonal Violence, 32*(14), 2083–2117.

Tene, O., & Polonetsky, J. (2014). A theory of creepy: Technology, privacy and shifting social norms. *Yale Journal of Law and Technology, 16*(1), 9–102.

Thomas, S. (2018). "What should I do?": Young women's reported dilemmas with nude photographs. *Sexuality Research and Social Policy, 15*(2), 192–207. doi:10.1007/s13178-017-0310-0

Trottier, D. (2012). Interpersonal surveillance on social media. *Canadian Journal of Communication, 37*(2), 319–332. doi:10.22230/cjc.2012v37n2a2536

Twist, M. L. C. (2018, June). *Digisexuailty: What the tech is it?* Invited Lecture, College of Sexual and Relationship Therapists, London, England, United Kingdom.

Twist, M. L. C., Bergdall, M. K., Belous, C. K., & Maier, C. A. (2017). Electronic visibility management of lesbian, gay, and bisexual identities and relationships. *Journal of Couple and Relationship Therapy: Innovations in Clinical Educational Interventions, 16*(4), 271–285.

Van den Bulck, J. (2004). Television viewing, computer game playing, and Internet use and self-reported time to bed and time out of bed in secondary-school children. *Sleep, 27*(1), 101–104.

Van Ouytsel, J., Walrave, M., Ponnet, K., & Heirman, W. (2015). The association between adolescent sexting, psychosocial difficulties, and risk behavior: Integrative review. *The Journal of School Nursing, 31*(1), 54–69. doi:10.1177/1059840514541964

Waasdorp, T. E., & Bradshaw, C. P. (2015). The overlap between cyberbullying and traditional bullying. *The Journal of Adolescent Health: Official Publication of the Society for Adolescent Medicine, 56*(5), 483–488. doi:10.1016/j.jadohealth.2014.12.002

Wade, A., & Beran, T. (2011). Cyberbullying: The new era of bullying. *Canadian Journal of School Psychology, 26*(1), 44–61. doi:10.1177/0829573510396318

Wehrenberg, M. (2018, December 13). *The new face of anxiety: Treating anxiety disorders in the age of texting, social media and 24/7 internet access.* PESI Webinar.

Weisskirch, R. S., & Delevi, R. (2011). "Sexting" and adult romantic attachment. *Computers in Human Behavior, 27*(5), 1697–1701. doi:10.1016/j.chb.2011.02.008

Willard, N. E. (2007). *Cyberbullying and Cyberthreats.* Eugene, OR: Center for Safe and Responsible Internet Use. Retrieved November 14, 2018, from https://dl.acm.org/citation.cfm?id=1396222

REBOOTING YOUR RELATIONSHIPS

SEVEN

What About the Internet Changes Our Relationships?

A Social Solution to a Social Problem

Up to this point in the book, we have covered many different areas of how technology affects our lives. We have covered the social. We have covered the physical. We know it creates problems. We know it provides solutions. Here is the list of where we have gone and what gets covered time and time again in presentations, books, and media:

- More persistent communications
- Internet, sex "addiction," and pornography
- Parenting challenges
- Surveillance
- Dopamine/brain changes
- Increase in autonomy
- Online infidelity
- Cyberbullying, cyberstalking, and electronic intimate partner violence
- Sexting
- Issues with privacy
- Mental health issues in children and adolescents
- Sedentary lifestyles
- Isolation
- Depression
- Increase in narcissism
- Increase in social anxiety

To see this list is overwhelming. This list alone is going to interfere with helping people change and use technology in productive ways, because of the sheer volume of what is in this . . . well, volume. We cannot ask people to address out-of-control technology-related behaviors, parenting, surveillance, physical changes in the brain, autonomy, and all of the other risks mentioned in one fell swoop. To do so is a grave mistake.

Unfortunately, attending to these topics in a topical manner and telling both therapist and the general population that these are the risks and they have to figure out a way to do things differently is confusing, and unfortunately, the status quo. Time and time again at conferences we attend, the presenter lays out the warning signs of all that is wrong with technology. The presenters tend to adopt a shock value orientation about all of the things that can potentially be negative about technology, sprinkled with a little information about neural networks and the brain from non-medical personnel who woo the audience into believing that these are contemporary findings, but in our view, it is all wrong. The layout of the overwhelming negatives makes it hard for any person to act and move forward with a true understanding of the impact of technology in a coherent fashion. The focal point of these presentations being on the problems with technology makes sense given that therapists often have their sights set on the problems people are experiencing in their lives and relationships—and technology is no exception. Therapists tend to have a more cautious and somewhat negative perspective of technology than much of the public at large (Funk, Kennedy, & Sciupac, 2016).

The other trend with technology is the people who are presenting the information are not well-versed in both the positives and negatives of new technologies. At mental health conferences, a common strategy in training other clinicians is reporting clinical anecdotes with warnings that the times are a-changin' and we must be cautious: after all, the digital age is different. For example, I (KH) was at a conference at which one speaker referenced "Pokemon Go." This individual suggested that that was a way to be able to connect with our younger generation. While that is a great start, understanding how technology can be used in our lives is more than asking about "Pokemon Go." It is about getting down to the nitty-gritty and how the Internet actually interferes, and enhances. We have to define the problem in terms of something we can do something about—our roles, rules, boundaries, relationship maintenance, initiation, and relationship termination.

There is yet to be one person outside of our earlier work (Hertlein & Blumer, 2013) to prevent an overall framework—a clear and coherent way to think about the impact of technology. We also have to think differently about technology. Wehrenberg (2018) discussed anxiety management, and removing the phones was her solution. Again, the evidence suggests that we are facing an epidemic and we need to rethink each part of what we are doing. Her solutions for managing the anxiety present in the millennial generation are to encourage volunteering, engagement in YouTube meditations, and other individually based strategies. But anxiety is not that simple, nor does it have a simple answer. This response of removing the phones and watching YouTube meditations does not explain the contributions the Internet makes in relationship initiation and maintenance. Wherenberg (2018) pointed out how we are in a new social anxiety, and that we are social creatures, but the strategies she poses for resolution are individual. This is not going to work and does not address the issue. Social anxiety demands a social solution. These are the same types of things that I (KH) discussed in 2005—and little has changed.

We need a social solution to this social anxiety problem, and the Internet and new media must be involved in that solution.

This is not to say that the involvement has to be immersive, pervasive, continual, and constant. It means that we develop a responsible and thoughtful approach to integrating technology in our personal lives, whether that is at the individual, couple, familial, or social level. The Couple and Family Technology (CFT) framework does just that (Hertlein & Blumer, 2013).

The Couple and Family Technology Framework

In the CFT framework, the ecological elements drive a relational system's structure and processes, specifically with regard to rules, roles, boundaries, intimacy, commitment, and other areas. Further, changes to only one level of structure do not necessarily mean there are changes to one level of process; rather, changes to one level of structure (roles, for example) can inspire changes in many levels of process, such as commitment, intimacy building, trust, and others. In other words, one specific change to structure does not predict a change in a specific process; rather, the specific changes to process are influenced by the structural changes as well as the context of the relationship, history between those involved, the stressors in the environment and also between the people involved, and other pertinent information.

Historically, scholars have relied on the Technology Acceptance Model (TAM; Davis, 1989), the uses and gratifications theory (UGT; Blumler & Katz, 1974), and, albeit limitedly, the sociotechnological model (SM; Lanigan, Bold, & Chenoweth, 2009) to explain human interaction with technology. These theories are comprehensive in their explanation as to why people are motivated to use technology and new media. The challenge still remains, however, in providing information and guidance as to how the use of technology impacts couples and families. As a general framework applied to understanding usage of a variety of applications, TAM describes the processes by which computer users adopt various emerging technologies, but was initially designed to address what affected technology usage in the workplace (Lu, Yu, Liu, & Yao, 2003). TAM is based on the assumption that people have particular beliefs about the ease of computer usage, which in turn affect their attitudes about computers and technology, thus affecting their behavior (i.e., increased intention to use that technology, which leads to actual usage of the technology) (Lu et al., 2003). The belief held related to the extent to which the technology in question is useful or easy to use is dictated to some degree by the external variables surrounding it. For example, Mary, a Latina woman in her 40s living in the Southwestern US, learns a new computer program that can help her manage her weight. She believes this program is easy to learn and, therefore, has developed a positive attitude with regard to the program. This positive attitude corresponds with an increased intention to use this type of technology (Burton-Jones & Hubona, 2006). Of the four stages identified (external variables influencing perceived usefulness and perceived ease of use, leading to attitude and behavioral intentions for usage), the most important relationship is that between the perceived usefulness and behavioral intentions (King & He, 2006). Specific variables appear to have a mediating relationship on the perceived usefulness and perceived ease of usage of technology (King & He, 2006). Some examples include: age, level of education, and prior experience (King & He, 2006).

The CFT framework is aligned less with TAM and more with domestication theory (Haddon, 2006). Domestication theory focuses on how families adapt to and, consequently, incorporate technology into their day-to-day life. As couples and families adopt technology into their lives, the developments made to technology change in response in order to enhance its utilities for families (Haddon, 2006). This approach fits more with our conceptualization of the role of technology and new media in family life because we see the integration of technology into people's lives as something that influences people's behavior rather than focusing on narrowing on intention of usage. In describing the process by which the Internet entered our homes, Bakardjieva (2005) noted:

> the boundaries between the world beyond the doorstep and the "private" life of the household were ceaselessly cracking and shifting. People were bringing in work from their offices and schools, friends and relatives were coming and staying, giving remote input and advice, demanding time and attention. The physical household was in actuality only a node in a much larger network of significant others, which, to a large extent, determined the nature and rhythms of its preoccupations. . . . Objects such as computers and modems were flowing across the public-private divide and along the interpersonal networks reaching far beyond the doorstep so that it was difficult to say exactly which object belonged to the particular household.
>
> (p. 66)

The same process is true for the CFT framework (Hertlein & Blumer, 2013). First, the three components of the model recursively influence one another. The ecological elements affect how structure and processes in relationships manifest because they affect both the structure and process of relationships. Further, the shifts in structure can affect changes to process, and changes to process can subsequently affect changes to structure, such as changes to boundaries, and consequently couple and family processes (Hertlein, 2012). According to Spears and Lea (1994), "[Computer-mediated communication] introduces the possibility of revolutionary social and structural changes in the ways that people communicate and relate to each other" (p. 427). One primary example is in the issue of accessibility (an ecological element) within computer-mediated communication as it relates to boundaries (a structural component) and power (a relational process) as described in the Social Identity Model of Deindividuation Effects (SIDE) proposed by Spears and Lea (1994). The SIDE model "is a theory of situated self-categorization, and tries to specify the situational conditions under which different self-categories will be salient and under which different self-categories will be salient and under which behavior normative to that category will be appropriate and possible" (Spears & Lea, 1994, p. 441). It has been applied to understand how we act in groups and how the computer can shape our interactions and what we present to others, based on the audience (Spears, Lea, Corneliussen, Postmes, & Haar, 2002).

Normative behavior turning into behavior that may be antinormative in groups is particularly prevalent when we observe increased accessibility in our digital world. Computers, new media, and technology make the ability to communicate with many groups of people at any given time easier than ever before in history because they increase accessibility (Spears & Lea, 1994). With increased accessibility, users of computers and other new media are afforded the opportunity to connect with others more broadly outside of their traditional social circle. New media allows users to transcend the typical boundaries and adopt new roles in other structures and groups that they would not be able to otherwise. For example, as the Internet creates equal opportunity for people to cheat (Hertlein & Stevenson, 2010), it creates an equalizing phenomenon (Dubrovsky, Kiesler, & Sethna, 1991) specifically in terms of power with regard to sex outside of the relationship. This phenomenon is related to Foucault's concept of the panopticon, or the concept that specific structural features of something contribute to control, surveillance, and equality (Spears & Lea, 1994). In another example of accessibility, other authors widely acknowledged the impact of the accessibility of social media on relationship developmental stages. For example, Brody, LeFebvre, and Blackburn (2016, p. 1) stated:

> The accessibility of information on SNS influences relationship development over time, aids in relationship maintenance, displays relationship dissolution, and reveals the multimodality of information between (online and offline) relationships. This means that our relationships in this digital age are more commonly going to integrate technology in how relationships are developed, maintained, and terminated.
>
> (Hertlein & Blumer, 2013)

Table 7.1 Theoretical Origins of Couple and Family Technology Framework

Class	Theory and Authors	Main Tenet	Limitations	Potential Applications for Relationships
Communication aspects	**Media richness** Daft and Lengel (1984) **Hyperpersonal CMC** Rabby and Walther (2002)	Different types of media have varying implications for task completion, speed, and clarity. Users can construct what they want to represent through text based-media, thereby increasing perceived intimacy.	Scope is limited to individual user characteristics and some application with intimacy, but there are not many studies on other applications; little consideration of other contextual factors that may be operating.	Couples who use Skype or other video-conference technologies to communicate would have an advantage over couples and families that use text-based communication methods; mediums that are rich in presentation may be augmented quite well in text-based media in the initial relationship development phase.
Social aspects	**Social penetration** Altman and Taylor (1973) **Social presence** Short, Christie, and Williams (1976)	Sharing both depth and breadth of experiences with another facilitates intimacy. Social presence is experienced through speed and interactions characterized by intimacy.	Social presence and its contribution to other processes in relationships (i.e., more than intimacy) are not considered.	Couples may have different perceptions of the circumstances in which depth would be more important to couple development than breadth; social presence may be a useful concept to discuss with couples who are concerned about their partner's online presence.
Developmental aspects	**Developmental model** Watt and White (1999) **Domestication theory** Silverstone, Hirsch, and Morley (1992)	Computers introduced changes in the way that we work, play, and interact with one another. The manifestation of the changes depends on the stage in the life cycle and other demographic information. Computers and other forms of new media influence family operations and, in so doing, change the way a family interacts with technology.	Limited attention to specific couple dynamics; do not include some of the information related to intimacy development in CMC relationships; heavy focus on computers and more focus needed on other forms of new media	The integration of computers and new media in relationships is, at best, a complex interaction. This perspective enables more opportunities for couples to experience challenges or opportunities for relationship enhancement.

A prime example of an ecological element's influence on the process and structure of relationships is in the case of anonymity. Postmes, Spears, and Lea (1998) discussed the concept of anonymity in computer-mediated communication and proposed that anonymous users may have a tendency to become deindividuated, meaning they more closely follow the norms of the group. The impact could also be opposite on the process: Haines and Mann (2011) found that anonymity changed the group dynamics when awareness was involved—in other words, in groups with more awareness of others' actions, there was a higher likelihood to feel indispensable. In either case, the implementation of new media and technology into relationships affects people's views of their role in the relationships, which can have direct implications for the subsequent actions and behavior within that group context. The theoretical origins of the CFT framework are presented in Table 7.1.

Another characteristic of the domestication model is the importance of symbolism and meaning. In other words, users of technology and new media will ascribe meanings to certain technology functions (Hynes & Rommes, 2005). This, too, corresponds with the CFT framework. In many cases, couples ascribe meaning to the applications, programs, and technologies used by their partners, particularly when it accompanies behaviors viewed negatively by their partners.

Theoretical Frameworks

There are several other frameworks that attempt to explain the interaction between the technology user and the computer (e.g., the technology acceptance model, TAM; Davis, 1989; uses and gratifications theory, UGT; Blumler & Katz, 1974; and sociotechnological model; Lanigan et al., 2009). Yet these models fail to articulate specific ways in which families interact with technology and how relationship processes are affected by technology. As such, the CFT framework represents one of the most comprehensive treatment approaches grounded in theory and empirical findings. The CFT framework (Hertlein, 2012) is grounded in the theories mentioned earlier as well as three prominent theories in family studies: Family Ecology Theory (Granic, Dishion, & Hollenstein, 2003), Structural Functionalism Theory (Johnson, 1971), and Interaction-Constructionist Theory (Berger & Kellner, 1970). The family-ecology perspective posits that factors in the external environment affect people. In the CFT framework, we operationalize such factors as the "ecological elements," or the seven elements specific to computers and new media that have transformative effects on relationships. The structural-functionalist perspective (Johnson, 1971) posits how one organizes themselves and how aspects in one's life influence one's organization.

As conceptualized within the CFT framework, ecological elements drive changes to how families organize and how they function. In many cases, changes to structure encourage positive and adaptive changes in family function; in other cases, structural changes can be detrimental. As discussed by Hertlein and Blumer (2013), "The determination as to whether technology and new media provides distance or closeness is best expressed as a function of (a) the type of activity (whether it is physical, psychological, or both), and (b) the target of the behavior (i.e., is it another person or an object?)" (p. 108). The third and final perspective laying groundwork for the CFT framework is the interaction-constructionist perspective (Berger & Kellner, 1970), which states our communication with others is composed of rituals, behaviors, and gestures, which are interpreted by others. To understand how these theories contribute to the CFT framework, see Figure 7.1 later in the chapter.

The Flexibility of the CFT Framework

The interaction of ecological elements, structure, and process is certainly a complicated one. It will also vary for each relational system depending on the unique elements and dynamics within the relationship. One of the advantages to the CFT framework is that it is succinct enough to be able to accurately describe the process for couples and families, but broad enough to be able to account for a host of issues. It functions as a meta-perspective to already existing theories. In other words, therapists working with couples from this perspective can continue to use the theories that best fit them, but do so underneath the umbrella of the CFT approach. It is a way to conceptualize how technology affects couple (and family) life rather than being prescriptive with regard to theoretical orientation.

Part of its flexibility rests on the fact that, as a way to think about cases, the CFT framework is broad enough to be adapted to couples of varied cultural and ethnic backgrounds. Every couple has differences in their values, rules, and the way that they define their relationship. For example, Sergi and Nadia, a heterosexual, white couple, both originally from Siberia, but now residing in the US, stated the computer is accessible and allows for affordable interaction, which leads them to feel more connected and supported in their relationship with family members in their country of origin; yet that same accessibility and affordability is concerning for others, like more rural couples. For instance, Johona and Lynxton, a couple of mixed gender identities (Johona identifies as a woman, and Lynxton identifies as two-spirit) and of First Nations backgrounds, live in a remote area in the desert Southwest of the US. They tend to view the accessibility that technology brings into their home with more suspicion and have developed more stringent rules with regard to its usage in the relationship.

Key Characteristics of Technology That Affect Relationships

There are several characteristics about technology and new media that affect relationships, offered to us by a host of scholars and researchers over the years. They include: acceptability (King, 1999); accessibility, affordability; anonymity (Cooper, 2002); approximation (Ross & Kauth, 2002); accommodation; ambiguity (Hertlein & Stevenson, 2010); and accountability (this text). See Table 7.2 for a list of the benefits and risks each of these areas introduces into relationships.

Table 7.2 Benefits and Challenges of Internet Characteristics

Ecological Element	Benefits to Relationship	Challenges to Relationship
Acceptability	• Acceptable way to meet and maintain a relationship.	• The acceptable nature of communicating with others online introduces more risk.
Anonymity	• Test the waters prior to becoming vulnerable in the early stages of relationship development. • Can monitor and edit reactions prior to reacting in ways that might be hurtful.	• Greater potential to hide behind the computer and edit one's authentic self. • May lengthen the time that it takes to feel vulnerable with partner.
Accessibility	• Routine access to partner. • More opportunity to develop greater levels of intimacy.	• Increased ability and potentially interest to monitor partner.
Affordability	• Long-distance relationships can thrive.	• May be easier to develop relationships with others that are virtually undetectable to primary partner.
Accommodation	• Can help one to test pilot things one wants to be online with perceived safety.	• Can create further divide between online and offline personas, resulting in some level of inauthenticity.
Approximation	• Create unique and creative opportunities to "date" one another.	• Relationship may be unrealistic in the offline world and only function because of the unrealistic online behaviors.
Ambiguity	• Can create opportunities to practice assumption of good intent.	• May contribute to discord and disagreement between couples on expectations and relational rules.
Accountability	• Many ways to take accountability—does not have to be face-to-face, which may be more difficult.	• Contribute to people divorcing themselves from their own behavior and actions.

"Everybody's Doing It": Acceptability

The Internet, engagement in new media, and ownership of more advanced technological gadgets are becoming more acceptable, within both our work and personal lives. For example, it is not uncommon for people in a place of employment to attend work meetings with a writing instrument, pad of paper, and smartphone or other portable electronic device. The placement of mobile phone numbers on business cards in addition to the office number is another example of how acceptable technologies are becoming in one's work life. "More people will become connected because device manufacturers will make it far easier and acceptable to purchase and use these devices" (quote from a participant; Raine & Anders, 2017, p. 5). The use of applications (apps) for medical management (termed "mHealth") is also very commonplace, for a wealth of medical conditions, not the least of which is management of Hepatitis C (Levine et al., 2015), tracking cervical cancer (Irwin, Nordstrom, & Pyra, 2012), early detection of prostate cancer (Sundberg, Langius, Blomberg, Isaksson, & Wengström, 2013), uncomplicated malaria (Otieno et al., 2014), and other conditions. The acceptability of use for psychological conditions rivals the medical applications, including acceptability for using apps to detect symptoms of schizophrenia (Applegate et al., 2014) and self-harm (Grist, Porter, & Stallard, 2018).

Other aspects of new media that are becoming acceptable include the presence of an account on Facebook, Twitter, and other sites that provide opportunity for social engagement. The sheer number and penetration of Internet usage discussed in Chapter 1 are one indicator of the acceptance of these technologies in our lives. People may be part of support groups online or chat rooms where they are dedicated to dealing with a particular topic and issue. For example, participation in online dating is increasing as an acceptable practice across a wide variety of demographic and social groups (Conway, Noë, Stulp, & Pollet, 2015; Moscaritolo, 2013). Using the Internet to pursue sexual interests is also becoming more acceptable (Albright, 2008). For instance, in terms of digisexuality, at one time using an online avatar within an interactive cybersexual environment was not necessarily an acceptable activity, but now it is more common and more acceptable (McArthur & Twist, 2017), and may even lead to sexual activity with robots.

As acceptability of using technology in one's life increases, people also gravitate toward what is acceptable in their peer group. At times, this can raise serious issues for relationships. Take the case of infidelity in couples, for example. Because the communication with a third party was carried out via Facebook, couples might try to solve the problem by eliminating Facebook completely, and may even be advised (wrongly) by therapists to do so (Hertlein & Piercy, 2008). Facebook is not the problem; it is an acceptable way to engage with the Internet, and as a consequence, perhaps infidelity is becoming more acceptable.

Acceptability refers to both the practice of using the Internet and web-based services for a variety of functions but also the extent to which the new relationships formed from an online interaction are becoming more acceptable themselves. Regardless of the application or form of new media, Madden and Lenhart (2006) were among the first of many authors who have written specifically about how common the Internet is becoming for the initiation and development of romantic relationships. The initiation of such relationships can occur within SNSs, but is certainly not limited to these sites. Implicit in the practice of forming relationships online is the acceptable nature of participating in an intimate relationship maintained primarily online. Because couples are able to interact virtually, there may be fewer instances where they actually get a sense of each other in day to day life. One of the things evading couples is the sense of "everydayness" present in face-to-face relationships. This has resulted in an alternative model of couple development where the couple spends time feeling each other out, going on a trip as their first physical encounter or meeting up for the weekend, and making a decision whether to proceed with the relationship. In some cases, this might make sense for a wide variety of couple relationships.

The acceptability of online relating has also increased the acceptability of being in a long-distance relationship and living away from extended family. Additionally, with the advent of video phoning and other similar capabilities, it is becoming more acceptable to move away from one's birthplace and central hub. As Bacigalupe and Lambe (2011) note: "Technology is used first to maintain preexisting relationships (e.g., children moving away from their parents, who remain in the home region) and then to build on their existing relationship despite the lack of a common place" (p. 17). The acceptability of incorporating these issues in a couple's life also requires some negotiation. For which families is it more acceptable to participate in online interactions? Are there some families that actually require or value significantly more highly the physical face-to-face time instead of face-to-face time conducted over the Internet?

Likewise, there are also certain other expectations within families affecting the couple with regard to Internet time. For example, a family's participation in online gaming may be an important point of sharing and family connection that they experience. Many people participate in massively multiplayer online role-playing games (MMORPGs), games facilitated by SNSs that they can play with their friends, and similar games on their cellphones. This provides an opportunity to interact with extended family and friends in a way that maintains the connection but that does not necessarily entail sending individual messages or emails to them. In short, it is a way of being connected while being disconnected. The acceptable nature of such gaming within one's social life often has direct and indirect implications for couple life. A direct implication relates to whom the interaction is with; the other implication is what is said and communicated within these games. For example, one partner may feel conflicted about their partner's daily contact with a former partner through these games—on the one hand, the partner is communicating little in the way of emotion and personal thought through playing games. On the other hand, there are many people with whom the game could be played—why choose one person who is a former partner?

The acceptability of these gadgets also has implications for boundaries and acceptable behavior within relationships. With regard to infidelity, heterosexual women are more likely to cheat when they are in the same social group as other like identity women who have cheated (Atwater, 1979; Buunk, 1980). With regard to application to families and children, it is more becoming the norm that teens and kids have their own cellphones (Campbell & Ling, 2009). Though this research was conducted in the late 70s and early 80s, it begs the question as to whether the same thing occurs for men, or for gay, lesbian, or bisexual-identifying (LGB) persons, or people of transgender experiences/identities. While we do not necessarily have this data, there is some scholarly information that shows that for many LGB persons in partnered relationships they do not believe it is acceptable for their partner(s) to participate in an online romantic relationship with someone outside of their partnership(s), nor to have online sex with someone other than them, because they believe it to be physically and emotionally damaging to their relationship(s) (Twist, Belous, Maier, & Bergdall, 2017).

One result of the notion that people who know others who cheat online and accept infidelity behavior is it may create hyper vigilance for a partner in the relationship. Part and parcel with this hyper vigilance is an increased sense of justification with regard to hacking a partner's account. In a world that is getting exponentially more technological, it is becoming more acceptable to tap into your partner's personal account should you become suspicious of their activities. For example, Molly and Desmond are of mixed-class and racial backgrounds who both live in London. They met through an online dating portal. After a month of exchanging emails and texting, they began meeting up for dates—first, group dates with friends and, later, dates with just one other. Within eight months of their first online encounter, they decided Desmond would move into Molly's apartment. Shortly after moving in, Desmond demanded that Molly provide him with her passwords for her email and social networking accounts and, likewise, provided her with his account information. While Molly was not interested in logging into his accounts, she began to notice periodically that he would log into her accounts and monitor the activity and behavior with her friends and colleagues.

Another element of acceptability is the fact that some websites are geared toward and create an acceptable environment for couples to participate in hurtful or damaging behavior. For example, some sites have been created to advertise that someone is a poor partner. Other sites advertise they are a site that develops acceptability around the practice of cheating on one's partner. Certainly, the people using these sites do not have to be married or even in a relationship; however, the idea that there are sites that create a context of acceptability for either cheating or potentially slandering one's partner certainly does not necessarily contribute to the health of a relationship or the individuals within it.

"Who Are You?": Anonymity Online

Anonymity means computer and Internet users can present themselves in any way they desire to the recipient on the other end of an electronic communication (Cooper, 2002). Using the Internet and other forms of new media presents one with the ability to present particular aspects about themselves to others without being challenged by the other people online with whom they are communicating or interacting. Because of this, the person who is anonymous has a higher degree of control in their self-presentation:

> Those engaging in online relationships can choose to present a detached attachment or absent presence characterized by features of oppositionality: distance/immediacy; anonymity/disclosure; deception/sincerity . . . in one line of text, an individual can transmit confessional self-disclosure while remaining anonymous.
> (Hertlein & Sendak, 2007, p. 2)

Retaining anonymity in Internet relationships can take many forms. Some people might choose to conceal their relationship status, their physical characteristics, or their immediate responses within interactions. In some cases, one may choose to omit or embellish physical characteristics of themselves, particularly if a face-to-face meeting does not appear to be on the horizon for a great deal of time. Further, if photos are exchanged, it is worth noting these photos may be edited by someone with a computer program as to appear perfect. This allows people developing relationships to be able to test the waters and gain acceptance prior to becoming completely vulnerable in a relationship. This is critical in relationship initiation, where often the physical characteristics block the development of any type of relationship from the start (McKenna, Green, & Gleason, 2002).

In addition to one's ability to hide personal attributes from others, anonymity also refers to when users can be anonymous with their exchanges and interactions. Unlike face-to-face interactions, communication via a keyboard allows the person typing to edit their responses as they interact with others. Nonverbal reactions of a receiver are not automatically communicated to the sender as they are in face-to-face interactions (Cooper, 2002). Instead, any communication or reaction by the receiver that is communicated back to the original sender can be carefully crafted as to hide any reactions that may not be viewed favorably by the other party. The ability for online interactions to provide users with a way to edit, delete, backspace, and think about messages before hitting "send" provides a cloak of anonymity with regard to their emotions, reactions, and, in some ways, authentic self. Anonymity may already present a problem in current relationships and will most likely continue to do so in the future. For instance, in the present we are not only deceived by humans online, we are also deceived by robots (via software), and in the future this will continue, but this kind of deception will not be contained to online technology-based realities; instead it will also come in the form of offline realities with technology like robots (McArthur & Twist, 2017).

The use of anonymity and limited disclosure of authentic reactions as a protective mechanism in relationships may assist a relationship in getting off the ground in the early stages, until such a time when the relationship is safe enough to handle how each person honestly feels about certain issues. Part of this may be due to the fact that as each person is getting to know the other, messages eliciting a negative reaction by the reader may be given the benefit of the doubt that the sender was not aware of how the message came across. For example, Anna and Sonja, a similar-gender Asian American couple in a committed relationship living on the West Coast of the US, came to treatment to manage Anna's recent anger outburst. When the therapist asked about their use of technology, Anna stated that Sonja's communications with her over email were short, abrupt, and read rather harshly. Anna, however, decided to look past the tone of the messages because she believed that Sonja was unaware of how the tone in the messages came across. After several months, however, Anna indicated the tone was becoming hurtful to her and that Sonja now needed to construct her messages differently and with a soft, supportive tone. Sonja expressed confusion at the new rules—if Anna was not upset before at her tone, why was she upset now? Clearly, if editing reactions continues beyond a certain point in a relationship, the couple may discover they do not have the level of intimacy or safety in the relationship they previously believed they had.

Anonymity has been tied directly to online infidelity. In research within an Internet chat room examining the key elements that contribute to affairs, Mileham (2007) found three: behavioral rationalization, effortless avoidance, and anonymous sexual interactionism. "Anonymous sexual interactionism" is the term used to describe the experience of treating the chat room as if it was a movie, watching things go by and, consequently, detaching oneself from one's behavior in the process. When one becomes detached from their own behavior, the result may be a "slippery slope," or progressively moving toward increasingly risky, problematic, and/or hurtful behavior. The same situation occurs more broadly within online news articles with a comments section following the article. Consider a recent article that you read in an online news source with a comments section after the article. It is likely that it did not take long for the comments to turn negative and personally attacking (perhaps three to four comments). The concept of anonymity in this paradigm is no different from the paradigm offered in the Milgram experiments of the

1960s. Along with the demand characteristics of the experts instructing the research subjects to complete their tasks, the separation of the individual from the person to whom they were administering the shocks and the inherent anonymity within that structure contributed to the likelihood of administering the shocks (Badhwar, 2009). Anonymity has a rather prominent place in the decisions one makes about engaging in a particular behavior. Anonymity has a rather prominent place in the decisions one makes about engaging in a particular behavior, and it can differ based on an individual or a couple's cultural background. For instance, people of LGB backgrounds will sometimes decide to not be "out" about their sexual orientation in offline (otherwise known as visibility management) and/or online (also known as electronic visibility management) environments out of a need for safety from bullying and violence (Blumenfeld & Cooper, 2010; Lasser & Tharinger, 2003; Twist, Belous et al., 2017; Twist, Bergdall, Belous, & Maier, 2017).

Me and My Shadow: Accessibility

One of the most common effects of the Internet is the experience of connection (Raine & Anderson, 2017). Accessibility means that we literally have the world in the palm of our hands. Recently, my (KH) husband was at a local car dealership waiting for a repair. In the waiting room with our 4-year-old son, he was joined by another man and his young child, approximately 2 ½ years old. The man pulled out a tablet computer and put it in front of his son to occupy him while the man began to work on his laptop. The boy turned to look at my son, and my son in turn turned to look at the boy. My son told my husband, "That boy is looking at me," and my husband went over to my son and saw what was on the tablet—Japanese anime pornography. The father of the other young boy noticed my son looking at the tablet and said to my husband: "Oh, he can watch that too if he wants." My husband politely declined and told my son to come with him. The other man peered out from his laptop screen and looked at the tablet. Upon realizing what was on it, he exclaimed "Oh my gosh! What are you watching?!?" and proceeded to change what was being portrayed on the computer. This scenario exemplifies the concept of accessibility—just about anybody can access the Internet and anything on it if given the proper connection and tools.

Cooper (2002) described accessibility as the characteristic of the Internet allowing for individuals to be able to access a wide variety of material. Specifically, he described accessibility as related to sexual material online in his book *Sex and the Internet*, and this description still applies today and will in the future. For instance, digisexual engagement (like accessing online pornography) while possible from virtually anywhere (particularly via smartphones)—workplaces, planes, schools, hospitals, etc. (Twist, Bergdall et al., 2017)—does not mean that accessing it is socially and/or legally allowed in such public settings, which most likely will not change even as digisexuality grows in the future (McArthur & Twist, 2017). In addition, accessibility can and does refer to a wide variety of electronic material, not just material of a sexual nature (Hertlein & Stevenson, 2010). One, for example, is the increased accessibility to our partners through emails, instant messaging, and other mechanisms (Cooper, 2002). Researchers have found that LGB individuals in partnered relationships report being very accessible to each other via technology (Twist, Bergdall et al., 2017). Because of this accessibility, almost all couples now have to negotiate the presence of media in their lives. Other elements of the Internet that have to be negotiated include access to others via SNSs, blogs, chat rooms, and websites. Internet-based search engines exponentially increase our accessibility in their ability to find any number of people through posted addresses, phone records, and related contact information.

The flipside of this increased accessibility is greater vulnerability (Raine & Anderson, 2017). The Internet allows us to be accessible to other people and entities. In other words, the Internet introduces people who are known to us and unknown to us into our couple and family relationships. These meetings can have some pretty challenging consequences. As Rymarczuk and Derksen (2014) state: "Facebook isolates at the same time as it exposes: it liberates the user from the constraints of distance yet confines him to a screen." Not only are people accessible to others at any given time, they are also available in any given place. A married, heterosexual, white, middle-class couple in their late 20s living on the West Coast of the US called for therapy related to his infidelity in their relationship. His wife discovered a trail of phone calls and text messages to other women demonstrating a clear emotional connection. He indicated this behavior had gone on for years, but had become more pronounced, and he had begun relationships with multiple women in the last year. After the first session, the couple seemed committed to making the relationship work. I (KH) felt pretty good about the case and was fairly hopeful they would be able to resolve these issues. The next week, the couple came in for their regularly scheduled session, and I asked about their assignment over the week. It was clear there was some tension in the room. When I asked what happened, the wife said they had argued in the car ride home from the last session. The wife disclosed while she was driving on the way home from the therapy session, she discovered her husband in the seat next to her was texting his girlfriend messages about how much he loved her. I looked at him seated on the couch and said "Dude—I'm trying to help you here." He just gave me a sheepish grin, looked down, and said "I know." This example introduces one of the most problematic elements for couples related to access. Not only is the access itself problematic in the cases where it constitutes betrayal because of who is accessed, but the access to another in front of the primary partner generates a more complicated and secondary betrayal—activities conducted in secret, yet right out in the open. Regarding the couple discussed in the preceding paragraph, the male partner was able to conduct his extramarital interactions outside of his partner's awareness while seated near her without drawing attention to himself.

This is especially problematic because one of the core components of infidelity is secrecy, and may very well be one of the first barriers couples need to navigate in their healing—processing the betrayal of the events in such a way that allows them to move forward without being suspicious of every action. In other words, accessibility may also be problematic for couples when one partner clearly does NOT have access to certain elements of their partner's life, a phenomenon common with each person having an individual cellphone, logins, and email addresses. Applications (apps) have even been developed to permit the saving of photos and messages in hidden locations on one's cellphone, detectable to no one but the owner of the phone. As a result, increased accessibility becomes synonymous with increased opportunities, a key variable in likelihood to engage in infidelity (Treas & Giesen, 2000).

We also believe the definition of accessibility should be broadened (Hertlein & Blumer, 2013). Cooper's (2002) definition of accessibility refers to the access that one in a relationship has to the outside world and its inhabitants. Accessibility can also refer to the fact that people in a relationship are accessible to others, not just that those in the relationship can access others. In other words, the Internet and other similar forms of new media introduce both people who are known to you and people who are not known to you in your relationship.

Recent updates in cellular technology have the capability to pinpoint one's location. This can have positive or negative implications for a couple. On one hand, it can be used to promote the development of trust in an already-struggling relationship. Trez and Caitlin, a Black American, heterosexual, upper-class couple in their 30s living in the Southeastern US, came to treatment to address Trez's constant infidelity throughout the duration of the relationship. One of the challenges to the couple's recovery process was that Trez's cheating happened while he was at work. Part of his job required that he travel to people's homes to conduct interviews. It was during these errands that he would also stop off to have sex with someone. The couple had to develop a solution to enable her to trust him enough so that he could still work and so that she could feel more trusting. The couple worked out an arrangement where when Caitlin needed him to respond to her or to check in, Trez would take a photo of where he was and respond immediately to her.

The Ultimate Cheap Date: Affordability

To carry on relationships via technology online is very affordable in the present (Cooper, 2002). For instance, in a study of LGB individuals, participants reported that their technologies were very affordable, with cellphones reported as the most affordable, followed by Internet services, and then computer maintenance (Twist, Bergdall et al., 2017). However, more sophisticated technologies are still fairly costly—like virtual reality, 3D printers, and digisexual equipment like sex dolls (McArthur & Twist, 2017). The direct cost for high-end sex dolls like RealDolls is currently between US$4,000 and US$15,000 (RealDoll, 2017). Presently, we cannot predict the cost of a digisexual companion, and currently these more sophisticated technologies are not affordable to average-income earning people (McArthur & Twist, 2017).

To carry on relationships online is very affordable (Cooper, 2002). The ease with which one can communicate, the multiple methods, and the fact that it is acceptable to have a way through which to communicate can all create problems. It was not uncommon in couple relationships plagued by infidelity to be discovered by a receipt, a charge on a hotel, or a bill from a gift. One couple, I (KH) worked with, Heath and Jess, a mixed-race couple in their 40s, divulged early in the course of couples therapy that even though they had an open relationship, Jess believed that Heath had violated their rules around the open nature of their relationship. She believed that he had "hooked up" with someone else and not told her. He denied hooking up with someone else and kept reminding her that if he had he would have told her. Every several weeks, we would make progress on the couple's communication patterns, their access to their feelings, and they would grow closer. Shortly after, Jess would once again begin to think about what she believed to be the discovery of an affair that was outside of their agreed upon relational parameters—this discovery was a charge from an upscale restaurant that her husband clearly went to with someone other than her.

Affordability also relates to some of the programs developed to organize romantic relationships with others, including partners other than ourselves. Many apps such as the ones described earlier that allow you to hide photos and messages from others on your phone can be downloaded for free. The same is true for opening virtually any email account—all you need is a password and a username. The cost, however, of participating in relationships that are affordable financially may not be affordable for relational health in the long run for certain couples. Recall the couple mentioned earlier in the chapter (Trez and Caitlin) who had a relationship characterized by online interactions separately and then vacations together. Certainly, while it is financially feasible to carry on a long-distance relationship, the end result may be that one loses a sense of reality within the relationship. That being said, there are just as many couples, if not more, for whom financial affordability allows them to have relationships that they would not otherwise be able to have because of being separated by distance or circumstance. Marco and Brian, a white, similar-gender, gay, middle-class couple, for example, began their relationship in the same town, but an academic opportunity opened up for Brian in another state. The affordability provided by the Internet and the ability to send each other daily journal entries complete with photos went a long way to sustaining the relationship and making it possible for them to develop a deeper level of commitment to one another, resulting in them deciding to live together and eventually marry upon Brian's return from out of state.

A World of Sims: Approximation

Approximation refers to the quality of the Internet that approximates real-world situations (Tikkanen & Ross, 2003). As graphics and computer technologies improve, the graphics and video projections become more lifelike and therefore more seductive. There are a number of online mechanisms by which people replicate their offline lives. An article in *Time World*, for example, cites an incident where one woman filed for divorce after the revelation that her husband was having virtual sex with another avatar within the game *Second Life* (Adams, 2008). In this way, one's engagement in certain sexual interactions across a medium approximating the offline world can result in a blurring of the lines between fantasy and action (Ross, 2005).

To date, the main group that has been examined with regard to the approximation phenomenon is men who seek similar-gender partners online (Cooper, Galbreath, & Becker, 2004). The rationale provided by the participants in the study was that they were engaging in that behavior as a way to manage their stress or anxiety. The more they engaged in this practice, the more it became a self-reinforcing strategy. The researchers concluded people perform these behaviors online because they do not feel it is the appropriate behavior in which to participate in their offline lives, yet it is perceived as "safe" when it is online because it provides a way of having an authentic and realistic experience without specific unwanted consequences. For example, one can engage in digisexual activities with someone without risk of becoming pregnant, or infected with viruses like the human immunodeficiency virus (HIV) or any other sexually transmitted infections (STIs). To a lesser extent, LGB individuals in partnered relationships have also been the focus of research on approximation. For instance, Twist, Belous et al. (2017) found that participants believed that email was the most approximating online expression of themselves in comparison to their offline expression of themselves. Furthermore, the participants did note there was a difference between online sex and offline sex—so they did not see online sex as a true approximation of sex offline (Twist, Bergdall et al., 2017).

Approximation is a very powerful element of computer and web-based technologies that introduces a different dimension into coupled relationships affecting both emotional and physical intimacy between partners. Participating in real-time conversations over instant messaging or text provides members of a relationship with timely information about a partner's current emotions, motivations, thought processes, and feelings in a way that only phone calls could accomplish. Further, the ability to visually see one's partner (or others) through real-time Internet channels has important implications for couples. Particular programs currently advertised have the ability to provide some level of sexual gratification through their ability to provide real-time visual and tactile stimuli. For example, one can purchase devices with the ability to connect to computers or tablet computers with a USB that are designed to physically stimulate one's genitalia. Upon connection, users visit a website to download or view short movies that are developed to move in sync with the device. Other developments to this same technology include a device for a partner to operate at their own computer to stimulate a partner remotely.

In some cases, approximation can interfere with a relationship because the interactions with others online can be highly realistic. As mentioned earlier, the ability to have one see another in a real-time sexual situation can be appealing. When a physical partner cannot be found, options on pornographic websites such as live cameras can fill in the gap. For example, Whitty's (2005) research found approximation played a part in the experience of betrayal in online infidelity. Because communications on the Internet approximated real-world situations, the experience of online betrayal mimicked offline betrayal.

The quality of approximation contributes to our understanding of different types of motivations of computer users, particularly with regard to sex. Three types of cybersex users have been identified: recreational users, sexually compulsive users, and at-risk users (Cooper, Delmonico, & Burg, 2000). Recreational users are those who utilize the Internet as a way to entertain themselves or because they are curious about different aspects of sexual behavior. These cases are most often not brought to therapy as a presenting problem, nor are they addressed in treatment when this behavior is revealed. The category of compulsive users includes those who participate in what some consider to be unhealthy and out-of-control sexual expressions, and the Internet is just one manner in which this is accomplished. The third group represents a vulnerable portion of the population—a group of people that, without the Internet, would not have a problem with what some consider to be at-risk sexual expressions. Yet, the Internet's accessibility creates opportunities for the at-risk user to participate in usage to gratify sexual needs. Individuals in this group are vulnerable to developing sexual compulsions when they are using the Internet to gratify themselves sexually in times of isolation (Delmonico, 1997).

Accommodation

Accommodation refers to the opportunity for a person to act a certain way offline, but have a different persona when it comes to their behaviors and activities online (Hertlein & Stevenson, 2010). As mentioned earlier, research conducted by Cooper et al. (2004) found the Internet is used to satisfy one's wants and needs when they do not believe they can get those needs met offline as in some research citing men seeking sexual connection with people of a similar-gender online, which may be an example of and related to using the Internet to approximate real-world situations. Such an activity, however, may be evidence of the concept of accommodation in that it is likely these men feel constrained to participate in these sexual activities in their offline lives.

This was similar to the findings of an earlier study on men who have sex with men, where the Internet was found to provide a way to experiment with having sex with someone of a similar-gender without having to identify as gay (Tikkanen & Ross, 2003). This desire to act in a certain way and the inability to do so create a conflict between one's ideal and real self (Higgins, 1987), leading to the exhibiting of incongruous behavior (Ben-Ze'ev, 2004). According to Hertlein and Stevenson (2010): "Many people feel the need for a secret life because they perceive their lives as rule-driven, confined, or constrained. Further, there are many who have the ability to risk or desire to seek out sensations that are now living routine (and by their report, 'boring' lives). The Internet provides greater opportunity for one to act a certain way in 'real time' but have a different persona when it comes to online behavior and activities, especially when there are no outward or obvious signs of this other, seemingly contradictory persona" (n.p.).

The crux of accommodation (in comparison to the previously mentioned ecological elements) is the distinction between one's "real" versus "ought" self as identified by Higgins (1987). Terrance and N'ysha, a Black American, mixed gender and sexual orientation couple in their 30s, came to treatment to improve the communication in their relationship. Over time, it became apparent that one of the issues in the relationship was N'ysha's report that they did not receive the same consideration from Terrance that he used to interact with his previous partner. N'ysha indicated that they felt that Terrance was "two different people"—with his previous partner he was compassionate, respectful, and complimentary, which N'ysha could see from his past social media posts, for instance. With themselves, however, he was short, business-like, and somehow detached, which N'ysha both experienced in his offline communication exchanges and saw in his displays of their relationship on social media. This difference in interaction left them feeling as if they were "second place," a feeling that they wanted to resolve. The concept that people can construct their communication in ways consistent with a view of themselves they prefer rather than whom they really are is defined as accommodation (Hertlein & Stevenson, 2010) and essentially refers to the Internet being another way in which people can portray themselves to be one way while really being another way.

Accommodation may not be a vulnerability for all relationships. The extent to which it enhances or detracts from a couple's relationship is largely dependent on the extent to which each individual has a discrepancy between their real self and their ought self (Higgins, 1987; see Table 7.3).

Table 7.3 Implications for Levels of Accommodation

	Match Between Real and Ideal Self	Partner B	
		Discrepancy	Similarity
Partner A	Discrepancy	• Significant challenges to emotional intimacy and relating. • Online communication may create confusion since both individuals are different online than they are offline.	• Partner B may experience difficulty trusting Partner A's behavior, depending on the level of discrepancy. • Preference in communication (online or offline) may depend on circumstances.
	Similarity	• Partner A may experience difficulty trusting Partner B's behavior, depending on the level of discrepancy. • Preference in communication (online or offline) may depend on circumstances.	• Couple will experience satisfying relationship both online and offline. • Intimacy levels will grow more quickly and deeply than in the other couple forms because online communication is used as an adjunct to the relationship and a way to continue to experience one another. • Self-disclosure online supports relationship development offline

For example, in relationships where there is not observed discrepancy in real versus ought self, the implication is that the relationship would be enhanced by electronic technologies. Couples would find more opportunities for interactions that are based on building emotional connections as well as building closeness through more frequent interactions. These couples learn to trust and be vulnerable to one another in any context, both online and offline. In other words, what you see is what you get with each partner in the relationship. In a study of LGB individuals in partnered relationships a high degree of congruity between one's online and offline self was reported. When the participants were asked if their online self was similar to their real-world self the majority reported that it was to a somewhat or high degree, and that their partners and non-partners were mostly aware of their online self (Twist, Bergdall et al., 2017).

Alternatively, a relationship in which partners experience a discrepancy between their real and ought self is on the opposite end of the accommodation continuum and is more complex. One element of the complexity deals with the manner in which the computer is used to express oneself. In most circumstances, it is the case where people who use the computer find it is a suitable mechanism through which they can express their true selves when they feel constrained in their day-to-day offline lives. One partner in a relationship may feel more security in their ability to express themselves in ways that they would not normally. Examples of this can be found in virtually every news story or posting online that allows space for people to post opinions and feedback; comments tend to turn to personal attacks on others very quickly. One of these might occur under the concept of anonymity discussed earlier as it is easier to comment negatively on something when that feedback cannot directly be associated with you. Part of this, however, is also reflective of the concept of accommodation—there are things that people really feel but that are not appropriate to express in their day-to-day offline lives.

A final type of relationship is one where a partner experiences the discrepancy with their online and offline lives and another partner is more similar and therefore relatively consistent. This dynamic in a couple can cause conflict because of difficulty in understanding another's perspective and the damage to the perception of trust in the relationship. The case of Reid and Toni, a mixed-race, middle-class, mixed sexual orientation, differing-gender couple from the Midwestern US, exemplifies this. Reid and Toni came to treatment indicating Toni had discovered Reid's online communications with a woman in another country. Most of the emails were characterized by graphic sexual content, description of particular sexual activities (such as including other men in sexual interactions), and other behaviors that Toni had never known were of interest to Reid. Toni was sad and angry that Reid positioned himself to be one way to others online and acted differently with her offline. In short, the computer allowed him to express what Toni came to believe as his true desires, while he acted in a way that was socially prescribed in his day-to-day life with her. In addition to the breakdown of trust in the couple relationship, Toni's individual psyche was also damaged. She came to see herself as someone whose decisions could not be trusted and found herself waiting for the other shoe to drop with Reid. The end result was impairment to her self-esteem and a pronounced amount of shame, which prevented her from seeking the social support to get through the relationship problems she would have otherwise used.

"I Didn't Technically Touch Them So It Doesn't Count": Ambiguity

Relational Ambiguity

Ambiguity is another element related to technology and new media creating specific issues in couple relationships. This concept refers to one of two types: relational ambiguity and technological ambiguity (Hertlein & Blumer, 2013). Relational ambiguity is any ambiguity around the evaluation of one's online behavior in regards to one's relationship. In many cases, members of a couple disagree on the valence of a behavior—that is, whether specific behavior occurring in the relationship related to the usage of Internet technologies is helpful, harmful, or neutral to the relationship. It is often the case that a partner participating in the behavior views it as neutral or positive, while another partner evaluating it from a distance views it as neutral or harmful. The greater the degree to which a behavior is defined ambiguously in the couple's relationship, the greater the degree of harm and the greater the potential for a disruption to the couple's intimacy processes.

One of the things most striking about the notion of relational ambiguity is exactly how many behaviors are ambiguous in the couple's contract. In days prior to new media's insertion in everyday life, couples were pretty clear on what, for example, constituted infidelity: intimate physical contact with a person other than one's primary partner (Thompson, 1984). Emily Brown (1991), a renowned scholar on infidelity, was among the first to acknowledge the potential of emotional infidelity to soon emerge in relationships. In fact, the emotional component of infidelity (either online or offline) is recognized by couple and relationship scholars (see, for example, Drigotas, Safstrom, & Gentilia, 1999). The advancements in technology, however, have increased the number of behaviors whose valence is quite ambiguous. We now have to make more decisions about what behaviors constitute appropriate behavior in the relationship and what behaviors cross the line. Despite the increasing amount of ambiguous online behavior, couples meeting today seem to fare no better at organizing conversations to either acknowledge or resolve the ambiguity prior to establishing a commitment with one another than couples who have committed together decades ago. For example, Ericka and Duane, of working-class Southeastern US backgrounds, both in their late 20s and heterosexual, sought premarital therapy five months prior to their wedding. The couple met through mutual friends and had spent approximately three years prior to becoming engaged, living together for the last two years. The conversations that emerged over the course of their premarital therapy revealed no areas where the couple seemed to have any problematic differences in opinion that would warrant further treatment or attention. Yet when the therapist introduced the area of infidelity and the definition as it relates to appropriate online behavior and boundaries in the relationship, the couple looked perplexed at one another and indicated they had not even thought about what those behaviors might entail. As the conversation unfolded, it became clear each had their own idea about how Internet infidelity would be conceptualized. The therapist assigned the couple to discuss the contract with one another over the week and return with some agreement on this element of their relationship contract.

It is not only the couples who have a recent commitment that are not establishing the definitions for appropriate online behavior in their relationship. Those who have had established relationships for some time generally do not revisit the original contracts they had with one another prior to the explosion of electronically based communication. In fact, many couples only revisit what would constitute appropriate behavior after there is some disagreement about the valuation of a particular behavior.

There are likely several reasons why couples, regardless of duration in their relationship, experience challenges with regard to establishing clarity with their relational contract. The relational contract is defined "as a set of implicit expectations that partners have concerning how they will define the relationship and interact with one another" (Birchler, Doumas, & Fals-Stewart, 1999, p. 256). First, the rapid development of software, systems, websites, and ways to communicate through electronic channels make it difficult to plan for every possible contingency within a relationship. For example, one cannot predict the amount of ways in which one might be contacted through the Internet by phone by others and what forms of interaction initiated by others will enter the couple's life. Second, this is further compounded by the fact that evidence seems to indicate that couples do not seem to address contracts within their relationships (Birchler et al., 1999). The inattention to the relational contract can result in differences in expectations and discord.

The most common issues related to relational ambiguity revolve around elements of infidelity: namely, what are the electronic behaviors that constitute infidelity in a relationship? Some couples define infidelity solely as physical contact with another person outside of the primary relationship. When both partners hold this definition, the problems of whether or not someone cheated are relatively clear, and any discord in couples seems to revolve around the betrayed partner claiming their partner participated in physical activity with another person outside the boundary of the relationship and the partner accused of such an activity denying there was any physical contact. Sal and Heather, a heterosexual, Latin American couple from the central region of the US, presented in treatment as a classic example of this phenomenon. Heather had discovered used condoms in their bedroom upon her return from a business trip. When she confronted Sal about her findings, he denied any involvement with someone else and claimed that he did not know how they got there.

In today's relationships, however, the clarity of the definition of infidelity behavior becomes murky when couples have to consider and agree upon the behaviors constituting infidelity. For instance, in the context of the current wave of digisexuailty there is a good deal of relational ambiguity around what constitutes cheating (McArthur & Twist, 2017). Researchers have found that half of partnered heterosexual adults report that they believe watching online pornography counted as cheating, while the other half did not (Thompson & O'Sullivan, 2016). With more potential problematic behaviors, the likelihood each partner will agree on each behavior is reduced. The potential for such an increase in problematic behaviors may only increase going into this next wave of digisexualities. When respondents in a YouGov (2013) poll answered whether they thought a person in a committed relationship having sex with a robot would constitute cheating, a little less than half believed that it would, about a quarter were unsure, and almost a third believed it would not constitute cheating. This demonstrates an ongoing issue of relational ambiguity for couples on what constitutes infidelity in the context of experiences with technology.

With more potential problematic behaviors, the likelihood each partner will agree on each behavior is reduced. In these cases, the discord in couples can revolve around a partner accusing another of a behavior and the other denying, both partners agreeing that the behavior occurred but disagreeing about whether it constituted infidelity, or situations where both are true. For example, Gracia made an appointment for her and her husband, David (both white, heterosexual, middle-class, Midwestern, and in their 50s), to treat his infidelity. Gracia viewed his interactions with other women online as a breach in their relational contract. David confirmed he did talk to other women online, but indicated these were friends from high school with whom he did not have nor did he ever have any romantic interest or history. David viewed Gracia as having changed the rules in the contract and was angry that she did not trust him. In this case, the couple's discord was less around the denial of events and more about the ambiguity around what constitutes stepping out of the relationship. In some cases, the definition of infidelity can include the viewing of pornography by one partner. While pornography has been around for a long time, in the past people viewing pornographic magazines did not seem to be classified as cheating to the extent that viewing pornography online is viewed today. First, pornography online has the ability to be interactive, where magazines or movies did not have that same quality. Advances in technologies such as live webcams may make the pornography more real and, therefore, more of a threat.

Another striking characteristic of relational ambiguity with regard to technology and behavior in couple relationships is that ambiguity of the valuation of online behavior seems to occur with approximately the same frequency in online relationships as in offline relationships. Kara and Mike, both in their 40s, biracial, middle-class, and heterosexual, each had a pattern of participating in serially monogamous relationships for years that eventually fizzled out. They were both ready to find a person with whom to spend the rest of their life. They met each other online through a dating website and participated in a long-distance relationship for approximately a year and a half. The relationship started relatively slowly, but once clarification was made to be exclusively involved with one another, the couple developed rules around the frequency of their online contact with one another. They did not, however, include a discussion of rules around permissible online behavior. When Mike observed certain activity on Kara's Facebook account from another, he categorized such behavior as a breach of the relationship contract; Kara, on the other hand, held the position that rules around this behavior were never part of the contract, and had she known about it, she would have done more to be clear with her friends about how to appropriately interact with her online.

This begs the question as to why couples whose relationships are conducted primarily online do not discuss the rules of the relationship with regard to online behavior, despite the fact this is their primary mode of interaction with one another. One reason could be the tentative nature of communication facilitated online. In the case of Kara and Mike, a disagreement about rules with regard to online behavior could have three potential negative consequences. One might be that either Kara or Mike might agree there are rules around the behavior but operate independent of those rules outside of the awareness of the other. Second, it might lead to the development of an argument between Kara and Mike, a couple who very much wants the relationship to be long lasting, but is also physically distant from one another. In this setting, Kara may fear that it is easier for Mike to end communication with her by walking away from the computer or ignoring texts/phone calls about the issue, a task more difficult to do when couples live in the same space. If she is not willing to take that risk, she may not be willing to start the conversation in the first place. A third consequence might be the development of a discussion lacking authenticity on the part of each partner. As described earlier in this chapter, one of the characteristics of online communication is that the user can type, write, backspace, and essentially alter their appearance. The sense of everydayness and spontaneity is lost as people think and organize what they want to say rather than being themselves and letting their expression show. In either case, the conversation may be avoided because of the lack of power one partner may feel by being connected only by a keyboard.

Technological Ambiguity

Another way ambiguity plays out in a relationship is with regard to the knowledge base of electronically based communication. Emoticons and abbreviations have certain meanings that are generally understood by users of these technologies to have particular meanings. It is also the case, however, many users might not be clear on what symbols, emoticons, or abbreviations stand for what. This ambiguity creates interesting scenarios for couple relationships as well. When I (KH) began sending instant messages, I began using this emoticon: ": x." I was under the impression that it was someone making a sick face, meaning "yuk." I used this fairly often in my communication with others online, men and women both, when something being discussed was not pleasant, such as a poor work schedule, difficulties within relationships, or other routine complaints. After about one and a half years, my husband texted me using that emoticon. Because we were not discussing anything unpleasant at the time, his "yuk" face seemed out of context. I asked him why he inserted a "yuk" face. He replied "That's not a yuk face. That means a kiss." I was shocked. I confessed I had been using it as a "yuk" face for nearly two years with my texting companions, both men and women. He laughed and said, "Well, now you know." While my husband was very calm and trusted that I was genuine in my lack of information about usage of symbols, there are many couples for whom the ambiguity around the use of symbols is dismissed as one partner clearly wanting to start up relationships with other people or can even count as evidence of cheating. In these cases, the couple has to rely on the trust that has already been built in the relationship as a way to determine whether there is a need for further exploration or whether the lack of clarity in using symbols is just one more example of one's lack of commitment to the relationship.

Technological ambiguity may also be characterized by lack of knowledge about the capabilities of technology and new media. For example, there may be software or phone applications used by one person to discreetly conceal one's activities. One's partner may be less familiar with such applications and therefore not be able to appropriately appraise a situation as problematic. Finally, technological ambiguity also frequently occurs in the context of text-based exchanges, as it can be difficult to decipher the tone and content of such messages as one still often lacks the ability to see the clear physicality of the intentions and emotions behind the messages. Such technological ambiguity often leads to more miscommunications and arguments via such media like texting than occurs offline, regardless of the gender or sexual orientations of the persons involved in the partnered relationship (Twist, Bergdall et al., 2017).

Accountability

One of the primary issues associated with technology in intimate relationships is the issue of accountability. This issue is one of the few that transcends various topical areas but may still be a major player in interactions. Accountability is a key issue in relationship maintenance. As couples struggle to navigate the use of power within the relationship, each individual has to take accountability for their own behavior. Though little has been written about accountability in clinical literature, accountability has been identified as critical in infidelity treatment (Bird, Butler, & Fife, 2007).

To some degree, accountability relies on one being aware of their own online behavior. Researchers to date have only focused on awareness of technology usage in adolescents (Hundley & Shyles, 2010). Hundley and

Shyles (2010) found teens experienced a high degree of temporal displacement while using technological devices—meaning that they were frequently not aware of the amount of time spent with their technology. In its application to technology in couples, accountability is an issue on two main levels. First, each member of the couple is accountable for their own behavior related to using electronically based communication to interact with others outside of their relationship. This includes regulation of whom each partner is contacting via outgoing messages as well as managing incoming contacts. Second, accountability also applies to people's online behavior regarding interactions with their partner. According to Postmes, Spears, and Lea (1998), "The notion that [computer-mediated communication] gives people a strategic freedom to express themselves because they are unaccountable has been identified as the cause of an ostensible increase in antinormative behavior in [computer-mediated communication] compared to face-to-face conditions" (p. 694). In other words, the amount of people you can communicate with relates to the sense of limited accountability.

A mixed-class, mixed-race, mixed-age, heterosexual couple, Hayden (42 years old) and Lucille (27 years old), were in couples therapy mainly because Hayden was angry at her for some of the conversations she had with a third party online. During the course of the conversation, it emerged that he had logged onto her email without her knowledge or permission, a clear violation of their relational contract. Such behavior complicates a case because those who place themselves in the position of monitoring their partner often assert the end justifies the means. Further, in cases where infidelity is discovered, both the couple and therapist experience the dilemma of knowing the partner logging into accounts did breach the trust, but are forced to attend to the more egregious issue of the sense of betrayal emerging from the problematic behavior. Take, for example, Margaret and Dan, a working-class, white, heterosexual couple who came to therapy because Margaret was distressed by her husband's participation in flirtatious chats with a co-worker and began monitoring his email communications. A conversation about accountability in violating the relationship contract goes by the wayside in order to manage the fidelity issue. Another dimension of the accountability problem is the decision around the degree to which a partner is required to report their behavior to a partner. It is not unusual for couples to have inconsistencies with regard to what rules around password usage they should implement in their relationships.

The accountability of one's behavior shifts, however, when there has been a breach of the relationship contract. A partner may feel the need to monitor another partner's interactions, which can have pronounced implications for the couple. In many ways, the desire to observe and monitor one's behavior while placing the accountability for such action on another party is adaptive and protective. Typically, this dynamic emerges in a relationship where one party has been hurt or betrayed by another's online activities and believes their partner's behavior warrants monitoring. For example, Angie and Zenn, a genderqueer, lesbian, mixed-race, middle-class, Northeastern US couple, presented to therapy, because Angie had logged onto Zenn's Facebook account to ensure they were not maintaining communication with a woman for whom they had previously expressed a strong level of attraction, despite their assurances that all communication had stopped. In other cases, this adaptive behavior may also be central to creating more issues for couples. In Angie's case, she and her partner had a very clear agreement about the nature through which Zenn would share their online activities with her—and her logging onto their accounts without their knowledge was not one of them. The pair had agreed to be forthcoming with specific and potentially contentious issues and to have the flexibility in their relationship to pose questions to one another appropriately. While Angie knew that her secretly logging into accounts would result in the termination of the relationship per her partner, her fear about their online activities, its consequences, and what meaning they gave it prevented her from adhering to her relationship agreement. The bottom line is that inattention to accountability may create an environment ripe for the development of a problematic power struggle in the couple's relationship, which can further contribute to relational discord. In short, just because you can do something does not necessarily mean you should.

The Couple and Family Technology Framework in Action

The characteristics of the Internet described earlier—acceptability, accessibility, affordability, anonymity, approximation, accommodation, ambiguity, and accountability—are one piece of a three-piece framework that, together, makes up the Couple and Family Technology framework. Together, these items make up the ecological elements of the framework.

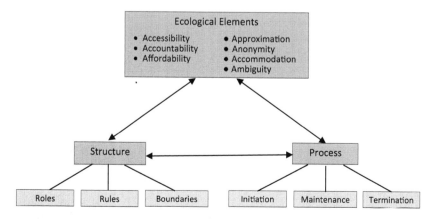

Figure 7.1 Couple and Family Technology Framework

In Chapters 8 and 9, we will present how the other entities (structure and process) are driven by these factors and how those changes to the structure and process of families affect couples and families. Before we move on, however, we are going to explore how some of these characteristics of the Internet have been evaluated in the contribution to challenges in couple and family life.

One of the earliest applications of the Couple and Family Technology (CFT) framework is to relationships where at least one person has online gaming problems (Hertlein & Blumer, 2013). This framework has been applied in this context to both couples and youth in a family system (Curtis, Phenix, Munoz, & Hertlein, 2017). With regard to couples and video gaming, Hawkins and Hertlein (2013) discuss how accessibility, affordability, and other characteristics of the Internet affect relationship roles. Specifically, roles can be affected through how those who play may be perceived as neglecting household duties/obligations, placing on another person in the couplehood a position of being that of a parent (telling the partner what to do) and the game-playing partner a position of being like a child, who is disobeying or not getting chores done. Boundaries and rules also are compromised because of the accessibility and affordability of these machines, as well as accommodation. Online games (particularly massively multiplayer online role-playing games or MMORPGs) allow a user to be whomever they wish to be—and they can use these games to accommodate whom they cannot be in their offline lives. Further, the accommodation may also cause issues with personality when one can be more aggressive online and then apply or transfer that behavior offline (Hawkins & Hertlein, 2013). In gaming and youth, Curtis et al. (2017) propose using the CFT framework to design interventions. For example, accessibility and affordability mean that youth can access gaming development and can create unique opportunities for families and children to design interventions and games in which they have a vested interest. Accommodation can be integrated with token economies to gain a child's investment in the behavior change process.

A second application of the CFT framework is in the case of adopted families (Black, Moyer, & Goldberg, 2016). In this case, people can use the accessibility of the Internet and its affordability to reach out to make connections with biological family members. For example, adoptive families can approximate connections with distant family members through reaching out via social media as they do with already existing relationships with their adoptive family. Further, the accessibility of others on the Internet may have implications for open adoptions, but also for closed adoptions when the adopted child searches for their biological parent despite the status of the adoption. In fact, about one-fifth of adoptive families had engaged in passive contact with birth family members and had established that contact through the accessibility provided by the Internet (Black et al., 2016). Further, because of the anonymity of the Internet, those doing the searching do not have to disclose their identity.

A third application of the CFT framework is in cases of sexual dysfunction where there is an Internet or online component. For example, approximation contributes to dysfunction in that we have an opportunity to play out what we wish to do online and not address what we need or want with our partners, thus compromising intimacy. Another element, accessibility, may contribute to dysfunction in that it may be a breeding ground for the development of behavioral compulsions, including the compulsive use of pornography. Finally, users can use the affordability, approximation, and accessibility of the Internet to find precisely what turns them on—without ever having to negotiate that with their partner (Hertlein, Nakamura, Arguello, & Langin, 2017).

A fourth application of the CFT framework is fostering improved scholarly and clinical attention to experiences of sexual orientation of minority individuals and relationships in online environments. Each of the ecological elements (detailed earlier) of the CFT framework have been researched in the context of LGB relationships, as well as clinically explored in the context of people with digisexual identities. In the case of the element of acceptability, there is research that has looked at comparisons between LGB and heterosexual relationships, examining how this element is perceived online across these relationships (Hertlein, Shadid, & Steelman, 2015).

Last but not least, one final application of the framework is in the area of couples and boundary-crossing online (Norton, Baptist, & Hogan, 2018). In this investigation, the authors evaluated actor-effects to determine the veracity of the CFT framework. In short, while acceptability does not play a direct role in relationship satisfaction, it may be because Internet activities are largely individual. Then when one's partner asks for information about online activities, such a request feels intrusive (as this is not acceptable since the Internet is generally regarded as a private activity) and, therefore, reduces relationship satisfaction (Norton et al., 2018). This is one of the first studies that lends preliminary evidence supporting the CFT framework (Hertlein & Blumer, 2013).

Conclusion

In this chapter, we presented our theoretical framework, the Couple and Family Technology (CFT) framework (Hertlein, 2012; Hertlein & Blumer, 2013), which we believe is the most useful way of conceptualizing and relatedly addressing technology in relationships. In doing so, we also provided a brief overview of several other frameworks that have been used in attempting to explain the interaction between technology and users. We also began to explain the different components of the CFT framework, with significant attention to the technology-based ecological elements. This framework is applicable to diverse family forms and is highly flexible with regard to understanding the impact of technology on relationships without rendering a decision about whether that impact is positive or negative—leaving the decision to the family.

References

Adams, W. L. (2008). *UK couple to divorce over affair on second life*. Retrieved from www.time.com/time/world/article/0,8599,1859231,00.html

Albright, J. (2008). Sex in America online: An exploration of sex, marital status, and sexual identity in Internet sex seeking and its impacts. *Journal of Sex Research, 45*(2), 175–186. doi:10.1080/00224490801987481

Altman, I., & Taylor, D. A. (1973). *Social penetration: The development of interpersonal relationships*. Oxford, UK: Holt, Rinehart & Winston.

Applegate, E., Palmier-Claus, J., Machin, M., Sanders, C., Ainsworth, J., & Lewis, S. (2014). Poster #T10 acceptability and feasibility of extended use of mobile phone technology to assess psychotic symptoms in DSM-IV schizophrenia patients. *Schizophrenia Research, 153*, S292.

Atwater, L. (1979). Getting involved: Women's first transition to extramarital sex. *Alternative Lifestyles, 2*, 33–68. doi:10.1007/bf01083662

Bacigalupe, G., & Lambe, S. (2011). Virtual intimacy: Information communication technologies and transnational families in therapy. *Family Process, 50*(1) 12–26. doi:10.1111/j.1545-5300.2010.01343.

Badhwar, N. K. (2009). The Milgram experiments, learned helplessness, and character traits. *The Journal of Ethics: An International Philosophical Review, 13*, 257–289. doi:10.1007/s10892-009-9052-4

Bakardjieva, M. (2005). Domestication running wild. From the moral economy of the household to the mores of culture. In T. Berker, M. Hartmann, Y. Punie, & K. Ward (Eds.), *Domestication of media and technologies* (pp. 62–79). Maidenhead: Open University Press.

Ben-Ze'ev, A. (2004). *Love online: Emotions on the Internet*. New York, NY: Cambridge University Press.

Berger, P. L., & Kellner, H. (1970). Marriage and the construction of reality. In H. Dreitzel (Ed.), *Recent Sociology, No. 2*. New York, NY: Macmillan.

Birchler, G. R., Doumas, D. M., & Fals-Stewart, W. S. (1999). The seven Cs: A behavioral systems framework for evaluating marital distress. *The Family Journal, 7*, 253–264. doi:10.1177/1066480799073009

Bird, M. H., Butler, M. H., & Fife, S. T. (2007). The process of couple healing following infidelity: A qualitative study. *Journal of Couple & Relationship Therapy, 6*(4), 1–25. doi:10.1300/J398v06n04_01

Black, K. A., Moyer, A. M., & Goldberg, A. E. (2016). From face-to-face to Facebook: The role of technology and social media in adoptive family relationships with birth family members. *Adoption Quarterly, 19*(4), 307–332. doi:10.1080/10926755.2016.1217575

Blumenfeld, W. J., & Cooper, R. M. (2010). LGBT and allied youth responses to cyberbullying: Policy implications. *International Journal of Critical Pedagogy, 3*(1), 114–133.

Blumler, J. G., & Katz, E. (Eds.). (1974). The uses of mass communications: Current perspectives on gratifications research. Beverly Hills, CA: Sage.

Brody, N., Lefebvre, L., & Blackburn, K. (2016). Social networking site behaviors across the relational lifespan: Measurement and association with relationship escalation and de-escalation. *Social Media Society, 2*(4), 1–16. doi:0.1177/2056305116680004

Brown, E. M. (1991). *Patterns of infidelity and their treatment*. New York, NY: Brunner/Mazel.

Burton-Jones, A., & Hubona, G. S. (2006). The mediation of external variables in the technology acceptance model. *Information & Management, 43*(6), 706–717. doi:10.1016/j.im.2006.03.007

Buunk, B. (1980). Extramarital sex in the Netherlands: Motivation in social and marital context. *Alternative Lifestyles, 3*, 11–39. doi:10.1007/bf01083027

Campbell, S. W., & Ling, R. (2009). Effects of mobile communication. In J. Bryant & M. B. Oliver (Eds.), *Media effects: Advances in theory and research* (3rd ed., pp. 592–606). New York, NY: Taylor and Francis.

Conway, J., Noë, N., Stulp, G., & Pollet, T. (2015). Finding your soulmate: Homosexual and heterosexual age preferences in online dating. *Personal Relationships, 22*(4), 666–678. doi:10.1111/pere.12102

Cooper, A. (2002). *Sex and the Internet: A guidebook for clinicians.* New York, NY: Brunner-Routledge.

Cooper, A., Delmonico, D. L., & Burg, R. (2000). Cybersex users, abusers, and compulsives: New findings and implications. *Sexual Addiction & Compulsivity, 7*(1–2), 5–29. doi:10.1080/10720160008400205

Cooper, A., Galbreath, N., & Becker, M. A. (2004). Sex on the Internet: Furthering our understanding of men with online sexual problems. *Psychology of Addictive Behaviors, 18*(3), 223–230. doi:10.1037/0893-164X.18.3.223

Curtis, M., Phenix, M., Munoz, M., & Hertlein, K. (2017). Video game therapy: Application of the couple and family technology framework. *Contemporary Family Therapy, 39*(2), 112–120. doi:10.1007/s10591-017-9409-y

Daft, R. L., & Lengel, R. H. (1984). Information richness: A new approach to managerial behavior and organizational design. In L. L. Cummings & B. M. Staw (Eds.), *Research in organizational behavior 6* (pp. 191–233). Homewood, IL: JAI Press.

Davis, F. D. (1989). Perceived usefulness, perceived ease of use, and user acceptance of information technology. *MIS Quarterly, 13*(3), 319. doi:10.2307/249008

Delmonico, D. L. (1997). Cybersex: High tech sex addiction. *Sexual Addiction & Compulsivity, 4*(2), 159–167. doi:10.1080/10720169708400139

Drigotas, S. M., Safstrom, C. A., & Gentilia, T. (1999). An investment model prediction of dating infidelity. *Journal of Personality and Social Psychology, 77*(3), 509–524. doi:10.1037//0022-3514.77.3.509

Dubrovsky, J., Kiesler, S., & Sethna, B. (1991). The equalization phenomenon: Status effects in computer-mediated and face-to-face decision-making groups. *Human—Computer Interaction, 6*(2), 119–146. doi:10.1207/s15327051hci0602_2

Funk, C., Kennedy, B., & Sciupac, E. (July 2016). *U.S. public wary of biomedical technologies to "enhance" human abilities: Americans are more worried than enthusiastic about using gene editing, brain chip implants, and synthetic blood to change human capabilities.* PEW Research Center; Information & Technology. Retrieved March 1, 2019, from http://www.pewinternet.org/wp-content/uploads/sites/9/2016/07/PS_2016.07.26_Human-Enhancement-Survey_FINAL.pdf

Granic, I., Dishion, T., J., & Hollenstein, T. (2003). The family ecology of adolescence: A dynamic systems perspective on normative development. In G. R. Adams & M. D. Berzonsky (Eds.), *Blackwell Handbook of adolescence* (pp. 60–91). Hoboken, NJ: Blackwell Publishing.

Grist, R., Porter, J., & Stallard, P. (2018). Acceptability, use, and safety of a mobile phone app (blueice) for young people who self-harm: Qualitative study of service users' experience. *JMIR Mental Health, 5*(1), e16. doi:10.2196/mental.8779

Haddon, L. (2006). The contribution of domestication research to in-home computing and media consumption. *The Information Society, 22*, 195–203. doi:10.1080/01972240600791325

Haines, R., & Mann, J. E. C. (2011). A new perspective on deindividuation via computer-mediated communication. *European Journal of Information Systems, 20*(2), 156–167. doi:10.1057/ejis.2010.70

Hawkins, B., & Hertlein, K. (2013). Treatment strategies for online role-playing gaming problems in couples. *Journal of Couple & Relationship Therapy, 12*(2), 150–167. doi:10.1080/15332691.2013.779100

Hertlein, K. M. (2012). Digital dwelling: Technology in couple and family relationships. *Family Relations, 61*(3), 374–387. doi:10.1111/j.1741-3729.2012.00702.x

Hertlein, K. M., & Blumer, M. L. (2013). *The couple and family technology framework: Intimate relationships in a digital age.* New York, NY: Routledge

Hertlein, K. M., Nakamura, S., Arguello, P., & Langin, K. (2017). Sext-ual healing: Application of the couple and family technology framework to cases of sexual dysfunction. *Sexual and Relationship Therapy, 32*(3–4), 345–353. doi:10.1080/14681994.2017.1397949

Hertlein, K. M., & Piercy, F. P. (2008). Therapists' assessment and treatment of Internet infidelity cases. *Journal of Marital & Family Therapy, 34*(4), 481–497. doi:10.1111/j.1752-0606.2008.00090.x

Hertlein, K. M., & Sendak, S. K. (2007, March). *Love "Bytes": Internet infidelity and the meaning of intimacy in computer-mediated relationships.* Paper presented at the Annual Conference of Persons, Intimacy, and Love, Salzburg, Austria.

Hertlein, K. M., Shadid, C., & Steelman, S. M. (2015). Exploring perceptions of acceptability of sexting in same-sex, bisexual, heterosexual relationships and communities. *Journal of Couple & Relationship Therapy, 14*, 342–357. doi: 10.1080/15332691.2014.960547

Hertlein, K. M., & Stevenson, A. (2010). The seven "As" contributing to Internet-related intimacy problems: A literature review. *Cyberpsychology: Journal of Psychosocial Research on Cyberspace, 4*(1). Retrieved November 10, 2012, from http://cyberpsychology.eu/view.php?cisloclanku=2010050202&article=3

Higgins, E. (1987). Self-discrepancy: A theory relating self and affect. *Psychological Review, 94*(3), 319–340. doi:10.1037/0033-295X.94.3.319

Hundley, H. L., & Shyles, L. (2010). US teenagers' perceptions and awareness of digital technology: A focus group approach. *New Media & Society, 12*(3), 417–433. doi:10.1177/1461444809342558

Hynes, D., & Rommes, E. (2005). 'Fitting the Internet into our lives': IT courses for disadvantaged users. In T. Berker, Y. Punie, & M. Hartmann (Eds.), *Domestication of media and technology.* Berkshire, UK: McGraw-Hill Education.

Irwin, T., Nordstrom, S., & Pyra, M. (2012). O326 acceptability of mobile phone technology for tracking cervical cancer in rural Guatemala. *International Journal of Gynecology & Obstetrics, 119*, S375–S376.

Johnson, H. (1971). The structural-functional theory of family and kinship. *Journal of Comparative Studies, 2*, 133–144. doi:10.1016/s0020-7292(12)60756-5

King, S. A. (1999). Internet gambling and pornography: Illustrative examples of psychological consequences of communication anarchy. *Cyberpsychology & Behavior, 2*, 175–193.

King, W. R., & He, J. (2006). A meta-analysis of the technology acceptance model. *Information & Management, 43*(6), 740–755. doi:10.1016/j.im.2006.05.003

Lanigan, J. D., Bold, M., & Chenoweth, L. (2009). Computers in the family context: Perceived impact on family time and relationships. *Family Science Review*, *14*(1), 16–32.

Lasser, J., & Tharinger, Dr. (2003). Visibility management in school and beyond: A qualitative study of gay, lesbian, bisexual youth. *Journal of Adolescence*, *26*(2), 233–244.

Levine, J. A., Cohen, S., Harkin, P., Guydish, J., Sorensen, J., & Masson, C. L. (2015). Acceptability of a mobile phone based Hepatitis C intervention. *Drug and Alcohol Dependence*, *156*, e127. doi:10.1016/j.drugalcdep.2015.07.349

Lu, J., Yu, C. S., Liu, C., & Yao, J. E. (2003). Technology acceptance model for wireless Internet. *Internet Research*, *13*(3), 206–222. doi:10.1108/10662240310478222

Madden, M., & Lenhart, A. (2006). *Online dating*. Pew Internet and American Life Project. Retrieved December 4, 2012, from http://pewInternet.org/Reports/2006/Online-Dating.aspx

McArthur, N., & Twist, M. L. C. (2017). The rise of digisexuality: Therapeutic challenges and possibilities. *Sexual and Relationship Therapy*, *32*(3/4), 334–344.

McKenna, K. Y, Green, A., & Gleason, M. (2002). Relationship formation on the Internet: What's the big attraction? *Journal of Social Issues*, *58*, 9–31. doi:10.1234/12345678

Mileham, B. L. (2007). Online infidelity in Internet chat rooms: An ethnographic exploration. *Computers in Human Behavior*, *23*(1), 11–31. doi:10.4103/0019-5545.5829

Moscaritolo, A. (2013, October 21). *Online dating now more socially acceptable.* PCmag.com.

Norton, A. M., Baptist, J., & Hogan, B. (2018). Computer-mediated communication in intimate relationships: Associations of boundary crossing, intrusion, relationship satisfaction, and partner responsiveness. *Journal of Marital and Family Therapy*, *44*(1), 165–182. doi:10.1111/jmft.12246

Otieno, G., Githinji, S., Jones, C., Snow, R. W., Talisuna, A., & Zurovac, D. (2014). The feasibility, patterns of use and acceptability of using mobile phone text-messaging to improve treatment adherence and post-treatment review of children with uncomplicated malaria in western Kenya. *Malaria Journal*, *13*(1), 44. doi:10.1186/1475-2875-13-44

Postmes, T., Spears, R., & Lea, M. (1998). Breaching or building social boundaries? SIDE-effects of computer-mediated communication. *Communication Research*, *25*, 689–715. doi:10.1177/009365098025006006

Rabby, M., & Walther, J. B. (2002). Computer-mediated communication impacts on relationship formation and maintenance. In D. Canary & M. Dainton (Eds.), *Maintaining relationships through communication: Relational, contextual, and cultural variations* (pp. 141–162). Mahwah, NJ: Lawrence Erlbaum.

Raine, L., & Anderson, J. (2017). *The internet of things connectivity binge: What are the implications?* Pew Research Center. Retrieved from www.pewInternet.org/2017/06/06/the-Internet-of-things-connectivity-binge-what-are-the-implications

RealDoll. (2017). *RealDoll* [home page]. Retrieved from www.realdoll.com

Ross, M. W. (2005). Typing, doing and being: Sexuality and the Internet. *Journal of Sex Research*, *42*, 342–352. doi:10.1080/00224490509552290

Ross, M. & Kauth, M. (2002). Men who have sex with men, and the Internet: Emerging clinical issues and their management. In A. Cooper (Ed.), *Sex and the internet: A guidebook for clinicians*, 162. New York, NY: Brunner-Routledge.

Rymarczuk, R., & Derksen, M. (2014). Different spaces: Exploring Facebook as heterotopia. *First Monday, 19*(6). doi:10.5210/fm.v19i6.5006

Silverstone, R., Hirsch, E., & Morley, D. (1992). Information and communication technologies and the moral economy of the household. *Consuming Technologies*, 15–31. doi:10.1111/j.1460-2466.1994.tb00706.x

Spears, R., & Lea, M. (1994). Panacea or panopticon? The hidden power in computer-mediated communication. *Communication Research, 21*(4), 427–459. doi:10.1177/009365094021004001

Spears, R., Lea, M., Corneliussen, R., Postmes, T., & Haar, W. (2002). Computer-mediated communication as a channel for social resistance. *Small Group Research, 33*(5), 555–574. doi:10.1177/104649602237170

Sundberg, K., Langius [Langius-Eklöf], A., Blomberg, K., Isaksson, A., & Wengström, Y. (2013). Feasibility and acceptability of an interactive mobile phone application for early detection of patient reported symptom distress in prostate cancer. *European Journal of Cancer, 49*, S280.

Thompson, A. E., & O'Sullivan, L. F. (2016). I can but you can't: Inconsistencies in judgments of and experiences with infidelity. *Journal of Relationships Research, 7*. doi:10.1017/jrr.2016.1

Thompson, A. P. (1984). Emotional and sexual components of extramarital relations. *Journal of Marriage and Family, 46*(1), 35–42. doi:10.2307/351861

Tikkanen, R., & Ross, M. (2003). Technological tearoom trade: Characteristics of Swedish men visiting gay Internet chat rooms. *AIDS Education & Prevention, 15*(2), 122. doi:10.1521/aeap.15.3.122.23833

Treas, J., & Giesen, D. (2000). Sexual infidelity among married and cohabiting Americans. *Journal of Marriage and Family, 62*(1), 48–60. doi:10.1111/j.1741-3737.2000.00048.x

Twist, M. L. C., Belous, C. K., Maier, C. A., & Bergdall, M. K. (2017). Considering technology-based ecological elements in lesbian, gay, and bisexual partnered relationships. *Sexual and Relationship Therapy, 32*(3/4), 291–308.

Twist, M. L. C., Bergdall, M. K., Belous, C. K., & Maier, C. A. (2017). Electronic visibility management of lesbian, gay, and bisexual identities and relationships. *Journal of Couple and Relationship Therapy: Innovations in Clinical Educational Interventions, 16*(4), 271–285.

Watt, D., & White, J. M. (1999). Computers and the family life: A family development perspective. *Journal of Comparative Family Studies, 30*(1), 1–15.

Wehrenberg, M. (2018, December 13). *The new face of anxiety: Treating anxiety disorders in the age of texting, social media and 24/7 internet access*. PESI webinar.

Whitty, M. T. (2005). The realness of cybercheating: Men's and women's representations of unfaithful Internet relationships. *Social Science Computer Review, 23*(1), 57–67. doi:10.1177/0894439304271536

YouGov. (2013, February 23). *Omnibus poll*. Retrieved from http://big.assets.huffingtonpost.com/toplinesrobots.pdf

EIGHT

Strengthening Roles, Rules, and Boundaries

Introduction

As mentioned in the previous chapter, the Internet and new media change many things about our relationships. The characteristics of acceptability, affordability, accessibility, anonymity, approximation, accommodation, ambiguity, and accountability affect both the structure and processes of relationships. In this view, structure of relationships is defined as the roles, the rules, and the boundaries of relationships (Hertlein & Blumer, 2013). The accessibility, affordability, and acceptability of the pervasiveness of the Internet have led to a new term—the Internet of Things. The Internet of Things can make both positive and negative changes to the roles, rules, and boundaries of relationships.

> So not only will the trend toward greater connectivity of people and objects continue, it will continue to change boundaries and dynamics of all sorts—personal, social, moral, political . . . . The [Internet of Things] reality represents both huge opportunity and huge vulnerability. They go hand in hand.
>
> (Raine & Anderson, 2017, pp. 5–6)

The Internet of Things has evolved into an Internet of entities. In other words, as the reach of the Internet has expanded, so have the devices that touch our day-to-day life. The Internet shapes, for example, what rules we have in terms of interacting with each other and interacting with parties outside of our primary relationships. Some of this was already in the chapter on couples, where couples indicate that they need rules in their relationship, particularly on phone usage, but do not believe that they are willing to implement the rules in their own relationship. So what really does happen with the Internet and roles, rules, and boundaries? And how do we use what is good about the Internet to create a structure for couples and families that is going to be growth producing instead of hampering or pathological?

Roles

There are a few ways that the structure of relationships has shifted and been altered in the Internet of Things (see Figure 8.1). The structure affects both couple relationships as well as those between parent, child, or even extended family, and other relational systems. One of the things that dictates structure are the roles that we each hold. For example, in many couples, there may be prescribed gender roles that influence behavior. An example is when men may feel they have to initiate interactions. That is a gender-linked situation. Similarly, the role of a parent has implied certain tasks, activities, and set of rules. These rules might include ensuring that their children attend school, ensuring that they are physically present for their children, and ensuring that they care physically and emotionally for the young people in their charge.

When it comes to technology and the roles in couples and families, there is some debate as to who holds the position at the top of the hierarchy. As it pertains to couples, the previous chapter details how technological ambiguity contributes to a member of a relationship being in a higher position of power. The more one can navigate technology, the more they can engage in activities outside of their partner's awareness—either on their behalf or to track their partner. In one sense, the traditional roles

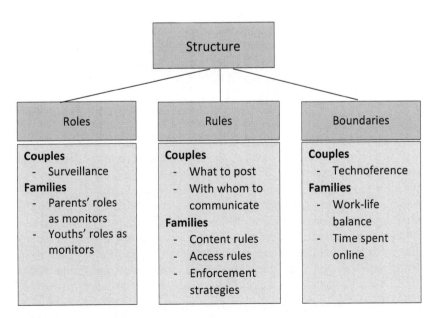

Figure 8.1 Relational Structure Areas Affected by Technology

of parent and child suggest that the parent is hierarchically higher than the child. This implies that they will be able to operate from a position of being the person who establishes the rules, because they know more. In the case of technology, however, at times these roles are reversed. Younger people may be more technologically competent as a consequence of their natural integration with technology at a young age, and therefore hold more power and have an ability to better dictate the rules related to phone usage—or more commonly find ways around the rules that have been put in place for their protection.

Rules

Rules in Couples

Relationships are defined and bounded by rules (Blevins, 1993). Rules in systems such as couples and families are manifested in the patterns of behaviors exhibited by members of a family and tend to give structure to how tasks are accomplished and emotions and values are expressed (Blevins, 1993). Rules dictate what behaviors are allowed, forbidden, and expected based on the context and roles (Caughlin, 2003). There are various types of rules in couple relationship typologies: two main types of rules include implicit and explicit rules (see Table 8.1). Implicit rules refer to rules where a couple makes, well, an inference about how to behave in a given context or situation (Minuchin, 1974). Implicit rules in couples develop out of spending time together and developing an understanding of each person's individual patterned behavior as well as the patterned behavior adopted as a couple (Meng et al., 2013). Explicit rules are those that are discussed by couples and agreed upon in an overt fashion (Steuber & Mclaren, 2015). Relationships function better when implicit rules are made explicit, as it gives the couple a better sense of boundaries and expectations (Petronio, 2002). Rules, however, may evolve with or without explicit acknowledgment. Nearly 80% of intimate couples agreed on rules for disclosure, yet only 25% discussed these rules. Further, when rules are broken, the result is reduced relationship satisfaction (Hosking, 2013), particularly if the rules that are broken are obligatory rules (or rules both members of the couple share agreement on) (Roggensack & Sillars, 2014). In addition, couples who understand rules but do not agree experience more conflict than those couples who agree to obligatory rules (Roggensack & Sillars, 2014).

In addition to the explicit and implicit typology of rules, there are also constitutive and regulative rules (Roggensack & Sillars, 2014). Constitutive rules refer to the definitions of certain acts. Regulative rules are those that govern behavior, expectations, and actions. In the case of the Internet, most of the ambiguity surrounds what constitutes problematic behavior, For example, is posting a selfie without anyone else in the photo considered a breach of the relationship contract? In some couples,

Table 8.1 Technology Examples of Types of Rules

	Implicit Rules	Explicit Rules
Constitutive Rules (conceptual)	One member of the couple has a specific idea of what constitutes online infidelity. They do not, however, share their idea and operate under the belief that their definition is somehow universal and, therefore, their partner would agree with them without overtly agreeing on this.	Parents express to a child/adolescent that they are not to "be inappropriate" online, but provide no clear guidance on what actions constitute appropriateness.
Regulative Rules (action-oriented)	One member of the couple has specific behaviors that constitute online infidelity. They evaluate their partner's actions one action at a time and may be oriented that those behaviors constitute infidelity, despite that those behaviors may be ambiguous or benign. These include both online (such as talking to someone of the romantic interest gender) and offline behaviors (not leaving the phone out in public areas in the house).	One member of a couple constantly checks their partner's account and becomes angry when they discover that their partner was messaging someone from their work. While the messages are benign, the claim is that they should have not withheld the conversation from their partner.

it is; in others, it is not. Is communicating with an attractive person online outside of one's relationship a breach or not? In many cases, implicit constitutive rules are developed from one's history (such as pathological jealousy from a previous relationship and poor modeling).

One of the more common issues in clinical settings is that the computer and new media influence how people respond to and uphold their relationship rules. A classic example is Internet infidelity. Due to the acceptability of using the Internet to foster relationships with many people in wide-ranging geographic locations and from varied backgrounds, there are more complexities introduced into the already-established relationship rules. To date, researchers have identified the presence of several rules specifically regarding cellphone usage. Duran, Kelly, and Rotaru (2011) investigated whether the rules of cellphones in relationships were associated with separation or merging. Although many participants indicated the rules for communicating via cellphone were not necessary within their relationships, other participants reported conflict regarding cellphone usage in their relationships. One reason for this conflict was related to a need to be autonomous and, therefore, having to separate oneself from a situation in order to achieve autonomy through the methods available through the structure of a cellphone (i.e., turning off the phone or ignoring the call). A second source of conflict was a need to merge with one's partner but with no means to access the other. In each case, one partner in the relationship had their own expectations of the rules regarding cellphone usage; conflict emerged when another partner did not share that expectation.

Miller-Ott, Kelly, and Duran (2012) found couples that enact certain cellphone rules experience increased relationship satisfaction. One group of rules for couples and phones are rules for managing responsiveness to a partner's texts or phone calls. For example, some couples may have rules around the length of time one waits prior to initiating a second contact. Further, individuals who rated themselves as having higher levels of satisfaction had some rules, but not a specific set of rules governing how to respond to a phone call (Miller-Ott et al., 2012). This is also consistent with research on texting and messaging norms, indicating that people believe that there is a norm dictating a response when one receives a message via cellphone (Laursen, 2005). Relationship satisfaction is also higher for couples who have rules for when and in what way to introduce emotionally charged content; in other words, couples fare better when there is a specific rule preventing partners from beginning arguments over the phone. Finally, couples experience greater satisfaction with fewer rules monitoring their usage of their cellphone placed upon them by their partner (Miller-Ott et al., 2012). Most couples, however, are not explicit about the rules applied in their relationship—a statement particularly true about couples having specific expectations around the sharing of information, but not sharing those expectations (Steuber & Mclaren, 2015).

Alongside negotiation of frequency and content of general interactions in a couple's relationship, the negotiation of rules in a relationship also occurs specifically with regard to emotional expression (Strzyzewski, Buller, & Aune, 1996). Partners in relationships more deeply developed tend to have worked out idiosyncratic rules in their communication that permit the expression of negative emotions such as hurt and pain, whereas individuals in the early stages of a relationship generally rely on cultural rules to determine how to express positive emotions while withholding negative emotions (Strzyzewski et al., 1996). This rule development becomes more confusing with increased usage of computers in one's life. According to Strzyzewski et al. (1996), "Emotion expressions may be considered highly personal information and too risky to share completely with new relational partners. Partners may also avoid positive emotions because they do not feel confident enough of the future relational trajectory" (p. 128). The same holds true for online relationships: the individual keeps negative emotions inside when there is fear that revealing the emotion might somehow jeopardize the relationship (Baker, 2007).

Interactions between people who communicate primarily via the Internet are best described as positive and open when emotions are expressed (Baker, 2007). In fact, partners may reveal more online more quickly than in offline relationships, having negotiated the rules around the expression of emotions early in the relational trajectory. Successful online couples appropriately use self-presentation, timing, setting, and selection of obstacles to resolve issues that would have otherwise prevented them from progressing as a couple (Baker, 2002).

With regard to social media, there are five groups of rules that couples generally observe: rules regarding communication channels, deception and control, relational maintenance, negative self-consequences, and negative friend consequences (Bryant & Marmo, 2012). The most common rules (both implicit and explicit) in couple relationships are around what to post and with whom to share information. In some couples, sharing information with ex-partners (or one ex in particular) is prohibited. Unfortunately, this is not usually discovered until one partner posts and the other becomes angry about the posting. Another type of rule group—rules around deception—is not often discussed in couples but is among the most important set of rules that a couple can discuss (Roggensack & Sillars, 2014). Most couples do not like when their partner tells them what to do. It upsets the power dynamic, and one may experience problems in perceived lack of control/threat in their own relationships, thus contributing to greater levels of conflict (Sanford, 2010). Here, the Internet characteristics of ambiguity, approximation, accommodation, and accountability play a significant part. Ambiguity is a key issue with the Internet, deception, and infidelity. When a couple has any ambiguity between each other regarding the agreement on what should be shared with whom or what behaviors, encounters, and messages should be disclosed, relationship discord cannot be far behind. In many cases, the presence of ambiguity and the meanings behind relationships stem from the perception of approximation. For example, many couples seek treatment for Internet infidelity. But what happens online is that we are ambiguous about the definition and therefore have different ideas about meaning and outcome based on how much we believe that behavior approximates real-world situations, thereby creating more conflict (Roggensack & Sillars, 2014). Ambiguity around what constitutes deception and infidelity is common (Roggensack & Sillars, 2014) and may mean that one person may inadvertently cross the line because of the ambiguity. In cases where there is a higher value placed on Internet behavior as approximating or mimicking offline behavior, the interactions online will be far more damaging than in cases where couples do not consider that behavior to be like offline behavior. In other words, the more one believes that online behavior mimics offline behavior, the more deceptive online behavior will appear to be.

Once online behavior deemed problematic is discovered, interpreting the meaning of the behavior/deception happens next. For example, when one discovers their partner has been communicating with someone else online, they may fear that their partner prefers the other individual and, by default, does not enjoy their current partnership. This meaning-making is in part the accommodation process whereby the partner offline may make some meaning that the person online is using the Internet to accommodate what they really wish to do in life but cannot because of the restrictions in their offline relationship. In other words, the betrayed partner makes meaning that they are holding back the online partner from what they would really like to be doing (and with whom they would like to be doing it). Another common example is the meaning-making around pornography usage. Many people report that when they discover their partner is viewing pornography online without involving them, they feel as if their partner is making comparisons to what they see online versus their offline relationship. Women in particular may also be fearful that their partner will see how they do not match up to the pornography actors (Grov, Gillespie, Royce, & Lever, 2011). Finally, when relationship rules are broken, the likelihood of revenge or retaliation increases (Boon, Deveau, & Alibhai, 2009), potentially altering the relationship dynamic.

Rules in Families and Relational Systems

Families are organizations defined and bounded by rules (Blevins, 1993). Family rules are manifested in the patterns of behavior exhibited by members of a relational system and tend to give structure to how tasks are accomplished and emotions and values are expressed (Blevins, 1993). With regard to the key characteristics of the Internet described in Chapter 7, the affordability of the Internet (for one) makes it easier for families to find ways to demonstrate their affection and values, and accomplish tasks. The Internet's approximation to real-world situations can set up a mock environment to test how youth are able to follow rules set up by parents and care providers and respect boundaries.

As a way to win the battle between roles and rules, parents have elected to identify content rules and access rules and manage their children's Internet usage through these rules. When parents are able to appropriately give some power to their children in decision-making, they help to foster their children's sense of competence (Brown & Mann, 1990). In one-parent families, for example, adolescents may be empowered to make more decisions, potentially as a way to compensate for not having another parent in their home (Brown & Mann, 1990). From Minuchin's (1974) structural perspective, this may mean that adolescents are shifted into a higher position in the family—combined with the notion that adolescents are more technologically advanced than their parents, it may mean that they adopt a higher role in the family in terms of the hierarchy. The role of a technology expert in the family has significant implications for the content rules in the family and how those rules are managed (Fletcher & Blair, 2016).

Another rule commonly established in families related to the Internet is time spent online. As noted in Chapter 1, there are several negative health effects related to the amount of time one spends online, including issues with dry eyes and declining eyesight, cervical problems, skin problems (particularly for women), wrist pain, hair loss, weight gain, and changes in the life cycle of a cell in the human body (Meena, Verma, Kohli, & Ingle, 2016). Research conducted by Cingel and Hargittai (2018) found that rules set up for health reasons have a positive impact on youth in terms of their grades in college; rules set up to limit computer time because it detracted from homework time, however, were inversely associated with good grades.

Surveillance of technology use among family members is becoming a huge endeavor and a common technique by which parents reinforce the rules established. Parental monitoring of youth technology use is a common activity (Martins, Matthews, & Ratan, 2017). Parents who have higher degrees of involvement with their children may, however inadvertently, end up with more negative outcomes as children feel that they are not able to be trusted (Martins et al., 2017). In addition, we have the issue of coveillance that is emerging in relationships. Coveillance refers to the fact that we are being observed by our community around us, and that this information can get back to our relationships without us intending for the information to get back. In some cases, parents and caregivers opt less for surveillance and more for coveillance and ask their online networked community to monitor their children's behavior.

If parents do not or cannot monitor their teens' technological use through the establishment of rules, it is still essential that they find some ways to help them manage their vulnerability to online perpetrators both known and unknown to them (Landau, 2008). This can include: (a) having bedrooms that are media-free zones, (b) encouraging comprehensive, informational, and positive media-education in the home and school environments, (c) supporting other forms of socializing and activities (e.g., athletics, reading, hobbies, traveling, writing, painting, playing musical instruments, etc.), and (d) modeling appropriate online behaviors and communications (Villani, Olson, & Jellinek, 2005). In terms of role modeling it is essential that caregivers select media and limit the time engaged with media to reasonable amounts (Villani et al., 2005). This includes modeling appropriate behaviors like following the rules of online communities. Modeling reduced Internet usage can be difficult for parents as they may not be willing to alter their own behavior (Johnson, 2017). Another challenge in the establishment of rules regarding technology usage is that parents and caregivers may need to follow them—and they often do not wish to do so. To not monitor parent use of technology, however, is detrimental to children, because the negative consequences of technology usage for parents and caregivers translate into negative consequences for their children (Hefner, Knop, Schmitt, & Vorderer, 2018).

Boundaries

The Internet and new media make us accessible to everyone—and also invite others into our world. Boundaries about sharing information with outsiders that were previously well established in the relationship may change when there are multiple channels for sharing information (Ward, 2006). In some cases, partners become more overprotective when they believe a boundary has been crossed; in other cases, users may feel smothered by their partner's behavior toward them, even though this may not be the partner's intent.

Problems can emerge in relationships because the Internet and new media introduce people who are both known and unknown to you into your relationship (Hertlein & Blumer, 2013). Two types of boundaries have been discussed in the literature with regard to technology and users: self-boundaries and dyadic boundaries (Joinson, Reips, Buchanan, & Schofield, 2010). Self-boundaries refer to those surrounding the individual affected by self-disclosures (Taylor & Altman, 1975, as cited by Joinson et al., 2010). Dyadic boundaries have historically related to the boundaries around how information is received by someone outside of the system. Those in relationships need to be aware of and attend to both types of boundaries. When couples are clear on both the self- and dyadic boundaries (what information is shared outside of the couple), problems are minimized. When partners only attend to one of the two, however, problems emerge. Parents and caregivers may experience discord with one another when one may be actively—and constantly—connected, via social media and other ways, to their family-of-origin. At the same time, the accessibility and affordability of the Internet make it easier to connect but also create more diffusion in the boundary between the relationship and the outside world.

Bakardjieva (2005) noted:

> the boundaries between the world beyond the doorstep and the "private" life of the household were ceaselessly cracking and shifting. People were bringing in work from their offices and schools, friends and relatives were coming and staying, giving remote input and advice, demanding time and attention. The physical household was in actuality only a node in a much larger network of significant others, which, to a large extent, determined the nature and rhythms of its preoccupations . . . . Objects such as computers and modems were flowing across the public-private divide and along the interpersonal networks reaching far beyond the doorstep so that it was difficult to say exactly which object belonged to the particular household.
>
> (p. 66)

The same process is true for the Couple and Family Technology (CFT) framework. Shifts in rules, roles, and boundaries can affect each other as well as the processes of relationship (to be discussed in Chapter 9).

Boundary development is hard enough without the inception of the Internet—people have long struggled with making sure that they are able to maintain appropriate distance from people who are not healthy and will push their boundaries.

Conclusion

The Couple and Family Technology framework (Hertlein, 2012; Hertlein & Blumer, 2013) is a useful tool for identifying what structurally changes in relationships as new technologies are introduced. As technology becomes more advanced, it will be up to us to continue to evolve this model to broaden its applicability.

References

Bakardjieva, M. (2005). *Internet society: The Internet in everyday life*. London: Sage Publications.

Baker, A. J. (2002). What makes an online relationship successful? Clues from couples who met in cyberspace. *CyberPsychology & Behavior, 5*(1), 364–375. doi:10.1177/0093650205285368

Baker, A. J. (2007). Expressing emotion in text: Email communication of online couples. In M. T. Whitty, A. J. Baker & J. A. Inman (Eds.), *Online matchmaking* (pp. 97–111). London: Palgrave Macmillan.

Blevins, W. (1993). *Your family, your self*. Oakland: New Harbinger

Boon, S., Deveau, V., & Alibhai, A. (2009). Payback: The parameters of revenge in romantic relationships. *Journal of Social and Personal Relationships, 26*(6–7), 747–768.

Brown, J. E., & Mann, L. (1990). The relationship between family structure and process variables and adolescent decision-making. *Journal of Adolescence, 13*(1), 25–37. doi:10.1016/0140-1971(90)90039-A

Bryant, E. M., & Marmo, J. (2012). The rules of Facebook friendship: A two-stage examination of interaction rules in close, casual, and acquaintance friendships. *Journal of Social and Personal Relationships, 29*(8), 1013–1035. doi:10.1177/02 65407512443616

Caughlin, J. P. (2003). Family communication standards and how are such standards associated with family satisfaction? *Human Communication Research, 29*(1), 5–40. doi:10.1111/j.1468-2958.2003.tb00830.x

Cingel, D., & Hargittai, E. (2018). The relationship between childhood rules about technology use and later-life academic achievement among young adults. *The Communication Review*, 1–22. doi:10.1080/10714421.2018.1468182

Duran, R. L., Kelly, L., & Rotaru, T. (2011). Mobile phones in romantic relationships and the dialectic between autonomy and connection. *Communication Quarterly, 59*(1), 19–36. doi:10.1080/01463373.2011.541336

Fletcher, A. C., & Blair, B. L. (2016). Implications of the family expert role for parental rules regarding adolescent use of social technologies. *New Media & Society, 18*(2), 239–256. doi:10.1177/1461444814538922

Grov, C., Gillespie, B. J., Royce, T., & Lever, J. (2011). Perceived consequences of casual online sexual activities on heterosexual relationships: A U.S. online survey. *Archives of Sexual Behavior, 40*(2), 429–439. doi:10.1007/s10508-010-9598-z

Hefner, D., Knop, K., Schmitt, S., & Vorderer, P. (2018). Rules? Role model? Relationship? The impact of parents on their children's problematic mobile phone involvement. *Media Psychology*, 1–27. doi:10.1080/15213269.2018.1433544

Hertlein, K. M. (2012). Digital dwelling: Technology in couple and family relationships. *Family Relations, 61*(3), 374–387. doi:10.1111/j.1741-3729.2012.00702.x

Hertlein, K. M., & Blumer, M. L. C. (2013). *The couple and family technology framework: Intimate relationships in a digital age.* New York, NY: Routledge.

Hosking, W. (2013). Agreements about extra-dyadic sex in gay men's relationships: Exploring differences in relationship quality by agreement type and rule-breaking behavior. *Journal of Homosexuality, 60*(4–6), 711–733. doi:10.1080/00918369.2013.773819

Johnson, D. (2017). *Parents' perceptions of smartphone use and parenting practices.* ProQuest Dissertations and Theses.

Joinson, A. N., Reips, U. D., Buchanan, T., & Schofield, C. B. P. (2010). Privacy, trust, and self-disclosure online. *Human—Computer Interaction, 25*(1), 1–24. doi.org/10.1080/07370020903586662

Landau, S. (2008). Privacy and security: A multidimensional problem. *Communications of the ACM, 51*(11), 25–26. doi:10.1145/1400214.1400223

Laursen, D. (2005). Please reply!: The replying norm in adolescent SMS communication. In R. Harper, L. Palen, & A. Taylor (Eds.), *The inside text: Social, cultural and design perspectives on SMS* (pp. 53–73). New York, NY: Springer.

Martins, N., Matthews, N., & Ratan, R. (2017). Playing by the rules: Parental mediation of video game play. *Journal of Family Issues, 38*(9), 1215–1238. doi:10.1177/0192513X15613822

Meena, J., Verma, A., Kohli, C., & Ingle, G. (2016). Mobile phone use and possible cancer risk: Current perspectives in India. *Indian Journal of Occupational and Environmental Medicine, 20*(1), 5–9. doi:10.4103/0019-5278.183827

Meng, K., Harper, J. M., Coyne, S., Larson, J., Miller, R., & Sandberg, J. (2013). *Couple implicit rules for facilitating disclosure and relationship quality with romantic relational aggression as a mediator.* ProQuest Dissertations and Theses.

Miller-Ott, A. E., Kelly, L., & Duran, R. (2012). The effects of cell-phone usage rules on satisfaction in romantic relationships. *Communication Quarterly, 60*(1), 17–34.

Minuchin, S. (1974). *Families & family therapy.* Cambridge, MA: Harvard University Press.

Petronio, S. (2002). *Boundaries of privacy: Dialectics of disclosure.* New York, NY: State University of New York Press.

Raine, L., & Anderson, J. (2017). *The internet of things connectivity binge: What are the implications?* Pew Research Center. Retrieved from http://www.pew Internet.org/2017/06/06/the-Internet-of-things-connectivity-binge-what-are-the-implications

Roggensack, K., & Sillars, A. (2014). Agreement and understanding about honesty and deception rules in romantic relationships. *Journal of Social and Personal Relationships, 31*(2), 178–199. doi:10.1177/0265407513489914

Sanford, K. (2010). Perceived threat and perceived neglect: Couples' underlying concerns during conflict. *Psychological Assessment, 22*(2), 288–297.

Steuber, K., & Mclaren, R. (2015). Privacy recalibration in Personal Relationships: Rule Usage Before and After an Incident of Privacy Turbulence. *Communication Quarterly*, 63(3), 345–364. doi:10.1080/01463373.2015.1039717

Strzyzewski, K., Buller, D. B., & Aune, R. K. (1996). Daily rule development in romantic relationships emotion management and perceived appropriateness of emotion across relationship stages. *Human Communication Research*, 23(1), 115–145. doi:10.1111/j.1468-2958.1996.tb00389.x

Taylor, D. A., & Altman, I. (1975). Self-disclosure as a function of reward-cost outcomes. *Sociometry*, 38(1), 18–31. doi:10.2307/2786231

Villani, V. S., Olson, C. K., & Jellinek, M. S. (2005). Media literacy for clinicians and parents. *Child and Adolescent Psychiatric Clinics of North America*, 14(3), 523–553. doi:10.1016/j.chc.2005.03.001

Ward, K. (2006). The bald guy just ate an orange: Domestication, work and home. In T. Berker, M. Hartmann, Y. Punie, & K. Ward (Eds.), *Domestication of media and technology* (pp. 145–164). Berkshire, UK: Open University Press.

NINE

Improving Relationship Launches, Runtime, and Crashes

Relational Intelligence in a Digital World

Rather than gaining knowledge from our own cognitive processes in our individual brains, in today's digital world we use other sources to supplement what we know and how we know it. Originally a term developed for other industries such as math and biology, extelligence refers to "cultural capital": widely available to us in media formats (Stewart & Cohen, 1997). In part, it describes intelligence that is socially constructed—but instead of a focus on the perspectives and viewpoints of others as equally valid, extelligence refers to the information and those perspectives that are provided to us via media in both digital and analog formats. Extelligence is developed through the process of "complicity"—that is, the integration of our internal knowledge systems with the external media knowledge.

In a digital world, not only is our general knowledge about things created through complicity, our knowledge around relationship rules, processes, and standards is also contextually (and digitally) informed; see Figure 9.1. We learn how to act, with whom to interact, and how to manage relationships through shared examples set up by production companies all the way down to the presentations and expositions of our peers and friends. Our relational intelligence both is a product of and contributes to the digital world in which we are embedded.

Relationship Formation

"To Swipe or Not to Swipe"

The online environment is a primary place for relationship initiation and formation. The first online matchmaking began in 1959 using a punch card system (Wrench & Punyanunt-Carter, 2017). There are now countless dating sites, not to mention at least two billion people worldwide

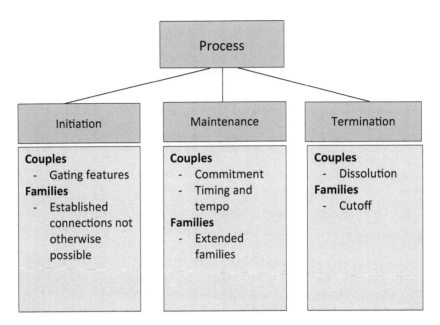

Figure 9.1 Relational Process Areas Affected by Technology

using social media and chat functions for other reasons who end up forming a relationship through these chat mechanisms (Finkel, Eastwick, Karney, Reis, & Sprecher, 2012). People in the United States in particular have shifted to beginning relationships in online dating (Smith, 2016). Nearly 20% of the adult population reports using dating sites, and a full one-third of people report using Tinder (Statista, 2017). This represents a growth of 5% in one year alone.

People in China and India have also taken to starting relationships via online dating (Schwartz & Velotta, 2018) such as through a Tinder-like dating application (app) known as Momo, which has over 91 million users (Li & Lipscomb, 2017; Ng, 2017). For those individuals who identify as lesbian or gay (LG), nearly 50% report using online dating, making this mechanism the predominant way in which these relationships are initiated (Rosenfeld & Thomas, 2010). Additionally, for bisexual and gay men online dating is reportedly the most common way that they meet partners for casual sex (Prestage et al., 2015). In terms of the intersectionality of age with online dating, 11% of teens used the Internet to start new relationships, 13% used it to maintain existing relationships, 13% used it for communication, 9% used it for maintaining long-distance relationship, 7% used it for establishing romantic relationships, and finally, 7% used it for making social comparisons (Borca, Bina, Keller, Gilbert, & Begotti, 2015). Online dating is also becoming increasingly popular for people in their later years of the lifespan (Davis & Fingerman, 2016; Gewirtz-Meydan, & Ayalon, 2018; Griffin & Fingerman, 2018).

In contrast to the increased engagement with online dating by people in each of the aforementioned groups, there are some populations whose online dating participation remains underwhelming (Schwartz & Velotta, 2018). Further, people in Japan, Singapore, and Indonesia have shown a relative lack of interest in online dating for myriad reasons (Schwartz & Velotta, 2018). Regardless, the governments in each of these countries are so worried about the potential of a future population drop-off that they have allocated funds into things like government-run dating sites (Ansari & Klinenberg, 2016; Schwartz & Velotta, 2018).

The characteristics of the Internet embedded in online dating also make relationship formation relatively easy online. According to Finkel et al. (2012), the Internet and websites provide three things to attract users and help users to make connections to others:

> Access to potential romantic partners
> Communication with potential romantic partners
> Matching with compatible romantic partners
> (Finkel et al., 2012, p. 4)

Two other processes that are involved in online dating sites include advertising to users that one is both unique and superior (Finkel et al., 2012).

Tinder, for example, was one of the first mainstream dating and "hook-up" apps to hit society using global positioning systems (GPS) to pinpoint nearby potential partners (Duguay, 2016; Wrench & Punyanunt-Carter, 2017). Part of the reason for Tinder's success was that it removed the vulnerability of anonymity discussed in Chapter 7 through a verification and authentication process. This step addressed the concern that many people had regarding the ability for people to pretend to be someone else (anonymity) online than who they are offline. In online relationships, there is a fear of people being dishonest and inauthentic in online dating scenarios (Toma, Hancock, & Ellison, 2008). At the same time, people who are sensitive to rejection use online dating, because they feel like they can be their more authentic selves (Hance, Blackhart, & Dew, 2018), thus supporting the notion of anonymity being a factor in online interactions.

For these reasons, the established view of dating apps and online dating tends to be negative (Rosenfeld, 2017). As reported in the preceding paragraph, approximately 20% of US people are using online apps for dating—but the remaining percentage is not necessarily finding dates. Rosenfeld (2017) asserts they are not dating at all—online or off. Translation: of the proportion of people who are eligible to date, most of them are using these devices and apps to accomplish this task.

For similar-gender couples, relationship formation is a little bit different. First, finding relationships online is the more common mechanism

by which LG individuals locate potential partners (Rosenfeld &
Thomas, 2012), though gay men still express concern around meeting
people online in regard to sexual health (Macapagal, Coventry, Puckett,
Phillips, & Mustanski, 2016). Second, part of what has to be mediated
in addition to the page itself is impression management—around one's
identity—otherwise known as electronic visibility management (Twist,
Bergdall, Belous, & Maier, 2017). Owens (2017) describes three categories of gay men's presentations on social media: Out and Proud,
Out and Discreet, and Facebook Closeted. Out and Proud refers to gay
men who use Facebook as a way to come out or advertise their sexual
orientation, as well as to celebrate their orientation. This type makes up
approximately 10% of gay men online. Out and Discreet men may use
specific functions within Facebook to disclose to certain people their
sexual orientation or denote their sexual orientation through relatively
subtle clues rather than overtly advertising it. These men (approximately 57%) may experience anxiety when others try to out them on
Facebook. Facebook Closeted refers to those who do not indicate their
sexual orientation on Facebook in any capacity. This group makes up
about 33% of gay men on Facebook and involves an active process
where men organize their Facebook pages to appear straight (Owens,
2017).

Other somewhat confusing data suggests that part of the reason people engage in online dating is the sense of control they have above and
beyond what they might experience in offline dating (Rochadiat, Tong, &
Novak, 2018; Tong, Hancock, & Slatcher, 2016; Vandeweerd, Myers,
Coulter, Yalcin, & Corvin, 2016). For example, computer users believe
they have the ability to control what type of information is shared—
age, ethnicity, socioeconomic status (SES), etc. in online environments
(Wrench & Punyanunt-Carter, 2017), thereby controlling risk in dating
(Vandeweerd et al., 2016). The sense of control, however, is actually an
illusion and tends to be associated with love and younger people's beliefs
about online dating (Borrajo, Gámez Guadix, & Calvete Zumalde, 2015),
though it has also been the perception in older women (Vandeweerd
et al., 2016).

After initial online interactions with a potential partner, the transition
to the first offline date is also critically important in the progression of
a relationship and considered a defining moment (Sharabi & Caughlin,
2017). Whether the relationship continues into development offline is
predicated on how well the first date goes (Sharabi & Caughlin, 2017).
Women also are more likely to feel like they have to protect themselves
more after an online interaction scenario as compared to offline interactions (Cali, Coleman, & Campbell, 2013). And while this study merely
examined perceptions of protection, some of us actually behaviorally
take steps to protect ourselves, including monitoring online disclosures
(Marwick & Boyd, 2010).

Being Facebook Official

Researchers have investigated how individuals initiate and certify their relationships as "official" (Fox & Warber, 2013), including differences in how people announce involvement in a relationship on Facebook. Consistent with previous research about women's investment in romantic relationships, women who had relationships that were "Facebook official" experienced those relationships as more serious and exclusive—and according to other scholars, may consider such a proclamation as a "digital wedding ring" (Orosz, Szekeres, Kiss, Farkas, & Roland-Lévy, 2014).

But becoming "Facebook official" is not the only way that couples make an overt commitment to one another. There are actually four processes that couples use to make such proclamation:

- Indication of relationship status via being "Facebook official." This is accomplished by using mechanisms already present in Facebook to indicate relationships.
- "Implied relationship disclosures" (Robards & Lincoln, 2016, p. 5). This means altering statuses, tagging people in photos, and removing photos without calling attention to these actions.
- "Intended absence of relationship traces"—meaning not implying any relationship and being careful about what is posted as to not lead anyone to believe that they are in a relationship.
- Revised relationship disclosures—this describes the process by which social media users make reversals to previous relationship disclosures. For example, one person may go back and edit their Facebook disclosures and profiles based on the preferences of their partner (Robards & Lincoln, 2016, p. 5).

Research in couple relationships noted the importance of similarity in couple relationships and the contribution of similarity in relationship satisfaction. When couples are similar in their communication and coping, the more mutually reinforcing their patterns become, and they are more satisfied in their relationships (Chow, Buhrmester, & Tan, 2014). For example, couples who are similar in the way they use Facebook relationally (i.e., post and tag one another) have higher levels of relationship satisfaction (Papp, Danielewicz, & Cayemberg, 2012).

First Comes Love, Then Comes Meeting

After the transition to the first date, there have been some challenges to the thought that relationships formed online are somehow of less quality than those formed offline (Turkle, 2012). The data, however, does not support this notion. In a longitudinal study beginning with over 3,000 heterosexual couples who met online, they had odds of transition to marriage nearly twice as high (1.98) as couples who met offline. When the data was weighted, the odds of transitioning to marriage were three times higher for online couples than offline couples—a highly statistically significant finding. People with college degrees and also those who identify as Evangelical and Fundamentalist Christian were also more likely to transition to marriage (Rosenfeld, 2017). Rosenfeld's (2017) explanation for this is that there is greater choice in online formats. With better choice, there is a potential for better matches, more information to make choices, and greater ability to select people who self-identify as ready for marriage in their profiles (Rosenfeld, 2017).

Further, because such a small percentage of married people are using dating apps and the Internet to find partners outside of their relationship, Rosenfeld (2017) suggests that the apps do not have a "destabilizing" effect on relationships (p. 16). Some might disagree. First, the percentage of men and women who report using apps to cheat on their partner is 16% for men and 12% for women. The judgment as to whether 16% and 12% are small is up to conjecture. Further, someone who has cheated on their partner with those apps may very much describe the lived experience as destabilizing for reasons described in Chapter 5 and by Hertlein, Dulley, Cloud, Leon, and Chang (2017). In an article describing recovery from infidelity, one of the issues that emerges is the inability to move past the infidelity because of the sheer presence of the communication channels to the other person—many of which can be hidden from a spying partner.

Relationship Maintenance

Development Across the Couple Lifespan

Social media usage has also been applied to Knapp's couple development life cycle (Brody, LeFebvre, & Blackburn, 2016). Knapp's stages include: initiating, experimenting, intensifying, integrating, and bonding. Technology, Facebook, and social media are critical in these stages (Bergdall et al., 2012). Initiating is easy online as there is the perception among Internet users that it is less of a risk since it would not be a face-to-face rejection, if rejection at all. Experimenting is facilitated by social media through the ability to reach out to more people than just one. The escalation of a relationship can be accomplished by the self-disclosure that occurs on social media, where relationships intensify more quickly than in offline relationships because of the emphasis on self-disclosure (Brody et al., 2016; Hertlein & Blumer, 2013). Finally, integrating and bonding are when a couple makes decisions to solidify their relationship through the expression of their status online or in other ways. For example, interdependence is created through being able to access one's partner through multiple devices and formats (Brody et al., 2016).

Technology's Contribution to Relationship Satisfaction

Despite the prevalent notion that technology destroys relationships, research also shows that many people who use email and spend time on the computer do not experience a loss of time with family and friends. In fact, they may spend even more time with family and friends, despite initially experiencing depression and loneliness at the outset of the computer entering their lives (Bargh & McKenna, 2004). From a relational communication perspective, the evidence would also seem to support that integration of technology in our lives may make the communication with others more desirable. This is especially the case in relationships that occur at a distance, which may increase as the possibility for greater distance and technological connectivity becomes more of a reality for humans, as when traveling or living in space (Peterson & Twist, 2017).

Technology also can help us have better sex (Macapagal et al., 2016). For example, people may use technology to look up information about improving their sex lives. This can include looking up date night ideas, findings articles that will spice up one's sex life, and looking up information on different sexual positions (Hertlein & Ancheta, 2014). Couples can also view online pornography together, send erotic pictures to one another, have a sexual relationship via webcam, and/or exchange erotic text messages. Phone apps also can be used to fulfill unmet sexual needs between partners (Macapagal et al., 2016). Consensually non-monogamous partners have greater ease in finding extra-sexual and relational partners through dating apps like OkCupid and Feeld. And partners with an erotic orientation (Twist, 2018) that is more kinky can use online social networking sites (SNSs) like FetLife to find partners to play with, and can learn more about kink/BDSM (bondage/discipline-dominance/submission-sadomasochism) techniques and activities via reputable educational websites like kinkacademy.com.

As we progress into more complex sexual technologies (sextech) more people will identify this way along a sextech orientation continuum (McArthur & Twist, 2017; Twist, 2018). A digisexual is one who prefers sexual experiences and relating via immersive technologies and who does not need (nor necessarily want) a human partner (McArthur & Twist, 2017). For digisexuals, technology does not mediate sex with human partners; the technology itself is the sexual partner. The implications of this are hard to predict at this early stage of theoretical and practical development. What may emerge are people who have transcended sexuality based on gender (after all what is the gender of a robot) and even based on being human, which might be considered a form of posthumanism or transhumanism (Belk, 2014; Ferrando, 2014; Ray, 2016). Posthumanism decenters humans through one's disappearance into networks and informational patterns (Hayles, 1999; Wolfe, 2010), and from this, transhumanism, or the point where humans have evolved beyond our current physical and mental limitations through such sophisticated technologies, may emerge (Huxley, 1968).

Some of the research relates to the role of computers and new media technologies on relationship satisfaction. Women, for example, experience greater relationship satisfaction with online dating than in face-to-face relationships (McKenna, Green, & Gleason, 2002). Satisfaction in relationships is also related to problem-solving strategies used by couples. For example, couples indicate that they can resolve their conflict more effectively if they can utilize asynchronous communication methods such as email because of its flexibility (Hertlein & Blumer, 2013). On the other hand, the emergence of smartphones into relationships is associated with decreased marital satisfaction and with wives' desire for their male counterparts to be more emotionally present (Czechowsky, 2008).

Another issue related to relationship satisfaction is the duration of technology-based communication. With such communication options, there are more frequent and often shorter communications (primarily through email) occurring any time of day (Wilding, 2006). This altering of the tempo has to also be negotiated by couples. For example, Mark and Shannon, a middle-class couple, came to treatment to improve their communication. Mark indicated Shannon was unresponsive to him during the day. Mark stated that the times he did call, Shannon answered abruptly and it was clear she did not want to speak to him. Shannon stated there was no reason for long conversations since Mark called frequently throughout the day. Mark, however, reported if the conversations were longer, he would not feel the need to call repeatedly.

The advent of technology in relationships also carries implications for sexual satisfaction. Research demonstrates that those who engage in out-of-control online sexual behavior run the risk of experiencing a reduction in their sex drive and desirability, have less offline sex, and subsequently feel less satisfaction than those who do not participate in out-of-control online sexual behaviors (Bridges, Bergner, & Hesson-McInnis, 2003). Couples who view online pornography together experience increased sexual satisfaction and a greater frequency of sex than those couples with partners who watch it independently. In addition, researchers have found that women who watch mainstream pornography by themselves develop uncertainty with regard to their own body, and tend to compare themselves to what they see in the videos, both physically and in terms of performance (Grov, Gillespie, Royce, & Lever, 2011). Men also report that they have sex less frequently when watching porn alone, but they also use it as a way to stimulate arousal (Grov et al., 2011).

Intimacy Development in Relationships With and Without Technology

In computer-mediated relationships the development and level of intimacy depend on how much the partners rely on self-disclosure. In some computer-mediated relationships, self-disclosure is used as a strategy to determine whether a person on the other end of the keyboard can be trusted with such information and vulnerability. Internet users have a tendency to engage in more self-disclosing behaviors than those in face-to-face relationships (Joinson, 2001).

One of the most significant points of debate regarding technology in everyday life is intimacy. What is technology's effect on intimacy—good? Bad? Or indifferent? There is some evidence to support the notion that computer-mediated relationships may augment the intimacy development process. The mere presence of more (and easier) ways to communicate with others may allow for greater levels of intimacy to be developed with others (Bargh & McKenna, 2004). In one study, three-quarters depended on mobile phones to interact with partners during the day (Kennedy, Judd, Churchward, Gray, & Krause, 2008). One area of investigation related to technology and relationships has centered around the role of electronic communication in social and familial relationships (Lanigan, Bold, & Chenoweth, 2009). Lanigan et al. (2009) conducted a survey study involving 103 participants including parents of children under 12, parents of children 12 and up, post-parenting families, and child-free couples. Their study explored family adaptability and cohesion, alternative use of technology time, and perceived impact of technology on family relationships. The majority of the participants (n = 79, 89%) reported that technology had impacted their family relationships (Lanigan et al., 2009). Further, just under half (n = 36, 45%) indicated computers had a mostly positive impact on their family life, whereas less than one-quarter (n = 16, 20%) reported a negative impact. The remaining participants indicated computers had both negative and positive impacts on family relationships (n = 19, 25%).

This is not the whole story. At least three studies conducted early in the days of mobile phones and email contradict this finding. One study found every email sent was responsible for 1 minute of lost family time (Nie, Hillygus, & Erbring, 2002). Another study found that the time spent together as a couple was negatively impacted once a smartphone arrived into the home (Czechowsky, 2008). Lanigan et al. (2009) also found that time spent on the Internet and computers was previously spent with family members. Finally, the ability to work from home may introduce challenges in attempting to balance work life and home life (Yao, Tan, & Ilies, 2017).

An argument, however, can be made in the opposite direction—that the use of the Internet, smartphones, and computers improves family communication and enhances intimacy. Technology can serve as a shared activity, function as a way to make family vacations and trips much easier and quicker to enable spending time with one another, and may facilitate household management and increased efficiency, resulting in more free family time (Lanigan et al., 2009). For example, when parents and children collaborate on technological activities together it can actually improve their communication (Mesch, 2006). Parents can now work from home, which would inherently create more time together and suggests a more supportive work environment (Fiksenbaum, 2014). Participation in social networking can also build intimacy for couples and family members. It provides a greater sense of connection, which can inspire offline interactions and meetings (Xie, 2007). In other words, it is not the devices themselves that may take time away from our relationships—it is the way in which they are used.

Studies over time have provided consistent evidence of this. In the early digital age, one study of undergraduate students involved meeting the same person offline as they met online—unbeknownst to the participant. The researchers found when the participants met the individual online, they liked that person better (McKenna et al., 2002). The more opportunity for communication, the greater the likelihood intimacy will develop (Henline & Harris, 2006). When studying family technology usage, Hodge and his colleagues found that there was a negative correlation between media use and family functioning, particularly when mobile phone usage was mediated by the parents (Hodge et al., 2012).

Another way these devices build intimacy is by providing the ability to share knowledge of the everydayness and intimate details of one's life. Mobile phones have the ability to "rat" you out—giving up your location, activities, and other individuals involved in those activities or at that location so that one can have more detailed information as to a partner's location and potentially activities (Ling & Campbell, 2009), in ways that are very affordable and anonymous to whoever might be watching (or tracking). For example, the dating app Tinder allows people to locate potential dating partners based on their physical location (Blackwell, Birnholtz, & Abbott, 2015). This type of knowledge about someone facilitated by mobile phones is termed "mobile intimacy" (Hjorth, 2013).

In addition to building intimacy, social media builds our networks (Manago, Taylor, Greenfield, Eccles, & Subrahmanyam, 2012). Networks can be geographically expansive and include key features of self-disclosure (and, consequently, intimacy development). In fact, those with larger networks on social media also report a greater degree of emotional support from their Facebook contacts and generally higher levels of satisfaction with their lives (Manago et al., 2012).

Building Intimacy Through Self-Disclosure

Many will agree that talking to others online is a welcome change in their lives, in part because of the ease and increased frequency of communication with partners. Unless conducted by video camera, however, the receiver has to interpret the sender's emotions, meaning, and motivation without observing any nonverbal cues accompanying the message. In relationships initiated offline, partners develop intimacy with one another through self-disclosure (sharing details of their lives and their personality) paired with observations in real-world (and unobtrusive) settings (Tidwell & Walther, 2000), where in computer-mediated relationships, intimacy is fostered through reliance on self-disclosure (Whitty, 2008).

Self-disclosure in relationships often follows a process where partners trust one another (Derlega & Chaikin, 1977, as cited by McKenna et al., 2002). The quantity and quality of self-disclosure in a relationship carry significant implications for the health of the relationship. More frequent disclosures are associated with greater emotional involvement in dating and greater levels of marital satisfaction (Rubin, Hill, Peplau, & Dunkel-Schetter, 1980, as cited by Yum & Hara, 2006). Research shows that relationships headed toward termination by one or both parties are characterized by fewer instances of self-disclosure. Further, when self-disclosure in relationships headed toward termination does occur, it is generally about superficial topics rather than topics related to emotions and relational content (Baxter, 1979).

Some have discovered that higher levels of self-disclosure to another online are associated with increased liking of that person along with matching communication styles and higher levels of commitment (Valkenburg & Peter, 2009). Part of how people transition into formal relationships is based on the level of disclosure occurring online. As mentioned in Chapter 5, disclosure is a primary method by which people maintain their relationship, both those primarily offline and those online (Thelwall & Vis, 2017). There are also elements of self-disclosure that can affect one's perception of the quality of the relationship. Specifically, the greater the depth of the self-disclosure and the more emotional the disclosure (i.e., the usage of stronger emotional words as opposed to weaker emotional words), the more positive one rates an online counterpart (Rosen, Cheever, Cummings, & Felt, 2008). Self-disclosure in relationships, however, can be a double-edged sword. As much as it can draw people together, it can also pull them apart. According to Schwab, Scalise, Ginter, and Whipple (1998), while self-disclosure inherently provides an opportunity to achieve intimacy, it is not free of risks because disclosure also carries with it the possibility of one being manipulated, embarrassed, exploited, or rejected. And since lonely individuals frequently suffer from a lack of social skills, the possibility of such adverse outcomes is genuine (Ginter, 1982) (p. 1264).

In a study on loneliness and self-disclosure, people who rated themselves as being lonely were indeed less likely to engage in self-disclosure across many settings, whether with strangers or friends (Schwab et al., 1998). This contradicts some of the conventional wisdom about computer users, which suggests people who use computers do so as a way of interacting with others without taking significant risks or becoming vulnerable in the same ways that might occur in face-to-face interactions.

In relationships mediated by the Internet and new media, self-disclosure may also occur as a means to an end; that is, to determine whether the person on the other end of the keyboard is trustworthy, one engages in a systematic process of self-disclosure. The development of intimacy also depends on what exactly is being disclosed. Intimacy develops more deeply in cases where individuals choose to disclose information of a personal and emotional nature as opposed to limited emotional content (Derlega, Winstead, & Greene, 2008). Much research has shown that computer users tend to engage in more self-disclosing behaviors than those in face-to-face relationships (Joinson, 2001). Further, it is likely self-disclosure is responsible for the heightened level of commitment experienced by partners in computer-mediated relationships (Yum & Hara, 2006).

The process of self-disclosure in online relationships is further aided by some of the ecological elements—not the least of which is anonymity (McKenna et al., 2002). The fact that the Internet provides anonymity may also contribute to the development of self-disclosure online. Research regarding self-disclosure and gender is generally mixed: some research contends that men are more likely to participate in self-disclosure than women; other research says that men are less likely to reciprocate high levels of self-disclosure; and finally, some says there is no difference (Klinger-Vartabedian & O'Flaherty, 1989). Despite the contradictions in likelihood of disclosure, there do not appear to be differences between men and women in terms of the depth of the disclosure (Joinson, 2001). Further, the status of individuals engaged in self-disclosing also bears some weight on how self-disclosure is perceived. Men as well as those in higher status positions are provided more latitude with self-disclosure and are viewed more positively. As a consequence, when those in positions of higher power disclose to those of lower status, those in the higher position are viewed as more attractive by those in lower positions because the disclosure is "viewed as a 'gift' which is offered to reduce power differentials" (Klinger-Vartabedian & O'Flaherty, 1989, p. 161). This also appears to be the case for disclosure in psychotherapy and clinical supervision (Barnett, 2011). In other cases, however, the timing of self-disclosure may impede a relationship. In investigating physician self-disclosure, for example, McDaniel et al. (2007) found that at times when physicians disclosed too early in a relationship, there was no evidence of a positive effect, and, in some cases, the disclosure appeared disruptive. For example, personal advertisements placed online tend to be longer than ads placed in a newspaper, presumably because of the reduced cost per word (Hatala, Milewski, & Baack, 1999). In fact, there is a negative correlation between one's level of self-disclosure on Facebook and one's age, with younger individuals disclosing more than older ones (Nosko, Wood, & Molema, 2010). For younger adults this level of self-disclosure may be dependent upon personality and culture (Chen & Marcus, 2012). Researchers have found that those young adults who disclose the least online are those from collectivistic cultures who are low in extroversion (Chen & Marcus, 2012). With the Internet, the anonymity of the person with whom one is communicating may provide an equalizing function for the nature of self-disclosure: one's social status and, in some cases, gender may be unobserved and unable to be assessed by the individual with whom one is communicating, thus creating an equal playing field where people initially meet. It is only after they are already invested in the relationship that some of these discoveries are made.

Empirical evidence demonstrates that anonymity via the computer can be beneficial to the development of trust and intimacy, even when theory suggests otherwise. Sztompka (1999, as cited in Henderson & Gilding, 2004) contends three elements contribute to trust-building in a relationship: accountability of the person with whom one is interacting, pre-commitment (a surrendering of one's own freedom as a demonstration of commitment), and the environment or situation in which the interaction occurs. Though the Internet can provide a setting through which one can feel connected, there are few channels through which the Internet provides an appropriate amount of accountability or pre-commitment. Because interactions may be anonymous, there is no way of accounting for the veracity of statements offered by individuals online, particularly as they relate to current emotional states, thus inhibiting accountability. Further, the structure of the Internet and new media creates a context where individuals can interact and build relationships with more than one person at a time, thus interfering with the emergence of pre-commitment in trust-building. The findings of Henderson and Gilding's (2004) investigation did reveal that accountability seemed to be one barrier in developing trust, but there was also evidence that computer users had found other ways to assess pre-commitment and their respective willingness to take risks in their relationships. One way that the computer can improve accountability is through the very nature of the Internet: online, one can find searchable, detailed information about other people, whether it is information specific to the individual or information about how that person behaves in a group (McKenna, 2008).

Another element of online self-disclosure is that there is a difference between directed and non-directed disclosures. Non-directed self-disclosure refers to the type of self-disclosure that reveals information of a personal nature, but not to any one person specifically. One example of this can be seen in blogging (Jang & Stefanone, 2011). Non-directed self-disclosures may also occur within the context of social media, such as in Facebook postings and profiles, or media such as Twitter. Although information is not directed at one person specifically in these formats, information of an intimate nature is nonetheless disclosed and can strengthen the ties to the individuals within the user's network. The frequency of the communication and the ability for other users to comment (an opportunity for some level of reciprocation, albeit limited) on a posting further contribute to the development of intimacy online (Jang & Stefanone, 2011).

Reciprocity in relationships is critical to the development of a trust-ing and intimate relationship, both online and offline, particularly if the reciprocity is in relation to self-disclosure (Laurenceau, Barrett, & Pietro-monaco, 1998). The Internet and new media both provide a forum for reciprocity. Equity theory asserts that as individuals in a relationship build trust, the development of that trust is predicated on the notion that each person in the relationship will make an equitable contribution to disclosing personal information in the relationship (Jang & Stefanone, 2011). Because of its accessibility at any time (both synchronous and asynchronous) and in many forums, the Internet provides many opportu-nities and greater degrees of reciprocation. This reciprocity, as explained by Yum and Hara (2006), is also evidence of social penetration theory (Altman & Taylor, 1973), briefly discussed in Chapter 1.

Another way in which technology and new media assist in develop-ing intimacy is people have a tendency to be more forthright in online interactions, especially when conducted over a web-camera program (Valkenburg & Peter, 2009). One likely reason may be that the physi-cal barrier of a digital screen prevents one from having to experience all of the consequences of personal online activities. Examples of this uninhibited behavior can be observed in daily postings and comments to online news stories or other material. This phenomenon is supported by research showing that computer users are more likely to engage in more aggressive and potentially conflict-causing communication than those who rely primarily on face-to-face methods (Dubrovsky, Kiesler, & Sethna, 1991).

Relationship Termination

Terminating a romantic relationship is a common phenomenon. Some scholars assert that couples who meet online are less likely to have mean-ingful, committed relationships compared to relationships formed offline. Nationally representative data, however, does not support this assertion (Rosenfeld, 2017).

To Block or Not to Block

We cannot discuss relationship endings in a digital age without cover-ing the issue of privacy, blocking, and social media. It's a well-known fact that people invoke blocking as a way to protect themselves from someone else being able to access them. This includes people who are highly abusive all the way down the continuum to the people with whom one does not wish to be involved. The motivation for blocking and the mechanisms for blocking evolve as the technology develops. Some of the more common motivations are related to personal safety. For example, if there is someone who has harassed you or ever been harmful to you in some capacity, blocking them prevents them from being able to see your activities. People often block significant others or family members in order to solidify emotional cutoff/closure in relationships. It not only prevents ongoing surveillance on both sides but is a protective factor when it comes to the temptation to continue to contact the person. Another side is one can unblock someone if staying away is difficult. Generally, social media and technology in general have made the end of a relationship a very blurred grey line, and no one has rigid enough boundaries (or will power) anymore to terminate the relationship completely. It can be gasoline for a co-dependent's fire.

Another reason for blocking someone, while not a common motivation, is to engage without disengagement. It is often the case that people try to get someone to pay attention to them through taking some action regarding the status of the relationship. If someone recognizes that they are blocked, that is likely to engage them. Like Nathaniel Hawthorne wrote in *The Scarlet Letter*, love and hate are the same thing because they both involve passion. The fact that someone is passionate enough to block you suggests that there is still some level of engagement. In many circumstances, the best option is to not respond, but of course, the reason that people may choose to block is to in fact get that engagement.

Once you have blocked someone, it is an auto block for both: the person being blocked cannot see things about the person who blocked them, and vice-versa. Blocking is not totally foolproof. What about in the cases of mutual friends? When a friend posts about another friend who has been blocked, the person who has been blocked can still be viewed by others, even the person who blocked them. Blocking someone is a very physical solution to a psychological problem. And in some cases that makes sense. We often employ physical barriers when we cannot use the psychological ones, and once we are able to use the psychological ones, the physical ones don't matter as much. The good news is that technology provides ways to physically block until the user can establish psychological boundaries.

"I Always Feel Like Somebody's Watching Me"

Breaking up is hard to do. And it is especially hard in a world where the final curtain call is not the cut off. As we discussed in Chapter 5, surveillance of anyone from perfect strangers to former partners is becoming more commonplace and accepted practice (Fulton & Kibby, 2017). Some common search terms include: an ex-partner's general social activities, the presence of a new partner, and the conversations the ex-partner is having with others (Tong, 2013). These searches are most commonly conducted when one is uncertain about why the relationship terminated (Tong, 2013).

"I Can't Forget You, Baby"

State dependent memory refers to superior memory for information that is retrieved in the same state as when it was learned (Lang et al., 2001, p. 695). In applying this information to social media in our relationships, we remember (and potentially search for) information congruent with our mood state. This can be damaging to one's personal well-being after a relationship ends. The Internet provides a way that one can fixate on someone else; search for photos and their memorabilia; and search for new information on a past partner as a way to feel that one is connected and potentially project onto them without the previous partner even knowing. It may stall someone's recovery process, take their attention and energy away from resolution, and keep them stuck emotionally as well as harm one's post–break up recovery. These findings are also true when one friends their ex-partner on Facebook. Those who remain Facebook friends with an ex feel less sexual desire, more longing for the ex-partner, and more negative feelings overall (Marshall, 2012). On the other hand, those who are not Facebook friends with former partners are more distressed than those who remained friends (Lukacs & Quan-Haase, 2015).

But it is not all bad. It is true that Facebook is a mechanism to remember potential sexual partners, most notably for men. This finding gives cause for partners to be somewhat jealous, as Facebook can be used to find alternative partners (Drouin, Miller, & Dibble, 2015). At the same time, those who are on Facebook do not perceive others on Facebook to be acceptable alternatives (Drouin et al., 2015). Further, just because one friends their ex-partner, it does not mean that they want to reunite with that partner (Marshall, 2012). At the same time, those who have the ability and engage in surveillance have a more difficult time with the break up, and ultimately may delete the ex to manage their feelings. This finding calls into question previous research that suggests the best path to emotional wellness is deleting the ex (Lukacs & Quan-Haase, 2015).

Conclusion

Relational development at this point in our history co-occurs with technology. We started with the role of technology in forming relationships with attention to online dating, the visibility of relationships online, and the intersectionality between meeting online and marriage. Next, relationship maintenance was discussed with attention to how technology contributes to relationship satisfaction, and the role of technology in developing and maintaining intimacy. The chapter closed with a discussion around how technology intersects with termination of relationships. In the upcoming chapter we address more advanced technology-based relational problems like technophobia and out-of-control technology-related behaviors, to name a few.

References

Altman, I., & Taylor, D. A. (1973). *Social penetration: The development of interpersonal relationships.* Oxford, UK: Holt, Rinehart & Winston.

Ansari, A., & Klinenberg, E. (2016). *Modern romance.* London, England, UK: Penguin Books.

Bargh, J., & McKenna, K. (2004). The Internet and social life. *Annual Review of Psychology, 55*(1), 573–590. doi:10.1146/annurev.psych.55.090902.141922

Barnett, J. E. (2011). Utilizing technological innovations to enhance psychotherapy supervision, training, and outcomes. *Psychotherapy, 48*(2), 103–108. doi:10.1037/a0023381

Baxter, L. A. (1979). Self-disclosure as a relationship disengagement strategy: An exploratory investigation. *Human Communication Research, 5*(3), 215–222. doi:10.1111/j.1468-2958.1979.tb00635.x

Belk, R. (2014). If you prick us do we not bleed? Humanoid robots and cyborgs as consuming subjects and consumed objects. In E. M. González & T. M. Lowrey (Eds.), *Latin American advances in consumer research* (Vol. 3, pp. 3–6). Duluth, MN: Association for Consumer Research.

Bergdall, A. R., Kraft, J. M., Andes, K., Carter, M., Hatfield-Timajchy, K., & Hock-Long, L. (2012). Love and hooking up in the new millennium: Communication technology and relationships among urban African American and Puerto Rican young adults. *The Journal of Sex Research, 49*(6), 570–582.

Blackwell, C., Birnholtz, J., & Abbott, C. (2015). Seeing and being seen: Co-situation and impression formation using Grindr, a location-aware gay dating app. *New Media & Society, 17*(7), 1117–1136. doi:10.1177/1461444814521595

Borca, G., Bina, M., Keller, P., Gilbert, L., & Begotti, T. (2015). Internet use and developmental tasks: Adolescents' point of view. *Computers in Human Behavior, 52*, 49–58. doi:10.1016/j.chb.2015.05.029

Borrajo, E., Gámez Guadix, M., & Calvete Zumalde, E. (2015). Justification beliefs of violence, myths about love and cyber dating abuse. *Psicothema, 27*(4), 327–333. doi:10.7334/psicothema2015.59

Bridges, A., Bergner, R., & Hesson-McInnis, M. (2003). Romantic partners' use of pornography: Its significance for women. *Journal of Sex & Marital Therapy, 29*(1), 1–14.

Brody, N., LeFebvre, L. E., & Blackburn, K. G. (2016). Social networking site behaviors across the relational lifespan: Measurement and association with relationship escalation and de-escalation. *Social Media + Society, 2*(4) doi:10.1177/2056305116680004

Cali, B. E., Coleman, J. M., & Campbell, C. (2013). Stranger danger? Women's self-protection intent and the continuing stigma of online dating. *Cyberpsychology, Behavior, and Social Networking, 16*(12), 853–857. doi:10.1089/cyber.2012.0512

Chow, C. M., Buhrmester, D., & Tan, C. C. (2014). Interpersonal coping styles and couple relationship quality: Similarity versus complementarity hypotheses. *European Journal of Social Psychology, 44*(2), 175–186. doi:10.1002/ejsp.2000

Czechowsky, J. D. (2008). *The impact of the Blackberry on couple relationships.* Doctoral dissertation, Wilfrid Laurier University, Canada. Retrieved from https://scholars.wlu.ca/cgi/viewcontent.cgi?referer=www.google.com/&httpsredir=1&article=2055&context=etd://

Davis, E., & Fingerman, K. (2016). Digital dating: Online profile content of older and younger adults. *Journals of Gerontology Series B: Psychological Sciences and Social Sciences, 71*(6), 959–967.

Derlega, V. J., & Chaikin, A. L. (1977). Privacy and self-disclosure in social relationships. *Journal of Social Issues, 33*(3), 102–115. doi:10.1111/j.1540-4560.1977.tb01885.x

Derlega, V. J., Winstead, B. A., & Greene, K. (2008). Self-disclosure and starting a close relationship. In S. Sprecher, A. Wenzel, & J. Harvey (Eds.), *Handbook of relationship initiation* (pp. 153–174). New York: Psychology Press.

Drouin, M., Miller, D. A., & Dibble, J. L. (2015). Facebook or memory: Which is the real threat to your relationship? *Cyberpsychology, Behavior & Social Networking, 18*(10), 561–566. doi:10.1089/cyber.2015.0259

Dubrovsky, V., Kiesler, S., & Sethna, B. (1991). The equalization phenomenon: Status effects in computer-mediated and face-to-face decision-making groups. *Human–Computer Interaction, 6*(2), 119–146. doi:10.1207/s15327051hci0602_2

Duguay, S. (2016). Dressing up Tinderella: Interrogating authenticity claims on the mobile dating app Tinder. *Information, Communication & Society, 20*(3), 351–367. doi:10.1080/1369118X.2016.1168471

Ferrando, F. (2014). Is the post-human a post-woman? Cyborgs, robots, artificial intelligence and the future of gender: A case study. *European Journal of Future Research, 2*(43), 1–17.

Fiksenbaum, L. M. (2014). Supportive work–family environments: Implications for work–family conflict and well-being. *The International Journal of Human Resource Management, 25*(5), 653–672. doi:10.1080/09585192.2013.796314

Finkel, E. J., Eastwick, P. W., Karney, B. R., Reis, H. T., & Sprecher, S. (2012). Online dating: A critical analysis from the perspective of psychological science. *Psychological Science in the Public Interest, 13*, 3–66. doi:10.1177/1529100612436552

Fox, J., & Warber, K. M. (2013). Romantic relationship development in the age of Facebook: An exploratory study of emerging adults' perceptions, motives, and behaviors. *Cyberpsychology, Behavior, and Social Networking, 16*(1), 3–7. doi:10.1089/cyber.2012.0288

Fulton, J. M., & Kibby, M. D. (2017). Millennials and the normalization of surveillance on Facebook. *Continuum: Journal of Media & Cultural Studies, 31*(2), 189–199. doi:10.1080/10304312.2016.1265094

Gewirtz-Meydan, A., & Ayalon, L. (2018). Forever young: Visual representations of gender and age in online dating sites for older adults. *Journal of Women & Aging, 30*(6), 484–502.

Ginter, E. J. (1982). *Self-disclosure as a function of the intensity of four affective states associated with loneliness.* Dissertation, The University of Georgia, Athens, GA.

Griffin, E., & Fingerman, K. (2018). Online dating profile content of older adults seeking same—and cross-sex relationships. *Journal of GLBT Family Studies, 14*(5), 446–466.

Grov, C., Gillespie, B. J., Royce, T., & Lever, J. (2011). Perceived consequences of casual online sexual activities on heterosexual relationships: A U.S. online survey. *Archives of Sexual Behavior, 40*(2), 429–439. doi:10.1007/s10508-010-9598-z

Hance, M. A., Blackhart, G., & Dew, M. (2018). Free to be me: The relationship between the true self, rejection sensitivity, and use of online dating sites. *The Journal of Social Psychology, 158*(4), 421–429. doi:10.1080/00224545.2017.1389684

Hatala, M. N., Milewski, K., & Baack, D. W. (1999). Downloading love: A content analysis of Internet personal ads placed by college students. *College Student Journal*, *33*(1), 124–129.

Hayles, K. N. (1999). *How we became posthuman: Virtual bodies in cybernetics, literature, and informatics*. Chicago, IL: The University of Chicago Press.

Henderson, S., & Gilding, M. (2004). "I've never clicked this much with anyone in my life": Trust and hyperpersonal communication in online friendships. *New Media & Society*, *6*(4), 487–506. doi:10.1177/146144804044331

Henline, B. H., & Harris, S. M. (2006). *Pros and cons of technology use within close relationships*. Poster presented at the Annual Conference of the American Association for Marriage and Family Therapy, Austin, TX, October 19–22, 2006.

Hertlein, K. M., & Ancheta, K. (2014). Clinical application of the advantages of technology in couple and family therapy. *The American Journal of Family Therapy*, *42*(4), 313–324. doi:10.1080/01926187.2013.866511

Hertlein, K. M., & Blumer, M. L. (2013). *The couple and family technology framework: Intimate relationships in a digital age*. New York, NY: Routledge

Hertlein, K. M., Dulley, C., Cloud, R., Leon, D., & Chang, J. (2017). Does absence of evidence mean evidence of absence? Managing the issue of partner surveillance in infidelity treatment. *Sexual and Relationship Therapy*, *32*(3–4), 323–333. doi:10.1080/14681994.2017.1397952

Hjorth, L. (2013). The place of the emplaced mobile: A case study into gendered locative media practices. *Mobile Media & Communication*, *1*(1), 110–115. doi:10.1177/2050157912459738

Hodge, C. J., Zabriskie, R. B., Fellingham, G., Coyne, S., Lundberg, N. R., Padilla-Walker, L. M., & Day, R. D. (2012). The relationship between media in the home and family functioning in context of leisure. *Journal of Leisure Research*, *44*(3), 285–307. doi:10.1080/00222216.2012.11950266

Huxley, J. (1968). Transhumanism. *Journal of Humanistic Psychology*, *8*(1), 73–76. doi:10.1177/002216786800800107

Jang, C. Y., & Stefanone, M. A. (2011). Non-directed self-disclosure in the blogosphere: Exploring the persistence of interpersonal communication norms. *Information, Communication & Society*, *14*, 1039–1059. doi:10.1080/1369118X.2011.559265

Joinson, A. N. (2001). Self-disclosure in computer-mediated communication: The role of self-awareness and visual anonymity. *European Journal of Social Psychology*, *31*(2), 177–192. doi:10.1002/ejsp.36

Kennedy, G. E., Judd, T. S., Churchward, A., Gray, K., & Krause, K. (2008). First year students' experiences with technology: Are they really digital natives? *Australasian Journal of Educational Technology*, *24*(1). doi:10.14742/ajet.1233

Klinger-Vartabedian, L., & O'Flaherty, K. M. (1989). Student perceptions of presenter self-disclosure in the college classroom based on perceived status differentials. *Contemporary Educational Psychology*, *14*(2), 153–163. doi:10.1016/0361-476X(89)90033-7

Lang, A. J., Craske, M. G., Brown, M., & Ghaneian, A. (2001). Fear-related state dependent memory. *Cognition and Emotion*, *15*(5), 695–703. doi:10.1080/02699930143000031

Lanigan, J., Bold, M., & Chenoweth, L. (2009). Computers in the family context: Perceived impact on family time and relationships. *Family Science Review*, *14*(1), 16–32

Laurenceau, J., Barrett, L. F., & Pietromonaco, P. R. (1998). Intimacy as an inter-personal process: The importance of self-disclosure, partner disclosure, and per-ceived partner responsiveness in interpersonal exchanges. *Journal of Personality and Social Psychology, 74*(5), 1238–1251. doi:10.1037//0022-3514.74.5.1238

Li, J., & Lipscomb, A. (2017). *Love on the cloud: The rise of online dating in China*. Retrieved October 15, 2018 from https://china.usc.edu/love-cloud-rise-online-dating-china

Ling, R., & Campbell, S. (2009). *The reconstruction of space and time through mobile communication practices*. New York, NY: Routledge

Lukacs, V., & Quan-Haase, A. (2015). Romantic breakups on Facebook: New scales for studying post-breakup behaviors, digital distress, and surveillance. *Information, Communication & Society, 18*(5), 492–508. doi:10.1080/13691 18X.2015.1008540

Macapagal, K., Coventry, R., Puckett, J. A., Phillips, G., & Mustanski, B. (2016). Geosocial networking app use among men who have sex with men in seri-ous romantic relationships. *Archives of Sexual Behavior, 45*(6), 1513–1524. doi:10.1007/s10508-016-0698-2

Manago, A., Taylor, T., Greenfield, P., Eccles, J., & Subrahmanyam, K. (2012). Me and my 400 friends: The anatomy of college students' Facebook networks, their communication patterns, and well-being. *Developmental Psychology, 48*(2), 369–380. doi:10.1037/a0026338

Marshall, T. C. (2012). Facebook surveillance of former romantic partners: Associations with post-breakup recovery and personal growth. *Cyberpsychology, Behavior & Social Networking, 15*(10), 521–526. doi:10.1089/cyber.2012.0125

Marwick, A. E., & Boyd, D. (2010). I tweet honestly, I tweet passionately: Twitter users, context collapse, and the imagined audience. *New Media & Society, 13*(1), 114–133. doi:10.1177/1461444810365313

McArthur, N., & Twist, M. L. C. (2017). The rise of digisexuality: Therapeutic challenges and possibilities. *Sexual and Relationship Therapy, 32*(3/4), 334–344.

McDaniel, S. H., Beckman, H. B., Morse, D. S., Silberman, J., Seaburn, D. B., & Epstein, R. M. (2007). Physician self-disclosure in primary care visits enough about you, what about me? *Archives of Internal Medicine, 167*(12), 1321–1326. doi:10.1001/archinte.167.12.1321

McKenna, K. Y. A. (2008). Influences on the nature and functioning of online groups. In A. Barak (Ed.), *Psychological aspects of cyberspace: Theory, research, applications* (pp. 228–242). Cambridge, UK: Cambridge University Press.

McKenna, K. Y. A., Green, A. S., & Gleason, M. E. J. (2002). Relationship forma-tion on the Internet: What's the big attraction? *Journal of Social Issues, 58*(1), 9–31. doi:10.1111/1540-4560.00246

Mesch, G. (2006). Family characteristics and intergenerational conflicts over the Internet. *Information, Communication & Society, 9*(4), 473–495.

Nie, N. H., Hillygus, D. S., & Erbring, L. (2002). Internet use, interpersonal relations, and sociability. In B. Wellman & C. Haythornthwaite (Eds.), *The Internet in every-day life* (pp. 215–243). Malden, MA: Blackwell. doi:10.1002/978047077429

Ng, B. (2017). *Momo rakes in millions live streaming*. Retrieved October 28, 2018 from http://www.ejinsight.com/20170825-momo-rakes-in-millions-with-live-streaming/

Nosko, A., Wood, E., & Molema, S. (2010). All about me: Disclosure in online social networking profiles: The case of Facebook. *Computers in Human Behav-ior, 26*(3), 406–418, doi:10.1016/j.chb.2009.11.012

Orosz, G., Szekeres, A., Kiss, Z., Farkas, P., & Roland-Lévy, C. (2014). Elevated romantic love and jealousy if relationship status is declared on Facebook. *Frontiers in Psychology*, 6. doi:10.3389/fpsyg.2015.00214

Owens, Z. D. (2017). Is it Facebook official? Coming out and passing strategies of young adult gay men on social media. *Journal of Homosexuality*, 64(4), 431–449. doi:10.1080/00918369.2016.1194112

Papp, L. M., Danielewicz, J., & Cayemberg, C. (2012). "Are we Facebook official?" Implications of dating partners' Facebook use and profiles for intimate relationship satisfaction. *Cyberpsychology, Behavior & Social Networking*, 15(2), 85–90. doi:10.1089/cyber.2011.0291

Peterson, R. B., & Twist, M. L. C. (2017). The space between us: Technology as an interplanetary bridge. *Sexual and Relationship Therapy*, 32(3/4), 366–373.

Prestage, G., Bavinton, B., Grierson, J., Down, I., Keen, P., Bradley, J., & Duncan, D. (2015). Online dating among Australian gay and bisexual men: Romance or hooking up? *AIDS and Behavior*, 19(10), 1905–1913. doi:10.1007/s10461-015-1032-z

Ray, P. (2016). "Synthetik love lasts forever": Sex dolls and the (post?)human condition. In D. Banerji & M. Paranjape (Eds.), *Critical posthumanism and planetary futures* (pp. 91–112). New Delhi: Springer.

Robards, B., & Lincoln, S. (2016). Making it "Facebook official": Reflecting on romantic relationships through sustained Facebook use. *Social Media + Society*, 2(4). doi:10.1177/2056305116672890

Rochadiat, A. M., Tong, S. T., & Novak, J. M. (2018). Online dating and courtship among Muslim American women: Negotiating technology, religious identity, and culture. *New Media & Society*, 20(4), 1618–1639. doi:10.1177/1461444817702396

Rosen, L. D., Cheever, N. A., Cummings, C., & Felt, J. (2008). The impact of emotionality and self-disclosure on online dating versus traditional dating. *Computers in Human Behavior*, 24(5), 2124–2157. doi:10.1016/j.chb.2007.10.003

Rosenfeld, M. J. (2017). Marriage, choice, and couplehood in the age of the Internet. *Sociological Science*, 4, 490–510. doi:10.15195/v4.a20

Rosenfeld, M. J., & Thomas, R. J. (2010, September). *Meeting online: The rise of the Internet as a social intermediary.* Unpublished manuscript, Department of Sociology, Stanford University, Stanford, CA.

Rosenfeld, M. J., & Thomas. R. J. (2012). Searching for a mate: The rise of the Internet as a social intermediary. *American Sociological Review*, 77(4), 523–547. doi: 10.1177/0003122412448050

Rubin, Z., Hill, C. T., Peplau, L. A., & Dunkel-Schetter, C. (1980). Self-disclosure in dating couples: Sex roles and the ethic of openness. *Journal of Marriage and the Family*, 42(2), 305–317. doi:10.2307/351228

Schwab, S. H., Scalise, J. J., Ginter, E. J., & Whipple, G. (1998). Self-disclosure, loneliness and four interpersonal targets: Friend, group of friends, stranger, and group of strangers. *Psychological Reports*, 82(3 suppl), 1264–1266. doi:10.2466/pr0.1998.82.3c.1264

Schwartz, P., & Velotta, N. (2018). Online dating: Changing intimacy one swipe at a time? In J., Van Hook, S., McHale, & V., King. (Eds.), *Families and technology: National symposium on family issues.* New York, NY: Springer.

Sharabi, L. L., & Caughlin, J. P. (2017). What predicts first date success? A longitudinal study of modality switching in online dating. *Personal Relationships*, 24(2), 370–391. doi:10.1111/pere.12188

Smith, A. (2016). *15% of American adults have used online dating sites or mobile dating apps*. Retrieved from www.pewInternet.org/2016/02/11/15-percent-of-american-adults-have-used-online-dating-sites-or-mobile-dating-apps/

Statista. (2017). *Online dating: Statistics & facts*. Retrieved from www.statista.com/topics/2158/online-dating/

Stewart, I., & Cohen, J. (1997). *Figments of reality: Molecules, minds, and multi-cultures*. Cambridge, UK: Cambridge University Press.

Sztompka, P. (1999). *Trust: A sociological theory*. Cambridge: Cambridge University Press.

Thelwall, M., & Vis, T. (2017). Gender and image sharing on Facebook, Twitter, Instagram, Snapchat and WhatsApp in the UK: Hobbying alone or filtering for friends? *Aslib Journal of Information Management, 69*(6), 702–720. doi:10.1108/AJIM-04-2017-0098

Tidwell, L. C., & Walther, J. B. (2000). Getting to know one another a bit at a time: Computer-mediated communication effects on disclosure, impressions, and interpersonal evaluations. *Human Communication Research, 28*(3), 317–348. doi:10.1111/j.1468-2958.2002.tb00811.x

Toma, C. L., Hancock, J. T., & Ellison, N. B. (2008). Separating fact from fiction: An examination of deceptive self-presentation in online dating profiles. *Personality and Social Psychology Bulletin, 34*, 1023–1036. doi:10.1177/0146167208318067

Tong, S. T. (2013). Facebook use during relationship termination: Uncertainty reduction and surveillance. *Cyberpsychology, Behavior & Social Networking, 16*(11), 788–793. doi:10.1089/cyber.2012.0549

Tong, S. T., Hancock, J., & Slatcher, R. (2016). Online dating system design and relational decision making: Choice, algorithms, and control. *Personal Relationships, 23*(4), 645–662. doi:10.1111/pere.12158

Turkle, S. (2012). *Alone together: Why we expect more from technology and less from technology*. New York, NY: Basic Books.

Twist, M. L. C. (2018, June). *Digisexuality: What the tech is it?* Invited Lecture, College of Sexual and Relationship Therapists, London, England, United Kingdom.

Twist, M. L. C., Bergdall, M. K., Belous, C. K., & Maier, C. A. (2017). Electronic visibility management of lesbian, gay, and bisexual identities and relationships. *Journal of Couple and Relationship Therapy: Innovations in Clinical Educational Interventions, 16*(4), 271–285.

Valkenburg, P., & Peter, J. (2009). Social consequences of the Internet for adolescents: A decade of research. *Current Directions in Psychological Science, 18*(1), 1–5. doi:10.1111/j.1467-8721.2009.01595.x

Vandeweerd, C., Myers, J., Coulter, M., Yalcin, A., & Corvin, J. (2016). Positives and negatives of online dating according to women 50+. *Journal of Women & Aging, 28*(3), 259–270. doi:10.1080/08952841.2015.1137435

Whitty, M. T. (2008). Revealing the "real" me, searching for the "actual" you: Presentations of self on an Internet dating site. *Computers in Human Behavior, 24*(4), 1707–1723. doi:10.1016/j.chb.2007.07.002

Wilding, R. (2006). "Virtual" intimacies? Families communicating across transnational contexts. *Global Networks, 6*(2), 125–142. doi:10.1111/j.1471-0374.2006.00137.x

Wolfe, C. (2010). *What is posthumanism?*. Minneapolis, MN: University of Minnesota Press.

Wrench, J. S., & Punyanunt-Carter, N. M. (2017). From the front porch to swiping right: The impact of technology on modern dating. In N. Punyanunt-Carter & J. Wrench (Eds.), *The impact of social media in modern romantic relationships* (pp. 1–12). Lanham, MD: Lexington Books.

Xie, B. (2007). Using the Internet for offline relationship formation. *Social Science Computer Review, 25*(3), 396–404. doi:10.1177/0894439307297622

Yao, J., Tan, N., & Ilies, R. (2017). Telecommuting and work-family conflict: The moderating role of work-family integration. *Academy of Management Proceedings, 2017*(1), 13717. doi:10.5465/ambpp.2017.13717abstract

Yum, Y., & Hara, K. (2006). Computer-mediated relationship development: A cross-cultural comparison. *Journal of Computer Mediated Communication, 11,* 133–152. doi:10.1111/j.1083-6101.2006.tb00307.x

TEN

Debugging Advanced Internet-Based Relational Problems

Decoding Technology and Relationship Error Messages

One of the first things I (KH) often hear in therapy is the accusation that a partner is "addicted" to the Internet. We believe this is a way to distance rather than confront the problem. More often than not, the people in the room are not addicted to the computer. Yet such words are used as a weapon against each other. When we talk about "addiction," what are we really saying? On the flipside, because of the nature of my (MLCT) clinical consultations—which focus on gender, sexual, erotic, and relational diversity (GSERD)—people I work with are at times very into sexual technologies (sextech), but may have partners who are afraid of the technology (technophobic) and thus are weary of such practices. But what is technophobia and how much of an issue is it really?

Out-of-Control Technology-Related Behaviors

Out-of-control technology behaviors have many characteristics of a behavioral addiction. Such behaviors are often conceptualized as being a form of one of two diagnoses in mental health—either a form of an "addictive" disorder or a form of impulse control disorder (Spada, 2014). When considered an "addiction," commonly referenced criteria include Internet use that is interfering with one's vocation or personal life (Spada, 2014). Ross (2006) offered a conceptualization of problematic Internet use among five criteria. These criteria include:

> Whether it is characterized by time online or the specific activities, the presence or absence of physical symptoms (which are more common in addiction than in infidelity), and the presence or absence of addictive properties such as speed and potency of information, or connection factors that play a part in maintaining the behavior. Another conceptualization is offered by Ross and

associates who conceptualize Internet addiction as having an impact on five major domains: "causing problems in everyday life; a sense of lack of control; feeling bad about sexual use of the Internet (dysphoria); a subjective awareness that things have reached the point of lack of control and addiction; and seriousness, a sense that this addiction requires professional intervention or treatment."

(p. 460)

In addition, out-of-control technology-related behaviors (Braun-Harvey & Vigorito, 2016; Twist & McArthur, 2017) seem to be associated with time spent online (Odacı & Kalkan, 2010). The more time spent online, the more likely one is to indicate problematic usage. Further, Internet "addiction" is viewed to have similar characteristics to other addiction categories, including withdrawal, conflict when asked to limit use, tolerance, relapse, changes in mood, loss of interest in previously pleasurable activities, and using the Internet for mood management (Sussman, Harper, Stahl, & Weigle, 2018).

Unfortunately, there is a great deal of incongruence in both the terminology and the criteria. For example, phrases such as "Internet addiction," "problematic Internet use," "compulsive Internet use," "Internet compulsion disorder," and "pathological Internet use" are used synonymously and interchangeably (Billieux & Starcevic, 2017). In fact, the American Psychiatric Association (APA, 2013) in the *Diagnostic Statistical Manual of Mental Disorders (DSM)-5* claims that Internet gaming disorder is synonymous with Internet "addiction" and Internet use disorder (American Psychiatric Association, 2013; Billieux & Starcevic, 2017), which, when considering the vast difference in those terms, is irresponsible. This makes the classification of Internet "addiction" (and consequently, treatment) fraught with conceptual and definitional issues (Ryding & Kaye, 2018). Moreover, with no clear definition of what are healthy technology-related behaviors and usage, it makes it virtually impossible to determine what are out-of-control, pathological, addictive, and/or phobic technology-related behaviors.

Technophobia

According to the Merriam-Webster Dictionary (n.d.), "technophobia" was first cited in 1947, and is defined as the fear or dislike of technology or complex devices, especially those of an advanced nature. There is disagreement as to whether this fear is irrational or justified in nature (Osiceanu, 2015). In the United States, such feelings and behaviors around technology started to first be observed during the Industrial Revolution, and have since been observed around the world across various societies.

Prominent computer educator, professor, and research psychologist Dr. Larry Rosen (1993) has identified and described three main types of technophobes: (1) uncomfortable users, who are slightly anxious about technology due to their lack of knowledge and information, (2) cognitive computerphobes, who appear non-anxious with technology, but who, internally, experience negative cognitions and distortions in relation to their technological engagement, and (3) anxious computerphobes, who experience classic anxiety signs and symptoms when engaged with technology.

In terms of the prevalence of technophobia, there is data that exists going back almost 30 years now. In a survey study of 3,392 first-year university students across 23 countries conducted between 1992 and 1994, Weil and Rosen (1995) found that 82% of Indian students, 58% of Japanese students, 53% of Mexican students, and 29% of US students reported high levels of technophobic fears. Moving forward, each year, beginning in 2014, a research team (Bader, Day, and Gordon) at Champman University has conducted a comprehensive, nationwide study of the fears of US persons. Their findings the first year were that of the 1,500 participants, technophobia was not one of the biggest fears, but rather that forms of technophobia (i.e., online identity theft, and government and corporate surveillance of Internet activity) were some of the top five things held as worries or concerns by people (Ledbetter, 2014). The following year, of the 1,541 random US sample of participants, Bader, Day, and Gordon found that technophobia (i.e., artificial intelligence, robots, and cyber-terrorism) was in the top five fears of people (Ledbetter, 2015). When participants were asked to rate their level of fear on a scale of 1 (not afraid) to 4 (very afraid), technophobia received the second highest average fear score—2.07; human-made disaster, with an average fear score of 2.15, was the only fear ranked higher (Ledbetter, 2015). By 2016, 2017, and 2018, however, technophobia was not ranked even in the top ten biggest fears of US participants (Wilkinson College, 2016, 2017, 2018).

The data has also shown that fear of US persons in general appears to be on the rise (Wilkinson College, 2018). Bader, Day, and Gordon speculate on this change, stating that in the era of the current US presidency (Donald Trump and administration), other fears have grown significantly more critical like fears for the environment, healthcare, government corruption, and shrinking wealth and thus have replaced technophobic fears (Wilkinson College, 2018). I (MLCT) would agree with this idea—that people have more important things to fear than technology, but I would also attribute such a decrease in technophobia to the growing everyday use of technology across US generations and overall populations.

"Let's Go Crazy"

Technophobia can and does have a major impact on the quality of life for individuals and relational systems (Brosnan & Thorpe, 2006; Nimrod,

2018; Osiceanu, 2015). For example, there is great difficulty in maximizing one's academic and employment opportunities at earlier and middle lifespan stages if one suffers from technophobia (Brosnan & Thorpe, 2006). In the later lifespan stage, those who experience technophobia often have fewer resources to cope with their declining health and losses of loved ones (Nimrod, 2018). Technophobia is therefore considered a threat to one's well-being across the lifespan (Nimrod, 2018).

Other negative effects of technophobia include poorer school performance, threats to job security, decreased happiness, and difficulty accessing one's social relationships/friendships (Nimrod, 2018). Negative relational system effects can include lack of partners met through online dating, decreased chances to relationally grow through digisexual engagements, less opportunity to develop attachment relationships via technology, decreased experiences with shared technology-based leisure activities with family and friends, and less opportunity to soothe one's anxieties and insecurities (and those of others) via digital attachments (otherwise known as digiattachments; Twist, 2018).

Some scholars have gone so far as to posit that technology usage is as important as literacy, and thus, the educational system needs to weight the importance of technological literacy equivalent to that of literacy around reading, writing, and mathematics (Osiceanua, 2015). Therefore, technophobia needs to be acknowledged as a problem, and steps need to be taken to reduce it across educational, employment, and home settings (Osiceanua, 2015).

Out-of-control technology-related behaviors have also been tied to a host of negative consequences (Eleuteri, Saladino, & Verrastro, 2017). For example, low motivation in students is associated with a lack of key aspects that would create success for one in academics, including intrinsic motivation, and the ability to master a task (Reed & Reay, 2015). Outside of academics, out-of-control technology usage is comorbid with somatoform disorders, suicidal ideation, sleep problems (as discussed in Chapter 1), immune system problems, anxiety symptoms, and conditions such as obsessive-compulsive disorder (Kim et al., 2016; Moretta & Guodo, 2018; Reed, Romano, Re, Roaro, Osborne, Viganò, & Truzoli, 2017; Shaw & Black, 2008; Stavropoulos, Gentile, & Motti-Stefanidi, 2016; Sussman et al., 2018; Taylor, Koerber, Parker, & Maitland, 2014; Tuzun Mutluer, Yener Orum, & Sertcelik, 2017).

There are also physiological responses after using the Internet for those who fit a profile of out-of-control pathological users—including increased heart rate and systolic blood pressure, increased sense of anxiety (either as an interpretation of the individual of the increased heart rate and blood pressure, or preceding the physiological changes), and depressed mood (Reed et al., 2017). This finding is further supported by research in neurobiology, which has uncovered impairment in the brain centers that regulate motivation, reward, memory, and cognitive control (Park, Han, & Roh, 2017). Like any construct in psychology, however, the relationship may be influenced by third variables. In the case of Internet "addiction," the anxiety and negative psychological outcomes are affected by one's coping style—the more negative your style, the more likely your computer use is problematic (Tang, Yu, Du, Ma, Zhang, & Wang, 2014). In fact, the ability to escape one's offline life is a major contributor to the development of Facebook "Addiction" Disorder (FAD), for instance (Brailovskaia, Rohmann, Bierhoff, & Margraf, 2018). Moreover, researchers using a German-based sample demonstrated that the personality trait of narcissism and negative mental health issues like depression, anxiety, and stress symptoms are positively related to the experiencing of FAD (Brailovskaia, Margraf, & Reed, 2017). Furthermore, this research seems to indicate that narcissistic people may be specifically at greater risk for developing FAD (Brailovskaia et al., 2017). Of course, because the findings are correlational in nature, it may also be the case that the experiencing of FAD puts people at greater risk for furthering their own narcissistic tendencies.

Out-of-control technology usage is also tied to psychiatric conditions—namely, substance abuse, mood disorders, and other impulse control disorders such as gambling (Kawabe, 2016; Ko, Yen, Yen, Chen, & Chen, 2012; Spada, 2014). Disorders that have demonstrated some association to out-of-control technology usage include major depression (Moreno, Jelenchick, & Breland, 2015), persistent depressive disorder (previously known as dysthymic disorder; Bernardi & Pallanti, 2009), generalized anxiety (Coyne, Padilla-Walker, Stockdale, & Day, 2011), and bipolar disorder (Tang & Koh, 2017). There has also been research substantiating co-occurrence with attention-deficit hyperactivity disorder (ADHD; Finlay & Furnell, 2014; Wu, Chang, & Tzang, 2014). Further research has tied alexithymia (the inability to identify emotions) and the experience of trauma to increased susceptibility to Internet "addiction" (Sussman et al., 2018; Taylor et al., 2014).

In children and adolescents, the criteria for determining if Internet use is problematic may be expanded to include using the Internet as a way to self-regulate, but doing so in a way that is maladaptive (Cole & Hooley, 2013; Haagsma, Caplan, Peters, & Pieterse, 2013; Kardefelt-Winther, 2014a; Oktan, 2011). Both cognitive and behavioral manifestations point to someone who cannot adequately regulate their emotions. Cognitively, an inability to self-regulate is characterized by obsessional thinking. The behavioral manifestation, then, is compulsive behavior (Caplan, 2010). In addition, the compulsion to use the Internet is fueled by an inability to feel that one has autonomy and mastery in their offline world (Casale, Lecchi, & Fioravanti, 2014). Family factors associated with Internet addiction in teens include poor communication (particularly about Internet use), parental drinking, family dysfunction, and family dissatisfaction (Lam, 2017).

The cognitive-behavioral theory of pathological Internet use (Caplan, 2002) states that pathological use arrests a variety of areas of one's functioning—emotional, cognitive, and behavioral. These effects can be observed both online and offline. For example, disruption in emotional functioning might be characterized by greater depression symptoms, anxiety symptoms, and sensitivity in interpersonal interactions (Alavi, Maracy, Jannatifard, & Eslami, 2011; Bodhi & Kaur, 2017; Caplan, Williams, & Yee, 2009; Chou et al., 2017; Ha et al., 2007). The association to depressive symptoms, according to Davis's (2001) model, suggests that individuals who are more likely to engage in pathological Internet use are those who have a predisposition to maladaptive cognitions, of which there are two types. One type—thoughts about the self—is those thoughts where the individual already has a pattern of rumination and this rumination extends to them thinking about their Internet use (Davis, 2001). Maladaptive cognitions held by the individual extend to ruminating about the evaluation of their offline interactions and their comparison to online interactions. For example, due to negative self-thoughts inspired by low self-esteem, an individual may convince themselves that they are more successful in interpersonal interactions online and may see themselves as unsuccessful offline, thus reinforcing their maladaptive cognitions (Davis, 2001). The other type is thoughts about the world, and, in the case of pathological Internet use, refers to when an individual holds global thoughts about the Internet such as "the Internet is the only place I am safe to be myself." In either case, the maladaptive cognitions further contribute to a dependence on the Internet and become self-reinforcing (Davis, 2001).

Additionally, in the cognitive-behavioral theory of pathological Internet use, the use is a multi-dimensional construct (Davis, 2001). This means that problematic use affects many areas of one's well-being. Pathological use is separated into two categories—specific problematic usage (SPIU) and generalized pathological usage (GPIU). SPIU refers to using the Internet to engage in certain activities in problematic ways, including online gambling, day trading, etc. (Caplan, 2002). These would be activities that could be done outside of the Internet and, without the advent of the Internet, would be accomplished in another way. GPIU, on the other hand, is more directly related to problems with technology's social communication components—that is, without the Internet, the person would not necessarily express problems related to communication (Davis, 2001). Sussman et al. (2018) claim individuals with anxiety in attachment and social interactions with others may be predisposed to Internet addiction, as the lack of anxiety to talk online may, without intention behind it, turn into a dependence as this is the only comfortable way to express oneself.

These categories are reminiscent of Al Cooper's categories of Internet cybersex users—at-risk, recreational, and compulsive users. At-risk users (Cooper, Putnam, Planchon, & Boies, 1999) are those users who would not have a problem with pornography and the Internet without the presence of the Internet. Cavaglion and Rashty (2010) describe the process of the at-risk user developing problems as beginning with a slow decline in the quantity and quality of interactions with others, including an eventual decline in work performance. A second type of user is defined as recreational (Cooper et al., 1999). This means the Internet provides a way to seek out cybersexual activities or facilitates the viewing of pornography, but the person uses this strictly for entertainment value and is in no way addicted to either the Internet or the sexual activity. This type can be the most difficult for couples to understand because a partner's usage might be recreational, but because of its sexual nature, it may be classified by their partner as being an addiction or compulsion problem, thus complicating the treatment process from the beginning. A third type of user is known as the compulsive user. Implications for couples where one partner is a compulsive user include a decrease in the amount of sex desired by the compulsive individual toward their partner (Schneider, 2000), a decrease in one's sense of sexual desirability, a reduced frequency in sexual interaction, and a decrease in sexual satisfaction (Bergner & Bridges, 2002; Bridges, Bergner, & Hesson-McInnis, 2003).

One final model that examines the complexities of Internet addiction and Internet gaming disorder is that which classifies such addiction as a spectrum disorder (Billieux & Starcevic, 2017). This view builds on previous research that identifies problematic gaming and problematic Internet usage as two very distinct phenomena (Király et al., 2014). Further, there are differences in motivation to engage in gaming and other online behaviors: for example, some motivations may be escapism, and other motivations may be excessive fantasizing, as in the case of cybersex (Billieux & Starcevic, 2017).

Only the Lonely?

One of the aspects commonly associated with those who use the Internet is its association to loneliness. The research early in the field of Internet users sought to explore what type of personality was associated with using the Internet. The prevailing hypothesis in the late 1990s and very early 2000s was the Internet had limited power and impact in our lives, and its users were afraid to interact with others—those with social phobias, who preferred a certain level of isolation, or who were socially inept (Ceyhan & Ceyhan, 2008; Ghassemzadeh, Shahraray, & Moradi, 2008). In fact, one of the key criteria for the definition of pathological Internet use, according to Davis (2001), is the perception that the Internet is one's only friend. Simsek, Akca, and Simsek (2015) have tied loneliness to a sense of hopelessness, which, in the case of out-of-control technology-related behaviors, becomes a reinforcer for becoming more dependent on using the Internet to manage the feelings of hopelessness and isolation.

As more and more people have been using the Internet, it is clear that it is no longer the case that "only the lonely" are the ones using the Internet—it is everyone. Researchers then started turning their questions to whether Internet usage leads to more isolation, and potentially more loneliness

(Kraut et al., 1998). This can be a very serious consequence. Brain scans reveal that remaining in a socially isolated state can induce certain changes in the brain (Cacioppo, Capitanio, Cacioppo, Hinshaw, & Albarracín, 2014). Heavy use of the Internet has also been found to increase depression and social isolation, despite the connectivity (see, for example, Puri & Sharma, 2016; Yao & Zhong, 2014). But is the Internet socially isolating, or are isolation and loneliness a precursor to Internet usage? The time one spends online away from others may not be time spent socially isolated if they are in fact engaging with others online. And in fact, that is what many seem to use the Internet for—social connections (Amichai-Hamburger, & Vinitzky, 2010; Zheng, Spears, Luptak, & Wilby, 2015). This contention might underlie why other researchers such as Takahira, Ando, and Sakamoto (2008) have found the opposite—that there is no impact to the perception of loneliness due to Internet usage. Further, in at least one study the Internet has been shown to improve quality of life, but can either increase or decrease loneliness to get there (Khalaila & Vitman-Schorr, 2018). In addition, the usual suspects that tend to contribute to Internet overuse (escapism, loneliness, and social anxiety) tend to lose their statistical significance when taking stress into account (Kardefelt-Winther, 2014b). Casale and Fioravanti (2011) noted that generalized pathological Internet use, as compared to specific pathological Internet use, seemed to be the one type predicted by a student's level of loneliness, but was not the type predicted by depression or self-esteem.

The Problem Behavior Theory has been applied to exploring young people's Internet use. Moving outside of the traditional models that associate certain personality characteristics such as loneliness and social anxiety with increased computer usage, the Problem Behavior Theory (Ko et al., 2008) takes an ecological approach. This theory posits that there are variables outside one's personality that create a fertile bed for the growth of Internet use problems—notably, behaviors and the environment. Both protective and risk factors serve to inhibit the development of problematic Internet use or accelerate it. For example, parental attitudes and behaviors may contribute to a youth being more likely to develop problematic usage (risk factor) or less likely (protective factor) (Lam & Wong, 2015). Finally, this model is a circular model: personality factors may influence environmental factors, which may in turn influence behaviors, and so on. This model has some support, as certain contextual factors such as support, bonding, work stress, religion, and style of parenting seem to be factors in the development and maintenance of Internet addiction (Lopez-Fernandez, 2015).

Sexual Technologies

Sextech is technology that is designed to enhance and innovate all areas of human sexuality and the human sexual experience (Gallop, 2015). In relation to sextech, some people are participating in digisexual activities, while others are adopting a full on digisexual identity (McArthur & Twist, 2017). Yet, some people see sexual participation and engagement with technology as a problem, like a technology or sexual "addiction" (Twist & McArthur, 2017).

Again, acting out sexual behaviors share many of the characteristics of a behavioral addiction. Yet, sexual "addiction" was not included in the *DSM-5* (APA, 2013) due to lack of sufficient empirical evidence, and related controversy among many in the medical and sexological fields. In addition, the term "sex addiction" is now regarded as pejorative, and viewed as condemning by many clinicians, and a few national governing bodies like the American Association of Sexuality Educators, Counselors, and Therapists (AASECT, 2016). AASECT (2016) recommend that its members not engage in practices that condemn or pathologize what appear to be consensual sexual activities and behaviors (e.g., engagement with online and offline pornography, frequent sexual self- or partnered-activity, etc.). Additionally, a review of the literature suggests that there is no evidence-based treatment for sex "addiction"; relatedly it is not considered a psychiatric diagnostic category, and by extension it is not something that needs to be "treated" (AASECT, 2016; Derbyshire & Grant, 2015).

Regardless of the term that is used to describe out-of-control sexual behaviors (OCSB), "sexual addiction/hypersexual disorder" is commonly used as an umbrella construct to encompass various types of problematic behaviors, including excessive masturbation, cybersex, pornography use, sexual behavior with consenting adults, telephone sex, strip club visitation, and other behaviors (Karila et al., 2014, p. 1). Furthermore, OCSB often leads to non-consensual non-monogamy and/or sexual promiscuity and interferes in one's sexual relationships.

One of the most common queries asked about OCSB is whether it is a distinct behavior that is qualitatively different from what is the norm, but in ways that are problematic, or if it is a problem on the extreme end of the "normal" range of sexual behaviors (Bancroft & Vukadinovic, 2004). In addressing this query, Braun-Harvey and Vigorito (2016) posit that OCSB can be either/or or both/and, because their way of seeing OCSB is tied to how a specific person envisions their own behavior. They suggest OCSB is a sexual health problem only if the sexual urges, thoughts, or behaviors feel out-of-control to that specific person (Braun-Harvey & Vigorito, 2016). To elaborate, a problem with sexual health means a problem with one's state of physical, mental, emotional, and social well-being in relation to sexuality, and sexual health is not merely the absence of dysfunction, disease, or infirmity (World Health Organization; WHO, 2010).

For a person to be sexually healthy it requires a respectful and positive approach to sexuality and sexual relationships, and the possibility of having pleasurable and safer sexual experiences that are free from discrimination, coercion, and violence. For a person to attain and maintain sexual health, rather than struggle with OCSB, the sexual rights of all persons must be respected, protected, and fulfilled (WHO, 2010). When individuals do struggle with OCSB, some of the ways it may serve a purpose in their lives is to provide them with the illusion of such behaviors serving as a mechanism for controlling their anxiety, stress, isolation, and/or solitude (Rathus, Greene, & Nevid, 2006). Although OCSB may seem to have these benefits, in reality often such behaviors are accompanied by feelings of low self-esteem, remorse, and fear of being found out in relation to their behaviors (Rathus et al., 2006). More often than not despite any of these adverse consequences, the person struggling with OCSB will continue their behavior (Rathus et al., 2006). OCSB might best be clinically explored as a lifestyle choice, or as an aspect of other relational and/or psychological issues (Braun-Harvey & Vigorito, 2016).

When one pairs OCSB with technology, matters become even more complex. For instance, concerns related to technology have yet to be diagnosable by the APA. Yet, people can and often do struggle with excessive, out-of-control, and potentially "addictive" technology issues and their effects on relationships (Hertlein & Blumer, 2013). Unfortunately, up until recently, these kinds of problems have been practically invisible in the mental and relational health community. With the rapid spread of technology, however, more people are now being adversely affected and becoming aware that technology can have both positive and negative effects on individuals and their relational systems. As detailed in this chapter, some of the various technological media that people experience issues with include, but are not limited to: video and online gaming, smartphones, and the Internet. Technology is also the medium needed to support out-of-control behaviors related to online pornography, video sex chats, and a range of other digisexual activities (Aaron, 2016; Delboy, 2015). Because of the current and ongoing lack of awareness on the part of clinicians toward better understanding and treatment of problems related to sextech or digisexuality, expanded assessment is necessary for clinicians to effectively attend to sextech-based behaviors (Blumer, Hertlein, Smith, & Allen, 2014). An assessment through which to do this is a focused genogram, more specifically one focused on sex and technology (Blumer & Hertlein, 2015; DeMaria, Weeks, & Twist, 2017; Hertlein & Blumer, 2013).

Video and Online Gaming

Relational Power-Ups

Online video gaming is now considered a mainstream activity in everyday life. As noted in Chapter 1, the sheer number of people participating in online gaming is growing at an astonishing rate. Couples and families have to make decisions about how this entity will play a part their lives. In 2011, I (KH) went to a large online gaming conference to recruit participants for a study on online gaming and relationships. As I handed out my advertisements for the survey, the conference attendees asked what I was researching. I responded I was interested to find out the ways in which gaming added to and complicated couple relationships. This reply was usually met with a story about how they or someone they knew was in a relationship where online gaming contributed substantially to the relationship's disillusion or success. For those who shared, it seemed there was not a middle ground—online gaming seemed to have one effect on the relationship or the opposite. The information I received at the conference lent support to what some research had already found: just over a third of couples disagree about whether online gaming is acceptable in their relationships (Helsper & Whitty, 2010). Certainly, the information mentioned in this paragraph was acquired from casual conversations soliciting research participants, and thus, it would not be appropriate to draw any scientific conclusions. But one theme became apparent: the impact of gaming on online relationships was also on the minds of the gamers attending the conference, not just the lone family researcher present.

Online video games are just one area in which couples may choose to participate independently and collectively, as well as with each other or with other people. Online video games refer to video games couples play interactively and online role-playing games. In some ways, online gaming can be helpful to couple relationships. It provides a safe place for the exploration of social interactions. For example, in some of the games that allow for text-based communication to other players, users can present their written text in a way that would present them most favorably. Other ways where games may be beneficial is in assisting people in developing relationships outside of a reliance on physical attributes because the users are generally only able to see one another's avatars (or characters) instead of the gamer. There may also be a sense of togetherness that is generated when playing with a partner or family members (Greitemeyer, Traut-Mattausch, & Osswald, 2012).

There is also some evidence to suggest that couple relationships are helped by online gaming because to be successful in the games, one has to be able to navigate social situations to collaborate with others in order to accomplish tasks in the game (Hertlein & Hawkins, 2012). Part of the way a gamer successfully navigates these social interactions is through developing a heightened understanding around gender roles. In online gaming, an avatar may or may not represent the characteristics of its owner. Additionally, the gender gap in an online role-playing game might disappear altogether since women can adopt masculine characters and vice versa. In some ways, the online world may provide a more equal playing field, or the notion of cisgender genders might break down altogether as more gender diverse options become available to users. Another benefit is the exposure to others who are geographically distant with the same or similar interests. Finally, those who participate in online fantasy games may have higher levels of creativity and the ability to fantasize outside of the gaming realm—namely within their physical relationship with a partner (Hawkins & Hertlein, 2013; Hertlein & Hawkins, 2012).

Relational Challenge Mode

Despite the benefits of online gaming in relationships, massively multiplayer online role-playing games (MMORPGs) have become vulnerable to attack because of their association with addiction characteristics, issues of player versus partner loyalty, number of hours spent on the game in one sitting, and one's willingness to pay for the service (Lu & Wang, 2008). One study cites problematic Internet behavior as a presenting problem in clinical practice (Mitchell, Becker-Blease, & Finkelhor, 2005), one element of which is online gaming.

One of the issues is around the elements of online gaming considered collective play. According to Zhong (2011): "Frequent participation in collective actions increases the chance of social interactions. However, it is unavoidable that sometimes online social interactions are accompanied with selfish, deceptive or ulterior motivations" (p. 2353). In this way, one may observe a partner interacting with others with increasing frequency and may develop suspicion around a partner's motives. It may also be the case that one's motives are trusted by a partner, but there is not the same assumption of good intent of the other gamer's motives.

Another relational challenge may be the ability to . . . well, relate. A meta-analytic review of video games found, independent of culture and gender, that engagement in violent video games is associated with increased aggressive behavior, increased aggressive thoughts, and lower levels of empathy (Anderson et al., 2008; Anderson et al., 2010). For example, after one year of playing violent video games, best friends were more likely to be aggressive to one another, even if they played together. This effect, however, was true for teen boys, but not for teen girls (Verheijen, Burk, Stoltz, Van den Berg, & Cillessen, 2018). Even playing games with profanity is associated with an increase in aggression levels (Ivory & Kaestle, 2013). In addition, the presence of online gaming addiction is associated with more problems with relationships with classmates, fewer friends, and less perceived family harmony (Wang, Chan, Sai-Yin, Wong, & Ho, 2014). With couple relationships, the implications of online gaming and addiction may be more profound. Those who participate in MMORPGs may play upwards of 22 hours per week (Yee, 2006). They also report having fewer friends and going out less frequently (Achab et al., 2011), but also increased social capital as a consequence of building relationships within the game (Zhang, & Kaufman, 2015). Couples are also aware of the negative impact participating in MMORPGs has on their relationship. According to researchers, for couples with one gamer, as well as couples where more than one partner games, partners report lower marital satisfaction, because they go to bed at different times. In addition, every couple in the study reported arguing over gaming issues and tied these arguments to reduced marital satisfaction, with those couples who had only one person gaming reporting lower satisfaction than in the relationships where more than one partner engaged in gaming (Ahlstrom, Lundberg, Zabriskie, Eggett, & Lindsay, 2012).

In a qualitative investigation specifically related to the experience of women whose husbands play *World of Warcraft* (a popular MMORPG), the researchers were interested in the relational issues that emerge as a consequence of partner gaming (Lianekhammy & Van De Venne, 2015). In the interviews about their experiences, the women discussed the impact to their family, their relationship, their feelings associated with the issues related to gaming, and their coping strategies. With regard to the family issues, commonly reported issues included conflict with finances, how the gaming affected the husband's job, lack of responsibility in the home including with children, and a change in the husband's behavior. Impacts on the relationship included wanting more attention for the non-gaming spouse, attention desired for the children, and a feeling that the priority was the video gaming, not the relationship (Lianekhammy & Van De Venne, 2015). Feelings expressed by the *World of Warcraft* "widows" included feeling hopeless, "fed up," angry, and distrustful of their partner. In fact, one of the coping mechanisms was mentioning divorce (Lianekhammy & Van De Venne, 2015).

The challenges associated with online video gaming could be explained by social presence theory (Short, Williams, & Christie, 1976). This theory posits that people who share experiences together are more likely than others to feel closer to one another because of the immediacy in their interaction. For example, Uma and Amar, a heterosexual, upper-class couple who both came from large families of East Indian descent, and whose marriage had been arranged by their families, came to therapy for relational enhancement. When the therapist inquired as to the development of their relationship over time, Amar cited that Uma was generally the first one who responded to his emails and he, in turn, responded to her quickly. They experienced each other as being reliable in their communication, more so than most others in their lives, and felt that the two of them immediately shared a bond characterized by mutual respect and shared family values.

The structure of online video gaming really makes social presence theory relevant. Online video gaming is characterized by (a) a specific number of challenges that have to be overcome in a game in order to be successful in progressing through the game's levels, and (b) the accomplishment of such tasks primarily through working in a group—an embedded opportunity for social interaction. Issues emerge when the online gamer is participating in online gaming and developing immediacy and intimacy with someone else and not providing those things to a partner. The net result may be the gamer being accused of spending more time and energy and having more positive feelings for online relations than for a primary partner. This can be even more problematic when one considers that the online associations for which the immediacy and intimacy may be developing are ones that may involve the player developing a romantic interest.

A highly developed sense of fantasy was previously classified as something online gaming may contribute to the positive nature of relationship. In some cases, however, when online video games are utilized as a strategy to avoid the tension and stress in one's offline life, it may interfere with creative problem solving, flexibility, and other issues, setting couples up to present with issues related to online gaming in treatment (Mitchell & Wells, 2007).

Action Point: A Case of Out-of-Control Online Gaming Behaviors

Online gaming addiction is more subtle and embedded in a couple's dynamics than it sounds. How do you know if you have a problem? It is not just the interference with activities. It is the time spent, and protection of the game over all other things, etc. The commonly stereotypic impression of online gaming addiction is that this individual does not bathe/shower, has no friends, is isolated, and spends all of their waking moments on the game playing. This is not an accurate representation. It looks more mundane than that and can really be discerned based on one's reaction to taking the game away—not even from them, but from someone else.

For example, Alan and Janet, a white, heterosexual, middle-class couple, presented to therapy with me (KH) for issues around online gaming. Alan has always played games, much to the chagrin of his wife, Janet, who always assumed he would grow out of it. There had been several times in the marriage when she had requested that he spend time with her (for example, staying in bed on Sunday mornings), but he always seemed to make time for his online friends (he elected to play with his gaming friends Sunday mornings instead), and her requests would go unanswered. In fact, he began to say things like "I have to keep that time open to play with my family" while his wife and son would sit downstairs, without him. Alan would engage in episodic barbs at his wife about the lack of sex, but seemed oblivious to the fact that his decision-making regarding her unmet needs and his decision to play games with strangers in favor of time with his wife had anything to do with unmet sexual needs. Further, because of Alan's work as an online instructor, he was tied to the computer at all times. Though he asserted that he only played with his friends Tuesday night, Saturday morning, and Sunday night (leaving his family to work around his schedule), he was actually tied to the computer more often. This might involve him playing games, and it also involved watching other people play video games—staring at a screen showing YouTube videos of people (young boys) playing computer games. These events would take place all day or all weekend, so Alan would abdicate his family in favor of these games as well.

At one point, Alan's son Joseph (age 9) started doing poorly in school. Janet suspended the video games until such time as Joseph brought up his grades. Once he lost his video games at home, Joseph was reprimanded and punished in school for using the Internet to look up video game music. The family hit a boiling point. Janet, having had enough of the games from both her husband's standpoint and her son's, told Joseph that he could no longer play video games the rest of the year and only when his report card came back with As and Bs would he be allowed to play again.

While both Alan and Janet agreed that Joseph was a totally different kid without the video games, Alan's inability to handle a consequence of no video games threatened his ability to relate to and work with his son to enjoy their relationship and help him to improve his grades. Alan, likely feeling threatened and ashamed that his own gaming behavior had contributed to the problems his son was having, cut himself off from the school problem in the family. Rather than change his behavior to be a role model for his son, Alan angrily told Janet and Joseph that he would no longer help with homework. He continued to spend every night in his office playing video games or watching other people play video games and left Janet to do the heavy lifting—hold down a full time job as a business executive, do all the homework with her son, etc. In fact, on nights when Janet was late at work or had meetings, Alan still refused to review Joseph's homework, thus setting him up for failure. When confronted by Janet about the fact that she was doing everything, he said, "I thought we agreed to give up and he was on his own." She replied that perhaps he was going to give up, but she would not since Joseph was only 9 years old and needed their guidance.

The salient elements of out-of-control online gaming behaviors in this case were: unmet needs; preference for spending time online instead of with Janet and Joseph; constant staring at a digital device through dinners, family recreation time, while driving, and in bed; anger at another personal interruption of computer games; and even watching others play computer games in favor of housework. In addition, Alan ended up needing glasses because he was no longer able to see distance given that his eyes had been negatively impacted by staring at a screen. Alan, aware that his eyes were changing, did nothing to remedy the situation. It was more important to stare at a screen than protect his own health. The way in which these actions affected the relationship included the following: both partners experiencing unmet sexual and emotional needs, resentment for the non-gamer toward the gaming partner for not being a satisfactory participant in the parenting and household responsibilities, lack of sleep for both partners, negative impacts to both partners' physical health, and providing a poor role model for a child around responsible ways to communicate and engage in leisure activity, and overall negative impacts to the relational system as a whole.

What the Tech Do We Do?

You Have Nothing to Fear, But Fear Itself

As we, and other scholars, have identified technophobia as a significant area of concern, it is important to give brief attention to what can be done about it. For instance, to address technophobia, many work environments offer support to employees to reduce anxiety-based technology issues (Osiceanua, 2015). Moreover, as those experiencing technophobia commonly have symptoms similar to people struggling from other kinds of phobias, the application of clinical treatments can also be effective in helping people manage or combat technophobia (Brosnan & Thorpe, 2006; Rosen, Sears, & Weil, 1993; Weil, Rosen, & Wugalter, 1990). For instance, technophobia has been successfully treated using systematic desensitization (Rosen et al., 1993). More recently, clinical research has found that when those experiencing technophobia are taught relaxation techniques to apply as a coping strategy, their technology-related anxiety is reduced, and their confidence with using technology is improved (Brosnan & Thorpe, 2006). In another more recent clinical study involving 89 Europe and US based university students, Brosnan and Thorpe (2006) found that even when just a single anxiety intervention session was conducted anxiety levels in the treatment group were significantly reduced when compared to the non-treatment/control group.

Winning Over Video Gaming Issues

Addressing video gaming issues comes from various frameworks and solutions. Because the etiology of problematic video gaming is multifaceted (Davis, 2001; Ko et al., 2008; Lam & Wong, 2015), the solutions also need to be multifaceted. Based on the diathesis-stress hypothesis, Davis (2001) considers pathological Internet usage as having both proximal and distal components. Proximal components are those that are an obvious link to problematic Internet usage, such as maladaptive cognitions (about both the self and the world), the social context of the Internet user (the presence of social support), and an inability to appropriately express oneself or regulate one's emotions (Haagsma et al., 2013). Distal causes may be an underlying level of pathology, an event that triggers the user, and potentially the presence of the Internet itself.

Managing Out-of-Control Technology-Related Behaviors

Parents/care providers can play a key role in assisting their children with moderating their Internet usage and avoiding some of the negative outcomes associated with Internet dependence. While many parents/providers may believe that it is their active monitoring of their children's Internet use that prevents them from falling victim to some of the negative consequences of such usage, the research actually supports using more strategies that rely on engaging technology to assist in the monitoring (Benrazavi, Teimouri, & Griffiths, 2015; Lee & Chae, 2007). This requires that parents/providers become more knowledgeable about the media to be able to use it to its utmost effectiveness.

Another important component is monitoring peer influences online. There is no question that children need their online activities monitored; however, in cases where parents/providers are not adequately monitoring, peer influences and affiliation can lead the youth toward a potentially deviant peer group, thus increasing the likelihood of developing out-of-control technology-related behaviors (Ding, Li, Zhou, Dong, & Luo, 2017).

Parents/providers also have to manage their own computer usage and be able to talk to their children about excessive Internet usage (Lam, 2017). Research by Lam and Wong (2015) found that those adolescents classified as moderate to severe problematic Internet users were three times more likely (in comparison to adolescents classified with normal Internet use) to have parents who were moderate to severe problematic users of the Internet themselves. In addition, parents can role model appropriate technology usage by being involved cooperatively in games. This does two things: first, it provides them a way to be able to continually monitor their children's online game-playing behavior. Second, as much as violent video gaming is associated with aggressive thoughts and behavior as mentioned earlier, (Anderson et al., 2008; Anderson et al., 2010), this increased aggression is somewhat mitigated when games are played cooperatively (Greitemeyer, Traut-Mattausch, & Osswald, 2012; Velez, Greitemeyer, Whitaker, Ewoldsen, & Bushman, 2016). Again, this is more than playing the games at the same time, in parallel; this means engaging in a task together during the game and being on the same team to accomplish a goal.

In cases where relational systems present with out-of-control technology-related issues, therapists can work with families to monitor and create a family plan using the *IMPROVE* tool (Tam, 2017). This acronym reflects a plan that, while geared more broadly toward excessive Internet use, can also be applied to video gaming issues in families. The first item is the Internet inventory, whereby the parent takes an inventory of the types of Internet use and the time their youth is using the Internet. The next item is Monitor Over Time, which refers to parental monitoring of the youth's Internet use, with particular attention to changes in patterns of Internet use. For example, a youth might increase the amount of time on social media or decrease game-playing time when the newness of a game wears off, and a parent needs to understand the baseline and be aware of the circumstances around changes in that pattern (Tam, 2017). Parenting Factors refer to how parents use their own technology to model appropriate behavior, and involve a parent's adopting a style that encourages rewards for appropriate Internet use. Real-World Activities ask parents to continually involve their children in offline activities, environments, and experiences. Other Mental Health Conditions include the presence of some of the conditions commonly co-occurring with out-of-control technology-related behaviors discussed earlier in this chapter, such as depression, anxiety, and events such as socioeconomic deprivation. Vulnerability Factors include attending to both external (such as major life events and trauma) and intrapsychic factors (like a narcissistic personality, low self-esteem, and a tendency to procrastinate) (Tam, 2017). Finally, Extra Help involves inviting other professionals into the picture to address the technology-related issue, including a pediatrician, psychologist, psychiatrist, and/or school counselor (Tam, 2017).

As aforementioned, the negative impact of violent video gaming can include impairments in one's ability to develop and express empathy, which may have significant and cascading implications for successful social interactions and prosocial behavior. To that end, assisting those who play to focus on strategies to improve the quality of their social relationships as well as moving them toward increasing positive emotions are key (Khazaei, Khazaei, & Ghanbari-H, 2017). Specific components of this IMPROVE program include focusing on assisting the individual with nurturing positive emotions, developing an ability to process maladaptive or negative emotions, and teaching forgiveness, hope, gratitude, satisfaction, and optimism (Khazaei et al., 2017).

Coping strategies suggested by partners in the Lianekhammy and Van De Venne (2015) study included joining in on the gaming, support from the community of people who also struggle with technology-related issues, recognition of the out-of-control component when appropriate, and reliance on the emoticons and electronic gestures they may receive from a partner (Lianekhammy & Van De Venne, 2015). Further, there has been some evidence that the strategies proposed by Hertlein and Hawkins (2012) could apply in these cases (Lianekhammy & Van De Venne, 2015). Such strategies include: increasing the use of fantasy to augment the relationship, inviting one's partner into the shared activity and working in a cooperative fashion (Hertlein & Hawkins, 2012), and developing clear expectations and appropriate communication patterns for addressing the lack of responsibility regarding the technology-related issues perceived by partners of people with the identifiable technology use issue.

Conclusion

While not common problems, issues such as technophobia, out-of-control sextech behaviors, and out-of-control video and online gaming can significantly affect a couple and family system. Some of these issues need to be addressed and managed individually, whereas others may be able to be addressed in a therapeutic relational context. As technology and the Internet continue to evolve, this list may grow. We need to continue to understand the intrapersonal and interpersonal mechanisms that contribute to the development and maintenance of such issues, which may potentially decrease any negative impact and potentially decrease the incidence of such issues.

References

Aaron, M. (2016). Review of sex addiction: A critical history. *Journal of Sex & Marital Therapy, 42*(1), 92–94. doi:10.1080/0092623X.2015.1106767

Achab, S., Nicolier, M., Mauny, F., Monnin, J., Trojak, B., Vandel, P., . . . Haffen, E. (2011). Massively multiplayer online role-playing games: Comparing characteristics of addict vs non-addict online recruited gamers in a French adult population. *BMC Psychiatry, 11*, 144. doi:10.1186/1471-244X-11144.

Ahlstrom, M., Lundberg, N., Zabriskie, R., Eggett, D., & Lindsay, G. (2012). Me, my spouse, and my avatar: The relationship between marital satisfaction and playing Massively Multiplayer Online Role-Playing Games (MMORPGs). *Journal of Leisure Research, 44*(1), 1–22. doi: 10.1080/00222216.2012.11950252

Alavi, S. S., Maracy, M. R., Jannatifard, F., & Eslami, M. (2011). The effect of psychiatric symptoms on the Internet addiction disorder in Isfahan's university students. *Journal of Research in Medical Sciences, 16*(6), 793–800.

American Association of Sexuality Educators, Counselors, and Therapists. (2016). *AASECT Position on Sex Addiction.* Retrieved from https://www.aasect.org/print/position-sex-addiction

American Psychiatric Association. (2013). *Diagnostic and statistical manual of mental disorders* (5th ed.). Washington, DC: APA

Amichai-Hamburger, Y., & Vinitzky, G. (2010). Social network use and personality. *Computers in Human Behavior, 26*(6), 1289–1295.

Anderson, C. A., Sakamoto, A., Gentile, D., Ihori, N., Shibuya, A., Yukawa, S., . . . Kobayashi, K. (2008). Longitudinal effects of violent video games on aggression in Japan and the United States. *Pediatrics, 122*(5), E1067.

Anderson, C. A., Shibuya, A., Ihori, N., Swing, E. L., Bushman, B. J., Sakamoto, A., & Saleem, M. (2010). Violent video game effects on aggression, empathy, and prosocial behavior in Eastern and Western countries: A meta-analytic review. *Psychological Bulletin, 136*, 151–173. doi:10.1037/a0018251

Bancroft, J., & Vukadinovic, Z. (2004). Sexual addiction, sexual compulsivity, sexual impulsivity, or what? Toward a theoretical model. *Journal of Sex Research, 41*, 225–234.

Benrazavi, R., Teimouri, M., & Griffiths, M. D. (2015). Utility of Parental Mediation Model on youth's problematic online gaming. *International Journal of Mental Health and Addiction, 13*(6), 712–727.

Bergner, R. M., & Bridges, A. J. (2002). The significance of heavy pornography involvement for romantic partners: Research and clinical implications. *Journal of Sex & Marital Therapy, 28*(3), 193–206. doi:10.1080/009262302760328235

Bernardi, S., & Pallanti, S. (2009). Internet addiction: A descriptive clinical study focusing on comorbidities and dissociative symptoms. *CyberPsychology & Behavior, 4*, 377–383. doi: 10.1016/j.comppsych.2008.11.011

Billieux, J., & Starcevic, V. (2017). Does the construct of Internet addiction reflect a single entity or a spectrum of disorders? *Clinical Neuropsychiatry, 14*(1), 5–10.

Blumer, M. L. C., & Hertlein, K. M. (2015). The technology-focused genogram: A tool for exploring intergenerational communication patterns around technology use. In C. J. Bruess (Ed.), *Family communication in a digital age* (pp. 471–490). New York, NY: Routledge.

Blumer, M. L. C., Hertlein, K. M., Smith, J., & Allen, H. (2014). How many bytes does it take?: A content analysis of cyber issues in couple and family therapy journals. *Journal of Marital and Family Therapy, 40*(1), 34–48. doi: 10.1111/j.1752-0606.2012.00332.x

Bodhi, V., & Kaur, J. (2017). Psychological correlates of Internet addiction among college students. *Indian Journal of Health and Wellbeing, 8*(11), 1404–1408. doi: 10.3928/02793695-20150309-02

Brailovskaia, J., Margraf, J., & Reed, P. (2017). Facebook Addiction Disorder (FAD) among German students—A longitudinal approach. *PLoS ONE, 12*(12).

Brailovskaia, J., Rohmann, E., Bierhoff, H., & Margraf, J. (2018). The brave blue world: Facebook flow and Facebook Addiction Disorder (FAD). *PLoS ONE, 7*(13), e0201484. doi; 10.1371/journal.pone.0201484.

Braun-Harvey, D., & Vigorito, M. A. (2016). *Treating out of control sexual behavior: Rethinking sexual addiction.* New York, NY: Springer Publishing Company.

Bridges, A. J., Bergner, R. M., & Hesson-McInnis, M. (2003). Romantic partners' use of pornography: Its significance for women. *Journal of Sex & Marital Therapy, 29*(1), 1–14. doi: 10.1080/00926230390154790Brosnan, M. J., & Thorpe, S. J. (2006). An evaluation of two clinically-derived treatments for technophobia. *Computers in Human Behavior, 22*(6), 1080–1095. doi: 10.1016/j.chb.2006.02.

Cacioppo, S., Capitanio, J. P., Cacioppo, J. T., Hinshaw, S. P., & Albarracín, D. (2014). Toward a neurology of loneliness. *Psychological Bulletin, 140*(6), 1464–1504. doi: 10.1037/a0037618

Caplan, S. E. (2002). Problematic Internet use and psychosocial well-being: Development of a theory-based cognitive behavioral measurement instrument. *Computers in Human Behaviour, 18*, 553–575. doi:10.1016/S0747-5632(02)00004-3

Caplan, S. E. (2010). Theory and measurement of generalized problematic Internet use: A two-step approach. *Computers in Human Behavior, 26*, 1089–1097.

Caplan, S. E., Williams, D., & Yee, N. (2009). Problematic Internet use and psychosocial well-being among MMO players. *Computers in Human Behavior, 25*, 1312–1319. doi:10.1016/j.chb.2009.06.006

Casale, S., & Fioravanti, G. (2011). Psychosocial correlates of Internet use among Italian students. *International Journal of Psychology, 46*(4), 288–298. doi: 10.1080/00207594.2010.541256.

Casale, S., Lecchi, S., & Fioravanti, G. (2014). The association between psychological well-being and problematic use of Internet communicative services among young people. *The Journal of Psychology, 149*(5), 1–18. doi: 10.1080/00223980.2014.905432

Cavaglion, G., & Rashty, E. (2010). Narratives of suffering among Italian female partners of cybersex and cyber-porn dependents. *Sexual Addiction and Compulsivity: The Journal of Treatment, 17*(4). doi: 10.1080/10720162.2010.535690

Ceyhan, A. A., & Ceyhan, E. (2008). Loneliness, depression, and computer self-efficacy as predictors of problematic Internet use. *CyberPsychology & Behavior, 11*, 699–701. doi: 10.1089/cpb.2007.0255

Chou, W. P., Lee, K. H., Ko, C. H., Liu, T. L., Hsiao, R. C., Lin, H. F., & Yen, C. F. (2017). Relationship between psychological inflexibility and experiential avoidance and Internet addiction: Mediating effects of mental health problems. *Psychiatry Research*, *257*, 40–44. doi: 10.1016/j.psychres.2017.07.021.

Cole, S. H., & Hooley, J. M. (2013). Clinical and personality correlates of MMO gaming: Anxiety and absorption in problematic Internet use. *Social Science Computer Review*, *31*(4), 424–436. doi:10.1177/0894439312475280

Cooper, A., Putnam, D., Planchon, L., & Boies, S. (1999). Online sexual compulsivity: Getting tangles in the net. *Sexual Addiction and Compulsivity, Journal of Treatment and Prevention*, *6*(2), 70–104.

Coyne, S. M., Padilla-Walker, L. M., Stockdale, L., & Day, R. D. (2011). Game on . . . girls: Associations between co-playing video games and adolescent behavioral and family outcomes. *Journal of Adolescent Health*, *49*(2), 160–165.

Davis, R. (2001). A cognitive-behavioral model of pathological Internet use. *Computers in Human Behavior*, *17*(2), 187–195. doi: 10.1016/S0747-5632(00)00041-8

Delboy, S. (2015). Evidence-based practice for sex addiction: A clinical case illustration. *Sexual Addiction & Compulsivity*, *22*(4), 273–289. doi:10.1080/10720162.2015.1072487

DeMaria, R., Weeks, G., & Twist, M. L. C. (2017). *Focused genograms: Focused intergenerational assessment of individuals, couples, and families* (2nd ed.). New York, NY: Routledge.

Derbyshire, K. L., & Grant, J. E. (2015). Compulsive sexual behavior: A review of the literature. *Journal of Behavioral Addictions*, *4*(2), 37–43. doi: 10.1556/2006.4.2015.003

Ding, Q., Li, D., Zhou, Y., Dong, H., & Luo, J. (2017). Perceived parental monitoring and adolescent Internet addiction: A moderated mediation model. *Addictive Behaviors*, *74*, 48–54. doi:10.1016/j.addbeh.2017.05.033

Eleuteri, S., Saladino, V., & Verrastro, V. (2017). Identity, relationships, sexuality, and risky behaviors of adolescents in the context of social media. *Sexual and Relationship Therapy*, *32*(3–4), 354–365. doi:10.1080/14681994.2017.1397953

Finlay, F., & Furnell, C. (2014, April). Internet addiction disorder/problematic Internet use and ADHD. *Archives of Disease in Childhood*, *99*(4), A145–146. doi:10.1136/archdischild-2014–306237.338

Gallop, C. (2015). What is sextech and why is everyone ignoring it? *Hot topics. HT.* Retrieved from https://www.hottopics.ht/14192/what-is-sextech-and-why-is-everyone-ignoring-it/

Ghassemzadeh, L., Shahraray, M., & Moradi, A. (2008). Prevalence of Internet addiction and comparison of Internet addicts and non-addicts in Iranian high schools. *Cyberpsychology & Behavior*, *11*, 731–733. doi:10.1089/cpb.2007.0243

Greitemeyer, T., Traut-Mattausch, E., & Osswald, S. (2012). How to ameliorate negative effects of violent video games on cooperation: Play it cooperatively in a team. *Computers in Human Behavior*, *28*(4), 1465–1470. doi: 10.1016/j.chb.2012.03.009

Ha, J. H., Kim, S. Y., Bae, S. C., Bae, S., Kim, H., Sim, M., . . . Cho, S.C. (2007). Depression and Internet addiction in adolescents. *Psychopathology*, *40*(6), 424–430.

Haagsma, M. C., Caplan, S. E., Peters, O., & Pieterse, M. E. (2013). A cognitive-behavioral model of problematic online gaming in adolescents ages 12–22 years. *Computers in Human Behavior*, *29*, 202–209. doi: 10.1016/j.chb.2012.08.006.

Hawkins, B. P., & Hertlein, K. M. (2013). Treatment strategies for online role-playing gaming problems in couples. *Journal of Couple and Relationship Therapy*, 12(2), 150–167. doi: 10.1080/15332691.2013.779100

Helsper, E. J., & Whitty, M. T. (2010). Netiquette within married couples: Agreement about acceptable online behavior and surveillance between partners. *Computers in Human Behavior*, 26(5), 916–926. doi:10.1016/j.chb.2010.02.006

Hertlein, K. M., & Blumer, M. L. C. (2013). *The couple and family technology framework: Intimate relationships in a digital age*. New York, NY: Routledge.

Hertlein, K. M., & Hawkins, B. P. (2012). Online gaming issues in offline couple relationships: A primer for MFTs. *The Qualitative Report*, 17(article 15), 1–48. Retrieved from www.nova.edu/ssss/QR/QR17/hertlein.pdf

Ivory, A., & Kaestle, C. (2013). The effects of profanity in violent video games on players' hostile expectations, aggressive thoughts and feelings, and other responses. *Journal of Broadcasting & Electronic Media*, 57(2), 224–241. doi: 10.1080/08838151.2013.787078

Kardefelt-Winther, D. (2014a). A conceptual and methodological critique of Internet addiction research: Towards a model of compensatory Internet use. *Computers in Human Behavior*, 31, 351–354. doi: 10.1016/j.chb.2013.10.059.

Kardefelt-Winther, D. (2014b). Problematizing excessive online gaming and its psychological predictors. *Computers in Human Behavior*, 31, 118–122. doi:10.1016/j.chb.2013.10.017

Karila, L., Wery, A., Weinstein, A., Cottencin, O., Petit, A., Reynaud, M., & Billieux, J. (2014). Sexual addiction or hypersexual disorder: Different terms for the same problem? A review of the literature. *CPD Current Pharmaceutical Design*, 20(25), 4012–4020. doi: 10.2174/13816128113199990619

Kawabe, K. (2016). Internet addiction: Prevalence and relationship with mental states in adolescents. *Psychiatry and Clinical Neurosciences*, 70(9), 405–412. doi: 10.1111/pcn.12402.

Khalaila, R., & Vitman-Schorr, A. (2018). Internet use, social networks, loneliness, and quality of life among adults aged 50 and older: Mediating and moderating effects. *Quality of Life Research*, 27(2), 479–489.

Khazaei, F., Khazaei, O., & Ghanbari-H, B. (2017). Positive psychology interventions for Internet addiction treatment. *Computers in Human Behavior*, 72, 304–311. doi: 10.1016/j.chb.2017.02.065

Kim, B. S., Chang, S. M., Park, J. E., Seong, S. J., Won, S. H., & Cho, M. J. (2016). Prevalence, correlates, psychiatric comorbidities, and suicidality in a community population with problematic Internet use. *Psychiatry Research*, 244, 249–256. doi:10.1016/j.psychres.2016.07.009

Király, O., Griffiths, M. D., Urbán, R., Farkas, J., Kökönyei, G., Elekes, Z., . . . Demetrovics, Z. (2014). Problematic Internet use and problematic online gaming are not the same: Findings from a large nationally representative adolescent sample. *Cyberpsychology, Behavior, and Social Networking*, 17(12), 749–754. doi: 10.1089/cyber.2014.0475.

Ko, C. H., Yen, J. Y., Yen, C. F., Chen, C. S., & Chen, C. C. (2012). The association between Internet addiction and psychiatric disorder: A review of the literature. *European Psychiatry*, 27, 1–8. doi: 10.1016/j.eurpsy.2010.04.011

Ko, C. H., Yen, J. Y., Yen, C. F., Chen, C. S., Weng, C. C., & Chen, C. C. (2008). The Association between Internet addiction and problematic alcohol use in adolescents: The problem behavior model. *CyberPsychology & Behavior*, 11(5), 571–576. doi: 10.1089/cpb.2007.0199

Kraut, R., Patterson, M., Lundmark, V., Kiesler, S., Mukopadhyay, T., & Scherlis, W. (1998). Internet paradox: A social technology that reduces social involvement and psychological well-being? *American Psychologist, 53*(9), 1017–1031. doi: 10.1037/0003-066X.53.9.1017

Lam, L. T. (2017). Parental mental health and Internet addiction in adolescents. In K. S. Young & C. N. de Abreu's (Eds.), *Internet addiction in children and adolescents: Risk factors, assessment, and treatment* (pp. 123–139). New York, NY: Springer Publishing Co.

Lam, L. T., & Wong, E. M. (2015). Stress moderates the relationship between problematic Internet use by parents and problematic Internet use by adolescents. *Journal of Adolescent Health, 56*(3), 300–306. doi: 10.1016/j.jadohealth.2014. 10.263

Ledbetter, S. (2014, October 20). *What Americans fear most—New poll from Champman University* [Web log post]. Retrieved from https://blogs.chapman. edu/press-room/2014/10/20/what-americans-fear-most-new-poll-from-chapman-university/

Ledbetter, S. (2015, October 13). *Americans top fears 2015* [Web log post]. Retrieved from https://blogs.chapman.edu/wilkinson/2015/10/13/americas-top-fears-2015/

Lee, S., & Chae, Y. (2007). Children's Internet use in a family context: Influence on family relationships and parental mediation. *Cyberpsychology & Behavior: The Impact of the Internet, Multimedia and Virtual Reality on Behavior and Society, 10*(5), 640–644. doi: 10.1089/cpb.2007.9975

Lianekhammy, J., & Van De Venne, J. (2015). World of Warcraft widows: Spousal perspectives of online gaming and relationship outcomes. *The American Journal of Family Therapy, 43*(5), 454–466. doi: 10.1080/01926187.2015.1080131

Lopez-Fernandez, O. (2015). How has Internet addiction research evolved since the advent of Internet gaming disorder? An overview of cyberaddictions from a psychological perspective. *Current Addiction Reports, 2*(3), 263–271. doi: 10.1007/s40429-015-0067-6

Lu, H. P., & *Wang*, S. M. (*2008*). The role of Internet addiction in online game loyalty: An exploratory study. *Internet Research, 18*, 499–519. doi: 10.1108/ 10662240810912756.

McArthur, N., & Twist, M. L. C. (2017). The rise of digisexuality: Therapeutic challenges and possibilities. *Sexual and Relationship Therapy, 32*(3/4), 334–344.

Mitchell, K., & Wells, M. (2007). Problematic internet experiences: Primary or secondary presenting problems in persons seeking mental health care? *Social Science & Medicine, 65*(6), 1136–1141. doi:10.1016/j.socscimed.2007.05.015

Mitchell, K. J., Becker-Blease, K. A., Finkelhor, D. (2005). Inventory of problematic Internet experiences encountered in clinical practice. *Professional Psychology: Research and Practice, 36*(5), 498–509. doi: 10.1037/0735-7028.36.5.498

Moreno, M. A., Jelenchick, L. A., & Breland, D. J. (2015). Exploring depression and problematic Internet use among college females: A multisite study. *Computers in Human Behavior, 49*(C), 601–607. doi: 10.1016/j.chb.2015.03.033

Moretta, T., & Buodo, G. (2018). Autonomic stress reactivity and craving in individuals with problematic Internet use. *PLOS ONE, 13*(1), e0190951. doi:10. 1371/journal.pone.0190951

Nimrod, G. (2018). Technostress: Measuring a new threat to well-being in later life. *Aging and Mental Health, 22*(8), 1080–1087. doi: 10.1080/13607863.2017. 1334037

Odacı, H., & Kalkan, M. (2010). Problematic Internet use, loneliness and dating anxiety among young adult university students. *Computers & Education*, 55(3), 1091–1097. doi:10.1016/j.compedu.2010.05.006

Oktan, V. (2011). The predictive relationship between emotion management skills and Internet addiction. *Social Behavior and Personality*, 39(10), 1425–1430. doi: 10.2224/sbp.2011.39.10.1425

Osiceanu, M. E. (2015). Psychological implications of modern technologies: Technophobia versus technophilia. *Procedia—Social and Behavioral Sciences*, 180, 1137–1144. doi: 10.1016/j.sbspro.2015.02.22

Park, B., Han, D. H., & Roh, S. (2017). Neurobiological findings related to Internet use disorders. *Psychiatry and Clinical Neurosciences*, 71(7), 467–478. doi:10.1111/pcn.12422

Puri, A., & Sharma, R. (2016). Internet usage, depression, social isolation and loneliness amongst adolescents. *Indian Journal of Health and Wellbeing*, 7(10), 996–1003.

Rathus, S. A., Greene, B., & Nevid, J. S. (2006). *Abnormal psychology in a changing world* (6th ed.). Upper Saddle River, NJ: Prentice Hall, Inc.

Reed, P., & Reay, E. (2015). Relationship between levels of problematic Internet usage and motivation to study in university students. *Higher Education*, 70(4), 711–723. doi:10.1007/s10734-015-9862-1

Reed, P., Romano, M., Re, F., Roaro, A., Osborne, L., Viganò, C., & Truzoli, R. (2017). Differential physiological changes following Internet exposure in higher and lower problematic Internet users. *PLoS ONE*, 12(5), e0178480.

Rosen, L. D., Sears, D. C., & Weil, M. M. (1993). Treating technophobia: A longitudinal evaluation of the computerphobia reduction program. *Computers in Human Behavior*, 9, 27–50. doi: 10.1016/0747-5632(93)90019-O.

Ross, M., Månsson, W., & Daneback, S. (2012). Prevalence, Severity, and Correlates of Problematic Sexual Internet Use in Swedish Men and Women. *Archives of Sexual Behavior*, 41(2), 459–466.

Ryding, F., & Kaye, C. (2018). "Internet addiction": A conceptual minefield. *International Journal of Mental Health and Addiction*, 16(1), 225–232. doi: 10.1016/j.chb.2016.03.041.

Schneider, J. (2000). A qualitative study of cybersex participants: gender differences, recovery issues, and implications for therapists. *Sexual Addiction & Compulsivity*, 7(4), 249–278. doi: 10.1080/10720160008403700

Shaw, M., & Black, D. W. (2008). Internet addiction: Definition, assessment, epidemiology and clinical management. *CNS Drugs*, 22(5), 353–365. doi:10.2165/00023210-200822050-00001

Short, J., Williams, E., & Christie, B. (1976). *The social psychology of telecommunications*. London: John Wiley & Sons.

Simsek, N., Akca, N., & Simsek, M. (2015). Internet addiction and hopelessness in high school students. *TAF Preventive Medicine Bulletin*, 14(1), 7–14. doi: 10.5455/pmb.1-1393401116.

Spada, M. M. (2014). An overview of pathological use. *Addictive Behaviors*, 39, 3–6.

Stavropoulos, V., Gentile, D., & Motti-Stefanidi, F. (2016). A multilevel longitudinal study of adolescent Internet addiction: The role of obsessive–compulsive symptoms and classroom openness to experience. *European Journal of Developmental Psychology*, 13(1), 99–114. doi:10.1080/17405629.2015.1066670

Sussman, C. J., Harper, J. M., Stahl, J. L., & Weigle, P. (2018). Internet and video game addictions: Diagnosis, epidemiology, and neurobiology. *Child and Adolescent Psychiatric Clinics of North America, 27*(2), 307–326. doi: 10.1016/j.chc.2017.11.015

Takahira, M., Ando, R., & Sakamoto, A. (2008). Effect of Internet use on depression, loneliness, aggression and preference for Internet communication: A panel study with 10-to-12-year-old children in Japan. *International Journal of Web Based Communities, 4*(3), 302–318. Retrieved from https://www.semanticscholar.org/paper/ Effect-of-internet-use-on-depression%2C-loneliness%2C-a-Takahira-Ando/47e 90dc2f77dff2409edddec215211d0c4c6b3f3

Tam, P. (2017). The IMPROVE tool: A resource to assist families and clinicians. In K. S. Young & C. N. de Abreu's (Eds.), *Internet addiction in children and adolescents: Risk factors, assessment, and treatment* (pp. 189–211). New York, NY: Springer Publishing Co.

Tang, C. S. K., & Koh, Y. Y. W. (2017). Online social networking addiction among college students in Singapore: Comorbidity with behavioral addiction and affective disorder. *Asian Journal of Psychiatry, 25*(c), 175–178. doi: 10.1016/j. ajp.2016.10.027

Tang, J., Yu, Y., Du, Y., Ma, Y., Zhang, D., & Wang, J. (2014). Prevalence of Internet addiction and its association with stressful life events and psychological symptoms among adolescent Internet users. *Addictive Behaviors, 39*(3), 744–747. doi:10.1016/j.addbeh.2013.12.010

Taylor, R. N., Koerber, R., Parker, J. D. A., & Maitland, S. B. (2014). Alexithymia and Internet abuse in young adults. *Personality and Individual Differences, 60*. doi:10.1016/j.paid.2013.07.203

Tuzun Mutluer, B., Yener Orum, T., & Sertcelik, S. (2017). Incidence of Internet addiction in adult attention deficit hyperactivity disorder. *European Psychiatry, 41*, S396–S397. doi:10.1016/j.eurpsy.2017.02.457

Twist, M. L. C. (2018, June). *Digisexuality: What the tech is it?* Invited Lecture, College of Sexual and Relationship Therapists, London, England, United Kingdom.

Twist, M. L. C., & McArthur, N. (2017). Introduction to special issue on sex and technology. *Sexual and Relationship Therapy, 32*(3/4), 249–268.

Velez, J., Greitemeyer, T., Whitaker, J., Ewoldsen, D., & Bushman, B. (2016). Violent video games and reciprocity: The attenuating effects of cooperative game play on subsequent aggression. *Communication Research, 43*(4), 447–467. doi: 10.1177/0093650214552519

Verheijen, G., Burk, W., Stoltz, S., Van den Berg, Y., & Cillessen, A. (2018). Friendly fire: Longitudinal effects of exposure to violent video games on aggressive behavior in adolescent friendship dyads. *Aggressive Behavior, 44*(3), 257–267. doi: 10.1002/ab.21748

Wang, C. W., Chan, C., Sai-Yin, H., Wong, P., & Ho, R. (2014). Prevalence and correlates of video and Internet gaming addiction among Hong Kong adolescents: A pilot study. *The Scientific World Journal, 87*, 46–48. doi: 10.1155/2014/874648

Weil, M. M., & Rosen, L. D. (1995). The psychological impact of technology from a global perspective: A study of technological sophistication and technophobia in university students from 23 countries. *Computers in Human Behavior, 11*, 95–133. doi: 10.1016/0747-5632(94)00026-E

Weil, M. M., Rosen, L. D., & Wugalter, S. E. (1990). The etiology of computer phobia. *Computers in Human Behavior, 6*, 361–379. doi: 10.1016/0747-5632 (90)90014-8

Wilkinson College. (2016, October 11). *America's top fear 2016: Champman University survey of American fears* [Web log post]. Retrieved from https://blogs.chapman.edu/wilkinson/2016/10/11/americas-top-fears-2016/

Wilkinson College. (2017, October 11). *America's top fear 2017: Champman University survey of American fears* [Web log post]. Retrieved from https://blogs.chapman.edu/wilkinson/2017/10/11/americas-top-fears-2017/

Wilkinson College. (2018, October 16). *America's top fear 2018: Champman University survey of American fears* [Web log post]. Retrieved from https://blogs.chapman.edu/wilkinson/2018/10/16/americas-top-fears-2018/

World Health Organization (WHO). (2010). Retrieved from www.who.int/reproductivehealth/topics/sexual_health/sh_definitions/en/

Wu, J. H., Chang, Y. C., & Tzang, R. F. (2014). Risks of abnormal Internet use among adolescents with attention-deficit/hyperactivity disorder. *Journal of Experimental & Clinical Medicine, 6*(6), 190–194. doi: 10.1016/j.jecm.2014.10.010

Yao, M. Z., & Zhong, Z. (2014). Loneliness, social contacts and Internet addiction: A cross-lagged panel study. *Computers in Human Behavior, 30,* 164–170. doi: 10.1016/j.chb.2013.08.007

Yee, N. (2006). The demographics, motivations and derived experiences of users of massively-multiuser online graphical environments. *Presence: Teleoperators and Virtual Environments, 15,* 309–329. doi:10.1162/pres.15.3.309

Zhang, F., & Kaufman, D. (2015). The impacts of social interactions in MMORPGs on older adults' social capital. *Computers in Human Behavior, 51,* 495–503. doi: 10.1016/j.chb.2015.05.034

Zheng, R., Spears, J., Luptak, M., & Wilby, F. (2015). Understanding older adults' perceptions of internet use: An exploratory factor analysis. *Educational Gerontology, 41*(7), 504–518. doi: 10.1080/03601277.2014.100349

Zhong, Z. J. (2011). The effects of collective MMORPG (Massively Multiplayer Online Role-Playing Games) play on gamers' online and offline social capital. *Computers in Human Behavior, 27,* 2352–2363. http://dx.doi.org/10.1016/j.chb.2011.07.014

ELEVEN

Measuring Technology's Impact on Relational Life

Assessment of Internet Impact in Daily Life: The Chicken or the Egg?

In Chapter 1, we presented information about how the Internet is associated with our physical and psychological selves, including changes to our sleep cycle, sleep habits, our sense of loneliness and social connectivity, etc. For youth in particular, more time online means less time in bed getting adequate sleep (Ferreira et al., 2017; Nose et al., 2017). We further reviewed articles that associated lack of sleep to a host of psychological problems, including depression, anxiety, substance abuse, and suicidal ideation (Lemola, Perkinson-Gloor, Brand, Dewald-Kaufmann, & Grob, 2015).

But these studies are correlational only. What is less clear is whether the choice to use Internet technologies and other forms of today's media before or instead of going to sleep is a function of something else that was not measured (also known as the third variable problem) or what the direction of the relationship may be. It is this lack of clarity that may also drive the inconsistencies demonstrated in the research about the impact of technology on our lives. For example, Amichai-Hamburger and Hayat (2011) found using the Internet was associated with a greater sense of connection to others, while other authors have uncovered associations between greater Internet use and loneliness (Stepanikova, Nie, & He, 2010). In determining the extent to which Internet usage is contributing to challenges in couple and family life, part of the conversation has to be whether Internet usage is a symptom of a larger problem or whether Internet usage is in and of itself the primary issue. Healthcare workers including therapists, physicians, nurse practitioners, counselors, social workers, and psychologists are left with the challenges of attempting to determine which came first: the proverbial chicken or the egg.

Perceived etiology of a presenting problem is critical in determining the scope of the problem and course of treatment. Case conceptualizations direct the treatment processes (Ridley, Jeffrey, & Roberson, 2017). The model by which we incorporate information into a case conceptualization is highly complex and is reliant on many things, including (but not limited to): the information obtained in the history/assessment phases of treatment, cultural/contextual considerations, and the theory from which the clinician selects to operate (Ridley et al., 2017). Of course, the clinician frequently has specific ways in which they gather information, which might also lead to a slant in how the information is conceptualized and packaged for treatment. Other factors that affect a clinician's judgment include how easily they can recall information, how similar the information is to other cases they have seen, their personal beliefs about a given topic (self-of-the-therapist factors), and being overly confident in what they see as the issue. Misspecifications in these levels may lead to misunderstanding about etiology, thus impairing treatment (Falvey, 2001).

Another element that also may influence treatment is the determination as to whether the presenting problem has a biological basis. Evidence of one's issues being rooted in biology has proven to reduce prison sentences, thus leading to the belief that the evidence of behavior that is tied to one's biology reduces blame and furthers empathy (Aspinwall, Brown, & Tabery, 2012). When applied to psychological or clinical settings, however, the reverse seems to be true: when clinicians focus primarily on the biology contributing to the problem, they are less likely to feel empathy for the clinical participant (Haslam & Kvaale, 2015). Clinicians retain some level of empathy if they keep in mind the confluence of factors contributing to one's symptoms, acknowledging the biological contribution and recognizing how that contribution interacts with the family/relational system dynamics, environment, etc. (Lebowitz & Ahn, 2014).

One's case conceptualization may also be affected by extra therapeutic factors. There are inconsistent findings around whether issues such as profession, demographic variables of the therapist, work setting, or education have an impact (Falvey, 2001). There is, however, good evidence to suggest that the intersectionality of factors such as gender, sexual orientation, religion, and/or racial/ethnic identity of the clinical participants and clinicians affects treatment retention, therapeutic alliance, and clinical outcomes (Blumer, Ansara, & Watson, 2013; Green, Murphy, & Blumer, 2010; Green, Murphy, Blumer, & Palmanteer, 2009; Staczan et al., 2017; Wintersteen, Mensinger, & Diamond, 2005).

Thus far, one study has examined the process of treatment decisions in cases of couple therapy with the Internet as an element in the presenting problem. Hertlein and Piercy (2008) examined the effect of client gender, therapist gender, and the association of the Internet in the assessment and treatment of infidelity cases. In this study, 504 licensed marriage and family therapists (LMFTs) were provided a script of a couple seeking treatment. The scripts were delivered via stratified random sample. One-quarter of the clinicians (all female) received a script of a female cheating on her male partner; a second quarter (also all female) received a script of a male cheating on his female partner. Another quarter (all male) received the script of a female cheating on her male partner. The final quarter (all male) received a script of a male cheating on his female partner. In addition, there were three different clinical scenarios, also distributed evenly to the respondents. One scenario described a case where one partner met and corresponded in a flirtatious manner with another individual and the email exchange was discovered in the trash by their partner. The second scenario was where an individual met someone online and ended up meeting this individual offline. The third scenario was where one person was watching pornography online. When the client who was involved with someone else or using pornography online was a man, the therapist tended to conceptualize the case as having a higher degree of sex "addiction" than when the identified client was a woman, and they were consequently more likely to assign individual treatment. Female therapists were more likely to connect the treatment to larger relational problems than male therapists (Hertlein & Piercy, 2008).

What is most surprising about this finding is despite the couple therapists clearly indicating they believed the problem was a couple problem (stemming from either a deficit in the relationship or other impaired processes), when the problem between the couple had some connection to a computer or the Internet, the participant therapists were more inclined to approve environmental changes (moving the computer to another room) than to employ a change that better reflected their original theory about why the couple was having the problems they were experiencing in the first place (Hertlein & Piercy, 2008).

So why the incongruence? Something almost *sinister* happens when a computer gets involved. When the Internet is introduced into the clinical setting, it leads clinicians to inappropriate conclusions about how to navigate treatment, potentially ascribing the Internet as the cause of the problem. Part of it may be due to the familiarity that the clinician themselves has with online technology or even their use of such technologies, their own degree of technophobia, and, as Falvey (2001) stated, their personal beliefs—in this case, about technology. For example, couple and family therapists (CFTs) are generally not comfortable with using the Internet as a service-delivery platform (Hertlein, Blumer, & Smith, 2014). In a survey study, CFTs reported they were uncomfortable with the Internet as the sole mechanism for delivery of therapeutic services (Hertlein et al., 2014). While this discomfort was experienced for treating individuals online (42% noted they were very uncomfortable with this modality for individuals in treatment), that proportion increased to 50% of CFTs expressing they were very uncomfortable with couples treatment delivered online and increased again for families (54.4% reported being very uncomfortable with this service delivery) (Hertlein et al., 2014).

CFTs, in particular, cling to the misguided notion that the therapeutic relationship, a key part of treatment, is significantly compromised when therapy is conducted in an online format, despite the empirical evidence to the contrary (Germain, Marchand, Bouchard, Guay, & Drouin, 2010; Glueck, 2013a, b; Hertlein & Earl, in press; Morgan, Patrick, & Magaletta, 2008; Twist & Hertlein, 2016). Why? It makes us, as relational therapists, feel better to think that in-person interactions cannot replicate ones facilitated by a heartless, soulless machine. As many as 61% of therapists surveyed reported that their perception was that the therapeutic alliance was weaker in therapeutic relationships developed online as compared to those developed offline (Hennigan & Goss, 2016). This perception persists despite evidence that most of the time, joining is not impaired by online therapy (Glueck, 2013b), regardless of presenting problem (Jenkins-Guarnieri, Pruitt, Luxton, & Johnson, 2015). In fact, in at least one study the therapeutic relationship was stronger online than offline (Knaevelsrud & Maercker, 2006).

When joining is not necessarily impaired, there may be a level of comfort around face-to-face therapy for clinical participants. In a study with young adults, a significant proportion reported a preference toward face-to-face therapy (Rogers, Griffin, Wykle, & Fitzpatrick, 2009). These results, however, are tempered by the fact that the authors did not use people in treatment. Moreover, individuals were screened out if they were not between the ages of 21 and 30 only. Rather, this sample of convenience included people recruited from Facebook not specifically in therapy and focused on their perception of being in different modalities of therapy. Further, those who indicated they preferred face-to-face might have responded to subsequent questions in a way that would endorse their previously espoused view.

There is some evidence that suggests that romantic relationships develop online more quickly than offline relationships and are characterized by more commitment and greater levels of intimacy because of the increased amount of self-disclosure that occurs in online relationships (Farci, Rossi, Boccia Artieri, & Giglietto, 2017; Hertlein & Blumer, 2013). Self-disclosure on the client's end is a key part of the therapeutic process and has been demonstrated to lead to powerful changes in personal relationships and life changes (Han & O'Brian, 2014).

The research indicating that effectiveness toward intention to change behavior in conversation is more likely to convince therapists that online therapy may not be ideal (Hammick & Lee, 2014). Finally, younger therapists saw the technology as less of a problem than therapists of a relatively older age in the Hertlein and Piercy (2008) study. While again not causal, it may be that the generational effect and comfort with using technology contribute to one considering the role of technology in treatment as less pathological when compared to clinicians of an older age, as they are generally less comfortable (Schreurs, Quan-Haase, & Martin, 2017). This is in part because comfort is based to some degree on increased digital literacy, which happens through more experience (Murray & Pérez, 2014). In the case of older individuals, if they are reluctant to adopt the technology, they will not have the experience of working toward greater degrees of literacy (Morris, 2007). It may be that therapists are operating from a different community, one described by Christopher Lasch (1979):

> Those who dig bomb shelters hope to survive by sur-
> rounding themselves with the latest products of mod-
> ern technology. Communards in the country adhere to
> the opposite plan: to free themselves on the dependence
> of technology and thus to outlive its destruction and
> collapse.
>
> (p. 4)

For all of the aforementioned reasons, it is important to conduct a thorough assessment as to what might be facing a couple or family system when the Internet is involved. It is not as easy as assuming the Internet is the problem, but at the same time, the Internet could be contributing in substantial ways to the difficulties. There are many survey tools designed to assess both the perception of Internet use as well as the extent it may remain problematic in one's life.

My Problem Is You(Tube)

Problematic Internet use is not a well-defined construct. For example, 5% of women in a Swedish sample self-reported their Internet use as problematic, whereas 13% of men in the sample reported the same. This proportion is consistent with another study by the American Psychiatric Association (APA, 2013), which put the rate of problematic Internet use at between 6% and 14%. Because the estimate of those reporting some level of out-of-control behaviors related to the Internet ranges from 0.3% to near 60% (Parsons, Severino, Grov, Bimbi, & Morgenstern, 2007), it is difficult to determine what proportion of them may actually be experiencing some kind of behavioral "addiction"; potentially 2% of the women and 5% of the men characterized their problematic use as serious (Hertlein & Cravens, 2014). The challenge in identifying problematic behavior is further confused by multiple terms—such as Internet dependence, addiction, and pathological Internet use (Cravens, Hertlein, & Blumer, 2013; Hertlein & Cravens, 2014).

Rather than working with strict definitions only, scholars in the field may focus instead on a cluster of behaviors. Bulut Serin (2011) found that problematic Internet use was tied loosely to gender (for instance, men seemed to have more of a problem than women). Those with higher levels of neuroticism were more likely to use the Internet for entertaining (as opposed to extroverts, who use it for connections with others); in addition, those with higher levels of neuroticism, psychoticism, and who practice more deceptive behaviors have higher levels of out-of-control technology-related behaviors. They may also be the same people who are dissatisfied with life—and in fact, score lower on the Life Satisfaction Scale (Diener, Emmons, Larsen, & Griffin, 1985).

Further, Jones and Hertlein (2012) outlined key differences between various types of problematic Internet behavior across four dimensions. One dimension is the parties that are involved. In Internet infidelity, the involved party is typically an identifiable third person. In so-called "Internet sex addiction," there may be interaction with others online, but not necessarily an identifiable third person. In "Internet addiction," there are no involved parties per se—instead, the issue is website surfing and usage. A second dimension is the view of the problem—whether the issue is time spent online (as is the case in "Internet addiction") or how that time is spent online (content is related to sexual behavior or content is about benign topics). A third dimension is whether physical symptoms are present, as having an "addiction" would imply co-occurrence of withdrawal and tolerance. A final dimension is exploring the extent to which factors such as speed, potency of information, and the importance of being connected to another individual are playing out.

Measuring "Addictive"/Compulsive Internet Use

The rise of the Internet and its insertion into our everyday life have created a near-dependence on the Internet to function in society. Businesses, social groups, and work settings function through a wide variety of software programs and systems with a heavy reliance on passwords, logins, and interactions through email addresses and text notifications. As a result, the discussion around Internet use and the problems associated with it are a mainstream topic in today's society.

The term "Internet addiction" was actually introduced in 1996 (Goldberg, 1996) and was compared to having the same characteristics as other addictions at the time, including tolerance when playing, symptoms of withdrawal when not using the Internet, and even impairment in one's academic, workplace, and relationship endeavors (Lortie & Guitton, 2013). The data on problematic usage, however, confirms that the individual's physiology and psychological state after using the Internet match those using opiates and alcohol (Reed et al., 2017). But, as scholars have used the term "Internet addiction" the term has become more confusing. Jones and Hertlein (2012), for example, argue that the criteria for Young's (2001) version of Internet addiction contains elements that do not involve the Internet. Young's criteria led to the development of the Internet Addiction Test, but this inventory focuses on tolerance, withdrawal, ignoring other activities, and using the Internet nearly constantly, all of which are not supported empirically (Cho et al., 2014).

Since the creation of the term, many other inventories have been developed. These include but are not limited to:

- Anxiety scale toward the Internet
  (Ekizoglu & Ozcinar, 2011)

- Assessment of the Italian version of the Internet Disorder Scale (IDS-15)
  (Monacis, Sinatra, Griffiths, & Palo, 2018).

- Compulsive Internet Use Scale (CIUS)
  (Meerkerk, Van Den Eijnden, Vermulst, & Garretsen, 2009)

- Arabic version of the Compulsive Internet Use Scale (CIUS)
  (Khazaalm et al., 2011)

- Japanese version of the Compulsive Internet Use Scale (CIUS)
  (Yong, Inoue, & Kawakami, 2017)

- Digital Media Use Assessment
  (Carson, Gansner, & Khang, 2018)

- Excessive use of microblogs in Chinese college students
  (Hou et al., 2014)

- Generalized Problematic Internet Use Scale (GPIUS)
  (Caplan, 2002)

- Internet Addiction Scale
  (Cho et al., 2014)

- Internet Addiction Scale
  (Nichols & Nicki, 2004)

- Internet addiction and mobile phone problem use
  (Beranuy Fargues, Chamarro Lusar, Graner Jordania, & Carbonell Sánchez, 2009)

- Korean Smartphone Addiction Proneness Scale for Youth
  (Kim, Lee, Lee, Karin Nam, & Chung, 2014)

- Measurement of Internet Addiction: An Item Response Analysis Approach
  (Zhang & Xin, 2013)

- Pius-A: Problematic Internet Use Scale
  (Boubeta, 2015)

- Problematic Internet Use Questionnaire
  (Demetrovics, Szeredi, & Rózsa, 2008)

- Problematic Internet Use Questionnaire Short Form
  (Demetrovics et al., 2016)

- Problematic Internet use

(Davis, Flett, & Besser, 2002)

- Problematic Internet usage scale

(Ceyhan, Ceyhan, & Gurcan, 2007)

- Revised Chen Internet Addiction Scale (CIAS-R) in Chinese Adolescents

(Mak et al., 2014)

- Smartphone Addiction Inventory (SPAI)

(Lin et al., 2014)

Lortie and Guitton (2013) evaluated the criteria included in 14 assessments for problematic Internet behavior. They found seven dimensions present in their review: compulsive use, negative outcomes, withdrawal symptoms, salience, mood regulation, escapism, and social comfort. The "core" of the questionnaires, however, was composed of three of these: compulsive use, negative outcomes, and salience. In addition, the authors were able to find evidence for six of the seven dimensions of having a diagnosis of behavioral addiction, as classified by the APA (2000) in the *Diagnostic Statistical Manual of Mental Disorders-IV-Text Revision* (*DSM-IV-TR*), and five of the seven classifying criteria in the *International Statistical Classification of Diseases and Related Health Problems-10* (*ICD-10*) (Lortie & Guitton, 2013). Some scholars have pared down problematic Internet usage into two factors—dependency and distraction (Jia & Jia, 2009). Still others have uncovered more nuanced factors in their operational definitions of problematic Internet use, such as issues in time commitments, emotional/psychological conflict, and difficulty managing one's mood (Widyanto, Griffiths, & Brunsden, 2011).

In a revision of the GPIU Scale (GPIUS2), three different Internet users were identified in relation to how risky their behavior was in regard to leaving them with a problem with their computer usage (Pontes, Caplan, & Griffiths, 2016). The authors summarized the three groups as such:

> Participants in the "low risk" class accounted for almost half of the sample (46.7%) and were characterized as experiencing very few PIU cognitions, behaviors, and/or negative outcomes. Participants with "medium risk" of PIU represented 40.7% of the total sample and tended to use the Internet more often as a way of enhancing their mood, as demonstrated by the markedly high scores on the mood regulation subscale of the GPIUS2. The third and final class comprised 12.6% of the total sample and featured participants showing "high risk" of PIU cognitions, behaviors, and negative outcomes due to Internet use.

(p. 830)

But, of course, this distinction makes no difference to people living with these types of users. In 2018, the World Health Organization tried for a classification of Internet gaming addiction (Revell, 2018).

Measurement Tools

What's in a Name?

As with many of the behavioral addictions, the determination as to whether a particular set of Internet behaviors is diagnosable is challenging. There are three commonly used diagnostic labels that are applied to out-of-control Internet usage: impulse control disorder, obsessive-compulsive disorder, and addictive disorders, with an "other" or "unspecified" condition (previously not-otherwise-specified in the *DSM-IV-TR*; APA, 2000; Juhnke & Hagedorn, 2006). Despite their similarities, behavioral addictions do not share all of the same properties as addictions related to substance abuse and differ from impulse control disorders. For example, both behavioral addictions and substance abuse may begin with an

> urge or craving state prior to initiating the behavior, as do individuals with substance use disorders prior to substance use. Additionally, these behaviors often decrease anxiety and result in a positive mood state or "high," similar to substance intoxication. Emotional dysregulation may contribute to cravings in both behavioral and substance use disorders.
>
> (Grant, Potenza, Weinstein, & Gorelick, 2010, p. 234)

Such disorders differ from obsessive-compulsive disorder in that obsessive-compulsive behaviors generally start out as more distressing and/or unacceptable, while addictive behaviors typically become more unpleasant over time as their participation is frequently motivated by avoiding withdrawal or positive reinforcement for continuing the behavior (Grant et al., 2010. Still, the APA (2013) has made little mention of behavioral addictions altogether in the *DSM-5*. Gaming disorder was included, and Internet gaming disorder was considered, but ultimately not included (Hertlein & Cravens, 2014).

Measuring Online Sexual Behavior

As with the "Internet addiction" inventories, there are also a host of inventories that attempt to measure so-called "sexual addiction" on the Internet, and most notably, the concept of cybersex. One of the areas that is assessed in cybersex is the intensity or severity (Hertlein & Cravens,

2014). One such inventory is the Preoccupied, Ashamed, Treatment, Hurt others, Out of control, Sad (PATHOS) scale (Carnes et al., 2012). Based on inventories that assess severity of alcoholism, PATHOS has six items that focus on how much time is spent pursuing sex online as compared to other activities; sadness, shame, or other negative feelings associated with this activity; one's awareness of the impact on others of their sexual online behavior; and whether one can govern their online sexual behavior. Other well-known inventories include the Internet Sex Screening Test (ISST) and the Online Sexual Addiction Questionnaire (OSA-Q) (Delmonico, 1997; Putnam, 2013). Both of these latter inventories attempt to assess the manner in which the online sexual activities disrupt day-to-day life. The OSA-Q, in particular, attempts to assess the characteristics associated with addiction in general, including withdrawal, tolerance, and cravings/compulsions to engage in sexual behaviors online.

Another common way for online sexual behavior to be assessed is through a clinical interview (Hertlein & Cravens, 2014). Such an interview not only enables the clinician to ask the client about their online sexual behavior, but also provides an opportunity to ask their partners and family/relational system members about their online sexual behavior (e.g., symptoms and issues they might observe. This may include how the identified patient engages in online interactions with others, the presence of sexual fantasies and how those play out in the couple's life, any secrecy in one's activities online, and the presence of any guilt and shame as a consequence of one's sexual activities online). For American Association of Sexuality Educators, Counselors, and Therapists (AASECT)–certified providers, however, a cautionary note is extended regarding the assessments and line of clinical interviewing one does with regard to exploring online sexual behaviors as it is considered unethical to use assessment tools and/or to frame one's clinical interviewing in a way that denotes a clinical participant is experiencing a "sex addiction" or an "online sex addiction" (AASECT, 2016). Instead, what is recommended is to work with the clinical participant(s) using a framework like the one proposed by clinicians Douglas Braun-Harvey and Michael A. Vigorito in 2016, which views online sexual behaviors as potentially being out-of-control behaviors in the context of looking at how a person and their partners are experiencing their sexual health and well-being.

The Rebirth of Slick: The Couple and Family Technology Assessment Revised

It is important to work toward understanding the role of the Internet, coping skills, personality and temperament, health, and moderating factors in the contribution to out-of-control technology-related behaviors. At the same time, to merely give an assessment to determine whether one person is out of control with regard to their Internet usage may not be sufficient for family/relational system members and partners who are in pain as a consequence of one's Internet usage. For example, if a therapist gives an individual inventory and comes to the conclusion that someone is "addicted," then what? Do the family and partner somehow become empathetic to the partner's plight? Does it matter what it is called if the behavior is the same? Further, the assessment of Internet "addiction" is not very easy (Pawlikowski, Nader, Burger, Stieger, & Brand, 2014).

Such work has inspired the development of relationally based Internet assessment tools. One example was developed by Campbell and Murray (2015). Known as the Technology and Intimate Relationship Assessment, it poses a series of questions about the respondent's use of technology, their partner's use of technology, whether this technology usage is a barrier to communication and intimacy, or whether the use of technology serves as a useful adjunct to the development and maintenance of intimacy in a romantic relationship. Scholars such as Carlisle, Carlisle, Polychronopoulos, Goodman-Scott, and Kirk-Jenkins (2016) consider Internet addiction a process addiction, and propose to measure it within that frame. Loosely defined, a process addiction is where "an individual compulsively engages in a particular activity despite suffering negative consequences after repeated attempts to stop. . . . Examples include addictions to activities such as gambling, shopping, nonparaphilic hypersexual activities, video games and Internet use" (Northrup, Lapierre, Kirk, & Rae, 2015, p. 342). One of the interesting things, however, from Northrup et al.'s (2015) research was that: (1) their Internet Addiction Test was not related to the gambling addiction test (which the authors surmise may have had something to do with the gambling test), and (2) cellphone usage was not correlated with any of the other technology constructs, which suggested perhaps misspecification in that construct as well.

Hertlein and Blumer (2013) provided an assessment of ecological factors related to the Internet, and we have revised it for this text. Rather than a tool to assess out-of-control technology-related behaviors this tool can evaluate where an individual's vulnerabilities and strengths lie in the context of Internet usage. Such knowledge will help individuals and families/relational systems identify areas for improvement and change. It is recommended that this revised assessment be used in combination with other assessment tools designed to assess relationship process and structure. This type of assessment would help to establish a closer relationship between teens and parents, while also helping teens cope with their internalizing behaviors that may be contributing to out-of-control technology-related behaviors (Van den Eijnden, Meerkerk, Vermulst, Spijkerman, & Engels, 2008). This type of assessment would also be helpful in working with lesbian, gay, and bisexual (LGB)–identifying individuals and partnerships in making decisions around management of ecological elements like anonymity and accommodation, which manifest often for LGB folks in the form of electronic visibility management (Twist, Belous,

Maier, & Bergdall, 2017; Twist, Bergdall, Belous, & Maier, 2017). This tool would also be beneficial to clinicians and their clinical participants in assessing common technology-based issues between couples like the interplay between online infidelity and electronic partner surveillance (Hertlein, Dulley, Cloud, Leon, & Chang, 2017). Honestly, it is our belief that this tool is the most comprehensive and fitting assessment for gaining information and effectively helping relational systems with virtually any technology-based concern with which they present.

The assessment we provide evaluates one's activities each month across the dimensions described in an earlier section of this book—the ecological elements, as well as the process and the structure of relationships. In addition, we have provided some questions for reflection regarding how one's family of origin and choice, and their technology usage, has impacted their own views and behaviors around sexuality. This tool can be used for developing understanding for couples and families/relational systems around why technology usage may persist in patterned ways across time and space in relational systems/families. See the Appendix for a full list of the assessment items.

Conclusion

In this chapter, we reviewed a variety of formal assessments and measurements of technology-related issues in the lives of individuals, couples, and families/relational systems. As researchers continue to explore these concepts, we expect this list of potential measures will grow exponentially. It is our hope that assessment will continue to focus not only on the specific Internet-usage behaviors, but also on the provided assessments related to the impact on one's familial and romantic relationships.

References

American Association of Sexuality Educators, Counselors, and Therapists. (2016). *AASECT position on sex addiction*. Retrieved from www.aasect.org/print/position-sex-addiction

American Psychiatric Association. (2000). *Diagnostic and statistical manual of mental disorders, DSM-IV-TR*. Washington, DC: American Psychiatric Association.

American Psychiatric Association. (2013). *Diagnostic and statistical manual of mental disorders* (5th ed.). Arlington, VA: American Psychiatric Publishing

Amichai-Hamburger, Y., & Hayat, Z. (2011). The impact of the Internet on the social lives of users: A representative sample from 13 countries. *Computers in Human Behavior, 27*(1), 585–589. doi:10.1016/j.chb.2010.10.009

Aspinwall, L. G., Brown, T. R., & Tabery, J. (2012). The double-edged sword: Does biomechanism increase or decrease judges' sentencing of psychopaths? *Science, 337*(6096), 846–849. doi:10.1126/science.1219569

Beranuy Fargues, M., Chamarro Lusar, A., Graner Jordania, C., & Carbonell Sánchez, X. (2009). Validation of two brief scales for Internet addiction and mobile phone problem use. *Psicothema, 21*(3), 480.

Blumer, M. L. C., Ansara, Y. G., & Watson, C. M. (2013). Cisgenderism in family therapy: How everyday practices can delegitimize people's gender self designations. *Journal of Family Psychotherapy, 24*(4), 267–285. doi: 10.1080/08975353.2013.849551

Boubeta, A. R. (2015). Pius-A: Problematic Internet use scale in adolescents. Development and psychometric validation. *Adicciones, 27*(1), 47–63. doi: 10.20882/adicciones.193

Braun-Harvey, D., & Vigorito, M. (2016). *Treating out of control sexual behavior: Rethinking sex addiction.* New York, NY: Springer Publishing Company.

Bulut Serin, N. (2011). An examination of predictor variables for problematic Internet use. *Turkish Online Journal of Educational Technology—TOJET, 10*(3), 54–62.

Campbell, E. C., & Murray, C. E. (2015). Measuring the impact of technology on couple relationships: The development of the technology and intimate relationship assessment. *Journal of Couple & Relationship Therapy, 14*(3), 254–276. doi:10.1080/15332691.2014.953657

Caplan, S. E. (2002). Problematic Internet use and psychosocial well-being: Development of a theory-based cognitive-behavioral measurement instrument. *Computers in Human Behavior, 18*(5), 553–575. doi:10.1016/S0747-5632(02)00004-3

Carlisle, K., Carlisle, R., Polychronopoulos, G., Goodman-Scott, E., & Kirk-Jenkins, A. (2016). Exploring Internet addiction as a process addiction. *Journal of Mental Health Counseling, 38*(2), 170–182. doi: 10.17744/mehc.38.2.07

Carnes, P. J., Green, B. J., Merlo, L. J., Polles, A., Carnes, S., & Gold, M. S. (2012). PATHOS a brief screening application for assessing sexual addiction. *Journal of Addictive Medicine, 6*(1), 19–34. doi:10.1097/ADM.0b013e3182251a28

Carson, N. J., Gansner, M., & Khang, J. (2018). Assessment of digital media use in the adolescent psychiatric evaluation. *Child and Adolescent Psychiatric Clinics of North America, 27*(2), 133–143. doi:10.1016/j.chc.2017.11.003

Ceyhan, E., Ceyhan, A. A., & Gurcan, A. (2007). The validity and reliability of the problematic Internet usage scale. *Educational Sciences: Theory and Practice, 7*(1), 411–416.

Cho, H., Kwon, M., Choi, J., Lee, S., Choi, J. S., Choi, S., & Kim, D. (2014). Development of the Internet addiction scale based on the Internet gaming disorder criteria suggested in DSM-5. *Addictive Behaviors, 39*(9), 1361–1366. doi:10.1016/j.addbeh.2014.01.020

Cravens, J. D., Hertlein, K. M., & Blumer, M. L. C. (2013). Online mediums: Assessing and treating Internet issues in relationships. *Family Therapy Magazine,* 18–23.

Davis, R. A., Flett, G. L., & Besser, A. (2002). Validation of a new scale for measuring problematic Internet use: Implications for pre-employment screening. *Cyberpsychology & Behavior: The Impact of the Internet, Multimedia and Virtual Reality on Behavior and Society, 5*(4), 331–345. doi:10.1089/109493102760275581

Delmonico, D. L. (1997). *Internet sex screening test.* Arizona: International Institute for Trauma and Addiction Professionals. Retrieved from: www.sexhelp.com/component/content/article/80-am-i-a-sex-addict/130-Internetsex-screening-iss

Demetrovics, Z., Király, O., Koronczai, B., Griffiths, M. D., Nagygyörgy, K., Elekes, Z., . . . Urbán, R. (2016). Psychometric properties of the Problematic Internet Use Questionnaire Short-Form (PIUQ-SF-6) in a nationally representative sample of adolescents. *PLOS ONE, 11*(8), e0159409. doi:10.1371/journal.pone.0159409

Demetrovics, Z., Szeredi, B., & Rózsa, S. (2008). The three-factor model of Internet addiction: The development of the problematic Internet use questionnaire. *Behavior Research Methods, 40*(2), 563–574. doi:10.3758/BRM.40.2.563

Diener, E., Emmons, R. A., Larsen, R. J., & Griffin, S. (1985). The satisfaction with life scale. *Journal of Personality Assessment, 49*(1), 71–75. doi:10.1207/s15327752jpa4901_13

Ekizoglu, N., & Ozcinar, Z. (2011). A study of developing an anxiety scale towards the Internet. *Procedia—Social and Behavioral Sciences, 15,* 3902–3911. doi:10.1016/j.sbspro.2011.04.392

Falvey, J. E. (2001). Clinical judgment in case conceptualization and treatment planning across mental health disciplines. *Journal of Counseling & Development, 79*(3), 292–303. doi:10.1002/j.1556-6676.2001.tb01974.x

Farci, M., Rossi, L., Boccia Artieri, G., & Giglietto, F. (2017). Networked intimacy. Intimacy and friendship among Italian Facebook users. *Information, Communication & Society, 20*(5), 784–801. doi:10.1080/1369118X.2016.1203970

Ferreira, C., Ferreira, H., Vieira, M. J., Costeira, M., Branco, L., Dias, Â., & Macedo, L. (2017). Epidemiology of Internet use by an adolescent population and its relation with sleep habits. *Acta Médica Portuguesa, 30*(7), 524–533. doi:10.20344/amp.8205

Germain, V., Marchand, A., Bouchard, S., Guay, S., & Drouin, M. (2010). Assessment of the therapeutic alliance in face-to-face or videoconference treatment for posttraumatic stress disorder. *Cyberpsychology, Behavior, and Social Networking, 13*(1), 29–35. doi:10.1089/cyber.2009.0139

Glueck, D. (2013a). Business aspects of telemental health in private practice. In K. M. L. Turvey (Ed.), *Telemental health* (pp. 111–133). Oxford: Elsevier.

Glueck, D. (2013b). Establishing therapeutic rapport in telemental health. In K. Myers & C. L. Turvey (Eds.), *Telemental health: Clinical, technical, and administrative foundations for evidence-based practice.* Elsevier insights (pp. 29–46). Amsterdam, Netherlands: Elsevier. doi:10.1016/B978-0-12-416048-4.00003-8

Goldberg, I. (1996). *Internet addiction disorder.* Retrieved July 8, 2018, from www.urz.uni-heidelberg.de/Netzdienste/anleitung/wwwtips/8/addict.html

Grant, J. E., Potenza, M. N., Weinstein, A., & Gorelick, D. A. (2010). Introduction to behavioral addictions. *The American Journal of Drug and Alcohol Abuse, 36*(5), 233–241. doi:10.3109/00952990.2010.491884

Green, M. S., Murphy, M. J., & Blumer, M. L. C. (2010). Marriage and family therapists' comfort working with lesbian and gay clients: The influence of religious practices and support for lesbian and gay human rights. *Journal of Homosexuality, 57*(10), 1–17.

Green, M. S., Murphy, M. J., Blumer, M. L. C., & Palmanteer, D. (2009). Marriage and family therapists' comfort level working with gay and lesbian individuals, couples, and families. *The American Journal of Family Therapy, 37,* 159–168.

Hammick, J. K., & Lee, M. J. (2014). Do shy people feel less communication apprehension online? The effects of virtual reality on the relationship between personality characteristics and communication outcomes. *Computers in Human Behavior, 33,* 302–310. doi:10.1016/j.chb.2013.01.046

Han, Y., & O'Brien, K. M. (2014). Critical secret disclosure in psychotherapy with Korean clients. *The Counseling Psychologist, 42*(4), 524–551. doi:10.1177/0011000014524600

Haslam, N., & Kvaale, E. P. (2015). Biogenetic explanations of mental disorder: The mixed-blessings model. *Current Directions in Psychological Science, 24*(5), 399–404. doi:10.1177/0963721415588082

Hennigan, J., & Goss, S. P. (2016). UK secondary school therapists' online communication with their clients and future intentions. *Counselling and Psychotherapy Research, 16*(3), 149–160. doi:10.1002/capr.12082

Hertlein, K. M., & Blumer, M. L. C. (2013). *The couple and family technology framework: Intimate relationships in a digital age.* New York, NY: Routledge.

Hertlein, K. M., Blumer, M. L. C., & Smith, J. M. (2014). Marriage and family therapists' use and comfort with online communication with clients. *Contemporary Family Therapy, 36*(1), 58–69. doi:10.1007/s10591-013-9284-0

Hertlein, K. M., & Cravens, J. D. (2014). Assessment and treatment of Internet sexuality issues. *Current Sexual Health Reports, 6*(1), 56–63. doi:10.1007/s11930-013-0011-5

Hertlein, K. M., Dulley, C., Chang, J., Cloud, R., & Leon, D. (2017). Does absence of evidence mean evidence of absence? Managing the issue of partner surveillance in infidelity treatment. *Sexual and Relationship Therapy, 32*(3–4), 323–333. doi: 10.1080/14681994.2017.1397952

Hertlein, K. M., & Earl, R. (in press). Internet-delivered therapy in couple and family work.

Hertlein, K. M., & Piercy, F. P. (2008). Therapists' assessment and treatment of Internet infidelity cases. *Journal of Marital and Family Therapy, 34*(4), 481–497. doi:10.1111/j.1752-0606.2008.00090.x

Hou, J., Huang, Z., Li, H., Liu, M., Zhang, W., Ma, N., . . . Zhang, X. (2014). Is the excessive use of microblogs an Internet addiction? Developing a scale for assessing the excessive use of microblogs in Chinese college students. *PLoS ONE, 9*(11), e110960. doi:10.1371/journal.pone.01109600

Jenkins-Guarnieri, M. A., Pruitt, L. D., Luxton, D., D., & Johnson, K. (2015). Patient perceptions of telemental health: Systematic review of direct comparisons to in-person psychotherapeutic treatments. *Telemed e-Health, 21*(8), 652–660.

Jia, H. H., & Jia, R. (2009). Factorial validity of problematic Internet use scales. *Computers in Human Behavior, 25*(6), 1335–1342. doi:10.1016/j.chb.2009.06.004

Jones, K. E., & Hertlein, K. M. (2012). Four key dimensions for distinguishing Internet infidelity from Internet and sex addiction: Concepts and clinical application. *The American Journal of Family Therapy, 40*(2), 115–125. doi:10.1080/01926187.2011.600677

Juhnke, G. A., & Hagedorn, B. (2006). *Counseling addicted families: An integrated assessment and treatment model.* New York, NY: Routledge

Khazaal, Y., Chatton, A., Atwi, K., Zullino, D., Khan, R., & Billieux, J. (2011). Arabic validation of the Compulsive Internet Use Scale (CIUS). *Substance Abuse Treatment, Prevention, and Policy, 6*(1), 32. doi:10.1186/1747-597x-6-32

Kim, D., Lee, Y., Lee, J., Nam, J. K., & Chung, Y. (2014). Development of Korean Smartphone Addiction Proneness Scale for youth. *PLoS ONE, 9*(5), e97920. doi:10.1371/journal.pone.0097920

Knaevelsrud, C., & Maercker, A. (2006). Does the quality of the working alliance predict treatment outcome in online psychotherapy for traumatized patients? *Journal of Medical Internet Research, 8*(4), 31. doi:10.2196/jmir.8.4.e31

Lasch, C. (1979). *The culture of narcissism: American life in an age of diminishing expectations.* New York, NY: W. W. Norton & Company.

Lebowitz, M. S., & Ahn, W. (2014). Effects of biological explanations for mental disorders on clinicians' empathy. *Proceedings of the National Academy of Sciences of the United States of America, 111*(50), 17786–17790. doi:10.1073/pnas.1414058111

Lemola, S., Perkinson-Gloor, N., Brand, S., Dewald-Kaufmann, J. F., & Grob, A. (2015). Adolescents' electronic media use at night, sleep disturbance, and depressive symptoms in the smartphone age. *Journal of Youth and Adolescence, 44*(2), 405–418. doi:10.1007/s10964-014-0176-x

Lin, Y., Chang, L., Lee, Y., Tseng, H., Kuo, T. B., & Chen, S. (2014). Development and validation of the Smartphone Addiction Inventory (SPAI). *PLoS ONE, 9*(6), e98312. doi:10.1371/journal.pone.0098312

Lortie, C. L., & Guitton, M. J. (2013). Internet addiction assessment tools: Dimensional structure and methodological status. *Addiction, 108*(7), 1207–1216. doi:10.1111/add.12202

Mak, K., Lai, C., Ko, C., Chou, C., Kim, D., Watanabe, H., & Ho, R. (2014). Psychometric properties of the revised Chen Internet Addiction Scale (CIAS-R) in Chinese adolescents. *Journal of Abnormal Child Psychology, 42*(7), 1237–1245. doi:10.1007/s10802-014-9851-3

Meerkerk, G., Van Den Eijnden, R. J. J. M., Vermulst, A. A., & Garretsen, H. F. L. (2009). The compulsive Internet use scale (CIUS): Some psychometric properties. *Cyberpsychology & Behavior: The Impact of the Internet, Multimedia and Virtual Reality on Behavior and Society, 12*(1), 1–6. doi:10.1089/cpb.2008.0181

Monacis, L., Sinatra, M., Griffiths, M. D., & De Palo, V. (2018). Assessment of the Italian Version of the Internet Disorder Scale (IDS-15). *International Journal of Mental Health and Addiction, 16*(3), 680–691. doi:10.1007/s11469-017-9823-2

Morgan, R. D., Patrick, A. R., & Magaletta, P. R. (2008). Does the use of telemental health alter the treatment experience? Inmates perceptions of telemental health versus face-to-face treatment modalities. *Journal of Consulting and Clinical Psychology, 76*(1), 158–162. doi:10.1037/0022-006X.76.1.158

Morris, A. (2007). E-literacy and the grey digital divide: A review with recommendations. *Journal of Information Literacy, 1*(3). doi:10.11645/1.3.14

Murray, M., & Pérez, J. (2014). Unraveling the digital literacy paradox: How higher education fails at the fourth literacy. *Issues in Informing Science and Information Technology, 11*, 085–100. doi:10.28945/1982

Nichols, L. A., & Nicki, R. (2004). Development of a psychometrically sound Internet addiction scale: A preliminary step. *Psychology of Addictive Behaviors, 18*(4), 381–384. doi:10.1037/0893-164x.18.4.381

Northrup, J., Lapierre, C., Kirk, J., & Rae, C. (2015). The Internet process addiction test: Screening for addictions to processes facilitated by the Internet. *Behavioral Sciences, 5*(3), 341–352. doi:10.3390/bs5030341

Nose, Y., Fujinaga, R., Suzuki, M., Hayashi, I., Moritani, T., Kotani, K., & Nagai, N. (2017). Association of evening smartphone use with cardiac autonomic nervous activity after awakening in adolescents living in high school dormitories. *Child's Nervous System, 33*(4), 653–658. doi:10.1007/s00381-017-3388-z

Parsons, J. T., Severino, J. P., Grov, C., Bimbi, D. S., & Morgenstern, J. (2007). Internet use among gay and bisexual men with compulsive sexual behavior. *Sexual Addiction & Compulsivity, 14*(3), 239–256. doi:10.1080/10720160701480659

Pawlikowski, M., Nader, I. W., Burger, C., Stieger, S., & Brand, M. (2014). Pathological Internet use: It is a multidimensional and not a unidimensional construct. *Addiction Research & Theory, 22*(2), 166–175. doi:10.3109/16066359.2013.793313

Pontes, H. M., Caplan, S. E., & Griffiths, M. D. (2016). Psychometric validation of the Generalized Problematic Internet Use Scale 2 in a Portuguese sample. *Computers in Human Behavior, 63*, 823–833. doi:10.1016/j.chb.2016.06.015

Putnam, D. E. (2013). *Online sexual addiction questionnaire (OSA-Q).* Retrieved from www.onlinesexaddict.com/osaq.html

Reed, P., Romano, M., Re, F., Roaro, A., Osborne, L., Viganò, C., & Truzoli, R. (2017). Differential physiological changes following Internet exposure in higher and lower problematic Internet users. *PLoS ONE, 12*(5), e0178480.

Revell, T. (2018). Gaming really can be bad for you. *New Scientist, 237*(3159), 10. doi:10.1016/s0262-4079(18)30012-5

Ridley, C. R., Jeffrey, C. E., & Roberson, R. B. (2017). Case mis-conceptualization in psychological treatment: An enduring clinical problem. *Journal of Clinical Psychology, 73*(4), 359–375. doi:10.1002/jclp.22354

Rogers, V. L., Griffin, M. Q., Wykle, M. L., & Fitzpatrick, J. J. (2009). Internet versus face-to-face therapy: Emotional self-disclosure issues for young adults. *Issues in Mental Health Nursing, 30*(10), 596–602. doi:10.1080/01612840903003520

Schreurs, K., Quan-Haase, A., & Martin, K. (2017). Problematizing the digital literacy paradox in the context of older adults' ICT use: Aging, media discourse, and self-determination. *Canadian Journal of Communication, 42*(2). doi:10.22230/cjc.2017v42n2a3130

Staczan, P., Schmuecker, R., Koehler, M., Berglar, J., Crameri, A., von Wyl, A., . . . Tschuschke, V. (2017). Effects of sex and gender in ten types of psychotherapy. *Psychotherapy Research, 27*(1), 74–88. doi:10.1080/10503307.2015.1072285

Stepanikova, I., Nie, N. H., & He, X. (2010). Time on the Internet at home, loneliness, and life satisfaction: Evidence from panel time-diary data. *Computers in Human Behavior, 26*(3), 329–338. doi:10.1016/j.chb.2009.11.002

Twist, M. L. C., & Hertlein, K. M. (2016). Ethical couple and family e-therapy. In M. J. Murphy & L. Hecker (Eds.), *Ethics and professional issues in couple and family therapy* (2nd ed., pp. 261–282). New York, NY: Routledge.

Twist, M. L. C., Belous, C. K., Maier, C. A., & Bergdall, M. K. (2017). Considering technology-based ecological elements in lesbian, gay, and bisexual partnered relationships. *Sexual and Relationship Therapy, 32*(3/4), 291–308.

Twist, M. L. C., Bergdall, M. K., Belous, C. K., & Maier, C. A. (2017). Electronic visibility management of lesbian, gay, and bisexual identities and relationships. *Journal of Couple and Relationship Therapy: Innovations in Clinical Educational Interventions, 16*(4), 271–285.

Van den Eijnden, R. J., Meerkerk, G., Vermulst, A. A., Spijkerman, R., & Engels, R. C. (2008). Online communication, compulsive Internet use, and psychosocial well-being among adolescents: A longitudinal study. *Developmental Psychology, 44*(3), 655–665. doi:10.1037/0012-1649.44.3.655

Widyanto, L., Griffiths, M. D., & Brunsden, V. (2011). A psychometric comparison of the Internet addiction test, the Internet-related problem scale, and self-diagnosis. *Cyberpsychology, Behavior and Social Networking, 14*(3), 141–149. doi:10.1089/cyber.2010.0151

Wintersteen, M. B., Mensinger, J. L., & Diamond, G. S. (2005). Do gender and racial differences between patient and therapist affect therapeutic alliance and treatment retention in adolescents? *Professional Psychology: Research and Practice, 36*(4), 400–408.

Yong, R. K., Inoue, A., & Kawakami, N. (2017). The validity and psychometric properties of the Japanese version of the Compulsive Internet Use Scale (CIUS). *BMC Psychiatry, 17*(1). doi:10.1186/s12888-017-1364-5

Young, K. S. (2001). *Caught in the net: How to recognize the signs of Internet addiction—and a winning strategy for recovery*. New York, NY: John Wiley & Sons, Ltd.

Zhang, J., & Xin, T. (2013). Measurement of Internet addiction: An item response analysis approach. *Cyberpsychology, Behavior, and Social Networking, 16*(6), 464–468. doi:10.1089/cyber.2012.0525

TWELVE

Developing Your Personal Technology Integration Plan With the Couple and Family Algorithm

Technology Integration Plan

Throughout this book, we have introduced a number of ideas that should convince you by now that technology is here to stay. When I (KH) typically lecture on this topic to clinicians, frequently their response is to "remove technology" and set a very physical boundary through limiting access. And when I (MLCT) give talks to instructors about how to manage technology in their university classrooms, usually their solutions to this problem are to tell students that either they cannot use their technology at all in the classroom or they can use it without restriction. The trouble with these solutions is that technology is here to stay, and these are not effective long-term answers to any of the concerns that it does and will present. Technology is now almost like the air we breathe or like a part of our genetic makeup. The integration of technology in our lives, then, should be thoughtful, with purpose, and support the strengths of a specific individual, couple, or family/relational system.

The Technology Integration Plan (TIP) describes a decision-making process by which couples, families, scholars, educators, family consultants, and mental health professionals can design ways to responsibly and effectively integrate technology in daily life. In the development of the TIP, we were informed by the work of Brian Primack, who proposes an algorithm whose abbreviation is "REAL." In this framework, "R" stands for "Renege Negativity." As we have seen in this text, not all social media experiences are created equal—some will be better than others. Therefore, engaging in social media activities that are positive as opposed to negative will better protect one's well-being (Primack et al., 2018). "E" stands for "Engage With Equilibrium." Sometimes using social media in passive ways is associated with depression; in other cases, it is associated with decreases in depression. The best way to manage, then, is to engage in some circumstances and be passive in others—achieving a balance in one's usage. "A" stands for "Actual Allies." As we read earlier in this text, having those you have not met on your friend list is associated with depression. Ensure that the people who are on your social media are ones who can support you. Finally, "L" stands for "Limit Time, Frequency, and Number of Platforms Used." These three distinct constructs are all important in managing the impact of social media use on one's well-being. More time on social media was related to more depression. While the average person uses approximately four platforms, those with significantly more depressive symptoms are using between seven and 11 (Primack et al., 2018).

In addition, the TIP is informed by the Couple and Family Technology (CFT) framework (Hertlein & Blumer, 2013). A particular relational system's (couple or family) TIP is a road map based on the CFT framework. One of the benefits to using the CFT framework is that it can be applied to diverse relational systems. At its core, the CFT framework does not advocate for one way or another of using the Internet and new media. The framework simply refers to the notion that technology affects process and structure—in some ways, the effect is positive, and in other ways, it is negative. In this model, the therapist reserves judgment about how the family should proceed with technology in their lives and instead assists the family with the implications and interventions congruent with their own beliefs and value system. In some families, for example, appropriate interventions may center around increasing boundaries between parents and their teens; in other cultures or family systems, it may be more appropriate to decrease the boundaries.

Take cellphones and secrecy—because cellphones are independent (as opposed to shared) devices, users have a certain amount of privacy regarding how they use the phone. Adolescents may opt to use the phone as one method of interacting with their peers in secret, but they may be at greater risk for cyberbullying in doing so. It may be a balance between honoring the teen's privacy and helping them bring down the guard to develop trust, and ultimately help protect them from threats.

1. Consider the Audience

The plan for integrating technology into one's couple and family life depends, in part, on who are the members of the relational system, and the behaviors the plan is designed to address. Is the focus the children? The parents? The partners? What is the relationship that is under investigation or in need of rehabilitation? One needs to consider who will be engaged in the discourse with others online, and how the audience will receive the discourse. Just because we are accessible in many ways, it is tempting to advertise one's position more broadly. On the other hand, there have to be some decisions made about whom the audience is and how we can make decisions in anticipation of the audience. One example is the concept of revenge porn. This is where information sent to one person in an electronic format is compromised because of relational fallout.

2. Maximize the Benefits

One of the primary benefits of social media is the ability to connect with others. Certain specific elements of the advantages include but are not limited to: connecting with new and established friends, sharing ideas, engaging in opportunities for volunteerism and community work, and collaboration for education and training (O'Keeffe & Clarke-Pearson, 2011). Other benefits are related to identity development and finding space to explore one's identity via videos, blogs, podcasts, electronic art media, etc. Other benefits described in Chapter 1 include the accessing of health information, which tends to spur individuals to have conversations with their doctors about conditions. Young people tend to be better at using the Internet for asking questions, are more likely to schedule appointments, and actually miss fewer appointments (O'Keeffe & Clarke-Pearson, 2011).

Altering of the boundaries may contribute to more communication among family members or with the outside world, depending on how the boundaries have shifted. For example, children with cellphones and diffuse boundaries in whom they may contact may have direct and immediate access to parents, siblings, and extended family members without having to go through their parents to navigate those connections. Such a structure may result in more communication with family. More communication with the outside world could involve children themselves receiving robocalls or from those who had the phone number of the previous owner of the line, an exchange in which they could conceivably be the receiver. The reorganization in roles, rules, and boundaries can also prompt changes in communication among family members and levels of closeness and support.

3. Consider the Motivations

One of the considerations is to engage in reflection on one's motivations in using technologies. Is the motivation to reduce anxiety? To connect with others? The honesty with which one can evaluate their motivations for phone usage may be key for understanding the rules that need to be developed in response to the motivations. For example, surveillance and using technology to monitor at a younger age may backfire and complicate relationships; at an older age, when the motivation is communication, such technologies may improve relationships.

The CFT framework may provide some insight into how accessibility, affordability, anonymity, approximation, ambiguity, accommodation, approximation, and accountability may give a clue of one's motivation for technology usage. For example, if the motivation for using technology for teens is to avoid processing painful emotions, parents might wish to develop a plan to help the teen use technology via accommodation to process their pain rather than using applications (apps) and search engines to avoid. Some examples of these apps include Moodpath, Calm, Headspace, Anxiety Relief Hypothesis, and iMood Journal. If the motivation for teens is to connect with others and this connection is occurring so frequently and intensely that it is impairing the completion of school assignments, one solution may be to set rules around accessibility and affordability of messaging functions. If, however, that accessibility is proving that it assists the teen with support, then the family may wish to consider increasing accessibility to those in-person resources.

Integration Ideas for Structure (Roles, Rules, Boundaries)

Boundary Tip 1: Check Your Email— Don't Let Your Email Check You

The ability for us to check our email instantly, whether it be for work or personal purposes, is helpful in our daily lives. The challenge in this, however, is not giving into those types of notification so that you remain in control of your own technology checking behavior. The scholarly literature is replete with studies attesting to the work-home interference now being a part of our daily lives when we have technology that keeps us virtually connected to work at all hours (Piszczek, 2017). One way to do this is to go into the settings on your phone and adjust the notifications so that you are not alerted to your work emails. Rather, you are the one who is in control of checking the work email when it is convenient for you. Once you establish this notification change and setting change, the next step would be to make rules for yourself about the circumstances under which you would check this work email. For example, you might make a decision that you are not checking the work email on weekends or on days off as you are not working. In addition, you may wish to explore the motivations that are contributing to your checking of email. Are you feeling like you are not being productive when you are in fact? Are you trying to avoid a situation with a partner or peer? Where do you feel it in your body?

Boundary Tip 2: Cover Your Private Parts (or Privacy Management)

Structure of relationships has a great deal to do with our computer and device usage. In a study by De Wolf, Willaert, and Pierson (2014), the roles one adopts have implications for the way in which privacy is managed. While this study had to do with groups and management of groups, families are inherently groups. The same results can be applied to families. Each member has to be clear about what their role is and make sure that they stay in that role. These rules should have clear roles in how privacy is managed (and by whom). Therefore, the same strategies that we use to manage individual privacy are not the same as for groups; as a result, families need to establish rules for individuals and make sure those rules are altered when in a family context.

Another interesting aspect of rules and privacy is the negotiation of such rules. The debates typically revolve around what information should be disclosed and what other information should be withheld. The conflict around someone disclosing outside of the identified rules can create issues for couples and family members (Petronio, 2002). In some cases, someone will disclose or give up private information in order to gain information. Online, this is often seen as giving up certain information to join a group. If you give up certain elements and ideas about you, then you can join the group. One issue is, however, that anonymity can prevent us from fact-finding any information disclosed to us that is assumed to be private.

The inability to maintain (or protect) privacy has pretty significant consequences. For example, people who use the Internet can fall victim to criminal endeavors. People who have malicious intentions may be fishing for information or fooling people into donating money. It may be the case that privacy is compromised and credit card information is stolen. Cybersecurity is quickly becoming a great business as a way to address some of these concerns. In relationships, there are significant implications for ambient apps as we may overtly (or covertly) observe former partners, present partners, and children via these apps. Privacy management varies based on who is using the Internet and in what capacity. Some data suggests that some users actually engage more privacy strategies because they acknowledge that other users around them may be lurking (Child & Starcher, 2016). Adolescents, in fact, rely more on texting and instant messaging rather than Facebook communication as a way to gain control over their privacy (Mullen & Hamilton, 2016). In addition, the extent to which one manages their privacy is somewhat dictated by gender and/or sexual orientation. For instance, men tend to engage in fewer privacy management strategies than women (Child & Starcher, 2016; De Wolf et al., 2014) and are more likely to use group privacy management strategies. And in comparison to their heterosexual peers, lesbian, gay, and bisexual (LGB)–identifying individuals and partnerships tend to employ a higher degree of privacy management strategies in non-queer-friendly online spaces as a form of electronic visibility management, in order to buffer themselves from things like cyberbullying (Twist, Bergdall, Belous, & Maier, 2017).

Finally, because youth and teens use technology differently than adults, we have to adapt our privacy management strategies in ways that are developmentally appropriate and consistent with their usage. For example, Jack and Jill, a, heterosexual, British American, middle-class couple, brought their 14-year-old daughter, Michelle, to therapy as a way to address her slipping grades and increasing isolation in her room away from the family. Part of her pattern of isolation was to be in her room, door locked, posting on Instagram. When her parents would ask her to come out of her room, she would come out of her room only wearing a bra. This evidence led her parents to believe photos of her in her bra alone were what she was posting on Instagram or sending in messages to others. To address the issue of her using her phone and engaging in risky behavior online, the parents elected to invoke a privacy management plan that limited her ability to use her phone. Her parents also began monitoring her Instagram account and were able to set limits on the types of posts that she could make.

Rule Tip 1: Develop a Rule for Your Family on Collective Privacy Management

Collective privacy management relates to the way in which people make decisions about and guard their privacy within a group. In individual settings, people are able to evaluate what they want to do in terms of putting their personal information out into the web. Individuals have to make careful decisions between having an online presence and the benefits from that while weighing what part of their privacy they have to give up to be able to participate (Wessels, 2015). While half of the people who have recently quit Facebook cite privacy concerns as the rationale for their quitting, the truth is the privacy concerns really have not made a dent in the type of Internet traffic that Facebook has experienced. In family and couple settings, the way in which the rules around privacy management are established requires that a negotiation occur and often is re-visited. In couples, there may be some negotiation around the types of pictures and the types of posts made. For families, awareness around policies dictates what is appropriate to put online and what is not. For example, there are a host of websites that set a minimum age such as 12 or 13 for one to be able to have an account. Families have to also make decisions about whether they are going to share photographs of their children that could be stolen or compromised. Be mindful that it is not just the individual parents whose privacy is compromised—it is also the youth. The compromises in privacy have to be considered because it is nearly impossible to withdraw totally from having your information online. Using the Internet and having online accounts are practices that are becoming unavoidable in today's world (Baruh & Popescu, 2017). Some have tried to manage online privacy concerns by closing social media accounts (Stieger, Burger, & Bohn, 2013).

Initiating Relationships

Rule Tip 1: Recognition of Gatekeeping in Online Dating

It is not within the scope of this text to outline all of the intricacies in the online dating world and the process of online dating. There are many books and articles written by fantastic scholars about this dynamic in couples. What we wish to accentuate here is that in initiating relationships, one quick tip is to understand the gatekeeping mechanism employed (often unconsciously) by online daters. Part of meeting online that interferes with interaction are the filters and limitations applied to dating. For example, those who are more sensitive to rejection are also those who indicate they use online dating more frequently so that they can feel free to be their authentic selves in such an environment (Hance, Blackhart, & Dew, 2018). This is in part due to the perception that online dating environments, because users can be selective, introduce more choice and convince the user they have greater control, autonomy, privacy, and confidentiality (Rochadiat, Tong, & Novak, 2018). First, the individual engaging in online dating has a chance to self-select what they present to others on the site in an effort to look more attractive (Toma, Hancock, & Ellison, 2008). Warranting is the process of producing information that may seem difficult to manipulate (Wotipka & High, 2016). This means that people who are viewing that individual's profile can feel confident that the information the poster presents is verifiable and accurate, thus generating a feeling of trust (Wotipka & High, 2016). This is a critically important process, as people who are looking to find mates online are not necessarily privy to accurate information—only the information that someone wishes to portray (Troyer et al., 2011).

Rule Tip 2: Recognition of the "Eight As"

As mentioned in the previous chapter, the use of the ecological elements from the CFT framework can assist one in managing and interpreting online interactions. These ecological elements (the eight As) include: anonymity, acceptability, affordability, accessibility, approximation, accommodation, ambiguity, and accountability. While we will not review the elements in their entirety here, we will make a few points as they relate to online initiation. The anonymity present in online interactions leads to an increase in the likelihood that one can engage in anti-normative practices. In other words, we may say things that we might not say in person, but can get away with it under the cloak of anonymity. We can also fake it until we make it—that is, deny any emotional reactions, downplay feelings, and simply not communicate them, thus hiding our feelings and limiting our vulnerability. Those who initiate relationships should consider that a text message is one small slice of one's experience, and there may be an undercurrent of thoughts and emotions of which the party is unaware, thus causing the anonymity to persist.

Maintaining Relationships

Intimacy Tip 1: Electronic Fantasy Dates

Another way to integrate technology in relationships is to use an electronic fantasy date. Integrating technology in this way allows for another way to be able to connect with one another instead of just through daily texts in short bursts of conversations. As the research shows, couples that use technology often talk more frequently during the day, but those conversations are shorter and have less depth. Electronic fantasy dates offer another way to keep the frequency of the communication going, but it is different as the conversation is throughout the entire day as an experiential activity that a couple can do together while they are separate (Hertlein, 2016). The electronic fantasy date relies on the CFT framework principles of accessibility and affordability to forge a stronger relationship via a greater sense of connectedness (Bargh & McKenna, 2004; Hertlein, 2016). In this activity, one partner begins by providing a thick, rich description of the date and an approximation of the date setting and accommodating one's desires with ambiguity, allowing the recipient room to use their imagination. There may also be a positive end of anticipation built up in the expectation of a message being received, providing a more positive feeling about one another throughout the day.

Intimacy Tip 2: Using Asynchronous Methods to Manage Conflict

Ocker and Yaverbaum (1999) outline strategies for how to increase the satisfaction and sense of collaboration in computer-mediated communication. Among these are (1) educating those using the services on the benefits of each type of communication, (2) providing education on how to use the programs correctly, and (3) increasing exposure to these types of communication. In their application to couples, the activities a therapist may present include some of these strategies. For example, therapists can describe the differences between synchronous and asynchronous communication among couples to help them to make an informed decision around how they want to design the use of technology in their relationship.

Another part of the conversation has to be the practicality of when to use which strategy. Take the example of Debbie and Jerusha, who were a similar-gender, middle-class, mixed sexual orientation couple of mixed racial/ethnic identities and backgrounds. Debbie, a 28-year-old writer, and

Jerusha, a 39-year-old advertising executive, came to therapy. Debbie indicated she often felt ignored by Jerusha during the workday, which resulted in her calling Jerusha repeatedly during the day in order to get the time and attention she felt she deserved. Yet according to Jerusha, the demands of her position did not leave her available to take Debbie's calls, and if she was able to take them, she was not generally present in a physical location to be able to conduct the kind of conversation that was desired by Debbie. As Jerusha put it, "she keeps smothering me. I do not understand where it's coming from because I've never given her any reason to doubt me, but it seems like that's all she does all day long. She doesn't see the damage it's doing between us, and I'm afraid at one point I'm just going to snap and leave." Debbie's history was just as complicated. She had been cheated on by her most recent previous partner, Barry, who had then left her for his affair partner, Shayna, moved out, and subsequently moved on and got married to Shayna shortly afterwards. She had a history of substance abuse and feeling insecure. She also had a history of being sexually abused, for which she had never received treatment, and all of these individual issues were also complicating her ability to trust her partner.

Part of therapy was to help the couple to have appropriate expectations around when Jerusha would be able to talk, but also to heighten Jerusha's awareness of Debbie's need for communication throughout the day. Part of what was helpful in this example was bringing awareness to the circumstances when asynchronous communication would serve the relationship better than synchronous communication, and vice-versa. For instance, in times when Debbie desired social support and connection, Jerusha needed to be aware of this need, and identify instances in which the need could be met through synchronous (not asynchronous) communication.

Intimacy Tip 3: Using Synchronous Methods to Obtain Support

Another way that couples can use technology is with regard to pregnancy and parenting. Research has found that parents feel that they experience more support from their partner if their partner is in more frequent communication via text or phone during a pregnancy. It also enables long-distance relationships be able to flourish in ways that were not possible ten or 15 years ago. The electronic fantasy dates (discussed earlier in this chapter) offer the same possibilities for couples to demonstrate a level of commitment and a connection to one another without necessarily spending a dime, paying for a plane ticket, or taking off work. In addition, using mobile phones as a tool to communicate with one another is associated with higher relationship satisfaction—in part due to calling and texting features—which establishes a set of relationship expectations (Hall & Baym, 2011).

Intimacy Tip 4: Ensure Online Friends Are Offline Friends as Well

Online friends are great, but what seems to be protective of people's mental health is whether offline bonds are also allowed to form and be cultivated. In many ways, online relationships are protective of depression symptoms for younger people. For example, Shensa and colleagues (2018) conducted a study examining the depressive symptoms and the number of friends on social media—and whether the friendships existed in person or online only. They found every 10% increase in the number of online-only friends was accompanied by a 9% increase in depression symptoms. Conversely, every 10% increase in offline friends who were also friends on social media was accompanied by a 10% decrease in depression symptoms. This research suggests that we have a sense of who among our social media accounts may be the type of friend that we can count on for support as opposed to those who may be friends in number only. In fact, it is the social support that we gain from online friends that is highly important to warding off depressive symptoms for adolescents and young adults (Frison, Bastin, Bijttebier, & Eggermont, 2018).

Such a finding also means that we can teach our children and peers to make sure to make connections in person before adding them to one's social networking site simply as a way to gain psychological support and to stave off depression symptoms. The net effect may yield fewer connections online, but in the case of depression, that may be a good thing. Another alternative may be to have two separate accounts—one for work and networking, and another that is purely social, which only contains the friends that someone has already befriended in an offline environment.

Trust Tip 1: Recovering From Online Infidelity

Online infidelity is incredibly pervasive in the age of the Internet. As discussed earlier in the book, a few characteristics of the Internet lend themselves to connections with others (both physical and emotional) to the exclusion of the primary partners. Unfortunately, there is also a sense of secrecy and suspicion that can contribute to infidelity recovery. One of the key issues that starts with couples in trying to rebuild after an affair is the crazy-making nature of the Internet. As posed by many people who are recovering from the betrayal of infidelity, there is a sense that the betrayed individual would not be able to trust whether their partner actually stopped the affair because there would be no evidence of it since it is so easy to delete and discard messages. In other words, the absence of the evidence is not evidence of absence (Hertlein, Dulley, Chang, Cloud, & Leon, 2017).

Just as much as technology may be the problem in the case of recovery, it also offers unique solutions. For example, it becomes very easy to share passwords as a way to share access with (and be open to) your partner so that they can check online to see one's usage. This solution, however, comes with a few caveats. While such access may provide security and manage the crisis of the discovery, it is not a long-term solution. In a situation where one person has the other person's passwords constantly, it would establish an unhealthy power imbalance in the relationship. Another solution some couples have employed includes taking photographs of where they are as a way to verify location when their partner makes a request. Again, like the password solution, the idea is to use such solutions temporarily until such a time that the couple is ready to move toward developing trust.

Another key piece to the recovery process is to come to an agreement about the breach that occurred. In many cases, one partner might consider their partner's usage of pornography to constitute cheating. In other relationships, it is physical affection with someone other than their partner. In other relationships, an emotional connection to someone outside of the relationship constitutes infidelity. Couples can also be misled about what constitutes infidelity when it involves a computer—there is a difference, for example, between sex "addiction," Internet "addiction," and infidelity. Couples need to think about the different criteria that would separate infidelity from another problem—whether that be the presence of an identifiable third person, time spent online, the presence of tolerance and withdrawal, etc. (Fincham & May, 2017; Jones & Hertlein, 2012).

Trust Tip 2: Managing Surveillance

A number of factors contribute to how parents make decisions to surveil their children and their technology use. To some degree, this has to do with the parents' own ability to interpret and utilize technology, their parenting style as to whether they tend to be more permissive or authoritarian, and, to a certain extent, their demographic background (Nikken & Schols, 2015). For example, parents who find themselves with lower socioeconomic status and lower levels of education have more difficulty surveilling their children's online behavior, perhaps because of a function of work schedules when their children are home. There are three primary methods of parental mediation. One of them is restrictive monitoring, where the parent places restrictions but is passive about the enforcement of such restrictions. Active monitoring involves a parent's continual engagement in reviewing what sites are visited and establishing rules around the sites, without allowing the children to develop age appropriate strategies or strategies around the increase or the usage (Collier et al., 2016; Padilla-Walker, Coyne, Kroff, & Memmott-Elison, 2018). Another key piece to managing surveillance is to recover from a privacy breach when it happens. One study showed that when there is a privacy breach between two people online, the person whose information was breached often blames the confidant rather than take responsibility for themselves. This occurs despite the evidence that these victims were not overtly taking measures to manage their information in a more secure way (Steuber & Mclaren, 2015).

Ending Relationships

Termination Tip 1: "Give Up The Ghost"

The quality of the Internet that allows termination without confrontation is the anonymity provided. Ghosting in relationships refers to blocking someone via electronic media subsequent to a period of routine interaction. Accessibility of communication via cellphones, anonymity, and accommodation facilitate ghosting. Further, ghosting can happen in the context of any relationship—romantic, peer-to-peer, or even professional, and can be painful to the recipient in any setting. While there is little research on this phenomenon, anecdotal evidence suggests that being the recipient of ghosting can contribute to feeling disoriented in a relationship, lowered levels of self-esteem, rumination on the events leading up to the perceived distancing, and withdrawal.

While it may be tempting to terminate a relationship without the consequences of having further communication, there may be other ways to end relationships in non-destructive, boundary-preserving ways. One of the reasons that people use technology and engage in ghosting is that it is easier to put up physical boundaries than psychological ones—and the physical boundaries serve as the boundary until they are not necessary. In the case of technology, however, once you establish physical boundaries through blocking or deleting, you may not even get to a place to address the psychological boundaries, thus inhibiting one's growth.

Termination Tip 2: Using the Benefits of the Internet to Structure Interactions

Outside of ghosting, there are other ways that the Internet and cellphones can provide ways to terminate relationships. One key way is to be able to say "no" without feeling guilty and to use technology to do so (Tom Tong & Walther, 2011). As mentioned in the CFT framework, one of the things that makes it easier to initiate relationships is the ability to be anonymous. We can edit, delete, and have our facial expressions hidden from those on the other side of the electronic interaction. This anonymity might provide protection from watching another person's reaction to rejection without having to resort to ghosting. Another opportunity is to use an approach that relies on the middle ground—in other words, rather than ghosting, sending a contact to voicemail when they call, muting their text message, etc. This would put the receiver of the messages in a position to retain control of the response.

Online Behavior and Children: Some Guidelines

Rule Tip 1: When Should My Child Be Granted a Cellphone?

As therapists, one of the most frequently asked questions we get is at what age should we start integrating technology in our children's lives. One specific example of this is at what age should children have their own cellphones? The answer to this question is, "It depends." It depends, because it is so complex. It requires a parent's attention to different areas of their child's life. At the same time, it is an important question, as the adults are still the gatekeepers of children's access to technology (Chiong & Shuler, 2010). Following are some of the main components of decision-making on this question.

Dimension 1: Developmental Age

Developmental age is different from chronological age. When we talk about chronological age, we are talking about the biological age of the child, that is, how many years since their date of birth. As we know, however, children develop at various trajectories. A number of elements can affect a child's developmental age, and they include parenting, temperament, learning styles, developmental delays or disorders, and the presence of trauma, just to name a few. There are a number of studies exploring the appropriateness of when a child begins school based on their developmental age rather than their chronological age (Hale, 1988; Nicholas, 1985). This as a factor in awarding a cellphone should be no different. Like a classroom, cellphone ownership requires that the user be in a developmental place where physically they can navigate the phone, mentally they can handle the complexity that goes into responding to incoming calls appropriately (both wanted and unwanted), and they have the ability to manage interference from phones if they are executing another task. In addition, as compared to non-delayed children, those with developmental delays tend to have more behavior problems as well as being more likely to develop a diagnosable psychological condition (Caplan, Neece, & Baker, 2015). More behavior problems in an offline world may also mean more behavior problems in their phone use. Parents should carefully consider where their child is in terms of developmental age and make a decision with this in mind.

Dimension 2: Maturity of Child

While there is not specifically a developmental age that would require or prohibit cellphone usage, it is one of the things that factor into one's emotional maturity. The higher the developmental age, the more maturity that your child may experience or demonstrate. Physical maturity is probably the least important determinant from a health and safety perspective in deciding whether your child should have a cellphone. Physical maturity relates to a child's motor skills—for example, the extent to which a child can write legibly, their coordination with getting dressed, appropriate muscle development, being coordinated enough to ride a bike, etc. In the case of cellphones, it is important that children have the physical maturity to be able to handle a phone. Cellphones are becoming larger (Barredo, 2014), and for people with little hands, this might prove challenging to hold in one hand. If you decide to purchase your child a cellphone, you may wish to bring the child to try on different sizes of phones and see what feels like a good fit physically.

Another consideration has to be the child's ability to remain safe while using their phone. For example, a series of studies point out the consistent executive functioning impairments when people use their phone and walk simultaneously—leading to unsafe practices (Haga et al., 2015; Lamberg & Muratori, 2012; Neider et al., 2011). Children with cellphones need to demonstrate some maturity around physically being able to manage the devices and engage in responsible behaviors to avoid unsafe circumstances. An assessment of physical maturity leads to identification of one's intellectual maturity. Questions parents can ask themselves in this regard include how well a child follows directions, how well they do in school, their ability to understand cause and effect, and their ability to understand differences between an offline and online life (a concept that may even be difficult for adults to comprehend). Children have to be able to understand, for example, the concept of physical safety when using their cellphones and be able to execute a parent's directive to limit cellphone use in certain conditions—such as in school, crossing streets, etc. Intellectually, children have to be able to separate the cellphone as a tool to accomplish tasks from an extension of whom they are as a person.

Emotional maturity is another type of maturity to be considered by parents evaluating their child's fit for a phone. Emotional maturity is characterized by a child's ability to exhibit patience, manage frustration, control their anger and express it in appropriate ways, and manage disappointment. Because of the accessibility of phones and anonymity, a child who becomes frustrated may respond by sending a quick emotional message without considering the impact of their words. Intersecting with one's emotional maturity is their social maturity. Social maturity means one's willingness to share with friends or peers, their ability to interact and play appropriately with others, their ability to be cooperative, and how well they get along with others. Emotional maturity has to be at a level high enough to interact effectively with one's peers.

The last area of maturity is the child's ethical and moral maturity. This type of maturity means a child's general level of kindness, their sense of helpfulness with others, their understanding of empathy with others, their ability to take accountability and responsibility for their actions, and their tendency toward honesty. Certainly, children who are unable to empathize, are mean toward others, and do not take accountability (which is easy to do in an online world where posts can be anonymous) are not the type for whom a cellphone would be appropriate, as the risk of engaging in cyberbullying may be likely.

Dimension 3: Perceived Need

There are also some circumstances that would require a cellphone for a child in today's day and age. For example, a parent may need access to their child when their child is away from them. If the relationship with their ex-partners is rather contentious, it may behoove the parent to get their child a cellphone as a way to communicate. Another perceived need may be a child's schedule. For example, if there is involvement in extra-curricular activities where they need to call a parent for a ride home, a cellphone might be a logical idea.

Dimension 4: The Presence of Safeguards

In some circumstances, parents may wish to safeguard their children from harmful information online. In other times, they may feel like the child might be able to regulate their own access. The extent to which one is able to provide safeguards for their children is also going to dictate whether they can get their child a phone. For example, if you feel reasonably confident that your child would be able to get around and remain safe, without a phone, you may wish to withhold a phone until necessary. This may be true for children who experience difficulty with boundaries set by parents regarding phone use. In that case, the best answer might be a flip phone rather than a smartphone to be able to protect them from that. The challenge of this, of course, is that many companies are no longer making flip phones. While this seems like a useful decision in terms of marketing, it makes it more challenging for parents to be able to provide a phone to their children because a smartphone is incredibly expensive, and is not able to protect them in the way that they wish.

Dimension 5: Examination of Parent Motivation

Parents are motivated in when and how they use technology in their couple and family life. In some cases, that use of technology may be as it is for many of us: a way to entertain ourselves when bored, or for those who use the Internet pathologically, a way to dissociate from feeling and processing events and emotions. There are also other situations where parents use technology as a pacifier for their children. For example, I (KH) was at a local store yesterday and a small girl (no more than 3 years old) was walking around the store with a tablet in her hand. The tablet was playing a cartoon, and the girl was walking through the store near her mother, watching the screen and interrupting the viewing by glancing up to grab and examine whatever toys were at her eye level. Once she examined a toy, she would zone out again in front of her screen while her mother walked in the vicinity around her. This also is not the first, second, or third time I have seen this behavior and decision-making from parents. Restaurants are another common place for implementing the electronic pacifier. Parents may decide that they wish to have a "quiet" night away from the kids, so they bring the family to a restaurant and place a screen in front of them, allowing the child to zone out while the parents talk. My view has been that this motivation from the parents' end results in children not being able to sit patiently in a restaurant, to learn appropriate behavior in a restaurant, and to process any emotions and adversity. In other words, rather than engage in parenting and administer discipline, parents may find it easier to put their children in front of a screen. Finally, it is important to be aware that a parent's own problematic mobile phone involvement will predict their child's usage (Hefner, Knop, Schmitt, & Vorderer, 2018). Parents need to be able to reflect on their own behavior and their own motivations and patterns with regard to mobile phone involvement.

There are also parents, however, who have appropriate and well-intentioned motivations. It may be to teach their children certain tasks with cellphones, apps, and technology. In such cases, the motivation that a parent brings to providing their child a cellphone is to prepare them to use one responsibly and to help children adjust to the changes to technology over time. This type of motivation is characterized by time spent with a child teaching them about cellphone safety and cellphone usage, and the phone is often introduced to the child in a progressive manner. In other words, the child is given a short time with the phone, and over time, as their skills develop and with more comfort, the child's access to the phone and apps slowly increases. In another study, parents acknowledged giving children a touchscreen as a way to provide rest for the child (Nikken & Schols, 2015).

Case in Point: A Tale of Two Kiddies

Tonight over dinner, my friend Laura and I (KH) were talking about this very topic—at what point should our boys get cellphones? Her son, 10 years old, has a cellphone. My son of the same age does not, nor am I interested in getting him one. She asked about how I came to the determination of when kids should get cellphones. I began to walk through with her the five aforementioned dimensions, and she and I talked about the differences between our children. For example, in the First Dimension, developmental age, it seems that her son is a little bit older developmentally than my son. Their birthdays are only a few months apart and her son is

286 Rebooting Your Relationships

a little bit older, which may make a bit of a difference in their presenta-tions. In the Second Dimension, maturity, her son also has a bit more advancement. We discussed how in his case, growing up with an older sister may have made him a little bit more mature earlier on, whereas my son, an only child, did not have those pushes toward maturity. With regard to the Third Dimension, perceived need, in her case, her son rides a bus to a school 40 minutes from their home. She and her husband, both busy professionals, have to arrange to meet him at the bus stop or also be alerted if he is going to be late. There are also times when her son has to let himself into the house or be by himself for short periods while she and her husband are trying to come home from work. On the other hand, my son goes to school close to our house—about a mile away. My husband also works from home, so we do not have the challenges Laura has with trying to coordinate schedules and making sure that somebody is at a bus stop or making sure that somebody is coordinating a schedule to get home. Therefore, there is some level of perceived need in Laura's house that is different than mine. In the Fourth Dimension, presence of safeguards, the boys are about the same. In some ways, my son might even be ahead in this category. My husband happens to be a software developer, so he is intimately aware of various ways to protect and moni-tor online behavior as a way to introduce safeguards. On the other hand, my friend Laura's son lives in a home with very intelligent parents and a cellphone-savvy sister, who would be able to provide the same safeguards to him. On the cellphone that he owns, he can only do limited things with that phone. Finally, the Fifth Dimension, motivation of the parents: in this area, it is probably a tie as well. In this regard, neither my husband, myself, nor my friend and her partner are interested in giving our kids a phone so we can do something else with our lives and with our time. We are interested in making sure that the kids use the phone in ways that are helpful and adaptive and not as a babysitter.

Rule Tip 2: Boundaries and Rules for Safeguarding Against Cyberbullying

Cyberbullying is a pervasive problem in today's technological culture. Cyberbullying is defined as "aggression that is intentionally and repeatedly carried out in an electronic context (e.g., e-mail, blogs, instant messages, text messages, social networks, chat rooms, online games, or websites) against a person who cannot easily defend" (Lee, 2017, p. 58; Kowalski, Giumetti, Schroeder, & Lattanner, 2014). It is driven by the vulnerabili-ties we described in depth in earlier chapters in this book. Accessibility, for example, is a primary driver in engaging in cyberbullying. Cyberbul-lying can take many forms including harassment, forwarding one's texts, instant messages, or emails to others inappropriately, outing someone (disclosing details about one person to others), and masquerading (pre-tending to be someone else and attacking someone online).

Certain factors described by the CFT framework lend themselves to the development of cyberbullying—specifically, that the technologies that facilitate cyberbullying are affordable and accessible to young people, who may be more likely to take more risks or assault others in online formats. Further, most of these activities can be conducted under the cloak of anonymity, making it difficult if not impossible to track down the perpetrator, and tough for parents to figure out whether their children are at-risk as messages can be (and often are) frequently deleted (Hertlein, 2017).

Parents and children can develop strategies to manage the ecological elements and restructure family roles to improve processes. For example, in what circumstances is the accessibility creating more difficulties for teens and kids? Are there changes the family can make to minimize these difficulties? For some families the solution may be limiting accessibility. Another family member may identify the solution as increasing accessibility for all family members. This might include a shared email address, a shared Facebook account, or shared smartphones for several members of the family. In this way, cyberbullying would be attenuated since the interactions would be with the whole family.

Strategies that address cognitions are also critically important. Once bullied, the victim may feel ashamed, disempowered, anxious, and afraid to respond for fear of retribution. Such feelings can affect the ways in which the victim interacts with family members, which may result in changes to structure. While education about cyberbullying can help normalize and reduce shame around the victim's response, it can also help the victim to avoid internalizing messages that would contribute to an impaired self-esteem. Cognitive approaches also assist the family in supporting the victim with self-care strategies to manage depression, anxiety, and with the development of assertiveness skills for use in the management of cyberbullying.

Another strategy for both those being bullied and their families is implementing appropriate coping skills. Depressive, emotionally focused, and avoidant coping skills are more likely to promote depression and future symptoms than other, empowerment-based strategies (with emotionally focused strategies to be more likely to be employed by the victim) (Völlink, Bolman, Dehue, & Jacobs, 2013). Implementing positive coping skills may help to reestablish closer relationships in the family and assist in maintaining boundaries helpful to healing and the reestablishment of safety.

Conclusion

We closed this book with a plan—the Technology Integration Plan (TIP)—for how to thoughtfully integrate technology into one's individual, couple, and family/relational systems. In applying the TIP, we recommended that technology users address these considerations first: (1) consider the audience, (2) maximize the benefits, and (3) consider the motivations. We then recommended ideas for integrating technology into the structure of relationships, as well as into the lives of children.

Our goal in this text, which we stated in Chapter 1, was to address the ways that technology shapes our individual and relational processes, and the advantages and challenges it poses in doing so. While we believe we have accomplished this goal, we also understand that our relationship with technology, as humans, remains complicated. Our hope, then, is that our readers find the information gleaned within the pages of this text helpful for making their relationship with technology at least less complicated, and at most the kind of relationship that offers them greater ease, clarity, and benefit in their lives.

References

Bargh, J. A., & McKenna, K. A. (2004). The Internet and social life. *Annual Review of Psychology*, 55(1), 573–590. doi:10.1146/annurev.psych.55.090902.141922

Barredo, A. (2014). Retrieved from https://medium.com/@somospostpc/a-compre hensive-look-at-smartphone-screen-size-statistics-and-trends-e61d77001ebe

Baruh, L., & Popescu, M. (2017). Big data analytics and the limits of privacy self-management. *New Media & Society*, 19(4), 579–596. doi:10.1177/14614448 15614001

Caplan, B., Neece, C., & Baker, B. (2015). Developmental level and psychopa-thology: Comparing children with developmental delays to chronological and mental age matched controls. *Research in Developmental Disabilities*, 37, 143–151.

Child, J. T., & Starcher, S. C. (2016). Fuzzy Facebook privacy boundaries: Explor-ing mediated lurking, vague-booking, and Facebook privacy management. *Computers in Human Behavior*, 54, 483–490. doi: 10.1016/j.chb.2015.08.035

Chiong, C., & Shuler, C. (2010). *Learning: Is there an app for that? Investigations of young children's usage and learning with mobile devices and apps*. New York: The Joan Ganz Cooney Center at Sesame Workshop.

Collier, K., Coyne, S., Rasmussen, E., Hawkins, A., Padilla-Walker, L., Erickson, S., . . . Eric, F. (2016). Does parental mediation of media influence child out-comes? A meta-analysis on media time, aggression, substance use, and sexual behavior. *Developmental Psychology*, 52(5), 798–812. doi:10.1037/dev0000108

De Wolf, R., Willaert, K., & Pierson, J. (2014). Managing privacy boundaries together: Exploring individual and group privacy management strategies in Facebook. *Computers in Human Behavior*, 35(C), 444–454.

Fincham, F. D., & May, R. W. (2017). Infidelity in romantic relationships. *Current Opinion in Psychology*, 13(C), 70–74.

Frison, E., Bastin, M., Bijttebier, P., & Eggermont, S. (2018). Helpful or harmful? The different relationships between private Facebook interactions and adoles-cents' depressive symptoms. *Media Psychology*, 1–29. doi:10.1080/15213269. 2018.1429933

Haga, S., Sano, A., Sekine, Y., Sato, H., Yamaguchi, S., & Masuda, K. (2015). Effects of using a Smart Phone on pedestrians' attention and walking. *Procedia Manufacturing*, 3, 2574–2580. doi:10.1016/j.promfg.2015.07.564

Hale, L. (1988). *The effects of developmental versus chronological age placement on students' self concept, class achievement, and school adjustment.* ProQuest Dissertations and Theses.

Hall, J. A., & Baym, N. K. (2011). Calling and texting (too much): Mobile maintenance expectations, (over)dependence, entrapment, and friendship satisfaction. *New Media & Society, 14*(2), 316–331. doi:10.1177/1461444811415047

Hance, M., Blackhart, G., & Dew, M. (2018). Free to be me: The relationship between the true self, rejection sensitivity, and use of online dating sites. *The Journal of Social Psychology, 158*(4), 421–429. doi:10.1080/00224545.2017.1389684

Hefner, D., Knop, K., Schmitt, S., & Vorderer, P. (2018). Rules? role model? relationship? The impact of parents on their children's problematic mobile phone involvement. *Media Psychology*, 1–27. doi:10.1080/15213269.2018.1433544

Hertlein, K. M. (2016). "Your cyberplace or mine?": Electronic fantasy dates. In G. R. Weeks, S. T. Fife, & C. M. Peterson's (Eds.), *Techniques for the couple therapist: Essential interventions from the experts* (pp. 182–185). New York, NY: Routledge.

Hertlein, K. M. (2017). Clinical practice in families of cyberbullying. In S. W. Browning & B. van Eeden-Moorefield's (Eds.), *Contemporary families at the nexus of research and practice* (pp. 255–265). New York, NY: Routledge.

Hertlein, K. M., & Blumer, M. L. C. (2013). *The couple and family technology framework: Intimate relationships in a digital age.* New York, NY: Routledge.

Hertlein, K. M., Dulley, C., Chang, J., Cloud, R., & Leon, D. (2017). Does absence of evidence mean evidence of absence? Managing the issue of partner surveillance in infidelity treatment. *Sexual and Relationship Therapy, 32*(3–4), 323–333.

Jones, K., & Hertlein, K. M. (2012). Four key dimensions in distinguishing Internet infidelity from Internet and sex addiction: Concepts and clinical application. *American Journal of Family Therapy, 40*(2), 115–125.

Kowalski, R. M., Giumetti, G. W., Schroeder, A. N., & Lattanner, M. R. (2014). Bullying in the digital age: A critical review and meta-analysis of cyberbullying research among youth. *Psychological Bulletin, 140*, 1073–1137. doi:10.1037/a0035618

Lamberg, E. M., & Muratori, L. M. (2012). Cellphones change the way we walk. *Gait & Posture, 35*(4), 688–690. doi:0.1016/j.gaitpost.2011.12.005

Lee, E. (2017). Cyberbullying: Prevalence and predictors among African American young adults. *Journal of Black Studies, 48*(1), 57–73.

Mullen, C., & Hamilton, N. (2016). Adolescents' response to parental *Facebook* friend requests: The comparative influence of privacy management, parent-child relational quality, attitude and peer influence. *Computers in Human Behavior, 60*, 165–172.

Neider, M., Gaspar, J., McCarley, J., Crowell, J., Kaczmarski, H., & Kramer, A. (2011). Walking and talking: Dual-task effects on street crossing behavior in older adults. *Psychology and Aging, 26*(2), 260–268. doi:10.1037/a0021566

Nicholas, R. (1985). *Developmental versus chronological placement: Comparative effects on self-concept, school achievement, and school attitude (gesell, transitional class).* ProQuest Dissertations and Theses.

Nikken, P., & Schols, M. (2015). How and why parents guide the media use of young children. *Journal of Child and Family Studies, 24*(11), 3423–3435. doi:10.1007/s10826-015-0144-4.

Ocker, R. J., & Yaverbaum, G. J. (1999). Asynchronous computer-mediated communication versus face-to-face collaboration: Results on student learning, quality and satisfaction. *Group Decision and Negotiation, 8*(5), 427–440. doi:10.1023/A:1008621827601

O'Keeffe, G. S., & Clarke-Pearson, K. (2011). Clinical report: The impact of social media on children, adolescents, and families. *Pediatrics, 127,* 800–804. doi:10.1542/peds.2011–0054

Padilla-Walker, L., Coyne, M., Kroff, S., & Memmott-Elison, S. (2018). The protective role of parental media monitoring style from early to late adolescence. *Journal of Youth and Adolescence, 47*(2), 445–459.

Petronio, S. (2002). *Boundaries of privacy: Dialectics of disclosure.* SUNY Series in Communication Studies. Albany, NY: State University of New York Press.

Piszczek, M. (2017). Boundary control and controlled boundaries: Organizational expectations for technology use at the work–family interface. *Journal of Organizational Behavior, 38*(4), 592–611.

Primack, B., Bisbey, M., Shensa, A., Bowman, N., Karim, S., Knight, J., & Sidani, J. (2018). The association between valence of social media experiences and depressive symptoms. *Depression and Anxiety, 35*(8), 784–794. doi: 10.1002/da.22779

Rochadiat, A., Tong, S., & Novak, J. (2018). Online dating and courtship among Muslim American women: Negotiating technology, religious identity, and culture. *New Media & Society, 20*(4), 1618–1639.

Shensa, A., Sidani, J., Escobar-Viera, C., Chu, K., Bowman, N., Knight, J., & Primack, B. (2018). Real-life closeness of social media contacts and depressive symptoms among university students. *Journal of American College Health,* 1–8.

Steuber, K., & Mclaren, R. (2015). Privacy recalibration in personal relationships: Rule usage before and after an incident of privacy turbulence. *Communication Quarterly, 63*(3), 345–364.

Stieger, S., Burger, C., & Bohn, M. (2013). Who commits virtual identity suicide? Differences in privacy concerns, Internet addiction, and personality between Facebook users and quitters. *Cyberpsychology, Behavior and Social Networking, 16*(9), 629–634.

Tom Tong, S., & Walther, J. (2011). Just say "no thanks": Romantic rejection in computer-mediated communication. *Journal of Social and Personal Relationships, 28*(4), 488–506.

Toma, C. L., Hancock, J. T., & Ellison, N. B. (2008). Separating fact from fiction: An examination of deceptive self-presentation in online dating profiles. *Personality and Social Psychology Bulletin, 34,* 1023–1036. doi:10.1177/0146167208318067

Toyer, R., Kilker, J., Bates, S., Sahlstein, E., & Traudt, P. (2011). *Factors of adoption: Initiating relationships using online dating sites.* ProQuest Dissertations and Theses.

Twist, M. L. C., Bergdall, M. K., Belous, C. K., & Maier, C. A. (2017). Electronic visibility management of lesbian, gay, and bisexual identities and relationships. *Journal of Couple and Relationship Therapy: Innovations in Clinical Educational Interventions, 16*(4), 271–285.

Völlink, T., Bolman, C. A. W., Dehue, F., & Jacobs, N. C. L. (2013). Coping with cyberbullying: Differences between victims, bully-victims and children not involved in bullying. *Journal of Community & Applied Social Psychology, 23*(1), 7–24. doi:10.1002/casp.2142

Wessels, B. (2015). Authentication, status, and power in a digitally organized society. *International Journal of Communication*, 9, 2801–2818.

Wotipka, C., & High, A. (2016). An idealized self or the real me? Predicting attraction to online dating profiles using selective self-presentation and warranting. *Communication Monographs*, 83(3), 281–302.

Index

Note: Page numbers in italics indicate a figure and page numbers in bold indicate a table on the corresponding page.